Man as Witch

Palgrave Historical Studies in Witchcraft and Magic

Series Editors: **Jonathan Barry, Willem de Blécourt and Owen Davies**

Titles include:

Edward Bever
THE REALITIES OF WITCHCRAFT AND POPULAR MAGIC IN EARLY MODERN EUROPE
Culture, Cognition and Everyday Life

Julian Goodare, Lauren Martin and Joyce Miller
WITCHCRAFT AND BELIEF IN EARLY MODERN SCOTLAND

Jonathan Roper *(editor)*
CHARMS, CHARMERS AND CHARMING

Rolf Schulte
MAN AS WITCH
Male Witches in Central Europe

Forthcoming:

Johannes Dillinger
MAGICAL TREASURE HUNTING IN EUROPE AND NORTH AMERICA
A History

Soili-Maria Olli
TALKING TO DEVILS AND ANGELS IN SCANDINAVIA, 1500–1800

Alison Rowlands
WITCHCRAFT AND MASCULINITIES IN EARLY MODERN EUROPE

Laura Stokes
THE DEMONS OF URBAN REFORM
The Rise of Witchcraft Prosecution, 1430–1530

Wanda Wyporska
WITCHCRAFT IN EARLY MODERN POLAND, 1500–1800

Palgrave Historical Studies in Witchcraft and Magic
Series Standing Order ISBN 978–1403–99566–7 Hardback
Series Standing Order ISBN 978–1403–99567–4 Paperback
(outside North America only)

You can receive future titles in this series as they are published by placing a standing order. Please contact your bookseller or, in case of difficulty, write to us at the address below with your name and address, the title of the series and one of the ISBNs quoted above.

Customer Services Department, Macmillan Distribution Ltd, Houndmills, Basingstoke, Hampshire RG21 6XS, England.

Man as Witch

Male Witches in Central Europe

Rolf Schulte
Historian, University of Kiel, Germany

Translated by Linda Froome-Döring

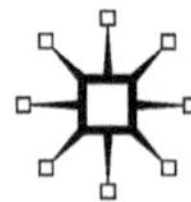

First published 2009 by
PALGRAVE MACMILLAN

Palgrave Macmillan in the UK is an imprint of Macmillan Publishers Limited, registered in England, company number 785998, of Houndmills, Basingstoke, Hampshire RG21 6XS.

Palgrave Macmillan in the US is a division of St Martin's Press LLC, 175 Fifth Avenue, New York, NY 10010.

Palgrave Macmillan is the global academic imprint of the above companies and has companies and representatives throughout the world.

Palgrave® and Macmillan® are registered trademarks in the United States, the United Kingdom, Europe and other countries.

ISBN-13: 978–0–230–53702–6 hardback

This book is printed on paper suitable for recycling and made from fully managed and sustained forest sources. Logging, pulping and manufacturing processes are expected to conform to the environmental regulations of the country of origin.

A catalogue record for this book is available from the British Library.

Library of Congress Cataloging-in-Publication Data

Schulte, Rolf, 1950–
Man as witch: male witches in Central Europe / Rolf Schulte; translated by Linda Froome-Döring.
p. cm.
Includes bibliographical references (p.) and index.
ISBN 978–0–230–53702–6
1. Witchcraft – Holy Roman Empire. 2. Warlocks – Holy Roman Empire. 3. Werewolves – Holy Roman Empire. I. Title.

BF1571.5.M45S35 2009
133.4′30810943—dc22 2008052860

Contents

List of Illustrations

List of Tables, Figures and Map

Tables

Figures

Map

Palgrave Historical Studies in Witchcraft and Magic

Series Foreword

The history of European witchcraft and magic continues to fascinate and challenge students and scholars. There is certainly no shortage of books on the subject. Several general surveys of the witch trials and numerous regional and micro studies have been published for an English-speaking readership. While the quality of publications on witchcraft has been high, some regions and topics have received less attention over the years. The aim of this series is to help illuminate these lesser known or little studied aspects of the history of witchcraft and magic. It will also encourage the development of a broader corpus of work in other related areas of magic and the supernatural, such as angels, devils, spirits, ghosts, folk healing and divination. To help further our understanding and interest in this wider history of beliefs and practices, the series will include research that looks beyond the usual focus on Western Europe and that also explores their relevance and influence from the medieval to the modern period.

Acknowledgements

The list of people I would like to thank for their help and advice is long. I am particularly grateful to Wolfgang Behringer (University of Saarbrücken), Heide Dienst (University of Vienna), Katrin Möller (University of Halle) and Olaf Mörke (University of Kiel) for their helpful suggestions. My thanks also go to Linda Froome-Döring for the care she took with the translation. But my greatest debt is to my wife, Christine, for her support and patience.

List of Abbreviations

AR	Administrative accounts (Amtsrechnung)
AP	Administrative records (Amtsprotokoll)
ADD	Archives du département Doubs/Besançon/France
ADH	Archives du département Haute Saône/Vesoul/France
AHL	Archiv der Hansestadt Lübeck/Germany
CCC	Constitutio Criminalis Carolina (Caroline Code)
HSA	Hamburger Staatsarchiv/Germany
EOW	*Encyclopedia of Witchcraft* (see selected bibliography)
ER	Expert report
KLA	Archiv des Landes Kärnten/Klagenfurt in Carinthia, Austria
KA	Church archives (Kirchenarchiv)
LAS	Archiv des Landes Schleswig-Holstein/Schleswig/Germany
Lg	Regional court (Landgericht)
Sg	Town or city court (Stadtgericht)
StA	Town or city archives (Stadtarchiv)

1
The Trial of Peter Kleikamp or – So Many Questions

February 1615. A judge in the sovereign's service orders the arrest of one Peter Kleikamp from the town of Ahlen, near Münster. He is accused of theft and sodomy; Kleikamp vigorously denies all charges. The court members then interview further witnesses and finally find some who seriously incriminate this destitute, 44-year-old unmarried man. According to their testimonies, Kleikamp had frequently been in contact with suspicious persons. This prompts the court to change the charge to one of witchcraft. On the grounds of the circumstantial evidence at hand it is not long before the prosecutors decide to use torture. The executioner applies instruments which crush the arms and legs of the accused, who is unable to withstand the agony and soon confesses to being a male witch, to having denounced God and the saints and sworn loyalty to the Devil. When renouncing God, he claims, he jumped backwards three times, whereupon Satan appeared before him in the shape of a black dog. The Devil had promised to feed him well, but also gave him herbs with which to poison calves and oxen. Simultaneously, he committed Kleikamp even admits to having slept several times with a female demon. He then became a werewolf, killing and tearing sheep to pieces in the dark of night. Together with his witches' company, consisting of four men and three women, he rubbed an ointment onto his skin at midnight, thus enabling them to fly to the heath close to Ahlen. Here they danced on a cord, and he beat the drum with a saw. Further, he states, his dead wife Sandera, who was a witch, had introduced him to the arts of witchcraft 16 years earlier.

In the eyes of the court this confession is evidence that Kleikamp was a destructive follower of the Devil and a member of an aggressive sect whose goal it was to secretly undermine Christian society. They see it as proven that he had worked maleficium and consciously formed a pact with the Devil. By attending the Sabbat he had become a member of a subversive group of felons whose moral standards represented the reverse of contemporary norms. Statements which do not tally with Kleikamp's confession are of no interest to the court. For example, Kleikamp confessed that in the guise of a werewolf he had bitten a sheep belonging to one of the witnesses; in fact, however, this witness did not even possess any such animals. Another witness was unable to recall a calf of his or any of his ancestors' ever being harmed as Kleikamp had claimed in his confession. In the end, he was condemned to death as a male witch on the grounds of his confession to witchcraft and poisoning. The trial had begun with a charge of theft and sodomy and ended with a conviction for witchcraft. A person who turned against the Christian community and made such a profane pact with the Devil deserved no sympathy. Not even if he was a man. Peter Kleikamp was burnt in public on 13 July 1615.[1]

This trial is characteristic of large numbers of court cases in early modern central Europe in which people were charged with and sentenced to death for witchcraft–the period of the witch-hunts.

A great deal of intensive research has been conducted on witchcraft in recent years, and both the results and the methods used to reach these results have been among the most controversially discussed topics among scholars of history. Methodologies reach from the more traditional social–historical and quantifying method to the historical–anthropological and the major research paths of the social control and denomination theses to feminist approaches where the line between explanation and transfiguration of the past at times becomes blurred.

From the beginnings of historical research into the witch persecutions scholars have asked why it was that women were comparatively frequently affected. For many years, the fact of this marked gender-specific assymetry appeared to be a foregone conclusion and one which historiography repeatedly confirmed for all but a few regions of central Europe, for Finland, the Baltic countries and Russia by the large number of regional studies which were being published. There is, however, still an ongoing discussion on the issue of gender orientation and today several approaches compete or coexist with one another.[2]

For a long time, research perceived men's prime role as that of the persecutor, and was largely oblivious to men as accused and executed victims. Gender analysis was concerned with associating women with witch trials and did not see men as the victims of this historical phenomenon.

The trial of Peter Kleikamp described above had all the marks of a classical witch trial and clearly contradicts the classic woman/witch paradigm. Without doubt, the majority of witch trials in most of the study regions seem to have targeted women – but minority cases also require explanations; in the context of a comparative gender study the case of Peter Kleikamp, which took place in what is now northern Germany, poses immediate questions such as the extent to which:

- Men were typically charged as werewolves in witch trials.
- A particular type of man (age, status, behaviour) was charged in witch trials.
- The sentences passed on men were milder or stricter than for women.
- The courts applied cumulative demonology to male suspects.
- Men were accused for similar reasons and in similar conflicts as women.
- Men remained the minority of accused in the various phases of the witch-hunts.

It is not possible as yet to provide anything approaching definitive answers to these questions. Some historians, both women and men, have registered the very evident fact that men did form a (minority) percentage of the people persecuted in the witch-hunts, for which they have given possible explanations; however, in many cases this research either presents hypotheses only or devotes little time or space to the approaches used in the discussion of men as victims of the witch-hunts. The following theories have recently been put forward:

- Male witches were closely related to female witches, and their involvement in the witch trials is to be seen as a kind of collateral damage or byproduct of the original trial[3] (relationship theory).
- Male witches figured more frequently in chain trials and mass executions, cases where the typical female witch stereotype broke down[4] (mass-trial theory).
- Male witches were not accused of the same offences as female witches or they were charged with less harmful types of witchcraft not involving diabolism[5] (difference theory).
- Male witches were most common in areas where witchcraft was more closely associated with heresy than with maleficent aggression[6] (heresy theory).

When my book *Hexenmeister. Die Verfolgung von Männern im Rahmen der Hexenverfolgungen von 1530 bis 1730 im Alten Reich* (Male Witches in the Witch-persecution of the Holy Roman Empire from 1530 to 1730) appeared in German in the year 2000 there were only a few published studies on this topic, and these were restricted to individual cases or regions. In my study, I looked into the trials of men accused and executed for witchcraft, thus opening up a largely unknown chapter in the history of Central Europe; male victims were no longer viewed as a peripheral phenomenon or quasi-pollutant of the female-focused witch paradigm but as a component which had developed in its own right.[7] The work aroused great interest, both among the lay public and researchers, though largely restricted to German-speaking countries, and two editions were published. In recent years, there has been more research into the male witch phenomenon, and in 2003 the Canadian historians Lara Apps and Andrew Gow published their general study on Europe as a whole. The authors again criticized both the fact that alleged male witches had been excluded from witchcraft research and the approaches used in the few studies in which this phenomenon had been acknowledged.[8] Apart from an analysis of contemporary literature on gender-specific observations the study contained little of their own empirical witchcraft research. With their hypothesis that the male witch was feminized in the early modern era, they reiterate and expand on an important and correct position which confutes previous arguments, and the criticisms brought forward by the two authors certainly served to fuel the discussion in witchcraft research. William Monter's contribution in the *Encyclopedia of Witchcraft*, on the other hand, is well structured and poses important questions but does not really reflect the current research status.[9]

The studies by Karin Amundsen, Malcolm Gaskill and Elisabeth Kent for the Anglo-Saxon field, Rune Hagen and Antero Heikkinnen for Scandinavia, William Monter for Normandy in France, and Valerie Kivelson for Russia have all discussed the significance of men as persecution victims. Wolfgang Behringer, Boris Fuge and Robert Walinski-Kiehl describe individual trials, while Robin Briggs, Alison Rowlands, Norbert Schindler and Karen Lambrecht investigated individual places or regions in the Holy Roman Empire.[10]

All these authors have contributed large or small pieces of the mosaic which have helped to bring light to the phenomenon male witch. Finally, in 2006 a conference on 'Witchcraft and Masculinities in the Early Modern World' was held at the University of Essex in the UK; the conference was attended by scholars from many different countries and many important issues were broached. The conference proceedings edited by Alison Rowlands and Jenni Grundy will be published in 2008.

'Man as Witch' does not aim to pretend to be able to address all the questions which arise in the light of the numerous trials of men in Central Europe, but does look into certain questions in greater detail:

- The men persecuted as so-called 'werewolves' in the Free County of Burgundy/Franche-Comté are the subject of Chapter 2. This chapter looks into the possibility that the historical werewolf phenomenon might be a male version of the female witch stereotype.
- The percentage of men persecuted in the course of the witch-hunts has only ever been estimated–at between 15 per cent and 25 per cent–dependent on author and work. Chapter 3 pools the results from a large number of studies on gender distribution, thus giving a quantitative survey of the breadth and intensity of this issue.
- Chapter 4 discusses the hypothesis that the number of men accused increased in the intensive phases of mass trials.
- Chapter 5 deals with the integration of the male sex in the witch image of contemporary theology and demonology.
- Chapter 6 discusses with a case-study of Schleswig and Holstein the gender-specific roles as portrayed in popular discourse on the crime of witchcraft and goes on to compare witch images in elite and popular culture.
- In Chapters 7 and 8 the focus is on actual persecutions in various parts of the Holy Roman Empire. Two territories were chosen in which the proportions of men among the persecuted were very different: in Holstein in present-day northern Germany, men played only a minor role as victims; in Carinthia in present-day Austria they represented the majority. These chapters also discuss whether men were only the secondary targets of the persecutors and investigate the extent to which they were associated with heresy and whether different magic realms and powers were ascribed to the two sexes.
- Chapter 9 discusses the working term 'male witch' and examines the extent to which the concepts of 'womanishness' and 'feminized men' can be applied to men persecuted as witches.
- The final chapter attempts to place the results of this investigation in the general social, religious and denominational context of the Early Modern era.

In order to improve the readability of this study, which works with numerous European languages, the spelling in unprinted sources has been very cautiously adapted to modern usage. As citations from printed early modern German, Latin, French and Danish demonology are also analyzed from a linguistic point of view, they are translated into English; however, the most relevant passages are given in their original form in the annotations to give readers the opportunity to scrutinize them for themselves. 'Man as Witch' is not only a revised and updated translation of the earlier German edition from 2000; it has been gratifying to note that the witchcraft research of the past eight years has broadened our knowledge of this dark period of European history, and many chapters have been expanded and parts rewritten for an Anglo-Saxon readership.

The problematic nature of the word 'witch'

Male witches (in German 'Hexenmeister' and 'Hexenmänner') are men or persons of male gender; witches are women or persons of female gender who were either explicitly charged with witchcraft or for whom the original sources imply that they were indicted for witchcraft. For the purposes of this definition it is irrelevant whether the trials ended in execution, banishment or acquittal.

A qualitative analysis requires clear terminology. The English word 'witch' is defined as 'esp. a woman supposed to have dealings with the devil or evil spirits and to be able by their cooperation to form supernatural acts'[11] or as 'a person, now esp. a woman, who professes or is supposed to practice magic, esp. black magic or the black art; sorceress' Thus, the modern English noun 'witch' clearly refers to the female sex, although the word has its etymological roots in both Old English male 'wicca' and female 'wicce'. The dual gender meaning of the plural 'wiccan' was, however, lost in early modern times so that there is today no male equivalent to the female 'witch'. So as to distinguish them from women, male witches in the 16th and 17th centuries were described as 'he-witches' or 'men-witches',[12] terms which did not, however, persist. The noun 'wizard' comes from the Old French and describes a magically active person, probably a "wise man", but not a male witch.[13]

The English words 'sorcerer' and 'sorceress' do not relate semantically to the early modern crime of witchcraft and thus cannot be used without ambiguity in this context. Other historians have attempted to solve this problem in translations for the Anglo-Saxon world by using the gender-overlapping term 'worker of harmful magic'.[14] As far as facts and circumstamces go, this term is totally correct, but seems nonetheless a rather abstract or even awkward rendering.

Other European languages have retained gender-indicative terms for witches: the French 'sorcier' (plural: 'sorciers') and the Latin 'maleficus' (plural: 'malefici') are used for a witch of either sex, but also for a man alone; the terms 'sorcière' and 'malefica' (plural: 'sorcières', 'maleficae') describe a female witch only. Both French and Latin grammar prescribe the use of the masculine plural form for a minority of male and majority of female persons, and distinguish between natural and grammatical gender.[15]

These are not the only European languages to have developed a gender distinction for the people guilty of witchcraft offences. German has 'Hexe' (female), but also 'Hexenmann/Hexenmeister' (male); Spanish has 'bruja' and 'brujo', Italian 'strega' and 'stregone'. In the Scandinavian languages Danish, Norwegian and Swedish we find, for example, the masculine 'trollmand/trollkarl/trulkarl' side by side with the feminine 'trollkvinde/trollkvinna/trulkonna', terms with easily identifiable common roots for all three languages. The Dutch courts used the terms 'tovares' for women and 'tovenaar' for men.

In order to avoid misunderstandings 'witch' is used throughout this study as a gender-neutral term, and 'male witch' and 'female witch' are used for precision and clarification where necessary.

Although the elaborated concept of witchcraft became established in Europe in the 16th century, in some regions official scribes, witnesses and defendants before the courts, theologians and jurists continued to use the traditional sorcery terms for the imagined crime: signified and signifier diverged. So as to avoid confusion the translation uses the appropriate expressions on the semantic level and not the lexical terms as recorded in the source material.

2
The Persecution of Men as Werewolves in Burgundy

Man is a wolf to man

(Thomas Hobbes, *Leviathan*, 1651)

In this sense Hobbes' thinking is wrong

(Denis Diderot, *Hobbisme, Encyclopédie ou dictionnaire raisonné* ..., Paris 1751–65)

The study begins by tracing the fate of some of the men persecuted as so-called 'werewolves' in the Free County of Burgundy or Franche-Comté. The central issue discussed in this chapter is to what extent the werewolf figure was potentially an alternative, male model to the 'witch' figure mainly attributed to women. The chapter goes on to discuss why this phenomenon occurred more frequently in Franche-Comté than in many other territories of the Holy Roman Empire and why it eventually became subsumed under the concept of witchcraft.

Jacques Bocquet, a werewolf, and the St Claude trials

On 5 June 1598 eight-year-old Loyse Maillat from the isolated hamlet of Courier suddenly began to crawl on all fours, her mouth twisted in strange contortions. Within a short space of time her body had stiffened almost to the point of paralysis; in gabbled sentences she accused another village resident of having struck her with a disease. She was referring to Françoise Sécretain, a 58-year-old woman who lived alone in extreme poverty in this remote village high up in the Jura mountains. A few days earlier, Sécretain had asked the family if they had somewhere for her to sleep for the night; as her husband was away at the time, the girl's mother had initially refused, but later relented.

When Sécretain was told of the accusation she sought help from one of the local cunning folk, a beggar known as 'Gros' Jacques Bocquet, who was later to be described by Henri Boguet, a judge located in the nearby town of St Claude, as '...one of the great male witches of his time'.[1] Jacques Bocquet advised the desperate woman to fetch some bread from the Maillats' home, keep it for three days and then attempt to sneak it into the girl's food; this, he maintained, would heal the allegedly enchanted child. The historical sources do not reveal whether or not Sécretain was able to perform this counter-spell but it is certain that the child did not recover at this stage. After a further four weeks her parents decided to seek help from a Catholic priest in St Claude. When the bewitched child, Loyse, declared that she was possessed by five devils, the cleric announced that he would perform an exorcism as an effective means of casting them out.

The next day all five demons simultaneously departed the girl's body after the priest had performed the rite of exorcism and the parents had prayed all night in the monastery of St Claude. Loyse Maillat recovered for all to see, but Sécretain was arrested and charged with witchcraft. After three days in a dungeon and an examination for the Devil's mark, her resistance broke and she admitted having made a contract and had sexual intercourse with the Devil, who had appeared to her in the form of a black man. Subsequently, she admitted visiting the witches' Sabbat where the participants had conjured hail showers. Here, she said, she had also seen 'Gros' Jacques Bocquet who had used a magic powder to cause the death of several cows. Finally, she admitted giving Loyse, who by this time had recovered from her sickness, some bread over which she had cast a spell.

Sécretain's was a classic confession in the sense of contemporary demonology, as she admitted to all the fundamental elements of witchcraft – from harmful magic, a pact with the Devil and intercourse with the Devil to participation in the witches' Sabbat. Her avowals initiated a wave of trials of people with alleged magic powers, at the end of which 19 men and women were indicted, 17 of whom were put to death.

As a result of the allegations made by Sécretain, Bocquet was also arrested and imprisoned (as Sécretain was), in a small, damp cell in St Claude, where his body was examined for witches' marks. As no stigma were found, this could not be used against him; he was, however, found to have a broken rosary.[2]

After questioning Sécretain and hearing her plea of guilty, the appointed judge, Henri Boguet,[3] a qualified jurist, began the interrogation with this new incriminating evidence. The historical sources do not make it clear whether the accused was tortured or only subjected to verbal interrogation; after some time, however, Bocquet confessed in detail to witchcraft and admitted having repeatedly used a magic powder to kill livestock and poultry.

In his confession he stated that he had often been able to make hail by beating water in a pot and had used this hail to destroy fruit before the harvest. Hailstones, he said, could also be made from a magic powder which was transformed into ice pellets in a water container. He also maintained that he was able to become a wolf by applying to his skin a greasy ointment which he had been given by the Devil. As a wolf, in French a 'loup-garou', that is a werewolf, he was able to attack other people, and to kill and finally eat them.

Not only he himself, Bocquet informed the court, was able to become a wolf; there were others in the area around St Claude, indeed entire packs of werewolves partook of these night-time meetings under the leadership of the Devil.[4] The judge appeared to be particularly interested in this part of Bocquet's confession and once he had established that the Sabbat participants all knew one another he focussed his interrogation on these nightly gatherings, concluding that participation in the Sabbat need not necessarily be physical but could also be in spirit, 'One can go to the Sabbat in the spirit'[5] Bocquet, when then asked to elaborate, gave the names of others who had allegedly entered into pacts with the Devil; their names cannot, however, be derived with any certainty from the court protocols or Boguet's report.

Bocquet, then, like Sécretain, made a similar confession, one difference being that she had not admitted to being a werewolf.

This and other testimonies by witnesses from villages around St Claude convinced Boguet of the existence of a witch community in the region and persuaded him to order arrests on a larger scale, in the course of which ten more people were committed to jail.

Boguet, the judge, devoted himself principally to the alleged cases of werewolves and thus went further than to merely expose the Devil's sect and its supposed subsection in St Claude. Boguet faced a major problem here, as majority opinion in Catholic theology since Augustine considered such transmutations to be impossible and to stem purely from the realms of fantasy.[6]

Boguet was aware of these standpoints, but when some of the accused began to demonstrate to him in the courtroom the behaviour of werewolves by running around the room on all fours, he began to doubt this doctrine: 'Together with our scribe Mr Claude Meynier, I have seen how those who I have enumerated moved around a room on all fours just as they did when I saw them in the fields.'[7]

When these prisoners testified that they were unable to transform themselves fully, since they did not have access to their magic ointment in prison, the judge's scepticism towards the official Catholic doctrine was intensified. Nonetheless, in this case the theologian in Boguet triumphed over the practically-minded man, and he arrived at a theoretical compromise: werewolf transformations have no bearing on reality, but the Devil is in a position to cause an illusion of such transformations.[8]

Boguet decided to follow this trial through and ordered further arrests to be made. Nine more suspects were apprehended: Clauda Gaillard, Thievienne Paget, Pernette Molard, Claude Soye, Clauda Jeanprost, Christophle d'Arenthon, Claude de la Tour, Claude Charlot and Claude Guillaume.[9] From here onwards the nature of the persecution changed; to Boguet the emergence of werewolves had come to represent a specific form of witchcraft which involved the brutish tearing asunder of human life. The 'werewolf witches' and the 'werewolf male witches' had to be eradicated. Boguet thus integrated the werewolf pattern into the witch paradigm, classifying the attacks on people and livestock as elements of harmful magic. He no longer deemed it necessary to prove that all the accused were guilty of werewolf activity; harm caused to humans and livestock was sufficient for a conviction.

Jacques Bocquet, the self-confessed werewolf, was condemned to death in 1598. This popular healer was burnt alive at the stake and was refused the mercy of being strangled prior to the burning, which would have spared him atrocious pain and suffering. According to Boguet's account, Bocquet went to the stake a contrite man, repenting his evilness.[10] All the others named by Bocquet and Sécretain were put to death – with the exception of one Christophe d'Arenthon, a child who did not even know his own name and was instead named after the village from which he came. Sécretain herself died in prison before she could be put to death.

In the course of the trial more news reached St Claude. A wolf, it was reported, had killed the son of a couple named Bridel. In the previous months there had been reports of attacks by wolves, but the current case was different in that the animal had no tail and had distinctly human hands on the underside of his paws – unmistakable features of a werewolf. The victim, 15-year-old Benoist Bridel, died as a result of the attack, and the villagers were quick to suspect a woman named Perrenette Gandillon of having appeared here in lupine form. Gandillon was seized, and stoned to death.[11] Her brother, Pierre Gandillon was at this point working on a small farm where he was subsequently arrested. At the time of his arrest, in the view of his pursuers, everything about his appearance signalized him as a wolf: his face, his hands and his legs were grazed and scratched, they thought, from running through the undergrowth of the forest, indeed his whole seemingly disfigured and inhuman appearance alarmed them: 'Pierre Gandillon was so disfigured as to bear no resemblance to a human being.'[12]

In the interrogation which followed Pierre Gandillon admitted he was an apostate from God, had succumbed to the Devil with whom he had had sexual intercourse, and had several times attended the witches' Sabbat. Those attending these nightly meetings had kissed the behind of the Devil – who appeared in the form of a he-goat – and had made plans to cause storms to destroy what was already a meagre harvest in this mountainous area. The Devil, Gandillon maintained, provided them with wolfskins and the ointment needed for the metamorphosis. Gandillon admitted having attacked and devoured a number of children from communities around the village of Nezen, thus confessing to lycanthropy.[13] His son Georges similarly admitted making a pact with the Devil and attending the Sabbat – but not to committing infanticide. As a werewolf he had only attacked goats, not people.

A glance at the reasons given by the court shows that the werewolf concept and the witch paradigm have now merged into one. The witches' Sabbat is seen as a meeting-place for werewolves who plan there crimes to be carried out at a later time:

> Thus because he attended the Sabbat and gatherings of male witches and witches. Also because he once transformed himself into a wolf with the aid of his aunt Perrenette Gandillon, who provided him with a wolfskin and smeared his stomach with a certain grease. This is how, with his aunt's help, he turned into a wolf, seized a goat, carried it away and devoured it in the house of the above-mentioned aunt.[14]

In this verdict a woman, Perrenette Gandillon, is named as the chief offender. The court's investigations singled her out as a particularly aggressive member of the alleged wolf pack, and the suspicions of the villagers culminated in a violent lynching. The court verdict also followed the testimony of Georges Gandillon, thus showing their belief that both genders are capable of magical transformation into an animal and of killing in this guise.

Georges Gandillon divulged further details regarding the activities of those in pact with the Devil. On Maundy Thursdays, he reported, he would experience a strange condition while in bed; he would regularly fall into a kind of deep sleep from which he would awake not refreshed but exhausted and extremely tired. Judge Boguet interpreted these periods of unconsciousness as times when he attended the Sabbat.[15]

Georges' sister, Anthoine Gandillon, who had also been arrested was indicted for witchcraft alone, and was not obliged to admit to lycanthropy.

Various evidence given in court caused suspicion to fall on another family, the Vuillermoz. In the preliminary inquiry 20 witnesses gave evidence against Guillaume Vuillermoz, stating that he had long been reputed to be a witch. Boguet also questioned his 12-year-old son, with the result that the boy further incriminated his father, saying that they had been to the witches' Sabbat together. A dramatic scene ensued between father and son in which Guillaume, aware of the gravity of the boy's statement, attempted to save them both from a conviction. In court he pretended not to recognize his son; even after Boguet ordered the boy to be undressed, Vuillermoz still refused to identify him as his son. The boy, however, repeated his incriminating words and his father broke down weeping, biting his lips and scratching his face, fully aware of the difficult position in which they both found themselves: 'Oh, my son, you will destroy us both…' he cried, while Boguet noted down in surprise: 'He spoke at times in a loving tone to his son.'[16]

Guillaume Vuillermoz was not to live much longer – the conditions of his imprisonment and perhaps, too, his despair was too much for him and he died in prison before his case could be concluded. He had not pleaded guilty. After long deliberations, the court ordered his son, Pierre, to be given strict religious instruction and schooling under the control of the Catholic church.[17]

In 1599 the Abbot of the monastery at St Claude, who had appointed Boguet to preside over these trials, ordered all the accused to be burnt at the stake on the market square in front of a large crowd. After this series of trials the werewolf prosecutions in St Claude came to a halt; in 1603, 1604 and 1608 there were further persecutions, but this time the accused were charged and convicted as witches and male witches.[18]

Jacques Bocquet – burnt at the stake in 1598 – was one of numerous men executed in the course of the witch-hunts of the 16th and 17th centuries. It was not because of his alleged activities as a werewolf that Bocquet met his violent death but because he was charged with and admitted having performed witchcraft. He admitted to large-scale maleficium, to having consciously entered into a pact with the Devil, to membership in the Devil's sect, but not to sexual intercourse with the Devil. The court integrated his activities as a werewolf into the general witch paradigm, subsuming this into a more comprehensive perception of witchcraft, and passing judgment on him in a classic witch trial. Bocquet, however, was no average agent of evil; his persecutors saw him as playing a leading role in what they imagined to be the local St Claude sub-section of the witches' sect and as the leader of the local werewolf pack, and, as such, as entertaining more direct contact with the Devil than anyone else. When Sécretain implicated him, this was the first time he had been denounced, but it was sufficient to focus the attention of the witch-hunters directly on his person.

On close examination, however, it becomes clear that Bocquet was not one of the maleficents; indeed his place was on the other side, as one who was able to apply counter-magic. Sécretain, who had been labelled a witch, turned to Bocquet as an expert magical healer in trust, hoping to be able to relay the suspicion into which she had fallen and to save the allegedly enchanted child. Bocquet advised her to use a resource behind which the imagery of contagion is apparent: eating another piece of bread charged with magic powers is expected to break the earlier magic spell cast by some anonymous person.

In her despair, Sécretain viewed Bocquet as a professional magician with a positive function. Boguet, the well-educated, cultured judge, on the other hand diabolized him; in his view, and this was in accordance with the generally accepted concept of demonology, both black and white magic stemmed from an evil pact. So, Boguet the learned witch-hunter demonized this popular cunning man – who might even be described as a practitioner of countermagic – classifying his doings as acts of magical aggression. Thus the healer became a male witch, and no longer able to withstand this suspicion of his person and crushed by the long interrogations, he confessed. Through the escalation dynamics inherent to many witch trials he incriminated other people. The end of it all was the stake at St Claude.

Another one of the numerous male victims of witch-hunts was Guillaume Vuillermoz who, as described above, died in prison before the end of his trial; he was not, however, one of the early modern professional cunning folk. He had allegedly performed harmful magic and was thus suspected of being a male witch. He, too, became an explicit suspect on the grounds of another person's testimony, and was tried for witchcraft. It is not difficult to conceive of the child's statements as part of a father–son conflict, since the boy must have been aware (at least as the trial progressed) of the danger in which he was placing his father. Vuillermoz, on the other hand, retained his paternal role, protected his son and to the very last refused to incriminate him, a fact which probably saved the boy's life. There is no record of the questions asked of Vuillermoz, but the principal charge laid against him makes it clear that he was prosecuted for attending the witches' Sabbat.

The alleged werewolf Pierre Gandillon admitted having sexual intercourse with a she-demon at the Sabbat. In his case, the full breadth of the witch paradigm was applied, including the charge of intercourse with a she-demon, a fact which also shows that this element of the witchcraft concept was not considered exclusive to female witches. Gandillon became a suspect because of his sister's testimony and because his appearance branded him as a potential werewolf. Living, as he did, in the mountainous forest far from St Claude and scraping an existence for himself and his family with a few livestock (probably goats) he bore all the signs of physical toil. Judge Boguet interpreted these as typical signs of incomplete lycanthropy. Just as a witch could be identified by her Devil's marks, so too were there characteristic marks by which it was possible to identify a werewolf.

The trial of the Gandillon family yields yet more insight. Perrenette Gandillon was stoned to death by the villagers, and this incident of lynching reflects the atmosphere which prevailed in the St Claude region at the end of the 16th century. The concept of the werewolf had deep roots among the residents of the Jura region of Franche-Comté, and werewolf hunts derived from the needs of a peasant population. Even Boguet, the well-educated jurist was unable to avoid having to analyze the reported and repeated attacks and the way they were interpreted as deriving from magical activities. He had begun to doubt the theological doctrines of the time and justified the way he dealt with the werewolf epidemic by transforming popular belief and ideas into a pattern which was theologically justifiable. The stoning of Perrenette Gandillon had already shown that in popular culture werewolves were no longer exclusively a male phenomenon; Boguet, along with the establishment, now also began to target women in his persecutions. Under the legal direction of Henri Boguet an increasing number of women came to be tried for lycanthropy. Of the ten people tried in 1598 for allegedly mutating into aggressive animals, seven were female.

What is more, Boguet's approach was directed against a clearly distinguishable group of people within the Jura population. Bocquet, popularly reputed to be, and described by Boguet as, knowledgeable of protective magic spells, could not be suspected by the villagers of harmful magic or destructive metamorphosis. However, Bocquet had migrated to the area from Savoy and so was not a local. The accused Sécretain, Vuillermoz, d'Arenthon and du Vernois were also immigrants to the region.[19] This example is indicative of the fact that witch-hunts in and around St Claude were aimed chiefly and unmistakably against families who had recently moved to the area and who as such clearly stood out from the rest of the population. The extermination of poorly integrated families thus acted as a valve for the werewolf fears of the locals.

Bocquet was probably also a victim of Calvinist–Catholic indirect cooperation. In his homeland Savoy (which at that time covered a larger area than the boundaries to which it has been restricted since 1601 and, at least as a geographical term, included parts of today's French-speaking Switzerland) the end of the 16th century was a period of intensive witch persecutions, some of which were described in demonological works. Lambert Daneau, a theologian from Geneva, described massive witch-hunts in Savoy and noted that large numbers of female and male witches had fled from persecution:

> ...in Savoy and its surroundings the witches and male witches are so densely [congregated] as to make it impossible to root them out, although there are avid searches and a no less rigorous judiciary, until 80 of them from a single town of the region have been burnt in one year.[20]

Another theologian, Johann Jakob Wick of Zürich, also reported on these trials. According to his chronicle there were at the end of the 16th century in Savoy:

> ...large numbers of witches and male witches, many of whom have been executed and are still being executed daily by the authorities in Bern and Geneva. A servant relates having seen many of them, large numbers of whom have been condemned, but many, too, have escaped.[21]

From all that has been handed down about the witch-finder Jacques Bocquet, he belonged to this latter group, having fled from the Calvinist, or possibly the more southern Catholic, part of Savoy across the mountains into Franche-Comté. Here, he managed to scrape an existence and perform some of his past practices, but it was not long before he was again accused – and this time the outcome was fatal. The cunning man was tried for witchcraft in the form of lycanthropy and condemned to be burnt at the stake.

Broken by the trial and Boguet's interrogations, both he and Georges Gandillon gave accounts of unusual states of consciousness. One of them reported attendance at the witches' Sabbat – but this attendance was not physical, it was 'en âme', that is in soul or in spirit. Gandillon recounted long periods of unconsciousness on certain days such as Maundy Thursday before Easter, from which it took him a long time to recover.

Such reports are reminiscent of the so-called 'Benandanti' from Friuli in the north of Italy, a mountainous area on the edge of the Alps, and in that sense similar to the Jura region. The Venetian Inquisition tracked down these people (whose name means as much as 'do-gooders') in the period 1575–1650 and tried them for heresy. Most of the Benandanti were men who had set themselves the task of protecting their villages from harm caused by witchcraft. They asserted that four times a year their spirits left their bodies and departed from their homes to fight the witches who were destroying their fertility and their harvests. To do this it seems they fell into a kind of trance. Inquisitors – such as Judge Boguet in Franche-Comté – interpreted these events as attendances of the witches' Sabbat. In long interrogations they succeeded in making some Benandanti, most of them men, dissociate themselves from their self-perception as godly warriors fighting against destructive magic; the result was a complete turn-around such that the men came to accept the perception the authorities had of them as witches and witchmasters.[22] And it was for witchcraft that they were prosecuted.

The parallels between the utterances of the Benandanti in Italy and those of the werewolves in Burgundy are purely descriptive, and it must be pointed out in this context that the statements laid down in Boguet's work and available to us today are not the original statements of the accused but are coloured by and interspersed with Boguet's own theological interpretations. Whether or not the countermagical expert Bocquet and the suspected male witch Gandillon saw themselves, similarly to the Benandanti, as chosen warriors who actively and regularly set forth in the services of the common good cannot be determined from the available Burgundy sources. What can be said is that, unlike in Friuli, no group structure existed, and we must assume that these were the deeds of individuals.

'Gros' Jacques Bocquet can be assigned more readily to the type of male healers found in other parts of the Empire, who were also victims of witch persecutions. In the Allgäu region of the Alps, the local witch expeller and seer Chonrad Stoeckhlin fell into trances, recounted trips in spirit between this life and the afterworld, visions which eventually brought Stoeckhlin himself under suspicion of witchcraft. His accounts set off a massive witch-hunt towards the end of the 16th century; he himself was tried for witchcraft and subsequently executed.[23]

Similar persecution patterns which began with accounts or denunciations of male magic specialists are also to be found in other regions of the Empire, as well as in France and Switzerland.[24]

Werewolf images

Werewolves were considered to be people who through some magic ritual had metamorphosed into wolves. The concept of animal metamorphosis is a cross-cultural one and is, indeed, one of the central myths of humanity. In Europe, as elsewhere, this concept was not restricted to specific animals.

With the exception of the north Germanic sagas in which the ability to metamorphose into wild animals was largely restricted to the gods,[25] no clear-cut picture of what constituted a werewolf emerged in Central Europe. In the 8th century, Bishop Boniface gave a baptism sermon in which he admonished his flock to relinquish their belief in such metamorphoses, comparing this to transgressions of the Ten Commandents:

> Listen, my brothers. You shall reflect well on what you proclaim at baptism. You have renounced the Devil and all his works and all his pomp. What then are the Devil's works? They are pride, idolatory, envy, murder, abduction, adultery, all vices, theft, false witness, robbery, gluttony, inebriation, slander, quarrelsomeness, anger, poisoning, the study of incantations and consulting soothsayers, and the belief in witches [in Classical Latin the term 'strix' denotes a bloodsucking witch, R. S.] and fictive wolves...These and other evil works are of the Devil.[26]

In the tradition of the church Boniface rejects lycanthropy as fictive, but at the same time his comments show that the concept of animal metamorphosis was widespread. However, it is not possible to infer any concrete werewolf images either from these sources or from the works of Burchard of Worms. From the latter, writing in the 11th century, we know that the term existed; his penitential stipulated that anyone confessing to believe in lycanthropy should be given ten days' penance on bread and water:

> Have you believed, as some are wont to do ... that some people, whenever they so wish, can transform themselves into wolves, 'werewolves' as the Teutons say, or into some other form? If you believe this ... you must do a penance of ten days on bread and water.[27]

This article again confirms that the werewolf concept must have been one of popular culture, since church Latin, the language of contemporary elite culture, knows no word for it and Burchard is thus obliged to use a colloquial German term in the text, adding 'as the Teutons say'.[28] The offence was considered neither serious nor minor as the penalty was precisely the same as that given for receiving the host at mass without previous abstinence.[29]

Burchard gives no more detailed record of what this concept meant to people of his time. Neither was the term used in contemporary court literature, so that no concrete description of the werewolf paradigm has been handed down for the German-speaking lands in the High and Late Middle Ages.[30] Nor is it possible to reconstruct how widespread it was. Only the etymological root from the Old High German 'wer' meaning 'man' points to a link between the 'man-wolf' and the male gender.[31]

More details about alleged werewolves can be found in sources and literature from the French-speaking areas of Central and Western Europe. In 12th century novels by Guillaume de Palerme a prince, turned by his stepmother into a wolf, cares like a mother for an abducted child, protects absconding young couples from their pursuers, and finally becomes a human being again.[32]

Two werewolves are also the focal point of two of Marie de France's verse narratives, known as 'lais'. Marie de France lived in England but was French-born and related French folk tales in the Norman and Breton tradition. In 'Bisclavret' she portrays a man as a victim of his wife. For reasons which are not described, the nobleman occasionally, but involuntarily, takes on the likeness of a wolf and confesses this secret to his wife. She, who is loved by another man, makes the most of this knowledge to permanently turn him into a wolf and thus to dispose of him. The bisclavret is finally able to escape his fate when the King and others are struck by the human-like, genteel, behaviour of the beast; thanks to another magic spell he is finally able to resume the form of a man. In the 'lai de Melion' a wolf leads his pack to lay waste to the entire land but is eventually also released from the spell which compelled him to this aggressiveness and he is fully transformed back into a human being. The thus liberated person was also male.[33]

Gervase of Tilbury, Marshall to the Holy Roman Emperor Otto IV wrote his Otia Imperialia (Recreation for an Emperor) for his patron; here, he related folklore and tales from the French-speaking region where he lived around 1214. He was also interested in werewolf reports and described two alleged animal metamorphoses in which men became wolves out of sheer despair. Their brutality caused fear and distress in the forests of the Auvergne and Vivarais; nonetheless, they were able, by chance, to cast off the spell by which they had been bound and revert to being non-aggressive human beings. One of the two, who had torn apart and eaten children, was released from his fate by having a foot cut off.[34] These tales reflect the basic constellation seen in Marie de France's narratives.

Gervase uses in his tales a term for human wolves which was later used in the 16th century Franche-Comté werewolf trials:

> We have seen in England that humans are often transformed into werewolves when the moon phase changes; the Gauls call this type of people 'gerulfi', and the English 'werewolf', 'were' in English meaning a man.[35]

The roots of the later French term '[loup]garou' can be discerned in the word 'gerulfus'. This seemingly Romanic term had developed from the concept 'leu warou'. Whilst 'leu' can be traced back to the Latin noun 'lupus', the second part of the word 'warou' is derived from the Franconian word 'wer' meaning man. Through an abrasion of the consonants and a sound shift, 'leu warou' became 'leu garoul'.[36] Gervase then re-Latinised this term and 'gerulfus', the French 'gerulfus' of the Middle Ages, became 'loup-garou', the early modern French word for this phenomenon. The etymology of the word 'loup-garou' then shows that in French-speaking regions the roots of the human wolf are clearly male.

An involuntarily brutal wolf also appears in a tale by William of Paris (known in France as Guillaume d'Auvergne) written around 1228. The wolf, who turned out to be a human male, was delivered from his fate by a saint. The author, a theologian and Bishop of Paris, presented this as an event which had occurred only in the imagination and not in reality: William of Paris considered the story a means of conveying the message that the belief in human wolves should be renounced and that any alleged transformation took place purely in the imagination. This was fully in accordance with the church doctrine of the time which considered animal metamorphoses impossible.[37] Werewolves were, doubtless, men but they did not exist in reality, being only figments of folkloristic imagination. Theologically, then, werewolves did not exist in the High Middle Ages.

The fact that the werewolf image was already distorted and mythicized by sagas suggests that the concept of werewolves was probably widespread in French-speaking regions and had not only negative but also ambivalent connotations. The ostracized, the desperate: these were the people who through betrayal and fate were forced against their will to become beasts whilst maintaining their human nature and characteristics, all of which again became predominant when the spell was broken. The view was that werewolves were victims – and men. A collection of folkloristic and popular sayings published in old French in the 15th century makes this quite clear: 'If it is a man's fate to become a werewolf, then it is very likely that his son will also do so. And if he has a daughter and no son, she will become a "mar", a "night mare".'[38] Spirits called alp or mar, it was thought, could, by creating a feeling of suffocation, cause bad dreams, so-called nightmares.

This lore from popular culture of the late Middle Ages only links the werewolf paradigm to the male gender under specific circumstances. The ability to metamorphose could be bequeathed patrilineally; this explains why people believed in the existence of werewolf families. The quote from this 15th century source, then, does not indicate that werewolves were always male, but does confirm that this was considered to be the case when the werewolf fate was passed down within a close family group.

By Early Modern times, however, male werewolves in the area around St Claude in Franche-Comté were no longer victims (as their counterparts in the Middle Ages had been), but had become evil-doers, indeed they were viewed as infinitely aggressive beasts. There was no longer anything positive to be found in them, all ambivalence had disappeared; the werewolf image had changed. The same applies to the female werewolves of St Claude, for by this time the alleged werewolves captured in this mountainous territory were by no means all male.

Jean Bodin and the Catholic devil-wolf

Belief in animal metamorphosis is based on the assumption that there are evil elements in human beings which can express themselves in the form of autonomous beings. Typically, such beings look like animals and lead a bloodthirsty nightlife. Almost the entire demonological literature of the Early Modern age rejected the idea of animal metamorphosis and declared such phenomena mere figments of the imagination.[39] Protestant demonology in particular, presented a uniform front, based on the teachings of Martin Luther.[40] Belief in werewolves was only able to assert itself in certain branches of Catholic demonology; Bodin, a supporter of the theory of absolute monarchy and a political thinker, played a major role here. He regarded animal metamorphosis as real, and in a chapter of his 'Démonomanie des sorciers' entirely devoted to this subject tried to prove in detail that it was really possible.[41]

Unlike the witch-hunter Boguet in Burgundy, Bodin and his works were highly respected. Boguet was not appointed to the 'Parlement', the chief provincial court (which consisted primarily of jurists) until shortly before his death, whereas Bodin was long considered an authority and cited as such in trials.[42] Under Bodin, and as a direct result of his influence and his detailed descriptions, the ambivalent werewolf image underwent a dramatic development from the unhappy being of the Middle Ages to the threatening devil-wolf of the Early Modern era. The Christian werewolf was no longer a product of the human mind or a trick of the devil; it had become very real, and beneath the wolf-skin were human beings who used magic arts to turn into fearful and threatening wild animals. Bodin cited contemporary reports to show how werewolves attacked children, tore them into pieces and devoured them. His reports went on to demonstrate that werewolves had developed a predilection for human buttocks, intestines and extremities, but that they also attacked livestock '... and cause[d] copious damage'.[43] The werewolves were in the Devil's service and their metamorphosis was one of Satan's works. As wolves they also had intercourse with female wolves '... with the same lust as they were accustomed to with women' and the human beasts gathered at night in remote and distant castles.[44] Bodin transposed the classic elements of Catholic teachings on witches to the old folkloristic werewolf image, showed werewolves to be real by citing numerous contemporary confessions or portrayals and attempted to prove this with reports from Ancient literature, extracts from the Bible and texts written by clerics.

Bodin's Christian werewolf, then, was diametrically opposed to the werewolf of popular culture; all positive or ambivalent aspects had now disappeared. Werewolves were now devouring, destructive and aggressive, had entered pacts with the devil, and were thus voluntary parties to a contract which designated them as cannibalistic variants of witches. Whereas the werewolf of the Middle Ages was an object, obliged by external forces and through no fault of his own to act this way, the new werewolf was an active subject, operating of his own accord, albeit in the service of Satan. In the past, werewolves had been loners; now they performed their evil deeds in packs, in acts of collective aggression. Whilst the unhappy and outcast werewolf of mediaeval popular culture waited for deliverance and acceptance back into the Christian community, the voluntary devil's agent was seen only to be attacking this community and working towards its destruction. For this agent there was no chance of repentance and reintegration. As other folkloristic figures previously characterized by ambivalence, the werewolf figure had now been demonized. It had become imperative that werewolves be eradicated and not that spells be broken. In short, the Christian werewolf had come to be a metaphor for the Devil who has invaded the Christian flock.[45]

Bodin's werewolf is a diabolical, demonized being – as is the witch figure. The difference was, however, that '...men mostly transform into wolves'.[46] Bodin was an influential demonologist and theoretician and his development of the werewolf figure alongside that of the male witch, created an additional, and this time primarily male, version of a witchcraft crime, whilst simultaneously legitimizing the idea that genuine attacks by wolves might be ascribed to magical human aggression.

Such teachings were readily accepted in regions where the ecological conditions provided favourable habitats for wolves, where it was easy to relate Bodin's doctrines to real occurrences. Even if the theological scepticism which still existed did not permit the idea of animal metamorphosis to become totally unchallenged reality, by transforming a werewolf prosecution into a distinctive variant of a witchcraft trial, persecution of werewolves had now been made possible.

By assigning the blame for an anonymous magical attack to a person in wolf's clothing, evil could be personified and eradicated, for the wolf could be hunted down, captured and killed.

Werewolf trials and werewolf panics

The first known werewolf trials in Franche-Comté were conducted by ecclesiastical Inquisition courts. In 1521 the Principal Inquisitor appointed by the Pope for this region travelled from Besançon to Poligny, a largish village in the south of the county to question and try several men. The accused admitted to having turned into wolves, attacked and mutilated several people. Two shepherds, Pierre Burgot and Michel Verdun, stated that they had entrusted themselves to the Devil because they were concerned about their flocks and their own livelihood; the Devil, they said, had promised to protect them and to give them money. They had transformed into wolves by applying to their skin an ointment given them by the Devil. In wolf form they had taken part in night-time werewolf gatherings, but, they said, the transformation had only been of short duration and they had returned to their human forms in a state of exhaustion. These two men and the other accused from Plasne, Michel Udon, Philibert Montot and Pierre Gros were executed in 1521 for practising magic, for murder and heresy.[47]

Thirty years later another Inquisition Court tried a certain Pierre Tornier for lycanthropy. Tornier, a man from the foothills of the Jura in the south of the territory, admitted that together with his wife and sister he had committed 15 murders. The accused in this case faced both werewolf and witchcraft charges,[48] clearly indicating that the court had already begun to draw parallels between the two crimes. All accused were burnt at the stake in 1551 without being granted the mercy of being strangled prior to the burning. They were to feel the excruciating pain of this gradual death and it was intended that the spectators should experience the agony of the dying as a 'show of death'. The church authorities thus made it clear that this was intended as a deterrent and an attempt to stave off a possible werewolf epidemic. Werewolves were no longer outcasts or outsiders; the time had come to take an active and ruthless stance against them.

The Parliament in Dôle criticized the way the trial had been conducted because they felt they had not been duly informed by the Inquisitors. This indicates that the secular authorities were not only stating their claim to the right to prosecute werewolves and witches, but were doing so very pointedly.[49] From this point onwards werewolves faced persecution by the secular authorities.

At the beginning of the 1570s attacks by wolves in Franche-Comté increased in number. A German-speaking student of Dôle University reported that wolves the size of donkeys had been seen to attack people and livestock in the forests.[50] In September 1573, the 'Parlement' of Dôle saw reason to introduce more suitable measures to counteract aggression by wolves. The Parlement was both court and administrative authority in Franche-Comté and as such a typically French institution with no administrative equivalent in any other territory of the Empire. Its members were recruited largely from the legal profession and were appointed by the Habsburg authorities on the recommendation of the Parlement. This Parlement, as all other similar institutions, remained the centre of secular authority during the 16th and 17th centuries, but after the French conquest of Franche-Comté and resulting French centralization it degenerated to become, in practice, a defunct body without decision-making powers.[51] In 1573, however, the Parlement issued a regulation permitting the people to be armed in certain areas of the county, not as a defensive strategy against wolves but as an offensive aimed at the increasing number of humans magically transformed into wolves:

> ... this court has permitted and permits the residents and inhabitants of the named localities and others, irrespective of the hunting statutes to assemble armed with clubs, halberds, pikes, arquebuses and other cudgels and without fear of punishment *to hunt down the named werewolves wherever* they might find, catch, shoot or kill them.[52]

In contravention of the otherwise binding statute which laid down the state's monopoly with regard to arms, the court, as representatives of the Habsburg rulers, permitted the peasants to carry weapons in a form of organized self-help in the fight against werewolves. The edict was renewed the following year without any fundamental changes to the wording or content.[53]

In 1573 an alleged werewolf was finally caught in the pursuers' trap. His name was Gilles Garnier and he lived in isolation with his wife and two friends near Cromary, north of Besançon in the densely forested region of Haute-Saône. This small group of people lived in a grotto in abject poverty, and so were at the very bottom of the lowest stratum of early modern society, and what is more had not long been in the region. Garnier came originally from the south of France but it is not known when he actually settled in the area. He was accused of '... the murder of several children who he had eaten and devoured as a wolf – and of other crimes and offences'.[54] Garnier admitted under questioning, but without torture, that he had attacked several children and had taken parts of their mutilated bodies back to his wife in their hermitage where they had eaten them on a Friday. This alleged werewolf, then, admitted not only to murder but to a sacrilege, to having eaten meat on a Friday, the day Catholics were required to abstain from meat. Garnier's confession was a classic witchcraft confession, the core of which was the Devil's pact to which he also confessed.[55] He was burnt as a male witch in 1574; the fate of the other accused is not known.

In legal terms, the werewolf has by this time been transformed into a special variant of witchcraft offence. Garnier confessed without being tortured, and the idea springs to mind that there might have been a real murderer concealed behind this wolf-devil. However, some of the scenes of crime were more than 60 kilometres from the hermit's dwelling and in view of his physical weakness, which seems to have been apparent at the trial, it appears very unlikely that he would have been able to cover such distances. In the course of the same trial another alleged werewolf by the name of Pierre Culfin[56] was arrested; this time, however, the accused did not admit to the charge and was released on the condition that he appeared regularly before a representative of the relevant authorities.

The next werewolf panic did not break out in Franche-Comté until 1598; this time it ended with 17 death sentences pronounced by Judge Boguet of St Claude. With these trials a change was seen in the gender of the accused werewolves: 70 per cent of those charged with lycanthropy in this ecclesiastical district were female. The werewolf paradigm was further feminized under the influence of massive witch-hunts in the entire region of Franche-Comté towards the end of the 16th century and remained thus until the end of the persecutions.

In the course of the werewolf panic at the end of the 16th century, a man was arrested in Baumes-les-Dames in the Doubs valley in 1599 and accused not only of night-time attacks in animal form but of moral offences such as incest with his mother. A witness was struck by his piercing eyes, which she said were reminiscent of a wolf's. He had a 'dangerous, hideous look. The way this sorcerer eyed me'.[57]

Another (female) witness also described Verjux' appearance, testifying '... a loathsome face, eyes which glowed like a cat's and were as large as a blade, [and that his] mouth [was] open like that of a wolf'.[58] A third witness said Verjux appeared to her like a wolf, who followed her at night to her farmstead and whose presence she felt to be menacing.[59] Verdux was initially suspected of witchcraft for three reasons: the animal-like features of his physiognomy; his reputation as someone who did not conform to the norm; and illnesses not explicable to the villagers. Suspicion led to trial. When convicted, Verjux attempted an appeal to the court at Dôle. The evidence was against him, but because he had not pleaded guilty to the crime, the court banished him from the country.[60]

In another case which occurred in 1605, two soldiers were chasing a wolf which had disappeared into a thicket when, not far from the place where the wolf had vanished, a man emerged from the bushes. He was immediately accused of being a werewolf. The accused, 50-year-old Jacques Valeur earned his living as a beggar and lived in a solitary forest hut in a large area of forest north of Dôle. Denying the soldiers'charge, Valeur defended himself but then suddenly took to his heels and fled, hence reinforcing the initial suspicion. Valeur himself said that he suffered from fainting fits and severe headaches and finally admitted during questioning that he might possibly have eaten several children while experiencing these attacks. The totally bedraggled appearance of this clearly mentally disturbed suspect served the court as additional strongly incriminating evidence, and Valeur was burnt at the stake in Dôle in 1605.[61]

In 1604/5 a local court rejected accusations by villagers who filed charges[62] against two neighbours for alleged night-time werewolf attacks. The court proceeded to turn the charge into one of witchcraft. The two women were subsequently condemned to death as witches. Another prisoner, Perrenette Glaon, however, was sentenced to death by burning for alleged lycanthropy because she '... [had] about 7 years previously transformed herself into a wolf and killed and eaten two children'[63] In this case, the court used the term 'loup' (wolf) in the masculine genus rather than the feminine 'louve'. This meant that women were now seen as being capable of turning themselves into brutal wild animals of the male gender and could be tried individually for this crime. Up until this point, courts had only brought such charges against women when they were suspected of committing these crimes in a group in which men were also involved. Perrenette Glaon was the first woman to be condemned for her alleged ability to turn into a brutal animal without having any connection with a mixed-gender pack of human wolves. Werewolves could now also bear feminine traits.

Several years later the case of Rolin Blanc came up; Blanc was a loner who, as Gilles Garnier in the previous century, lived in a forest hut or possibly a grotto. Blanc had been suspected of a tendency towards animal metamorphosis for some time before a local court decided in 1612 that there were grounds for this accusation and had him arrested. He was burnt at the stake the same year.[64]

Another case in Jonvelle took a rather different turn. The seigneurial court, which was independent of the 'Parlement' in Dôle, believed it had discovered a group of werewolves within its jursidiction. Eighteen-year-old Francois Gousset was accused by almost the entire village of being '... commonly known as a male witch and sorcerer'.[65] A witness, Jean Thevenot, testified that he had recognized him in the form of a 'large [fat] dog and black animal which immediately disappeared and which caused him great alarm'.[66]

Illustration 2.1 A wolf, or perhaps a werewolf, attacks two men just outside the town gate; the fact that one of the men is armed does not deter the aggressive attacker. (Woodcut in Johann Geiler, known as Geiler of Kaisersberg, 'De Emeis', 1516. Johann Geiler preached in Strasbourg Cathedral, and in contrast to later theologians, Geiler thought of werewolves as personified devils and not as metamorphosed humans.)

In the course of the trial, however, the original accusation became increasingly peripheral. The court no longer focussed on the alleged damage caused by Gousset but on his alleged participation in the collective crime of witchcraft. His possible participation in the Sabbat was closely scrutinized. Both in terms of content and in a formal sense the werewolf charge became subordinate to a classical witchcraft charge. For some time, a werewolf charge had been viewed as grounds for prosecution in its own right; this had now definitively changed. The images of witch, male witch and werewolf had not only merged into one, but the more powerful witch image had absorbed the werewolf paradigm. Gousset admitted that as a werewolf he had killed a goat, but went on to tell how he had killed a far larger number of animals through witchcraft.[67] In the view of the prosecution Gousset caused considerably more damage as a male witch than as a werewolf.

Other similar cases also occurred in Jonvelle not long after Gousset's execution. Gérard Horriel, Aymé Boutteiller and Jeanne Horriel were accused of having used magic to strike several people with diseases. The damage they had allegedly transmitted by magic ranged from deafness, to mental suffering and mental illness in the form of a state of possession.[68] The charge of animal metamorphosis played only a subordinate role in this case and, interestingly and uniquely, referred here to a bull. The court's official prosecutor accused the three persons of 'having transformed themselves into wolves and other red-coated animals or bulls'.[69]

A further similar case was that of Adrien Veille, an old man from the village of Montmorot. He was suspected of lycanthropy but was actually charged with witchcraft. It is not known how the case ended, but the evidence was clearly insufficient for a conviction and it is possible that Veille was released from custody.[70]

In 1632 the 'Parlement' in Dôle renewed the edict on organized wolf and werewolf hunts for large areas of Franche-Comté after hearing reports of wolf attacks on people and livestock. In fact, the authorities went even further this time and ordered paid hunters to be appointed. When wolves were sighted near a village, the church bells were to be rung and the villagers were to assemble and be counted. This way, thus the reasoning of the jurists, it would be easier to identify any absentees as werewolves.[71]

A year later, however, the same authorities in Dôle amended the edict and deleted the term 'werewolf'; the human element had now been eliminated. Scepticism towards the concept of werewolves had gained the upper hand amongst the elite of Franche-Comté and this was reflected in amendments to official regulations. The werewolf had now officially disappeared at least in the more accessible regions of the county and from the procedures of the higher courts, but the witch and male witch lived on as objects of persecution and indeed suffered severely in the massive witch-hunts of the mid-17th century which followed a period of relative calm between 1635 and 1655.

Local courts, however, continued to pursue werewolf accusations made by the people. In 1633, for example, a beggar by the name of Claude Beljacquet was indicted for committing brutal night-time deeds as a werewolf; the Parlement, however, intervened in the case and exiled Beljacquet from the country, thus implementing the new form of the edict.[72] In 1657 a local court accused Renobert Bardel from the village of Ougney in the centre of the county of werewolf metamorphosis. In this case, there was no intervention by the Parlement, but Bardel was actually convicted for witchcraft and not lycanthropy.[73] His two children and his mother died at the stake with him.

The concept of the werewolf remained particularly alive in the inaccessible regions of the Jura, where several cases of alleged lycanthropy came before the courts. Whereas, in Bardel's case the werewolf concept appeared solely in the statements of the witnesses, including a son's witness against his father, in the mountainous regions where there was little communication with more populated areas the werewolf paradigm still held strong both among the local peasant population and local judges and thus appeared in the official prosecutions by the local courts. In particular in the jurisdiction of St Claude, which had its own imperial penal code, alleged animal metamorphoses continued to play an important role in some court cases. In 1643 a beggar named Claude Chastellan was arrested. Like others accused in the witchcraft trials of the earlier witchhunt period prior to 1600, he had migrated from Savoy and so did not belong to one of the established peasant families; in today's terms he was a 'foreigner'. Under torture he confessed to a pact with the Devil, to attending the witches' Sabbat, to killing people and to lycanthropy. He was convicted of lycanthropy and burnt at the stake in St Claude in the same year.[74]

Another court condemned Claude Gaillard from Chavéria to death in the course of a major witch trial in 1661 and he was the only one of the accused to be indicted primarily for harmful magic and subsequently, in the course of the same trial, for lycanthropy. Initially, he only admitted membership in a Devil's sect but towards the end of the questioning he confessed to his alleged cannibalistic crimes; the court scribe merely noted down, in unusually brief form, 'He sometimes used a skin to turn into a wolf and – thus transformed – he fetched children.'[75] As in many witch trials in Franche-Comté by this time the charges of maleficium and even of aggressive lycanthropy, played only minor roles. Seven of the twelve charges against Gaillard were related to attendance of the witches' Sabbat, and it was this which became the judges' main focus of attention, with a total of five people thus charged. All the accused – two men and three women – died at the stake in Chavéria.

Women also continued to be charged with aggressive behaviour in conjunction with wolf metamorphosis; the pattern of werewolf charges in Franche-Comté had clearly acquired gender-neutral traits. In 1660, for example, Renoberte Simon, a woman from Chapelle d'Huin an isolated village high up in the Jura mountains, was charged in an individual trial with animal metamorphosis. She was, however, released after refusing to admit to the charges.[76]

Three years later, charges of lycanthropy were made for the last time in this region in a case which aroused a great deal of interest. In the village of St Hymetière (situated at an altitude of 800 m in the foothills of the western Alps) there had been a large number of thefts, armed robberies and even murders. After a protracted inquiry had brought nothing to light, suspicions began to centre around three brothers, Mathieu, Claude and Aymé Mathieu, and the local judge ordered their arrest. In the course of the trial, the charge of lycanthropy was added to those of violence and brutality. Yet, even in this remote area, far from any main road, lycanthropy now only played a subordinate role. Of the 126 charges placed against Mathieu Mathieu, the alleged werewolf crimes concerned the court for only a very short time and remained on the periphery of what was in fact the trial of a male witch.[77] The brothers were generally considered belligerent and argumentative. One female witness incriminated Claude and Mathieu Mathieu by testifying that she had recognized them raiding a house.[78] Initially, the men admitted to none of the charges, although they did disclose their tendency to physical violence when they frankly admitted beating and maltreating their wives.[79] The court subsequently decided to employ torture in order to enforce a confession, with the result that all three brothers admitted a range of witchcraft crimes, including robbery commited with the help of magic. When they finally also admitted to having made a pact with the Devil, the death sentence seemed to be sealed. The case was, however, appealed to the Parlement in Dôle – the responsible authority for such appeals in Franche-Comté – where the death verdict was overturned by a majority of the jurists and the trial declared unlawful. The judges justified their decision by saying that attendance at the Sabbat, as admitted by the accused, might have been a product of the imagination, and that the use of the 'pricking test' was not permissible as a means of obtaining evidence. The court was thus obliged to release the three brothers[80] and the last alleged werewolves returned to the Jura forests from whence they had come.

In summary, then, the werewolf trials began in 1521 with the death sentences for heresy pronounced by the Inquisition courts and ended in 1663 with acquittals before secular courts. In the course of less than 150 years the werewolf paradigm had changed completely. Starting in 1550, but more frequently from 1590 onwards, the courts integrated the werewolf charge into the witchcraft trials, defining it as a particularly brutal kind of maleficium. In the 17th century this interpretation became an integral part of demonology and was accepted by both the lower and the highest courts. The werewolf degenerated to one of many variants of maleficium and thus became a subordinate aspect of the witchcraft trials. The werewolf went and the witch came (see Figure 2.1).[81] The werewolf hunt had effectively become a witch-hunt. In 1550 there was almost one werewolf trial for every two witchcraft trials, by 1600 this

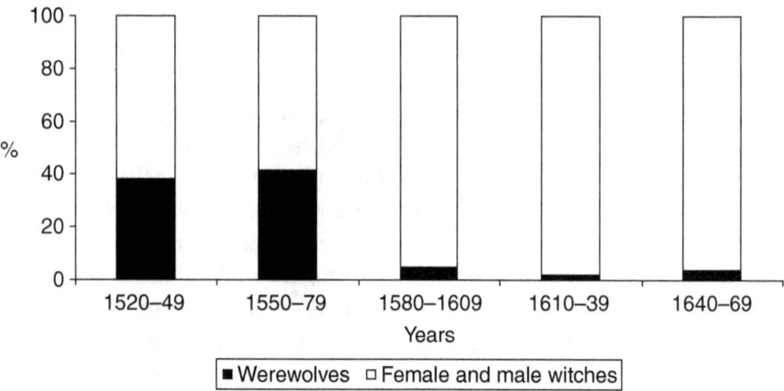

Figure 2.1 Witchcraft trials with/without werewolf charges: Franche-Comté, 1520–1669 (%)

figure had gone down to one in four, and with the turn of the century the proportion further decreased with the increase in the number of classic witchcraft trials. However, this does not mean that werewolves disappeared entirely from the history of Franche-Comté. Werewolves remained a symbol of a sinister threat representing dark, life-devouring forces, but as such returned to the realm of popular culture whence they had sprung.[82] The edict amended by the Parlement in 1633 initially reflected only a change of opinion in learned circles, but it removed the legal basis for werewolf charges, thus effecting a turnaround in legal practice.

This was not the only change which took place in the character of the werewolf paradigm. Described by Ginzburg as a '... symmetrical primarily male version of the ... primarily female ecstatic cult'[83] werewolves eventually lost their dominantly male character. At the end of the 16th and throughout the 17th century the werewolf image in Franche-Comté was unmistakably gender-neutral. In the period 1520–70, 78 per cent of all alleged werewolves were men; between 1580 and 1670, 48 per cent were women.[84]

A further point for consideration is that most of those accused of lycanthropy came from the lowest echelons of society, a fact which did not escape the attention of Judge Henri Boguet in St Claude.[85]

Franche-Comté: ecology, economy and social control

The werewolf panics and the comparatively large numbers of werewolf trials in Franche-Comté are unique in Central Europe.[86] In other regions, legal cases against alleged werewolves were rarely anything more than isolated and individual cases. The other regions where a significantly higher number of werewolf cases came before the courts were Austria, as well as Nassau and its neighbourhood,[87] so that werewolves and their persecution by the authorities remained a marginal phenomenon in the Empire. Non-specialized sources still cite figures of up to 30,000 persecuted werewolves;[88] such figures do not bear scrutiny or comparison with original sources and, with our current knowledge, must be regarded as myths.

From 1548 to 1678 Franche-Comté was formally a part of the Holy Roman Empire and formed part of the Burgundian Circle of the Empire. From 1598 onwards, however, the region was ruled by an Archduke from Brussels as part of the Spanish Netherlands. Nonetheless, Franche-Comté remained politically independent and as Lucien Febvre, founder of the French Annales School, proudly remarked of his homeland, '...neither were the inhabitants Spanish under a Philip II, nor were they German under a Charles V'.[89] Culturally, this land with its 400,000 inhabitants was French, politically it was a classical border-country uniting aspects of each of the two states' organization. The norms of the Carolina, the Imperial Penal Code, influenced jurisdiction in Franche-Comté; however, the judicature, the Parlement, resembled French institutions.[90] Thus it is not surprising that Flemish-, German- and French-speaking students registered at the University of Dôle.

Dense forests are still a typical feature of the landscape in Franche-Comté today. In the 16th century, the chronicler Gollut wrote in Besançon in 1590, it was possible to 'traverse the entire county under trees'.[91] With the exception of the Doubs valley, the fertility of the soil was so low that only marginal cultivation of the land was possible and only small and undemanding animals could be kept as livestock; most of the population lived from wood felling,[92] with willow culture playing an important role. In all parts of the county other than the valley of the Doubs, sheep farming was a major source of income, in contrast to most other regions of Central Europe where livestock farming did not play a central role in this period of history.[93] Mountains, forests, low population density in many areas of the territory and a large number of sheep as ideal prey made this a suitable habitat for wild animals, and in particular for wolves. Given these conditions, it is not surprising that werewolf trials also became a part of the witch-hunts in Franche-Comté; due to the large numbers of real wolves and the threat they posed to the local population and their livelihood, people came to identify these animals with the evil of harmful magic. The type of harmful magic conjectured depended on the ecological and economic structure of the respective region. The werewolf paradigm then represents the maleficium variant typical of witch persecutions in early modern Franche-Comté.

The intensified persecution of werewolves as well as of witches and male witches must be viewed in conjunction with a weakening of the economy from 1590 onwards. First heavy production losses heralded the crisis of the 17th century and were the cause of high corn prices in Burgundy and other areas and, to make matters worse, were accompanied in the Alpine regions by long winters and cold summers.[94]

There were fewer werewolf trials after the death of the sovereign Phillip II. Under his successor Albert of Austria an intensive Counter-Reformation began. The goal of this new policy was to enhance and strengthen Catholic teachings among laypeople and also among the clergy through the introduction of new orders to the country. At Albert's insistence, Jesuits, Capuchins, Carmelites and Ursulines set up monasteries in Franche-Comté. These orders supported the rulers' desired programme of new religious and denominational control. A 'renaissance catholique'[95] went hand in hand with early modern social disciplining – as expressed by a plaque which the sovereign ordered to be prominently placed in the town hall of Besançon. 'Foelicitatis Obedientia mater'[96] – obedience (or subservience) is the mother of happiness.

However, werewolf persecution did not ensue from the culture of the elite but had been established in the region for a long time, as Judge Boguet remarked in his demonological work.[97] The concept of maleficium in the form of lycanthropy was widespread amongst the general population. This was reflected in the accusations made by many of the victims and witnesses of alleged lycanthropy, as the trials portrayed in this chapter show. The initiative to pursue and prosecute alleged werewolves did not only come from above, as in St Claude, but also from below – as many other trial documents show. The Catholic concept of witchcraft strengthened in Franche-Comté as the Counter-Reformation gained ground. Bodin's work 'De la Démonomanie des Sorciers' in which, contrary to majority demonological opinion, he attempted to prove in theory the possibility of animal metamorphosis, was placed on the Pope's list of heretical works in 1596 and from then on no longer provided a basis for werewolf indictments. The werewolf had served its time, and with Catholic teachings on witchcraft, the witch and male witch became the dominant figures. The witch paradigm became an integrative force, subsuming all other patterns. In 1604 the Archduke in Brussels issued a decisive edict which provided a legal framework for far-reaching witch persecutions:

> All those who in this age of circumspection [self-responsibility] are convinced that they have voluntarily attended devilish and detestable meetings or Sabbats of the male witches and the witches, or who outside of these [meetings] bring illness to people or animals or practise magic, will receive the death penalty.[98]

Albrecht of Austria as the territorial sovereign stipulated specifically that the death penalty for witchcraft crimes applied to both genders.

The werewolf simply had to change its name and live on in the guise of the female witch *and* the male witch. It was not necessary to invent a new male version of the witch, for in Burgundy the gender-specific characteristics of the werewolf had already waned.[99] The closer the werewolf image came to the witch paradigm, the less this image bore clear resemblance to specific male or female roles.

3
Male Witches on Trial: An Empirical Approach

> I am an unhappy man and pain has made me admit to things which are not true...
> I have nothing to do with these things
>
> (Niclas Fiedler, tried and executed as a male witch in Trier, 1591)

The persecution of large numbers of male witches was not restricted to the free county of Burgundy. To date, however, witchcraft research has only estimated the percentage of men persecuted throughout Europe. This chapter draws together the results of micro and regional analyses and the data they provide on gender distribution in witch trials, compares the absolute numbers of men and women involved and, finally, looks into possible reasons for the marked differences between the different regions.

The individual fates behind the figures

In order to ascertain the percentage of male witches persecuted and executed it is necessary first to determine the total number of executions. In the past it was popular to quote numbers in their millions, but these have now been proven to be unrealistic and it is currently estimated that around 28,000[1] to 40,000[2] executions were carried out in the Holy Roman Empire of German Nations. However, not all those tried for witchcraft were condemned to death; since the advent of quantitative methods in witchcraft research it has become evident that not all trials ended in death and that any assumptions to the contrary must be consigned to the realm of myths. Indeed, the 'execution rates' varied considerably from region to region; whilst 84 per cent of trials in the Catholic county of Hohenberg in southwest Germany ended in the death sentence,[3] in nearby Protestant Württemberg the figure was only about 33 per cent.[4] In other regions, though, the relationship between religious allegiance and the number of death sentences was the reverse: in the Catholic Imperial City of Cologne only 38 per cent[5] were condemned, whereas 80 per cent of the accused met their death in the Protestant city of Kiel.[6]

Witch trials are not, then, synonymous with the death sentence; depending on the respective ruler, territory, court or even type of trial the accused had varying chances of escaping the death penalty and being released from custody. These people are not immediately apparent in the persecution figures, as these generally refer to executions; yet they, too, were victims. A release from custody in the early modern period cannot be equated to an acquittal in the modern sense of the word and is even further removed from our understanding of rehabilitation. The accused who were not executed remained in social isolation, were stigmatized[7] and lived in constant fear that suspicions would be revived. The residual distrust remained. Exile was tantamount to a life on the roads – in frugal early modern society this frequently meant a life, and consequently death, in almost inconceivably wretched circumstances.

Witch trials often resulted in physical casualties. The commonly used strappado torture method must have led to the tearing of articular ligaments in the shoulders or, when additional weights were fixed to the victim's legs to dislocation of the hip joints. The use of thumbscrews caused not only excruciating pain but also bone fractures. Torture, then, frequently caused irreparable physical harm. In an agrarian society, victims of such practices were no longer fully employable and in the crisis-filled society of early modern times this generally meant there was no escaping a life of material and social destitution.

Trial protocols classically used as sources in research on witch-hunting generally tell us little about the fate of the accused who were released or banished, or indeed of that of their families. Some examples from the north of the empire (an area which will be discussed in more detail below) serve to provide a less abstract basis for an assessment of these issues.

In 1533 a man from Tønder in the Duchy of Schleswig-Holstein begged in desparation for the court to rehabilitate him and his brothers and sisters and thus to relieve them of an old blemish on their characters; their mother had been burnt as a witch many years previously, and since her conviction her children had time and again found themselves suspected

Illustration 3.1 Torturing an accused man by hoisting him up by the arms whilst one of the executioners stretches his body downwards and others beat him with rods. Other instruments of torture can be seen on the floor: the iron 'collar' (below the left foot of the accused) and the frequently employed leg screws (bottom right). (Copper engraving from: Hermann Löher 'Most Melancholy Complaint of the Pious Innocents', Amsterdam 1676. In 1636, the court assessor Löher fled from his encounters with witch persecutions in the Electorate of Cologne to the Netherlands, where he recorded his experiences of witch trials of women and men. In: Alte Bibliothek, St Michael's Grammar School, Bad Münstereifel)

of witchcraft. The court, however, merely confirmed the legality of the execution and failed to contradict the clearly untrue rumours which had led to these suspicions.[8] In the same region, in 1577, a man whose wife had been burnt as an alleged witch also appealed to the court, arguing that the sentence had exposed himself and his 'poor, bereaved and unhappy children to insult, mockery and scorn'.[9] Another woman fled from Mecklenburg, where she had been accused of witchcraft, to Holstein, but was not able to flee the rumours and was indicted again; stigmatization was effective across borders and over long distances.[10] In another case, a 14-year-old girl was forced to watch her parents being burnt at the stake after being condemned as witches, and was subsequently threatened with the same fate if she did not fulfil the accepted norms of a moral life.[11] Individual husbands and whole village communities refused to accept women who had been accused, but acquitted, of witchcraft back into their homes or villages;[12] here Schleswig-Holstein is no exception and such reactions were recorded in many different regions.[13] Added to the personal and social stigmatization the victims suffered was the constant control exercised by the court over their future lives which, doubtless, had to conform rigidly to the social norm. This mental stress was often aggravated by the physical consequences of the trials. In one case, a woman attempted to evade a witchcraft charge made by a seigneurial court by fleeing to Kiel, a town with its own jurisdiction. She was nevertheless tried by the town council and tortured, after which one half of her body was paralyzed and she was no longer able to walk.[14] Another woman who was acquitted in a witchcraft trial after two torture sessions in the town of Flensburg in 1608 bore clearly visible physical signs of this treatment.[15] A frail 70-year-old woman from Saxony-Lauenburg who was only able to walk with the help of crutches was banished after a trial. Such a sentence was tantamount to a sentence of death as this woman would have been unable to survive without help from others in a strange land.[16]

The list of such cases could be continued; it is the concrete background to such individual fates which so clearly demonstrates the enormity of the terror with which the witch-hunts pervaded early modern society. There were many facets to death sentences in witch trials. The death penalty did not have to be pronounced as such; death could come in the form of a 'social' or 'material' execution arising from ostracism from the community, or it could come in instalments as deprivation reduced survival chances.

Men were also struck by such fates. A case in 1658 is recorded in which a man from the island of Fehmarn was subjected to repeated accusations of magic after being acquitted in a witchcraft trial. A peasant from Holstein saw a slander action as his only chance when he again found himself at the centre of suspicion 28 years after he had first been suspected and taken to court for witchcraft. Suspicions had remained latent all these years and had come to the fore again after almost a generation.[17] Such stigma were hard to eradicate.

The above examples show that it was by no means only the people executed who were the victims of persecution. If we accept Levack's figure of approximately 50 per cent death sentences in witch trials throughout Europe (but excluding Germany and Poland)[18] then it appears that the estimated numbers of persecution victims cited at the beginning of this chapter are considerably higher than the estimates given at the beginning of this chapter would indicate. The following statistics therefore work with a broader interpretation of the term 'victim'. When speaking of persecution or persecution victims throughout the book, this includes anyone taken to court for witchcraft, whatever the outcome. Execution rates as a benchmark for persecution are only meaningful to a point and should be complemented by numbers of accused – in as far as this can be expressed in statistical terminology.

One means of determining the proportion of men persecuted for witchcraft would be the so-called 'Hexen-Kartei' [Index of Witches] commissioned by Heinrich Himmler, the Nazi SS 'Reichsführer'. The Index was compiled between 1935 and 1944 and listed 34,000 witch trials throughout Europe. However, it is not possible to make a projection from these data, as the evaluation of the records was inadequate and large groups of sources were ignored.[19] The only alternative, then is to meticulously examine and bring together all empirical research undertaken to date – a painstaking exercise. The description which follows here is based on the results or evaluation of relatively new research which has investigated a broad set of materials to address a number of pre-defined objectives; these materials include not only court records but also execution lists, diaries, acquittal papers or chronicles. I have not made systematic use of local historical sources or contributions which have no explicit academic background or are based on chance data. As quantitative methods have gained international acceptance and are widely used in witchcraft research,[20] there is a large amount of data available for the empire, although numerous regions have not yet been investigated.

There is, incidentally, no indication that the authorities deliberately destroyed files in order to distort or balance statistics in terms of gender-specific differences. Even though no absolute figures are available, the statistics collected to date do permit us to draw conclusions regarding the relative numbers of men and women persecuted. However, anyone who is aware of the incomplete nature of early modern sources knows that any quantification can only be made with considerable reservations. Consequently, the following does not make any claim to completeness in the sense of having covered all witch trials; my aim is simply to show the trends. This also means that any figures beyond the decimal point have no real significance and thus were rounded up or down. These reservations are a necessary part of the attempt to convert archive material into statistical values; reducing a source to data presented in a table can be problematic and should only be seen as an approximation.

The individual fates behind the graphs

Historians who operate with quantitative methods aim not only to record historical phenomena in figures but to describe these phenomena in specific ways, that is in tables, diagrams, curves in graphs and so on. Representing numbers or proportions in this way can, however, considerably distort the facts or make them seem falsely unambiguous.

Let me back this up with an example from historical witchcraft research. In an important publication, the proportion of men persecuted as witches in the city of Vienna is given as 41.5 per cent.[21] This figure is, as will be shown later, very high and far above the relative average. The quality of this information, however, is relativized when the absolute number of cases is known; in the course of the 200 years in which persecutions occurred in Vienna, five men out of a total of twelve persons were accused.[22]

This example shows that percentages can give false impressions if the data set used is too small. The significance of any data given increases as soon as relative and absolute figures are combined.

Other sources of distorted information are graphs in which one or other of the axes is extended or shortened as in, for example, bar graphs and line graphs. In order to avoid misleading impressions arising from proportions or graphs, I adhere to the following rules: Relative and absolute numbers in a given data set are presented in combination with one another. In line and curve plots the length of the horizontal x-axis is two to three times that of the vertical y-axis. Both axes always begin at zero.

The study area: the Holy Roman Empire of German nations

The area investigated is the so-called Holy Roman Empire in its borders of 1648; this empire encompassed the whole of central Europe, as well as parts of southeastern and western Europe. Even after the Peace of Westphalia (1648), when certain regions such as Switzerland and the northern Netherlands finally became formally independent, the Holy Roman Empire remained the largest state in Europe in terms of area. It reached from the North and the Baltic Seas across today's Slovenia to the Mediterranean, from the English Channel far into present-day Slovakia. Various languages were spoken: German in numerous countries, Flemish in the Spanish Netherlands, French in Franche-Comté and Lorraine, Danish in Holstein, Italian in the southern Alpine areas and Slavonic languages in the eastern and southeastern regions.

The name of the empire is derived from claims made by the rulers of the Middle Ages who strove to pursue the tradition of the ancient Roman Empire, for according to a prophecy in the Old Testament, the world was to collapse after the downfall of four large empires.[23] For this reason, Popes from the early Middle Ages onwards conferred the honour of the title 'Emperor' on Charlemagne and a number of his successors in order to ensure the endurance of the fourth empire, and thus making them the patrons or protectors of Christianity in the occident. The term 'of German Nations' was first found on an official imperial document in 1486 and was not in common usage until the 16th century.

Because of both its pre- and its supranational character the empire never became a national state in the modern sense, unlike its neighbouring states Spain, France or England. The Holy Roman Empire is not, then, identical with Germany, which only existed as a united nation after 1871; what is more, there was no concept of a German nation in the early modern period.[24] In 1519, as the witch-hunts were beginning in Europe, Charles I of Spain, who had been brought up in the Netherlands and spoke little German, was elected leader of this empire. As the French philosopher Voltaire mocked in the 18th century, this state was 'neither holy, nor Roman, nor an empire' – nor, one should add 'entirely German'.

The emperor was at the head of the political system but he had yielded wide-reaching powers to the regional and local rulers, the so-called imperial estates: Princes, Prince-Bishops, Dukes, Margraves, Landgraves, Abbots, Grand Masters of Orders, Counts, Councils of Imperial Free Cities and even local knights had begun in the late Middle Ages to transform their territories into autonomous individual states. Although the borders of the empire were determined by commitments laid down in old feudal law, contemporaries did not view these lines as rigidly as modern cartography would suggest. In the 16th and 17th centuries the empire became a patchwork of 300 quasi-sovereign states and 1500 local estates belonging to minor territorial lords whose rulers determined their subjects' religious allegiance: subjects had to follow the belief of their ruler. Following Catholicism and Lutheranism, Calvinism was introduced as a third religious denomination in some territories. After 1580 the secular Catholic territories such as Bavaria and Inner Austria existed alongside ecclesiastical Catholic Prince-Bishoprics such as Würzburg and Trier, Protestant-Lutheran territories such as the Electorate of Saxony and Württemberg or Protestant-reformist territories such as the Electorate

Map 1 The Holy Roman Empire (1648)

of Palatinate.[25] The Imperial Free Cities were mixed-denominational islands within these territories.

Nonetheless, the Emperors Maximilian I and Charles V were able to consolidate the Emperor's authority and implement a number of reforms. By means of several juridical regulations and the introduction of central organs of jurisdiction, such as the Imperial Chamber Court or Imperial Aulic Council, and of a central Imperial Penal Code they were able to stipulate common legal principles and regulations with respect to legislation and the dispensation of justice in the individual territories of the empire. These standardization measures generally contributed to the development of a common concept of justice[26] and played an important role in the witch-hunts throughout the Holy Roman Empire.

Justice: the Caroline Code

The new Penal Code which Charles V wished to introduce had first to be accepted by the assembly of the estates of the empire, the Imperial Diet. After protracted debates and at the fifth attempt the Diet finally agreed to a central law; the *Constitutio Criminalis Carolina,* named after Charles V and abbreviated to CCC or *Carolina,* remained valid into the 18th century.[27]

The Caroline Code, then, standardized law enforcement in this multi-faceted empire; only a few regions, such as the Spanish Netherlands, proved an exception to this. The new Criminal Code nonetheless did justice to the individual princes, for individual, regional criminal proceedings were also still permitted, provided they did not contradict this new imperial regulation in spirit or content.

The CCC adopted the new demonology in as far as it declared alleged witchcraft a crime liable to public prosecution so that charges were no longer placed by one individual against another but the state authorities were required to prosecute a supposed witch or male witch on their own initiative. The old axiom of Germanic popular law, Where there is no complainant, there shall be no judge, the principle of accusatory procedure, was not precluded by the Carolina, but it was complemented by this new and different inquisitorial procedure. As allegations of witchcraft were now primarily to be officially pursued, this meant that the function of complainant and judge had been merged into one. In other words, witchcraft was now considered a contravention of the God-given general order of things, and no longer as an injury committed against another individual.

§109 of Charles V's Caroline Code stated that burning was to be the punishment for proven maleficium. This paragraph did not, however, include the devil's pact or the witches' flight as criminal offences. Men and women were equal before the law in witchcraft charges. §44 of the Caroline Court Code laid down that anyone was to be suspected of sorcery who offered to teach magic, threatened or (allegedly) practised maleficium, who consciously had contacts with others suspected or known to practise magic, who used real or verbal magic charms or was reputed to employ magic. This left a great deal of room for interpretation. Torture was legitimized in §60 of the CCC, thus detaching the circumstantial evidence named above from actual evidence so that through the use of force, a confession as the queen of all evidence might be obtained. In keeping with the new theory on evidence, the Code did, however, stipulate in §52 that material evidence of the use of sorcery should also be sought. To counteract earlier arbitrary acts of justice, §219 obliged the courts to obtain external expertise. In the case of ambiguous evidence, then, local courts were obliged to obtain advice from, for example, the law faculties of universities before employing torture.[28]

The authors of the Carolina also made other attempts to restrict the use of torture, whilst at the same time leaving the final decisions to the individual judges. There were, however, no regulations for witchcraft or any other trials which stipulated a maximum duration for torture sessions or stated whether a victim could be repeatedly subjected to torture. The use of torture not only solved any problems arising from insufficient evidence but also made it possible to condemn almost anyone suspected of a capital crime. The trial specifications laid down in the CCC, however, diverged widely from the practice of the witch persecutions. Although the Imperial Chamber Court did attempt to prevent deviations from the legislation, it had only very limited power to intervene in the witch trials of the individual territories.[29] Many territorial sovereigns did not accept the Code's definition of the crime of witchcraft, nor did they define the crime in their own legislation, with the result that conventional legal traditions and political requirements influenced the persecutions in the various territories.

Torture was the 'core' of the trials and as its use was not properly restricted, many courts tended to make 'short work' of the accused. The majority of cases then did not reflect the pattern envisaged by the CCC but were more akin to the procedure proposed by the Dominican monk Institoris in his infamous *The Hammer of Witches* written in 1486. Torture was ordered to be used if no tangible circumstantial evidence was available, the credibility of witnesses was not investigated, repeated use of torture was described as a continuation of the original torture, and no opportunity was given for a victim to retract a plea of guilty. The courts, then, failed to observe the stipulations of the CCC, and broken arms, dislocated joints, bloody bodies, fainting attacks, and death from disease in the cold and damp of the dungeons were, thus, all common accompaniments of witchcraft trials in the Holy Roman Empire.

Sorcery trials, gender and the late Middle Ages

Traditional sorcery trials of both female and male suspects, the main element of which was maleficium, were held throughout the entire Middle Ages.[30] The word 'witch' was used for the first time in 1377 in a register of offences, and mentioned again in 1402 in the context of a death sentence by burning which took place in Schaffhausen in present-day Switzerland.[31] From the sources available today, we can deduct that more than two decades later, there was a massive wave of persecutions in Valais (Switzerland), in the Dauphiné (France) and in the Savoyan Alps (Italy).[32] From 1430 onwards, witch trials became increasingly distinct from heresy and sorcery trials. The accused were charged with infanticism followed by cannibalism, charges which had not been made in heresy trials.[33] With the Council of Basle (convoked in 1431) as the intellectual discussion arena and with the beginnings of book printing, the new witch definition spread to numerous regions of the empire. After 1435, charges of alleged magical aggression elicited changes not only in the nature but also in the number of witchcraft trials.[34] Persecution was no longer of an individual nature but appeared to be working in a kind of network, heralding the mass executions of the 16th and 17th centuries.

The new facets of the witchcraft paradigm became obvious in the first part of the 15th century. The complete pattern is reflected in the trial held in 1438 of Pierre Vallin, an old man from La Tour du Pin in southeast France. He confessed under torture to the Devil's pact, an infanticide, weather magic and to the witches' flight, in short to all the elements of a sophisticated witchcraft trial.[35] This early trial, which dates from the years in which the concept of a witchcraft offence was only just emerging, also indicates that, in contemporary thought, both men and women could belong to the new sect. The judge, Claude Tholosan, who wrote a tract summarizing his experiences as a judge in the Dauphiné, describes almost without exception a gender-neutral offence, since he nearly always uses the Latin masculine plural (the grammatical form used to describe mixed gender groups) in his depictions of the witch community.[36] A contemporary witness, the chronicler Hans Fründ reports of numerous 'man und wip', men and women, who were burnt in the course of the first major witch trials around 1430.[37]

In the trials of the late Middle Ages there was a transformation in the witch stereotype; women and not men were increasingly being charged with sorcery offences. On the basis of a study which examined almost 900 sorcery and witchcraft trial records in Europe, we can assume that about three quarters of those tried between 1300 and 1349 were male, but that this proportion sank to one quarter in the period 1450–99.[38] These gender proportions remain representative even though this investigation has since been complemented by more detailed recent research. The development can be particularly clearly seen in the Swiss trials of the 15th century: whereas the Inquisitor Ulric de Torrenté saw men as representing two thirds of the target group in his persecutions, the witch concept increasingly came to be associated with women in the second half of the century, albeit with asynchronous developments in the various regions.[39] Despite these developments, men formed the majority (out of a total of 34) of those accused in the well-known 'vauderie d'Arras' mass trials of 1459–61 in the Duchy of Burgundy.[40] These trials – distinguishable from other trials of the late Middle Ages by the new criterion of the devil's pact – possessed no explicit gender-specific character.

The west: Franche-Comté, Montbéliard, Lorraine, the Saar region, Electorates of Mainz and Trier, Luxembourg, Eifel-Counties, Spanish Netherlands

After a number of different affiliations the free county of Burgundy, known since 1366 as *'Franche-Comté'* and its capital Dôle, formed part of the Burgundian Circle of the Empire from 1515/1548–1678. Franche-Comté remained almost untouched by the Reformation and was Catholic for the entire period of the witch persecutions. From 1530 onwards the territorial sovereign permitted the use of torture and in 1604 imposed the death penalty on maleficium and alleged visits to the witches' Sabbat; these rulings by the reigning Archdukes went far beyond the imperial legislation of the CCC. When the territory became part of France in 1678, Louis XIV ordered an end to be put to all witchcraft trials.[41] There is evidence of 795 people tried for witchcraft in Franche-Comté between 1434 and 1676; 33 per cent (or in absolute figures, 262) of the accused were men. The execution rate was 60 per cent for women and 55 per cent for men.[42] With a population of around 400,000 and a total of approx. 800 trials Franche-Comté was an area with a roughly average level of persecution.

The Principality of *Montbéliard* (German Mömpelgard) belonged to the empire from 1535–1793. The ruling dukes of Württemberg established Lutherism here,[43] with the result that part of the population still adheres to the Protestant-Lutheran church today. At least 205 witch trials took place in this small territory between 1554 and 1661; 82 per cent of the accused were women and 18 per cent men, the execution rate was 78 per cent for men and 74 per cent for women.[44] It should be noted that Württemberg's own legislation – which was stricter than the CCC – was applied in witchcraft offences.

The Duchy of *Lorraine* formally belonged to the Holy Roman Empire and its Upper Rhine circle, but in fact it was politically and judicially independent. Its rulers were prominent members of the Catholic French

League and as such had strong dynastic ties with Bavaria, the prime Counter-Reformation force in the empire. The Bishoprics of Metz, Toul and Verdun, however, came under French administration between 1552 and 1559. Lorraine had its own territorial legislation and jurisdiction which were, however, influenced by the CCC.[45] With 3000 accused and a conviction rate of 90 per cent and a population of about 400,000,[46] Lorraine must be classified as one of the persecution hotspots. We can assume a proportion of 72 per cent women to 28 per cent men.[47] Regional studies[48] confirm this figure, as the proportion of men fluctuated in the various districts of Lorraine between 20 per cent and 36 per cent.

The mixed-denominational region known as the *Saar Region* included parts of northern Lorraine, the county of *Nassau-Zweibrücken*, parts of the Electorate of *Trier* and other locally ruled areas. The CCC formed the legal basis of the witch persecutions but was complemented by special decrees and legal traditions. Of 591 accusations in total, 28 per cent were male, whereby there was a difference between Catholic regions (29 per cent) and Protestant regions (20 per cent). The execution rate of 91 per cent for men was slightly higher than that for women.[49] The Saar region was thus an area of intensive persecution.

The greatest persecution in German-speaking lands took place in the Electorate of *Trier* at the end of the 16th century. As records are scarce, we can only base assumptions as to the number of victims and gender relations on those records which are available. A local magistrate, Claudius Musiel made meticulous lists of over 400 people executed and 1300 people named in trials within the eight years from 1586 to 1594; of those executed, 94 – that is 27 per cent – were men. We can assume that for the area around Trier the proportion of men was somewhat higher, in the region of 33 per cent.[50] Two other regional studies confirm that the proportion of men accused of witchcraft was around 25 per cent and 30 per cent respectively.[51] Like many other territories in early modern times, the Catholic *Electorate of Mainz* with its centres Mainz and Aschaffenburg, was not a self-contained, enclosed territory. This electorate played a special role in that the Bishop of Mainz simultaneously held the position of Archchancellor of the empire. The region's modified version of the CCC provided the legal basis for the territory's witch persecutions. Between 1601 and 1629, 965 people were executed, 24 per cent of them male.[52] In Miltenberg 46 per cent of those executed were men[53]; the execution rate following the 239 trials was 87 per cent for males and 77 per cent for females.[54] With a total of about 2000 accused, the Electorate of Mainz was also one of the empire's hotspots of witch persecutions.

In the Counties of *Blankenheim and Gerolstein* in the Eifel Mountains, which were ruled by the Catholic house of von der Manderscheid, Counter-Reformation and witch-hunts were initiated pretty much simultaneously. Of 259 proven witch trials between 1580 and 1638, 246 (that is, 95 per cent) ended with the death penalty.[55] 80 per cent of those burnt were women and 20 per cent men.[56]

The *Spanish Netherlands*, inherited in 1477/1543 by the Habsburg dynasty, and the Free County of Burgundy formed the Burgundian Circle of the Empire. Although the treaties of 1548 secured the Spanish Netherlands the continued protection of the empire, the territory was exempt from imperial laws and decisions of the Imperial Chamber Court, and as such, was more of an ancilliary to than an integral part of, the empire. In 1551 Charles V handed over these sovereign territories to the Spanish Habsburg line. After 1648 the southern part of the territories remained under Spanish and thus ultimately Catholic sovereignty. There is some justified dispute as to whether the territory belonged to the Holy Roman Empire but it is beyond the scope of this work to discuss such issues. Since it did, however, formally belong to an institution of the empire, the data for this region are used in this evaluation; this is not intended as an attempt at defining the real boundaries of the empire. Despite their initial scepticism, towards the end of the 16th century, the authorities tightened the witchcraft laws, declaring witchcraft a crime against God and King.[57] Torture was already widely used long before this time, in witchcraft as in other trials. In the 1590s two decrees were issued on behalf of the King (who had next to nothing to do with their content, it was the Secret Council in Brussels that dealt with such matters) intended as a means of regaining a grip on trials that were getting out of hand.

Recent, as yet uncompleted, critical studies indicate that the number of men accused in the Duchy of Luxembourg was considerably higher than assumed to date. Between 1560 and 1683 approximately 3000 trials took place in this part of the Spanish Netherlands. Courts pronounced 2000 death penalties, and about one quarter, or possibly more, of those suspected were men.[58] In the small County of *Namur* the data available shows 366 accused between 1509 and 1646; 92 per cent were women and only 8 per cent men.[59] As the sentences were not recorded for a decisive number of trials, it is not possible to calculate the execution rate.

In the *Cambrésis* territories (part of the Lower Rhine Imperial Circle), *Artois, Lille-Orchies* and *Tournai* which were partially French after 1659, 245 death sentences were pronounced for witchcraft between

1550 and 1700.[60] In Cambrésis, 18 per cent of a total number of 294 charges were against men, but the execution rate of male witches in the same region was higher at 60 per cent than that of female witches at 46 per cent.[61]

The county of *Flanders* was also a member of the Burgundian Circle of the Empire although legally parts of the county remained a fief of the French king into the 16th century; it was also one of the most urbanized territories in Europe. The court records often make no distinction beween sorcery and witchcraft trials. In the 285 trials which can definitely be classified as witchcraft trials, 209 of the accused were women (73 per cent) and 76 men (27 per cent).[62]

The southwest: Baden-Baden, Ellwangen, Hohenberg, Hohenlohe, Hohenzollern, Mergentheim, Swabian-Austria, Further Austria, Vorarlberg, Vaduz, Württemberg

The data for this scattered region in the southwest of the empire is best presented in a table.[63]

In the entire southwest, the rules of the CCC formed the legal basis of the witch persecutions. From 1567 onwards, the Protestant territory of *Württemberg* punished alleged pacts with the Devil even when no maleficium was involved, thus intensifying the laws valid throughout the empire. The Electorate of *Palatinate*, a Calvinist territory, rejected witch trials, whereas regional trial patterns appeared to be common in Vorarlberg.

In the principality of *Vaduz (Liechtenstein)* approximately 200 people were taken to court and accused of witchcraft. The percentage of men executed in the period 1598 to 1689 was high at almost 40 per cent, and for the most severe period of persecution between 1669 and 1680 it was as high as 60 per cent.[75]

The southeast: 'Bavaria', Salzburg, 'Austria'

The region designated *'Bavaria'* in this study was not as heterogeneous as the southwest of the empire, but was nonetheless divided up among various rulers. The Catholic Duchy of Bavaria – an Electorate after 1623 – was the centre of the German Counter Reformation. Other large territories in the region were: the Catholic Prince-Bishoprics of *Passau, Augsburg, Eichstätt, Freising,* the Prince-Abbey *Kempten* and the split denominational county of *Oettingen,* as well as various smallish Calvinist lands.

Table 3.1 Witch-hunts in the south-west: distribution – men and women, 1530–1730

Territory	Denonimation	No. of persecution victims	Women persecuted (%)	Men persecuted (%)	Execution rate women (%)	Execution rate men (%)
Baden-Baden[64]	mainly Catholic	244	77 (1626–31 only)	23 (31)	95[1]	–
Baden-Durlach	mainly Protestant	low level of persecution	–	–	–	–
Württemberg[65]	Protestant	600	85	15	ca. 33[1]	–
Electorate of Palatinate[66]	Reformist	hardly any witch trials	–	–	–	–
Further Austria (Alsace, Breisgau, Hagenau,Ortenau)[67]	Catholic	1.522	89	11	–	–
Vorarlberg[68]	Catholic	170	80	20	–	–
Swabian-Austria[69]	Catholic	528	91	9	79	51
Hohenzollern[70]	Catholic	154	94	6	–	–
Hohenlohe[71]	Protestant	81	74	26	92	8
Ellwangen[72]	Catholic	>437	80 (78)	20 (22)	–	–
Mergentheim[73]	Catholic	584	84	16	68	59
Rottweil[74]	Catholic	287	72	18		

Note: [1]Overall rate; applies to both sexes. Percentages in parentheses are those given by Midelfort.

At the peak of the witch-hunts around 1590, the Duchy of *Bavaria* had no homogeneous legal foundation of its own for the juridical processes involved. The legal groundwork was finally completed at the beginning of the 17th century, but had, despite its severity, few drastic consequences.[76] From 1586 to 1730 the Duchy of *Bavaria* saw about 1500 people accused; in the entire region covered by Bavaria today, 3250 witch-trials and over 900 executions were carried out in this period.[77] 'Bavaria' then was not one of the areas of most intensive persecution.

Unfortunately, no precise figures are available for the gender relationships in the witch persecutions of the southeast part of the empire, an area which has been investigated by one of the most renowned scholars in the field of German witchcraft research. Nevertheless, certain figures can be established. In the first major witch-hunt around 1590 the number of female victims in the Duchy of Bavaria is estimated at about 80 per cent.[78] In part of a later phase, from 1608–16, the proportion of men tried before Bavarian regional courts rose to 25–35 per cent and increased again in the 1629–30 period, this time to over 50 per cent.[79] A regional study for the 17th century shows that the gender proportion must have increased similarly in Lower Bavaria. In the area around Mitterfels men increasingly became the victims of persecution; there were 102 arrests of men between 1584 and 1737. This represented a high 63 per cent of all persecution victims, but was surpassed by the figures for the Prince-Bishopric of *Freising* where 97 per cent out of a total of 60 people accused between 1715 and 1717 were male.[80] In other, smaller 'Bavarian' territories the gender profile appears to have been clear: In the Prince-Bishoprics of *Augsburg* and *Eichstätt* 99 per cent out of 100 accused and 85 per cent out of 279 accused, respectively, were female. A major surge of trials was initiated by the denunciations made by the herdsman Chonrad Stoeckhlin, accused as a male witch in the village of Oberstdorf on the edge of the Alps.[81]

In the Protestant Margravates of *Franconia*, which came to Bavaria in 1623, 113 witch trials have been verified for the 16th century, only 7 per cent of which involved men.[82]

One of the largest mass trials in the history of witchcraft was held in a part of the Bavarian Circle of the Empire, the Prince-Archbishopric of *Salzburg*. In the so-called 'Sorcerer Jack trials', which took place from 1675 to 1681, about 200 people were charged with witchcraft, approximately 70 per cent of them male. Between 124 and 141 people died either in the course of the trial or by execution order.[83] Further research has shown that, even apart from these mass trials, a high proportion of those persecuted in Salzburg were generally male (60 per cent).

Illustration 3.2 Five male witches and one female witch are being burnt, an alleged delinquent broken on the wheel: the execution of members of the Gämperl or Pappenheimer family and two other 'accomplices' in Munich in 1600. The youngest son is being forced to watch the event (top right). Having no fixed abode, these vagrants roamed the countryside and villages, earning a living by emptying cesspits, or by begging. The Pappenheimers became the scapegoats for a large number of alleged crimes; under torture they confessed to murdering over 100 people, although not a single body was actually found. They also admitted to numerous cases of arson, theft and witchcraft, and finally also named more than 400 alleged accomplices. Duke Maximilian of Bavaria decided to make this case a precedent, intending it to serve as a deterrent to other vagrants (Stadtmuseum Munich, Grafiksammlung M I/532.)

At 79 per cent the execution rate for men was considerably higher than that of women (45 per cent).[84]

The duchies of *Carinthia, Carniola, Styria,* the Arch-Duchy of *Austria,* and the County of *Tirol* had belonged to the Austrian Circle of the Empire since the 16th century. The House of Habsburg and the empire held the territories together; after gaining Bohemia and Hungary in 1526, Austria's position tended to be as an ancillary to, rather than a ruling party of, the empire. A complete Habsburg state as such did not exist until the Tirol line died out in 1665, a date which is still relevant for this study because the most drastic period of witch persecution in Austria (with the exception of Tirol) did not begin until the middle of the 17th century, after the process of re-Catholicization had been completed.

Regional police regulations provided the legal basis for persecutions. Whereas sorcery was not a capital crime in Tirol until 1573, the authorities in Styria adopted the relevant articles of the CCC almost literally. Although the Carolina was the basis for legal proceedings from 1532 onwards, the authorities were slow to transfer the terms to the Territorial Court ordinances. The Ferdinand III Code of 1656, the Ferdinandae, helped to unify court proceedings and served as an archetype for other regional legal codes in the Austrian Habsburg hereditary lands. It specifically named visits to the witches' Sabbat a criminal offence, thus intensifying the persecution of alleged witches.[85]

Witch trials in Austria continued into the middle of the 18th century when the Empress Maria Theresa finally put an end to them. Shortly before her decree became law in 1758, she wrote, 'It is certain that witches are only to be found where ignorance is rife. Where efforts are made to be rid of ignorance, no more will be found. This man [Polak, an accused

Illustration 3.3 The execution of a male witch. Simon Altseer of Upper Bavaria admitted under torture to sacrilege involving the host, to causing sickness, committing murder and working weather magic: because of the particular severity of these crimes, the old man was first mutilated by the executioner. After this comes death at the stake – the fire can already be seen blazing. Death by burning was the most common type of death penalty imposed for witchcraft in Central Europe, for men as for women, with the exception of the Habsburg territories where the delinquents were usually first beheaded and their bodies then committed to the flames (Leaflet from 1666, in: Stadtmuseum Munich, Grafiksammlung M I/320.)

witch] is no more one [a witch] than I am ...'.[86] This not only challenged the theoretical foundations of witch persecutions but referred to a specific case in which a male witch was under trial. It is not surprising that she spoke of a male witch, since in the majority of the Austrian hereditary lands men were more frequently charged with witchcraft than in other territories.

In *Upper Austria* more than three quarters of those indicted for witchcraft were men; 77 per cent[87] out of a total of 56 victims for the period 1570–1780. In *Lower Austria* the total number of accused between 1528 and 1730 was 120, 34 per cent of them men.[88]

The majority of witch-hunts in *Carinthia* were also primarily aimed at men; 68 per cent of a total of 218 accused between 1492 and 1765 were alleged male witches.[89]

In *Styria,* where almost one-third of all the trials in the Habsburg hereditary lands took place, figures for the 200 years from 1546 to 1746 show that 39 per cent out of a total of 879 accused were men.[90]

The waves of witch-hunts in *Tirol* and the *Bishopric of Brixen* occurred earlier than in other Austrian territories. Here there are records of 242 cases filed against 420 persons. If we ignore the small number of children implicated and the problems involved in distinguishing between sorcery and witchcraft trials, men composed 48 per cent of the total. Numerous sagas still popular in these Alpine regions today which tell of legendary sorcerers such as 'Hans Kachler' and 'Pfeifer Huisele' can be traced back to men actually condemned as male witches[91]

Carniola (which covered part of today's Slovenia) stands out among the Austrian territories in that the witch concept was more female-oriented, although the proportion of 85 per cent given for a total of 495 accused is somewhat dubious, since no gender was mentioned for over a quarter of the trials.[92]

Generally speaking, the 'Austrian' authorities were comparatively lenient in their treatment of persons who had allegedly made pacts with the Devil; approximately one in two were spared the immediate terror of persecution.[93] On the basis of the figures given here, and allowing for total numbers of persecuted in relation to size of population, it can be said that Lower and Upper Austria, Tirol and Carinthia were areas of relatively light but not insignificant persecution. Styria, on the other hand, with over 1000 trials, was an area of average persecution.

The east: electorate of Saxony, Silesia

In the course of the 16th century the Prince Electors built *Saxony* up into a tightly organized, exemplary Protestant territory. The terms of the so-called Saxon legal constitutions formed the basis for statutes passed after 1572. They contained strict regulations regarding witchcraft which transcended those of the Carolina, in that Devil's pacts were punishable by burning at the stake even if no harm to another human being had ensued as a result. 905 individuals were charged, 663 of them women and 208 of them men, that is a relation of 77 per cent to 23 per cent, plus a small number of trials for which the gender of the accused is unknown. 87 per cent of the accused women were condemned to death, as against only 13 per cent of the men.[94] This considerable difference might be explained by the fact that men were primarily charged with sorcery rather than witchcraft crimes.

From 1526 onwards *Silesia* belonged to the Habsburg block of territories. Jurisdiction for witchcraft offences was exceptional here in that it was based on local patterns and Saxon legal traditions, although it must be emphasized that here, too, inquisition trials had become the predominant procedure.[95] It is difficult to say definitively to which denonimation Silesia tended, as the population remained firmly Protestant, whilst the ruling class were predominantly Catholic; furthermore, the so-called Sovereign's Dispatch of 1601 declared equal rights for both religions. It was not until after the Peace of Westphalia that Catholicism again began to assert itself. In total, 960 people were accused of witchcraft in the Silesian territories; the period of persecution stretched from 1450 to 1757 but culminated in the years 1550 to 1675. 11 per cent of the accused were male and 89 per cent female, the execution rate being slightly lower for male than for female witches.[96] Such figures do not point to an intensive level of persecution, although it may be interesting to note that a unique and gruesome construction, known as a burning oven was developed in this area in order to increase the intensity of the burning process.

The central region: Prince-Bishoprics of Würzburg and Bamberg, Hesse, 'Thuringia', Electorate of Cologne, Paderborn

The Catholic Prince-Bishopric of *Würzburg* was affiliated with other Counter-Reformation forces in the empire and was responsible for what was conceivably the most extreme witch-hunt in the empire. To date there has been no investigation covering the whole of this high intensity area, where about 1200 people were burnt at the stake. A contemporary execution list for Würzburg for the years 1627–29 gives us an indication of the extent of the terror.[97] In 29 mass executions – known as 'burnings' – 116 people were put to death in only three years, 49 per cent of them female and 51 per cent male. One third of these victims were children – a gruesome fact which should also not be overlooked from a statistical point of view. The witch persecution in Würzburg also saw clergy – from simple curates to canons and provosts – among its victims.[98]

The neighbouring Catholic Prince-Bishopric of *Bamberg*, for a time ruled by the same people, was also an area of intensive persecution. The legal foundation here was the 'Constitutio Criminalis Bambergensis' passed in 1507, which bore considerable similarity to the CCC and foresaw the death penalty for maleficium. Records survive of 780 persons, 74 per cent of them women and 26 per cent men, accused of witchcraft between 1595 and 1680. The courts in Bamberg condemned 61 per cent of all alleged witches and male witches to death and did not stop at leading personages of the town, such as the Mayor Johannes Junius and the Chancellor of the Prince-Bishopric, Dr Georg Haan. The persecutions only subsided when the Emperor and the influential Imperial Aulic Court addressed the severity of the town's procedure, and they finally drew to an end when the town was occupied by Swedish troops.[99]

The rulers of the small county of *Büdingen* attempted to establish Calvinism as the state religion from the end of the 16th centuy onwards; part of the population, however, refused to accept this and remained Lutheran. 485 accusations of witchcraft can be proven for the period 1532 to 1699. My own laborious calculations based on the names of the victims came up with a proportion of 10 per cent of men and 86 per cent women among all those accused. The execution rate must have been high for both sexes.[100] With over 400 executions, Büdingen, this small reformed region, was without doubt a persecution hotspot.

Despite its unsettled history as a Lutheran and from 1603 onwards Calvinist state, the Landgraviate of *Hesse-Kassel* employed the CCC as the legal basis for witch persecutions. The records tell of 214 witchcraft trials between 1544 and 1760. As in Büdingen, the large majority of cases were female; only 13 per cent of those accused were male.[101] The execution rate at just under 30 per cent was low and this alone justifies placing this region in the low intensity category. In *Hesse-Darmstadt* there was only one major wave of persecution which lasted from 1582 to 1590 and involved 37 victims, almost without exception women.[102]

The counties of *Nassau* lay between their Lutheran and Catholic neighbours and, as a second reformed power together with the Palatinate played an important role in the 16th and 17th centuries. Again, the CCC was commonly used here, but it was also complemented by regional legislation. As in Lutheran Württemberg, not only maleficium but also a Devil's pact even without any harmful outcome was punishable by death[103] so that we can assume a penal law based on belief or opinion. From 1573 to 1713, 411 people were accused of witchcraft; 12 per cent of these were male and 88 per cent female. The execution rate for women was 65 per cent and somewhat higher than for men (58 per cent).[104] Such figures in this small territory are indicative of high intensity persecution.

The present-day federal state of *Thuringia* consisted in the 16th and 17th centuries of several territories. In this region, the centre of the Reformation, the basic legal principles were founded on the CCC, and about 1565 people were persecuted between 1526 and 1731. The percentage of men was about 13 per cent; the execution quota for both genders about 75 per cent.[105] With such a high number of victims Thuringia must also be classified as a hotspot, a territory of high intensity persecution.

The Catholic Electorate of *Cologne* consisted of two major areas, both ruled by the same person: the Duchy of *Westphalia* and the Archbishopric of *Cologne* in the southern Rhineland. A code of procedure for witchcraft trials was passed in the two territories in1607 and 1628, respectively, intensifying the regulations of the CCC and in particular making it easier for the judicial authorities to employ torture. Special witchcraft commissioners were employed by the Prince Elector and played an important and brutal role in the trials.[106]

In the Duchy of Westphalia alone, 1140 trials were held, ending in 914 executions during the period 1508 to 1732.[107] If the cases where no gender was given are discounted, the average proportion of persecuted men in a total of 800 trials was 37 per cent, a figure which rose to well over 50 per cent in the last two decades of the 17th century.[108] Westphalia, then, is also one of the core regions with high intensity persecution. The proportion of men was probably even higher as there are numerous trials in which it is no longer possible to determine the gender of the accused.

The small imperial Lordship of *Wildenburg upon Sieg* experienced an intense witch-hunt between 1574 and 1681 in which 195 people were taken to court; of these, 110, that is 56 per cent,were men.[109] In the mixed denominational *Ruhr-Lippe region* 198 people died as a result of persecution, 82 per cent of them women and 18 per cent men.[110]

The population and rulers of the neighbouring Prince-Bishopric of *Paderborn* were primarily Catholic. Trials of 260 people took place here between 1510 and 1702; 30 per cent of the accused were male,[111] so

Illustration 3.4 Pronouncement of the death sentence on the male witch Holger Lirtz (on the right, with hands folded) from Rheinbach in the Rhineland, and a woman accused with him. The background shows the next stage: their journey in the executioner's cart to the place of execution. (Copper engraving from Hermann Löher, 'Most Melancholy Complaint', 1676, in: Alte Bibliothek, St Michael's Grammar School, Bad Münstereifel.)

that the region can be classified as one in which persecution was of medium intensity.

The northwest: Lippe, Brunswick-Wolfenbüttel, Minden, Münster, Schaumburg, Osnabrück, Verden

The County of *Lippe* and its capital, Detmold, covered an area of only 1200 square kilometres and formed a reformed enclave surrounded by Lutheran and Catholic territories. From 1564 to 1681 local magistrates persecuted 221 people. In the town of Lemgo, which had its own jurisdiction independent of the sovereign's influence, records have been found of 209 people tried for witchcraft.[112] Such high numbers mean that this county was clearly an area of high intensity persecution. No gender-specific data are available for the county as a whole. In Detmold, however, the proportion of men was 24 per cent,[113] in the small town of Horn only women were tried and executed and in Lemgo the proportion of women was also very high – over 90 per cent between 1628 and 1637.[114]

Unlike its neighbour the Prince-Electorate of Cologne, the Prince-Bishopric of *Münster* pursued relatively few witch trials. With a population of 200,000 and 450 trials from 1550–1700, of which 170 led to the death sentence, it should be classified a moderate zone. The proportion of men among those executed was, however high at 33 per cent.[115]

The Prince-Bishopric of *Osnabrück* passed to Protestant dynasties in the 16th century and remained under Lutheran rule until 1623 when it was taken over by Catholic sovereigns. Records have survived of 90 people tried between 1588 and 1691; 12 per cent of these were male. The execution rate of 40 per cent for male witches was more lenient than for their female counterparts.[116] The Prince-Bishopric, then, was an area of low intensity persecution. This was in contrast to the Protestant town of Osnabrück where 276 women – and only 2 men (0.7 per cent) – were tried for witchcraft between 1561 and 1639.[117]

After 1640, one part of the County of *Schaumburg*, which lay on the border between Lower Saxony and Westphalia, passed to the Landgraviate Hesse-Kassel, whilst the other part remained independent and under reformed influence as the County of Schaumburg-Lippe. Only 5 per cent of the 118 trials from 1552 to 1659 involved men.[118] The overall figures were, however, high for a small territory, so that this Calvinist county should be considered an area of intensive persecution.

The Bishopric of *Minden* was secularized in 1648 and when it passed to Brandenburg also came under the influence of reformed forces. At least 91 executions were carried out here between 1530 and 1680[119]; it is, however, no longer possible to reconstruct the gender proportions. In the City of Minden, which had its own jurisdiction, 126 trials are known to have taken place from 1603–84; 90 per cent of the accused were women.[120]

In *Brunswick-Wolfenbüttel*, after 1568 a Lutheran territory, 90 per cent out of a total of 225 accused were women, and only 10 per cent men.[121] Although the numbers persecuted were almost certainly a good deal higher, Brunswick-Wolfenbüttel should be considered a region of moderately intense persecution.

The Swedish Queen Christina put an end to the witch trials in the Lutheran Bishopric/Duchy of *Verden* in 1649. The Lutheran Superintendent and assiduous persecutor, Heinrich Rimphof, wrote a work here aimed against the influential work 'Cautio criminalis' by Friedrich Spee, an opponent of the witch-hunts. 127 people were charged with witchcraft in this territory, only 6 per cent of them as male witches. The execution rate for women was 56 per cent, and for men 50 per cent.[122]

The north: Holstein, Saxony-Lauenburg, the Principalities of Mecklenburg

The Protestant duchies in *Mecklenburg* were among the hotspots of witch persecutions. Records survive of around 3950 persons on trial between 1570 and 1777.

Bearing in mind that both parts of this territory were sparsely populated – the population in the 16th and 17th centuries was about 200,000 – and despite the fact that only one in two trials ended in execution and one in three defendants were released, this must be classified an area of intense persecution, in clear contrast to the other regions of northern Europe. The female witch image dominated; men constituted only 15 per cent of the accused. The courts condemned 55 per cent of the accused women and 45 per cent of the accused men to death; men and women had equal chances of acquittal.[123]

In the Bishopric of *Ratzeburg*, which is identical with part of present-day Northwest- Mecklenburg, 10 per cent of the persecuted were men, 90 per cent women.[124]

For the territories in the far north of the empire, the Duchies of *Holstein and Saxony-Lauenburg*, records survive of 439 people tried for witchcraft between 1530 and 1735. The majority were women; only 12 per cent of the total were tried as male witches. A similar development was noted for the Duchy of Schleswig, a state associated with Holstein but which, as a Danish fiefdom, no longer belonged to the empire. Men constituted 7 per cent of the accused; the execution rate in Holstein and Saxony-Lauenburg was 45 per cent for men and 60 per cent for women. These figures indicate that this was a region of average intensity persecution.[125]

The towns and cities

About 3 per cent of the empire's population lived in cities at the beginning of the 16th century, one in four lived in a town. However, the terms 'town' and 'city' are deceptive; of the ca. 4000 so-called conurbations the majority were small or very small settlements which, due to their agricultural orientation, had not developed urban structures and scarcely differed from villages. Almost 30 towns/cities had populations of over 10,000 and can thus be classified as urban societies.[126]

On the whole, the early modern cities of the 16th and 17th centuries showed little inclination towards witch persecutions.[127] Thus, a gender-specific analysis should be avoided here purely from a methodological point of view, since the numbers involved are generally so small. The gender profile in the larger towns will, then, only be mentioned when the data are statistically relevant.

In Lutheran *Hamburg*, a city with ca. 40,000 inhabitants, research to date shows the persecution to have been low level;[128] the proportion of men appears to have been slight. This also applies to the second largest northern Hanseatic city, *Lübeck*, with ca. 28,000 inhabitants and considerable territories in the surrounding region. My own research revealed 64 people accused here between 1544 and 1693. The percentage of male witches was similar to that of the surrounding non-urban territories.[129] Calvinist *Bremen* showed equally little zeal with regard to persecution, and in 1603 the Archbishop of Bremen put an end to persecutions in the areas under his rule. From 1503–1751, 62 court cases were filed for witchcraft, 35 per cent of the accused were male.[130] The fact that 96 trials were conducted in the Imperial City of *Cologne* from 1446 to 1665 contradicts the image of an urban society with low-level persecution; however, the comparatively low execution rate of ca. 40 per cent indicates that the city was not overly zealous in its pursual of witches. The percentage of men at 11 per cent was also low here.[131] No burnings are known to have taken place in the city of *Frankfurt* (population: 17,000),[132] although there were anti-Jewish pogroms. The strictly Protestant *Nurmberg* saw only a small number of trials (including trials of men), indicating that the council did not advocate systematic persecution. Other cities such as *Augsburg* remained similarly resistant to persecution. The first record of an execution here was in 1625, after which persecution gained in severity. The gender proportions are unknown.[133] For the city of *Vienna* with its 40,000 inhabitants only seven witch trials are known to have occurred in 250 years. The percentage of men given here as 41.7 per cent must be regarded as statistically misleading, since the numbers involved were so low as to make an evaluation unjustified. The picture is different in the city of *Bruges* in the Spanish Netherlands, a large Flemish city with a population of 27,000, and, with the exception of a Calvinist interim period from 1578 to 1584, Catholic. Here, the figure of at least 134 trials between 1522 and 1687 means that the empirical evidence can more readily be used for a gender-specific statistical evaluation. My own evaluation of the trial register shows that the proportion of men was 29 per cent.[134]

Certain small and medium-sized towns, on the other hand, did tend towards more massive persecutions,[135] some of which can be explained by sovereignty conflicts between the towns and the surrounding territories.[136] In some, but by no means all, of the towns of this type, the female bias of the witch persecutions waned noticeably.

In *Korbach*, a town with a population of 3000 and a high execution rate, the proportion of men in the 44 witchcraft trials was 36 per cent.[137] In the town of *Luxembourg*, nearly one in two accused were male,[138] and in the Imperial town of *Esslingen*, the witchcraft commissioner Hauff was responsible for a wave of intensive persecution in which 42 per cent of the 72 accused were not female.[139] Despite its position in a persecution hotspot within the Prince-Bishopric of Würzburg and its proximity to Bamberg, the Imperial town of *Schweinfurt* retained a moderate level of persecution, particularly with regard to the execution rate. Of 55 indictments in the period 1608–1723, almost 55 per cent were male. At 30 per cent, the proportion of males incriminated between 1430 and 1723 in the five Franconian Imperial towns *Rothenburg, Weissenburg, Windsheim, Schweinfurt* and *Dinkelsbühl* was above average.[140]

A large number of towns and cities, then, formed enclaves within persecution regions and cannot unconditionally be included in a gender-specific analysis. Nevertheless, there were differences even between the larger Imperial Cities. In the small and medium-sized towns with their predominantly agrarian structures, some of which suffered under intense persecution, the proportion of men varied enormously, from 0.75 per cent in Protestant Osnabrück to almost 50 per cent in Catholic Luxembourg. This does not, however, mean that this disparity between the denominations is generally applicable, as the legal and geographical as well as the socio-economic status of a territory played a greater role in determining the level of persecution; further research is required to clarify these issues. For this reason, the above figures on the extent and gender-specificity of witch persecutions in towns and cities will not be incorporated into the rest of this investigation. Nevertheless, it should not be forgotten that the witch paradigm in urban society was not homogeneous and that the gender profile of the victims varied considerably.

Trials of male witches: a quantitative comparison

A comparative approach for the early modern period is made difficult by the empirically problematic nature of the available statistics. Issues such as gaps in the records, the changing quality of historical source material, and the inaccuracy of figures in contemporary records (including several cases of exaggerations), from a time period where statistics were unknown, are commonly acknowledged problems. Therefore, the statistical discussion must be restricted to what historical investigation has mutually accepted and to what is possible at this stage of research. Even then it is not always possible to ascertain exact numbers, and existing data have to be complemented by scholarly estimations based on a close analysis of the relevant sources.

The statistical approach to this question was based on an analysis of data from 82 witchcraft monographs of regional persecutions in the Holy Roman Empire, published before 2007. All monographs that were included in this analysis had to satisfy high scholarly standards and be systematically structured; these specifications were made to avoid correct conclusions being drawn as a result of inaccurate statistics. However, the results can only be regarded as a provisional overview as there are still many gaps in the research for many imperial territories in the early modern period; statistical analyses are even lacking for some of the hotspots in the regions that experienced the greatest number of witch-hunts.

There is some discussion as to the data for Lorraine in the region designated 'west' in this study. Several studies have come up with a comparatively high proportion of men in the witchcraft trials, so that the figure of 28 per cent cited in the research by Briggs seems to be a realistic estimate. For the entire 'western' region which stretched from Franche-Comté north as far as the Spanish Netherlands, a total of 8200 verified cases of persecution are known, in which the proportion of men was 27 per cent. For the southwest region, the figures (18 per cent of 1080 people executed were male) given by the American historian H.C.E. Midelfort, the mentor of witchcraft research in Germany, provide a solid basis, although more recent research has shown the number of executions to be considerably higher. For this reason, the 18 per cent has been applied to the total of 3229 executions[141] which have been verified for southwest Germany and complemented by the results of more recent research. This raises Midelfort's minimum percentage slightly, as in the trials of this region alleged male witches were condemned to death less frequently than their female counterparts. Research to date (excluding the cases for which gender proportions could not be determined) shows that the proportion of men accused in the whole Habsburg complex – including the Prince-Archbishopric of Salzburg and the County of Tirol – was about 45 per cent. Gender-specific data for Bavaria in the 'southeast' region is only sporadic and not available for the region as a whole; however, the data which does exist here and for the other areas of this region is reliable, so that it is possible to assume a total of 3600 persecution victims and 35 per cent of trials in which alleged male witches were charged. By contrast, the 'eastern' region saw a total of about 1800 persecutions which were clearly aimed to a far greater extent at women (83 per cent). The present state of research for the 'central region' provides evidence of over 5000 witchcraft trials, in over 23 per cent of which men were the accused. As far as the 'north' and 'northwest' are concerned, there were comparatively few men among the accuseds; the number of accused here was 1600 (north) and 4200 (northwest), representing a non-female proportion of 13 per cent and 14 per cent, respectively.

Based on the results of qualitative studies, the statistics for the Holy Roman Empire as a whole can – provisionally – be summed up as follows:

The data in Table 3.2 clearly demonstrate the undisputed gender-specific dimension of the witch-hunts, as over three quarters of those tried were women. They do, however, also show that the proportion of men persecuted was almost one in four. This overall proportion of male witches given above is likely to increase slightly as a result of new figures soon to be published in a study on the persecution hotspot Luxembourg with its relatively high numbers of male victims.[142]

This value is, of course, an arithmetic mean and a representative value only, which as such tells us nothing about the average dispersion, because extreme values can have a considerable influence on the distribution. Evaluations to date have shown high regional variance in gender terms. Whilst the percentage of men persecuted lay at 68 per cent in the Duchy of Carinthia, a region with a low level of persecution, in Schaumburg, an area of more intense persecution, the rate was only 5 per cent. Absolute outliers, in statistical terms, were the rates in the

Table 3.2 Witch persecution in the Holy Roman Empire: proportion of male witches, 1530–1730

Region	**Persecution victims (total)**	**Persecution victims (male)**	**%**
West	ca. 8200	ca. 2200	ca. 27
Southwest	ca. 3700	ca. 800	ca. 22
Southeast	ca. 3600	ca. 1250	ca. 35
East	ca. 1800	ca. 300	ca. 17
Centre	ca. 5200	ca. 1200	ca. 23
Northwest	ca. 1600	ca. 200	ca. 13
North	ca. 4200	ca. 600	ca. 14
Holy Roman Empire	ca. 28,300	ca. 6550	> 23

city of Osnabrück (0.2 per cent) and Upper Austria (69 per cent). In the majority of regions researched, the proportion of men persecuted lay between 10 per cent and 35 per cent, this then being the range of the most frequent distribution from which the extreme cases have been eliminated.

This distribution was also apparent in structurally similar landscapes and territories, as the following examples from the Habsburg territories show. Whereas in Carinthia the majority of those persecuted were male, the opposite was the case in its near-neighbour Vorarlberg. Although the 'Alpine territories' from Styria to Franche-Comté can be described in general as regions with a relatively high proportion of male persecution, this does not apply to all regions in these territories.

For a long time, both historical research and public opinion had at the most perceived male witches to be a marginal issue. One might well also ask why these victims have received so little attention, for practice shows that suspicion and persecution were by no means homogeneous in gender terms; this question, however, goes beyond the scope of the present study.

Quantitative comparisons: punishment

Some studies report that women were punished more severely than men in the witchcraft trials. This statement, however, requires more differentiated argumentation.

To date, persecution has been defined in terms of people accused and tried before the courts. In a narrower definition of the term, victims are those condemned to death, i.e. the people who had no chance before the courts and were sent to the stake. In order to determine the extent of gender-specific persecution it can be useful to distinguish more closely between the number of charges and the number of executions. A useful indicator here is the so-called execution rate, which shows the probability of a charge resulting in the death penalty or, conversely, in acquittal or banishment. Such a figure gives the proportion of those tried for witchcraft who were actually condemned to death. Execution rates alone tell us little about persecution and should be complemented by the accusation rates, as presented in detail above.

The data given in other studies together with the data personally calculated from information in other analyses permit more precise conclusions for a fair number of territories. In 10 of these, the execution rate – however cynical this term might sound – was higher for women than for men. The opposite was true for six other cases (which, admittedly, do not constitute the majority): Montbéliard, Cambrai, Mainz, Luxembourg, Salzburg and the Saar region, where there was a tendency to punish alleged male witches more severely than women accused of the same crime. In the view of the courts in these territories, this allegedly major offence could only be atoned by death – in most cases by burning. In Mainz, for example, it was barely possible for men to escape condemnation as alleged witches, whereas women were more frequently acquitted.

Male witches and religious denomination

In a series of structurally homogeneous Catholic territories, geographically distant from one another, as well as in a good number of Bishoprics the number of male witches accused and persecuted was above average. The figures for numerous predominantly Protestant regions with equally heterogeneous political, economic and geographic structures,

Table 3.3 Persecution of male witches and religious denomination (figures show proportion of men persecuted as a % of total persecutions)

Catholic territories		**Protestant territories**	
Upper Austria	69	County of Ansbach	7
Lower Austria	34	Duchy of Brunswick-Wolfenbüttel	10
County of Baden-Baden	31	County of Büdingen	10
Bishopric Bamberg	26	County of Hesse(n)-Darmstadt	3
Counties of Blankenheim	20	County of Hesse(n)-Kassel	13
Prince-Abbey Ellwangen	20	Duchy of Holstein	12
County of Flanders	27	Duchy of Mecklenburg	15
Duchy of Carinthia	68	Bishopric of Minden	10
Electorate of Mainz	24	Principality of Montbéliard	18
Bishopric of Münster	33	County of Ostfriesland	5
Principality of Vaduz	40 (approx.)	County of Nassau	12
Duchy of Lorraine	28	Duchy of Saxony-Lauenburg	12
Duchy of Luxembourg	>25 (approx.)	County of Schaumburg	5
Bishopric of Paderborn	30	Bishopric of Ratzeburg	10
Bishopric of Salzburg	58	'Thuringia' (mostly Protestant)	13
Duchy of Styria	34	Bishopric Verden	6
County of Tyrol	48	Western Pomerania[143]	11
Vorarlberg	20	Duchy of Württemberg	15
Duchy of Westphalia	37		

however, are below average. This shows that persecution took place regardless of denomination, but that intensity and gender proportions varied between Protestant and Catholic regions. For example, in the so-called 'Zauberer-Jackl' (Sorcerer Jack) trials in the Prince-Bishopric of Salzburg, about 80 per cent of the victims were men. In the Protestant territory of Mecklenburg, with its large-scale witch-hunts, men made up only 15 per cent of those persecuted.

The proportions of men in the Catholic territory of Franche-Comté and its neighbouring territory, the Protestant Principality of Montbéliard show remarkable divergences, as do the regions of the Saar district, where the sources show a rate of 20 per cent for men persecuted in Protestant as against 29 per cent in Catholic regions. The significance of the denominational differences increases when non-secular Catholic regions and Protestant regions are compared.

There are, however, some cases which prove the contrary. Of the Catholic regions these are: the Bishoprics of Eichstätt and Augsburg in the southeast, Namur and Cambrai in the west, Swabian-Austria or Mergentheim in the southwest. Of the Lutheran territories, the Electorates of Saxony and Hohenlohe present a contrast in terms of the gendering of witch persecution. It is also necessary to differentiate within the Protestant camp, for the authorities in some reformed territories, as exemplified by some Swiss regions, sought a high proportion of their victims among males. As far as the reformed block goes, there seems to be no uniform tendency; in persecution hotspots such as the Calvinist counties of Lippe and Nassau, figures show that witchcraft was clearly most strongly associated with the female gender, whereas the authorities in the Electorate of Palatinate succeeded in suppressing almost all witchcraft suspicion among the population.

A higher level of persecution of men is evident not only in the non-secular Catholic territories but also in numerous secular Catholic regions. Comparatively low levels are found primarily in Protestant territories. It can, then, be hypothesized that there is a relationship between denomination and gender distribution. Such a correlation implies a parallel but does not automatically signify causality. Possible causality is dealt with later in Chapter 5 of this study.

Excursus: other European countries

Any attempt to compare different regional and geographical persecution patterns in the European context meets with problems, not least because of the discongruities in the various legal processes. In England

Illustration 3.5 The illustration shows men in Finland or Lapland selling wind to mariners. The picture was part of a report by the Swedish Catholic Bishop of Uppsala, Olaus Magnus (true name, Olof Måsson) who depicted the Finns and Sami ('Lapps') as particularly well-known and skilled sorcerers. These men would make three magic knots in a rope; when the mariners undid the first knot a breeze would get up, when they undid the second, a stronger wind, and the third would then unleash a storm. (Woodcut from: Olaus Magnus, *Historia de Gentibus Septentrionalibus*, 1555, Book III, Chapter 16.)

torture was forbidden, in Denmark a person accused of witchcraft was not permitted to testify against anyone else suspected of the same crime. In France, the appeal courts gave the accused wide-reaching opportunities to appeal against the decisions of local courts, and in Venice and Spain the Inquisition courts of the church were primarily out to find heretics and not witches. These circumstances all influenced the gender-specific aspect of witch trials, because, for example, traditionally men were more frequently persecuted as heretics, or because financial constraints meant that only a relatively small number of accused (more men than women) were in a position to appeal to the higher courts.

Since there is no uniform basis or background against which to make comparisons, a statistical analysis for Europe, such as presented for the Holy Roman Empire where the legal system had a foundation common to all territories – albeit with many local modifications – can lead to severe misinterpretations.

In recently Christianized regions or in areas where Christianity had not become the dominant religion until comparatively late, other cultural patterns played central roles. It has been shown for Iceland, for example, that the predominant concept of witchcraft was that it was free of the gender connotations very clearly expressed in the Christian concept of intercourse with the Devil.[144] Although this concept of women's magical abilities was not unknown in Iceland, the witch paradigm there was different from that in western Europe in that it was almost exclusively men who were persecuted. Between 1604 and 1670 the courts of this thinly populated island prosecuted 120 people for witchcraft, only 10 of them women. In Estonia the majority of those accused were also male. A study for Finland – written in Finnish and thus attracting little attention – has been available for some time and demonstrates a clear male majority in witchcraft persecutions in some regions of the country. It may also be interesting to note that the author disputes any clear-cut connections which might be conjectured to have existed in Finland between shamanist beliefs, male shamanist village healers and the witch-hunts.[145] Figure 3.1 can be derived from the data[146] in this study:

Witch persecution – or more accurately, the persecution of male witches – in Karelia did not begin until early in the 17th century, comparatively late in a European context, and reached its climax at the end of the same century. In the initial period, persecution victims were exclusively male, and this witch stereotype remained even during the major witch-hunts after 1680. The gender proportions for Finland, then, can be assumed to be the reverse of those for other European regions.

Table 3.4 provides some of the pieces necessary to put together the mosaic of persecution gendering in a European context and shows the

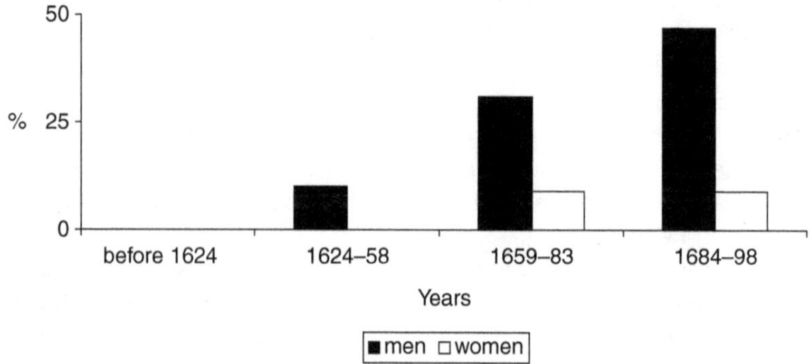

Figure 3.1 Finland, Karelia: witchcraft persecutions – numbers of accused, 1624–98

Table 3.4 Europe: witch persecution – men and women

Region/territory	Time period	Absolute no. of accused[148]	Women as % of total no. of accused[149]	Men as % of total no. of accused
Iceland	1593–1720	186	8	92
Norway	1551–1760	863	80	20
Sweden				
Southern Sweden	1635–1754	53	80	20
Mora	1668–76	(only maleficium)	85	15
Estonia	1520–1729	205	40	60
Finland	1520–1699	710	51	49
Denmark	1500–88	134	76	24
	1609–87	463	89	11
Netherlands (Northern)				
Province of Groningen		54	89	11
Province of Holland	1501–1620	193	95	5
England				
Home Circuit (Essex, Herefordshire, Kent, Surrey, Sussex)	1560–1701	474	90	10
Scotland	1560–1709	2710 (recent research shows this number is too high)	85	15
France				
'Parlement de Paris' (supervising criminal court for northern and central France)	1565–1640	1.288	48	52

Continued

Table 3.4 Continued

Region/territory	Time period	Absolute no. of accused[148]	Women as % of total no. of accused[149]	Men as % of total no. of accused
Toul (French since 1556)	1580–1630	135	70	30
Burgundy	1580–1642	159	48	52
Provence	1580–1628	103	71	29
Normandy	1564–1660	381	27	73
Holy Roman Empire (1648)[150]	1530–1730		77	23
Switzerland				
Bishopric of Basel	1571–1670	189	95	5
Fribourg	1607–83	162	64	36
Neuchâtel	1568–1675	259	81	19
Genf	1537–1662	240	76	24
Waadtland/Pays de Vaud	1580–1653	1700	65	35
Graubünden/Grisons	1590–1779		80	20
Spain				
Castile	1540–1685	456	71	29
Aragón	1600–50	120	31	69
Italy				
Republic of Venice	1550–1650	714	69	31
Friaul	1596–1785	magical arts:597	42	58
		maleficium:180	78	22
Piedmont	1292–1742	242	80	20
Siena	1588–1657	198	100	0
Hungary	1213–1800	4.089	87	13
Croatia	1360–1758	245	94	6
Russia	1622–1700	136	32	68[151]

diversity and complexity of this historical phenomenon from a broader perspective.

Although there are limits to the degree of comparison possible, the European dimension nonetheless demonstrates the equivocality of the gender aspect. Witchcraft on a European level was not necessarily gender-linked; the witch paradigm was also applicable to men.

Male patterns dominated in Iceland, Estonia. The sources also point to a high percentage of men in France. Persecution was less gender-specific in Spain and most of Italy, where the non-secular Inquisition courts ruled, in which the witchcraft concept found only limited acceptance. In most Protestant regions such as Sweden, Denmark, the Netherlands, England or Scotland, the witch-hunts concentrated on women. Calvinist Switzerland is a special case; here a number of regions, such as the 'Pays de Vaud' suffered massive persecution involving a high percentage of men. The political situation specific to this area was clearly a reason for the massive persecution of alleged witches and also of numerous male witches here.[147]

4
Witch-hunts and the Male Witch: A Chronology

> I am an honest man, a child of God...I am now a frightened man. I should not be driven away from God. On the Day of Judgment I want to prove to God that I am not a witch.
>
> (Statement made by Michael Heisch at his trial in Esslingen in 1603; he was later executed as a male witch)

> The devil makes the same pact with the witches and the sorcerers...
>
> (Statement of the Catholic suffragan bishop of Bamberg, Dr. Jacob Feucht, 1570)

This chapter deals with the temporal dimension of the persecution of male witches, this time drawing a chronological timeline rather than giving a statistical cross-section of the data. The chapter begins with a discussion of whether there were in fact peaks in the persecution of alleged male witches, and then looks into a theory on trials of male witches in the light of regional persecutions in territories with different denominations.

The 17th century

Quantitative methods are, despite all the problems with historical sources and unknown or unrecorded cases, an expedient way of depicting tendencies in persecution patterns. Again, I do not claim to cover all the trials which took place in a particular region; the data presented are intended as a guide to the relations between the various regions and historical periods.

Gender relations changed in the course of time: whereas witchcraft was still considered a gender-neutral crime in the late Middle Ages, the proportion of men persecuted grew from low at the beginning of the early modern era to high in the course of the 17th century. This is borne out by the figures for a number of territories for which data is available for the entire or large parts of the 16th and 17th centuries[1]:

During the same period the gender relations also changed in the Protestant regions; however, the changes were much less marked and the category 'woman' remained the decisive factor in witchcraft accusations in these regions. In the Calvinist county of Büdingen, for example, the proportion of men increased from 3 per cent to 17 per cent[2] and in the Lutheran Duchies of Holstein and Saxony-Lauenburg from 10 per cent to 15 per cent[3] in the period under discussion.

In the course of the 17th century the courts increasingly assimilated men as potential agents of the devil into their witch concept, leaving behind the phenomenon of the 16th century when women had represented the vast majority of the people persecuted and executed. Although in the witch-hunt around 1590 the female witch stereotype was still dominant, magical aggression at this point still being considered an almost exclusively female domain, the following century saw a general increase in the number of men affected. In some Catholic regions this tendency went so far as to almost reverse the gender proportions. The case whereby the majority of victims were women had become out of date, and the witch image in these regions took on male features; witch-hunts were now aimed increasingly at men.

It was, then, not the first major witch-hunt of 1590 but the second and third peaks around 1630 and 1660 which demonstrate the beginnings

Table 4.1 Proportion of male witches among the total number of people persecuted in the 16th and 17th centuries

Territory	Period	% of Men	Period	% of Men
Duchy of Westphalia	1570–89	16	1650–99	46
Electorate of Mainz	Entire 16th Century (and up to 1604)	8	Entire 17th Century	28
Prince-Archbishopric of Salzburg	Entire 16th Century	34	Entire 17th Century	70
Duchy of Carinthia	Entire 16th Century	18	Entire 17th Century	71
Duchy of Luxembourg	1500–80	3	1606–85	30

of the tendency, in some areas of the empire, to break through – and in some cases even to level – gender-specific barriers. This tendency was less pronounced in predominantly Protestant regions. As a whole, however, this gender development should be seen in a wider setting; both age and social structure of the trial victims also varied considerably in the 17th century. In one of the last massive witch-hunts in southern Germany, the so-called Sorcerer Jack trials, both gender and age proportions confirm this development; at the time of the trial three quarters of the accused were under the age of 23, and many of them became known as the 'magic lads' on account of their youth.

Mass trials

The American historian Eric Midelfort has given a plausible explanation for the increase in the persecution of men as the witch-hunt period progressed. The 'Midelfort thesis' is frequently quoted and accepted in historical research today.[4] He writes:

> In summary, it is fair to say that, as a hunt developed, the number of men suspected usually rose, and that from the 1620's on men were generally more prevalent. One stereotype had broken down, a stereotype by which society had been able to hunt its hidden enemies without inviting social chaos ...[5]

Midelfort uses examples from southwest Germany to develop his thesis and names the late phase of a persecution wave in Würzburg between 1626 and 1629 to demonstrate the increase in the number of men accused.

Midelfort sets store by a size model for witchcraft trials, distinguishing between small trials with up to three executions, 'small panics' with between four and 19 executions and 'major wtich hunts' with over 20 executions.[6] He argues that it was in the course of such large trials that men were increasingly accused of and executed for witchcraft. These mass trials saw the collapse of the characteristic description and understanding of a witch as 'poor, single and old'. Midelfort cites Würzburg trials with over 15 accused, in which almost half of those executed were men, to show that an increasing number of men were being accused and burnt. Three quarters of the people executed in the large-scale so-called 'burnings' (more than 20 people) in this city were men or boys.[7] The 'Midelfort thesis', then, states that the number of victims who, in terms of age and sex, corresponded to the traditional stereotype victim decreased in proportion to the size of the trial. Midelfort's data can be expressed in Figure 4.1.[8]

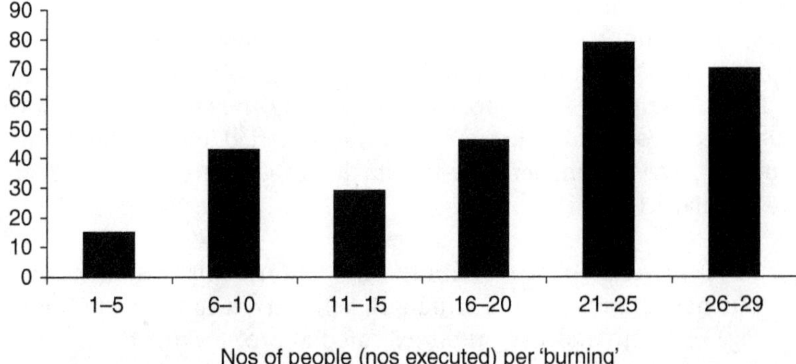

Figure 4.1 Percentage of men in witchcraft trials: Würzburg, 1627–29 (group size – proportion of men)

This trial-type classification has been – and still is – extremely fruitful in witchcraft research but it does not fully represent the reality of the witch persecutions and hence is only of limited use in analysing the connection between mass trials and the persecution of men.

First, since this method classifies as small all trials which began with a large number of accused but which culminated in just a few executions, it does somewhat distort the picture, for such trials also bore the features of a 'major hunt'.

Secondly, waves of persecution stretched over a number of years. Midelfort's decision to classify some cases as major but others as independent and individual trials, possibly even when they came before the same judge, should thus be rethought.

Thirdly, denunciations – whether extorted or voluntary – which led to further arrests, have the attributes of a composite trial which could satisfy the classification requirements of a major hunt in Midelfort's terms. Here, too, the division seems artificial. The background of widespread fear which arose from the mental strain of a familiar trial reduced the inhibitions potential accusers might have harboured, and had the capacity to cause denunciation campaigns and mass persecutions. It is difficult to discern any organized connection between these initiatives and the respective original trials. A witch panic could take the form of chain trials, linked by the exacted denunciations, or of numerous seemingly unconnected individual trials which the court records do not show to be linked with one another. It is impossible today to determine with any precision the internal connections between trials, and a definition of what constitutes a witch trial is a specific problem in witchcraft research. In the case of the Würzburg 'burnings', it is hard to see the validity of Midelfort's classification, since these all took place within such a short space of time.

In the 'Index of witch-people, executed by the sword before burning', a contemporary list of executions carried out between 1626 and 29[9], the chronicler lists two major executions between 2 and 16 February 1629:

> In the twenty-eighth burning...six persons: Mistress Knertzin, a butcher; Babel Schütz, a blind girl; Schwartz, a canon from the village of Hach; another canon executed at 5 o'clock in the morning and burnt with Mistress Bar; Ehling, vicar; Bernhard Mark, vicar at the cathedral was burnt alive.
>
> In the twenty-ninth burning, seven persons:
>
> A baker; the innkeeper (the keeper of the Klingen Inn); the reeve of Mergelsheim; the bakerwoman from the Ochsentor; the plump noblewoman; a clerical doctor by the name of Meyer from the village of Hach; and a nobleman called Junker Fleischmann. A Canon from Hach was also secretly executed at about the same hour and burnt with Mistress Bar, Paulus Vaecker. Since then there have been two burnings.
>
> Dated 16th Feb. 1629.
>
> But there have been many different burnings since.

According to the dates given, the burnings took place within a space of two weeks. It is not evident from the index whether the executions represent the sentences passed at a single trial of 17 or more people or from a number of separate trials. The distinction between small and mass trials cannot, therefore, be made without reservations for Würzburg in the period 1626–29. Nonetheless, it is clear that the witch stereotype collapsed here in those years, for the death penalties pronounced by the Würzburg courts appeared to make no distinction between such people as tradespeople, (the 'bakerwoman'), and nobles (the 'noblewoman' or the 'Junker Fleischmann') or Catholic clerics (the 'Canon of Hach'). Even children were caught in the mills of clerical justice (the 'blind girl').

The category 'major hunt' would appear, then, to pose too great a problem to be used as a basis for examining the connection between mass persecution and persecution of males. For this reason I have chosen to use the absolute number of persecutions per year classified into decades as an indicator of the intensity of persecution. This method makes it possible to investigate both a cumulation of individual trials and legally interlinked trials which formed part of mass trials.

The witchcraft trials of the 16th century, i.e. of the so-called first hunt, are not well documented. Sources improve, however, for the second, and even more so for the third wave around 1660, although records of some regional and local developments in the late 16th century are well preserved. Despite the dynamics they unfurled, the chain trials (i.e. series of trials each initiated by denunciations in previous trials – did not, on the whole, show any marked tendency towards breaking the witch gender stereotype, for even as the hunts escalated, there was no pronounced increase in the numbers of men affected. Even the mass, uncontrolled persecution in the Prince Bishopric Trier did not necessarily lead to more accusations of male witches; in 1586, for example, a large panic broke out in the district of Pfalzel, in rural Trier, in the course of which 118 women but only 2 men were arrested. One exception to this can be derived from the excellently preserved records of mass persecution (approximately. 400 people in 10 years) for the independent territory of the Abbey of St Maximin near Trier which demonstrate that in this small region the witch stereotype was no longer valid by the end of the 16th century; one third of those condemned to death here were men.[10] Yet in the so-called Schongauer trial of 1589–92 with 58 accused, a classic major hunt in Midelfort's sense, only two men were accused – and later released.[11] The hunts in southwest Germany took a similar course: the victims of the mass trials of Wiesensteig in 1562–63 and 1583 were all women, and of the 130 people accused in Rottenburg between 1578 and 1602 not one was male.[12]

These few examples show that, at least until the early 17th century, mass persecution was not connected with a breakthrough in the witch stereotype.

The hunt for new 'offenders'

In the following, the connection between mass persecution and a higher proportion of male victims will be investigated chronologically using selected processes in individual territories. The data chosen represent well-researched regional witch-hunts which permit a chronological timeline presentation of the gender issue rather than statistical cross-sections of the data.

In the terms of empirical social research, then, what we are using here is a pre-selected sample which does not pertain to systematically confute previous theories, and is only valid for the respective regions analyzed. Nonetheless, it can open up new perspectives. Again, it must be stressed that due to the nature of the sources for the Early Modern period, the following data can only be viewed as statistical orientations with limited representative value.

The Duchy of Westphalia provides a very good example of the tendency of witch persecutions to come in 'waves', a phenomenon which has been dealt with in some detail in the literature.[13] The intensity of the persecutions in Westphalia make this one of the hotspots. The first wave can clearly be seen in Figure 4.2 to have occurred in the 1590s, the second in the 1620s and the third in the 1660s; in each of these three periods the proportion of male victims rose.

If the same data is presented in a graph which shows the gender distribution in terms of proportions, it becomes clear that the relations between the numbers are constantly changing and that the proportion of men shows a continuous upward trend rather than an adherence to the periodical persecution cycles. Figure 4.3 demonstrates that whereas in the 16th century this proportion reached 40 per cent, it had climbed to over 50 per cent by 1660 and generally remained at a high level until the end of the century, even in times of fairly low-level persecution around 1645 and post-1660.[14] These figures, then, indicate a change in the stereotype of the female witch, clearly showing the gender development which took place in Westphalia, where by the end of the period in question, the majority of the accused were men. However, this does not imply that the victim prototype of earlier years collapsed, particularly in the years of high-level persecution, but rather demonstrates a tendency towards a levelling of the proportions of men and women.

A similar development can be seen in another persecution hotspot, the Prince-Bishopric of Bamberg. The percentage of male victims climbed from 1610 onwards, increasing significantly in the period of intensive persecution from 1620–30.[15] Between 1620 and 1629 one in three accused witches was male. The development of the gender proportions among the victims shows that there was a continuous change in the relations, with the female witch stereotype losing in importance, but nonetheless remaining relevant.

In the Bishopric of Bamberg, where prominent male representatives of the upper classes such as the burgomaster and the chancellor, were executed, the proportion of men accused of witchcraft did not exceed 40 per cent of the total in the high intensity periods in which there were literally 'deluges' of trials (Figure 4.4).

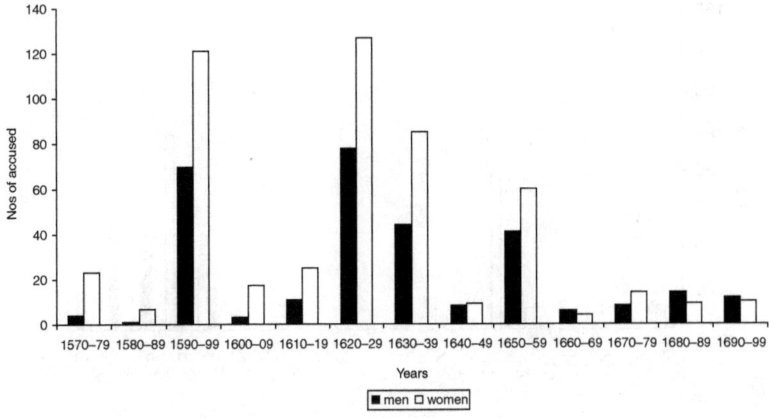

Figure 4.2 Westphalia: witchcraft persecutions by sex – 1570–1699

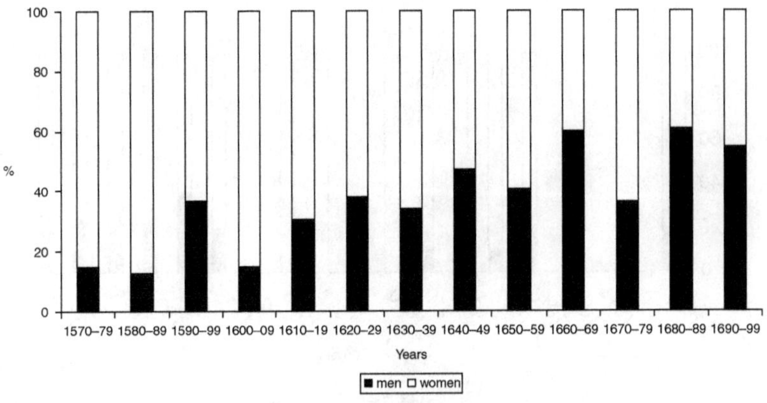

Figure 4.3 Westphalia: witchcraft persecutions by sex – proportion of men and women, 1570–1699 (%)

The development in the Electorate of Mainz was almost identical. The proportion of men among the accused rose in the intensive phase of persecution between 1604 and 1629, but never rose above about one third of all victims.[16]

Bamberg, Mainz, and Westphalia (which was ruled by a Prince Bishop) belonged to the non-secular Catholic territories and at the same time were among the zones which made the most extreme use of violence in

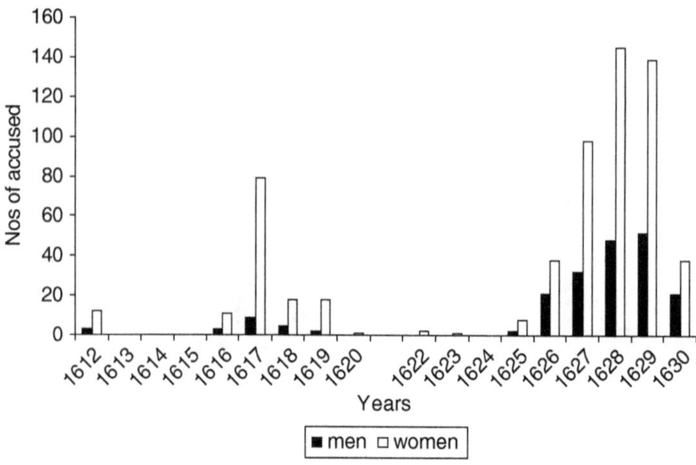

Figure 4.4 Prince-Bishopric of Bamberg: witchcraft persecutions by sex – nos of men and women, 1612–1630

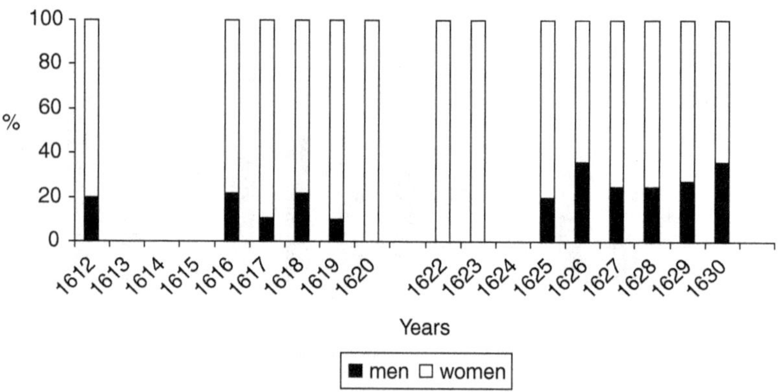

Figure 4.5 Prince-Bishopric of Bamberg: witchcraft persecutions by sex – proportion of men and women, 1612–1630 (%)

witchcraft trials. A connection between mass persecution and a high proportion of males can best be verified for these regions.

An analysis of regions with an average degree of persecution intensity, such as Franche- Comté, gives a different picture, for here the proportion of men did not grow consistently. Instead, it remained at a relatively high level of approx. 30–45 per cent and indeed even fell during the large panics of 1600–09. It then rose to ca. 45 per cent in the following protracted phase

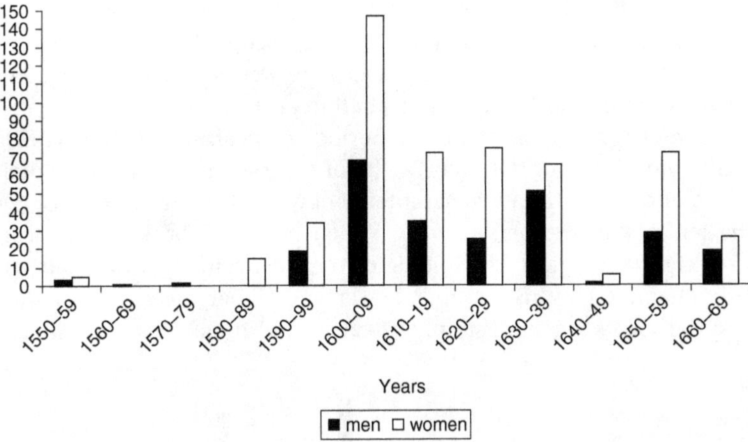

Figure 4.6 Franche-Comté: witchcraft persecutions by sex – nos of men and women, 1550–1669

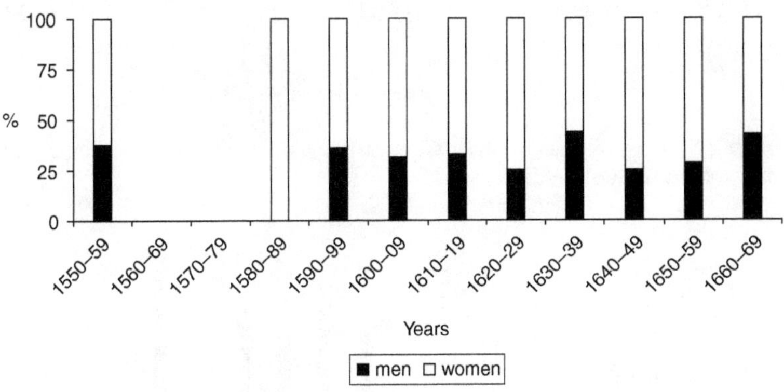

Figure 4.7 Franche-Comté: witchcraft persecutions by sex – proportion of men and women, 1550–1669 (%)

of arrests between 1630–39, only to decline again considerably in the last wave of persecutions.[17] From the beginning there was no homogeneous witch type evident in the Catholic Free County of Burgundy; the gender distribution was much more even and only changed gradually throughout the entire period of witch trials. The graphs below, incidentally, demonstrate that the 'wave movement' in witch persecution, as exemplified by Westphalia, cannot be generally applied to other regions.

Figures 4.8 and 4.9 show data from a region with a low persecution rate. In no one decade were more than 24 people tried, let alone executed; that is to say that on average there were two trials a year in a territory which was by no means small in area.

Figure 4.8 clearly shows three periods of peak persecution (1620s, 1650s and 1690s) for the Arch-Duchy of Austria, but these denote more an up and down than a general tendency, for it is the continuity and the tenacity of the persecutions, which persisted for 220 years from 1540 right through to the middle of the 18th century, which particularly characterize this region.[18] Lower and Upper Austria again show that Catholicism cannot simply be equated with mass persecution, and

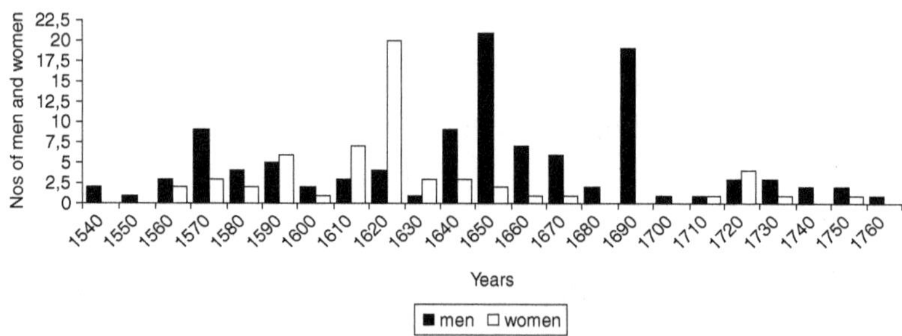

Figure 4.8 Lower/Upper Austria: witchcraft persecutions by sex – nos of men and women, 1540–1769

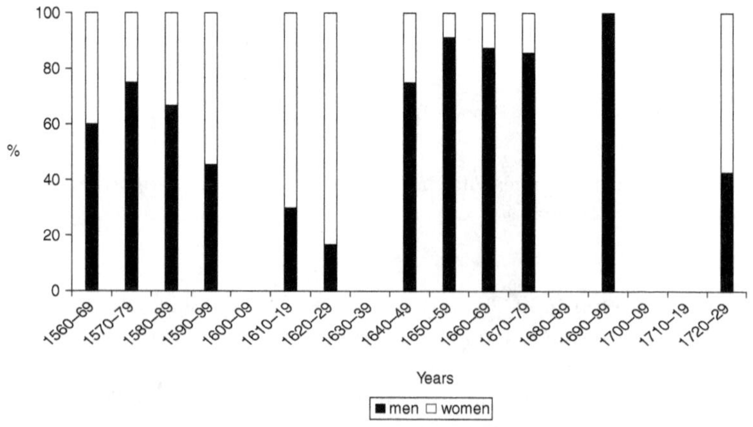

Figure 4.9 Upper/Lower Austria: witchcraft persecutions by sex – proportion of men and women, 1560–1729 (%)

Protestantism with a low level of persecution. The relation of the different religious denominations to the historical phenomenon of witch persecution followed more complex patterns.

From the beginning of the trials, the emphasis in the Arch-Duchy was on male witches and it was not until the phase which saw increasing trial numbers in the period up to 1629 that this male stereotype began to decline, with the proportion of men falling to below 20 per cent at the peak of the persecutions. In the ensuing period, however, it again rose, reaching ca. 90 per cent between 1650 and 1659. In the third wave of persecutions in the Arch-Duchy, there was not one woman among the accused. Persecution of witches no longer bore any relation to the female sex and in this respect, this region represents an exception within the Holy Roman Empire.

By the standards of the empire as a whole, it is possible to say that the female witch stereotype broke down and, indeed, was even reversed in this territory and that there was no correlation between mass persecution and a higher percentage of male victims. Here, the low level of persecution was connected with the breaking up of the female witch stereotype.

The county of Büdingen is considered a Protestant high persecution territory[19] on a level similar to that of the Catholic Prince-Bishoprics. The witch persecutions here culminated in the 1590s, 1630s and 1650s, a clear affirmation of the three persecution waves generally described in witchcraft research. As early as 1560, prior to a relatively mild persecution period, there was an increase in the number of witchcraft trials. In the intensive periods and particularly in the 1630s and 1660s, when there was a massive increase in persecution, the absolute numbers of men accused seem at first glance to have risen.

These observations become less evident in a diagram depicting the gender proportions, because the percentage of men fell in the intensive periods but rose instead in the periods of below-average intensity. From 1630 to 1639, a period when a large number of trials were held, the proportion fell to 9 per cent from an average of 12 per cent for the period 1620 to 1629 when few trials were held (Figure 4.11). An increase in the number of alleged male witches is not seen until towards the end of the witch-hunts, when the proportion climbed to 25 per cent. For the entire period, the numbers of men accused in this territory of high-level persecution remained fairly low; in this Calvinist county, then, the female witch stereotype remains essentially unchanged.

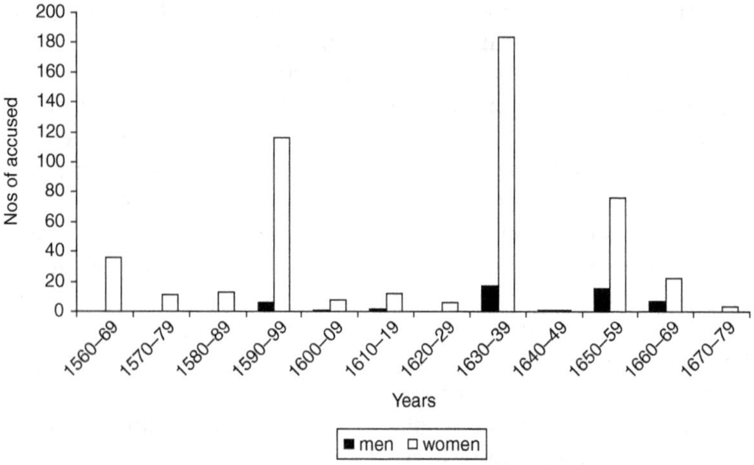

Figure 4.10 County of Büdingen: witchcraft persecutions by sex – nos of men and women, 1560–1679

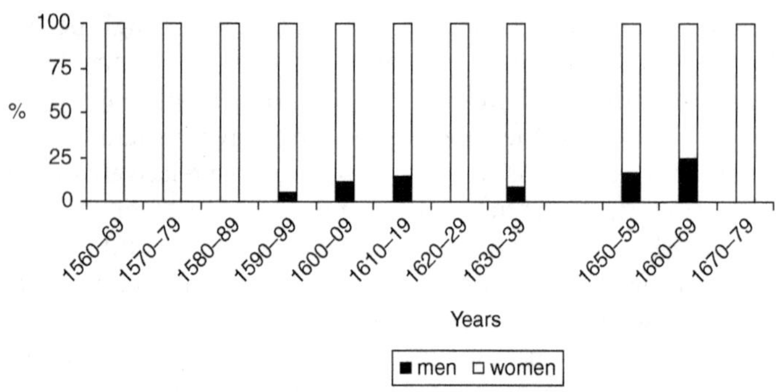

Figure 4.11 County of Büdingen: witchcraft persecutions by sex – proportion of men and women, 1560–1679 (%)

The same observations can be made for a further Calvinist county, the County of Schaumburg in the northwest of the empire. This county has previously been the subject of a study and can also be classified as a persecution hotspot. With the exception of a few precursors of the witchcraft trials prior to 1560, the proportion of men remains constantly under 10 percent, not even increasing in the periods of higher intensity from 1600–09 and 1650–59 (Figure 4.12). The data currently available shows that trials were directed exclusively against women in the years 1620–40.[20]

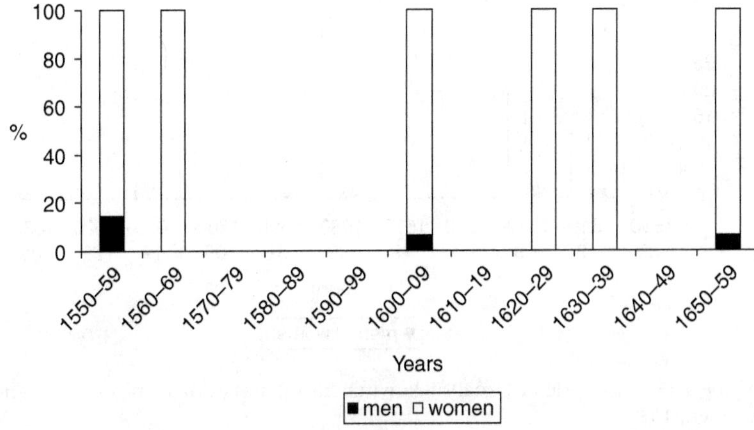

Figure 4.12 County of Schaumburg: proportion of men and women, 1550–1660 (%)

As in numerous other Protestant territories, the trials in the Lutheran Prince-Bishopric of Osnabrück, a territory with low-level persecution, began relatively early – around 1540. This makes it comparable with the Arch-Duchy of Austria where trials began equally early and remained endemic until 1760. In the early 'peak' periods, the proportion of men was consistently low, never exceeded 15 per cent and, indeed, fell to 8 per cent in the second wave of persecutions around 1590. There is no evidence of a man being tried for witchcraft after 1600.[21] Male witches either did not exist here or their numbers were reduced to a minimum, and men clearly played no more than a very minor role in the witchcraft allegations for this territory.

The two Duchies of Holstein and Saxony-Lauenburg have been chosen as representative of territories with average-level persecution. In these territories, together with several other smaller Protestant lands, there is evidence of 453 witchcraft trials between 1530 and 1735; bearing in mind that the combined population of these territories was ca. 300,000, this was clearly not an area with low-level persecution.[22] In contrast to some other Protestant territories, particularly in southwest Germany, persecution increased rather than decreased in the post-1600 period. Persecution also began comparatively early in Holstein, increased rapidly from 1560 to 1580 and culminated in a surge of persecutions around 1615 and a third peak around 1650–60. Persecution in the northern part of the empire shows clear parallels with that in Denmark up to 1630, which also peaked around 1560 and 1610–25.

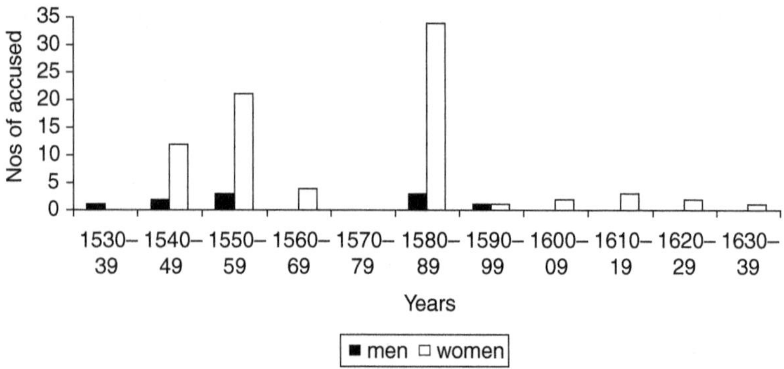

Figure 4.13 Bishopric of Osnabrück: witchcraft persecutions – nos of men and women, 1530–1639

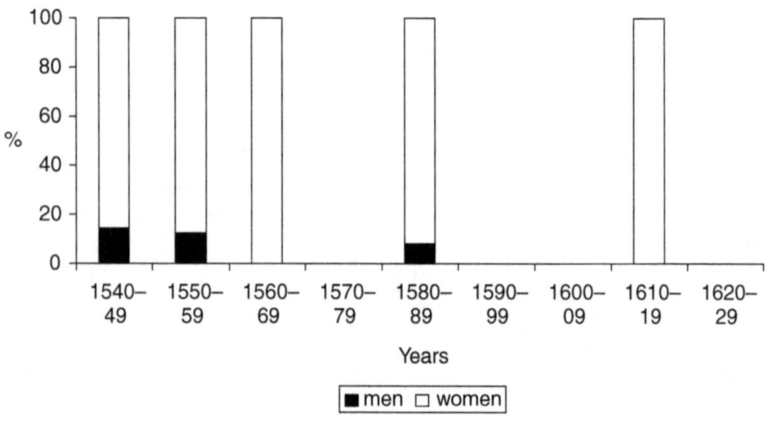

Figure 4.14 Bishopric of Osnabrück: witchcraft persecutions – proportion of men and women, 1540–1629 (%)

In contrast to other areas, however, the peaks are less evident because the number of trials rarely fell to an extremely low level. The numbers of men accused increased in the periods of high-level persecution, as Figure 4.15 shows.

The high proportion of men accused in the early years of the persecutions around 1540 and 1550 is represented correctly on Figure 4.16, but can easily create a false impression if the fact is ignored that the total number of trials was only 11. The percentage of men accused as witches remains relatively low at 5–10, rising above this figure in the

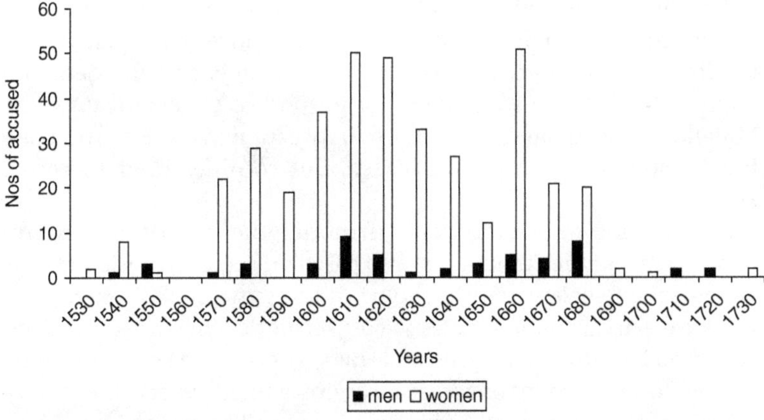

Figure 4.15 Duchy of Holstein and Saxony-Lauenburg: witchcraft persecutions – nos of men and women, 1530–1730

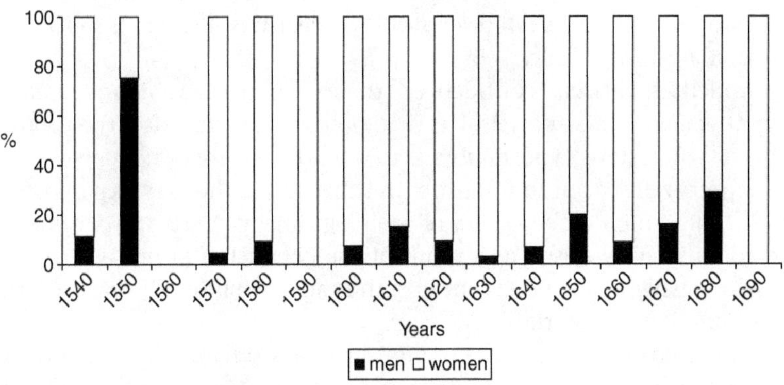

Figure 4.16 Duchy of Holstein and Saxony-Lauenburg: witchcraft persecutions – proportions of men and women, 1540–1690 (%)

witch persecutions of 1610–20 and 1650–60, but hardly ever reaching the empire's average of 25 per cent. It was not until the very end of the persecution period that a tendency towards a change in these relations became apparent. It cannot be denied that there is some connection here between more severe persecution and a higher proportion of men; however, the developments in the gender-specific nature of trials were limited and percentages of men below average in comparison with the rest of the empire. The classic female witch stereotype only began to fade as the will to prosecute receded.

It is significant that the evaluation of data from the various persecutions analysed here clearly demonstrates once more that there is no direct, mechanistic connection between intensity and denomination. However, this study does not purport to systematically refute Midelfort's postulated correlation between mass persecution and higher proportions of men accused, but confines itself to certain areas.

For the non-secular Catholic territories the evaluation confirms Midelfort's pathbreaking thesis (also based on these territories) of a collapse of the female witch stereotype in the sense of an erosion of the gender-specific contours. In these core territories there was a tendency towards a levelling of the gender barriers, although the gender relationship within the groups of accused was not actually reversed.

This evaluation cannot, however, assume validity for the secular territories discussed here. It is striking that the comparatively high proportion of men was unrelated to any persecution cycles in the Catholic regions of Franche-Comté or parts of the Austrian territories. In the low-intensity regions of Lower and Upper Austria, the witch stereotype was, if anything, male.

Midelfort`s 'crisis of confidence'[23] theory is both plausible and remains unaffected by this analysis. His theory postulates that after the rupture in the witch stereotype, doubts as to the now disfunctional persecution phenomenon began to intensify and that it was the very expansion of the trials which robbed them of their legitimacy. A crisis of confidence could also have arisen as a result of the expansion of prosecutions to include new social and age groups, thus again shaking the basis for the legitimation of the trials.

In the Protestant counties of Büdingen and Schaumburg, the Prince-Bishopric of Osnabrück (Lutheran until the 17th century) and the Lutheran Duchy of Holstein, the gender-specific characteristics changed little; witchcraft remained a female-specific crime, even if developments towards the end of the period meant that the female stereotype became less dominant in certain areas.

It would, then, seem likely – even though this study discusses only a pre-selected sample of data – that the denominational factor played a role of considerable importance not in the intensity of the witch persecutions but in their gender specificity. It is emerging that in the Catholic territories,[24] especially those ruled by prince-bishops with political aspirations, the witchcraft trials were more closely related to men than in the Lutheran or, with exceptions, the Reformed territories, in which there were only slight changes in the gender proportions of those arrested.

The question now arises as to whether there is a connection between the different gender specificities of the witch persecutions and the differences in the witch paradigms of the respective denominations. This will be discussed in Chapter 5.

5
Men as Potential Witches in Demonological Treatises

> A woman impudent and mannish grown is not more loath'd than an effeminate man
>
> (Shakespeare, Troilus and Cressida, 1602)

In this chapter, the perspective moves to the witch image in important contemporary theological and demonological works. Following the theory expounded by the French philosopher Foucault and quite commonly applied in historical research that discourse constitutes social communication, the present chapter investigates the degree to which the male sex was integrated into the witch image of elite discourse. At the same time, I look into possible denominational differences in the gendering of persecution. Finally, this chapter investigates the theoretical background to the gradual change in gender proportions in territories of different religious convictions, as determined in earlier chapters.

Witchcraft notion

The scholarly witchcraft notion of the early modern persecutions consisted of four central elements:

1. Maleficium
2. Devil's pact
3. Intercourse with the Devil
4. Witches' flight and witches' Sabbat

The following analysis works with this elaborated – or cumulative – concept.

The history of the witchcraft notion has been described so often that only a broad outline will be given here.[1] In the Early and High Middle

Ages theological literature denounced popular belief in magic as superstition and, with the help of secular ruling authorities, attempted to suppress 'heathen' customs. It was not the sorceress ('stria' or 'striga') herself who was persecuted but women who were designated thus by other people. The rejection of the idea of flight and the punishment of magical practices found their way into Church law via the text collection the 'Canon Episcopi' – recorded by Abbot Regino of Prüm – and Burchard Bishop of Worms' 'Corrector'. The position of these two authors had a decisive influence on the stance of the church right into the Late Middle Ages. The 13th century saw a gradual reevaluation of these magical practices, the effects of which were increasingly viewed as dangerous. The theoretical backgound to this was the view developed by St Augustine, a Doctor of the Catholic Church, that magical manipulation is not in itself efficient, but only when practised in contract with the Devil. In the course of the 13th century, other clerics, in particular the Dominican Albertus Magnus and his scholar and later Church Doctor, Thomas Aquinus, added to the Devil's pact concept the notion of intercourse with the Devil. The idea which combined the Devil's pact and intercourse with the Devil with a belief in the reality of magically induced harm had become a firm component of theological literature; apostasy from God and the Christian church necessarily preceded the pact with the Devil.

Once this position on the reality and threatening nature of magical practices had attained majority consensus in the church, a new element emerged and church theologians began to transfer the responsibility for the organization of nocturnal gatherings previously attributed to heretical movements to the alleged workers of magic themselves. Magic, heresy, and the folkloric nightflight, elements previously considered to be independent of one another, were combined in the theological discourse to make a comprehensive synthesis, with the result that by the 15th century people who allegedly practised magic were perceived as members of an organization of a heretical nature. Magic, once primarily seen as a single offence committed by individuals, was from now on a comprehensive offence committed by far more people. The sorcery of the Middle Ages – punishable but not life-threatening – had become witchcraft, the highly destructive magic of a conspiratorial sect of maleficent people.

Male witches – 'literally unthinkable'?

The two phases in the theological evaluation of magic beliefs and actions corresponded to differences in the gendering of these offences.

In the Middle Ages magic was not a gender-specific offence specifically attributed to women; for between the dual-gender 'magi' (magicians) or 'sortilegi/sortilegae' (sorcerers/sorceresses) and the generally single-or female gender 'malefica/ae' (female witches) lay a profound intellectual and mental development.

The question is, was this change of paradigm also accompanied by a *complete* reversal of gendering? Stuart Clark asserts that the 'gender' aspect did not play a substantial part in the demonology of Early Modern Europe and that its importance has thus been exaggerated.

> On the whole, however, the literature of witchcraft conspicuously lacks any sustained concern for the gender issue; and the only reason for the view that it was extreme and outspoken in its antifeminism is the tendency for those interested in this subject to read the relevant sections of the Malleus maleficarum and little or nothing else.

A few pages later, he adds, 'For it was literally unthinkable, at this level, that witches should be male.'[2]

On the basis of a number of common works on witchcraft in Central Europe this chapter analyses the role allocated to men in the demonology of the 16th and 17th centuries. Thus, in the following I make no pretence to an analysis of the gender issue in demonology in its entirety. The aim is rather to reshape the focus of the investigation by looking into a possible integration of the male sex in the learned witch paradigm. The elements of the witchcraft concept as propagated by theologians and demonologists who were well-known throughout Central Europe, were examined according to the following criteria

- Conceptual elements
- Implicit and explicit gendering
- Reception of these concepts in persecution practice

To avoid misunderstandings, texts were first analyzed in the original language in which they were written. Where necessary, several editions were checked to verify the consistency of the texts. Because of the meticulous linguistic analysis involved, I have avoided using abridged translations or English versions of demonological literature which do not sufficiently distinguish gender-specific differences. This applies particularly to the translations by such problematic experts as Montague Summers so frequently used in historical research.[3]

A representative of the transition period: Johannes Nider (1437)

Nider was born around 1380, joined the Dominican order in 1402, took up an appointment as Professor of Theology in Vienna in 1425, and later became prior of several Dominican monasteries. He played an active role in the Council of Basle, whence the witchcraft concept was spread to large areas of Europe. It was in this period that Nider wrote his treatise 'Formicarius' – as the title suggests, a comparison of an idealized view of ants and their social structures with human existence in contemporary society. It is not until the fifth book that he reflects on crimes of magic and witchcraft.

The treatise was written in dialogue form and although it does not give a precise witch concept, it does contain basic, albeit unsystematically presented elements, of later cumulative demonology teachings. He describes traditional harmful magic, the pact with the Devil and the existence of a new and threatening anonymous sect which met in churches to renounce God and the Catholic faith and to make pacts with the Devil. There is no explicit mention of the idea of the Witches' Sabbat. With Nider, learned Catholic discourse of the Late Middle Ages makes the transition from the heretical to the witchcraft offence through the synthesis of the individual elements.[4] In Nider's work, witchcraft is no longer the traditional individual crime but a composite crime practised by an increasingly large group of people.

Nider himself describes the members of this harmful confederacy as follows:

> One speaks of the witch [*'maleficus'*, clearly masculine singular and not concealed by a plural form, R.S.] who deals ill, does not truly keep the faith, and these both in the form of magic arts which through superstition and actions harm his neighbours, and that such people are found in abundance.[5]

This depicts the 'maleficus' as a heretical harm-doing person, and we should note that, when naming heresy and maleficium as the characteristics of this newly 'discovered' diabolical alliance, Nider uses the male singular noun 'maleficus' and not the female equivalent 'malefica'.

As evidence of the reality of witchcraft crimes, Nider cites witnesses who tell of trials of alleged witches and male witches. In their statements they give detailed descriptions of the accused. Nider repeatedly mentions persons of 'utriusque sexus' (Latin for 'both sexes') who practised infanticide and cannibalism, this being the reason why they were prosecuted and burnt as male and female witches, though some had fled:

> Nevertheless I will provide you with some examples and some information pertaining to your question…some of which I have from Mr Peter, a citizen of the city of Bern in the Diocese of Lausanne. He has burnt *many witches of both sexes* and driven others to flee the land…There are, then, or have recently been *witches of both sexes* around Bern who have a disposition contrary to that of human nature and even more contrary to the nature of all animal species, with the sole exception of the wolves. They devour children of their own genus and are wont to eat them.[6]

The other eye witness reports cited give almost equal numbers of men and women as witches; in sections 4 and 7 there is even a preponderance of male culprits.[7] Admittedly, Nider expressly emphasizes the evil nature of a particular old woman, a soothsayer, but he goes into far more textual detail on the alleged malpractices of male witches, whose names he records as 'Hoppo', 'Scavius' and 'Scaedeli(n)'. According to Nider, Scaedlin killed a large number of children before they were even born, thus causing their mothers to have miscarriages; similarly, he killed livestock young before birth by placing snakes under the doorsteps of the victims' houses. Of the other two criminals Nider says that they either allegedly transformed into harm-bringing mice or brought calamities to people, livestock and harvests. They were also able to "de loco ad locum per aera…transineare", that is to rise up into the skies and fly from place to place.[8] Although the witches' flight is insinuated in Nider's text, the actual trials of the three male witches evidently still bore some features of traditional sorcery trials.

For those who would like to implicate Nider in the connection between misogyny and witch persecutions, this work of his does not provide a good foundation.[9] The image drawn of women in the Formicarius is an anomalous one: some are portrayed as credulous and debauched, making them easy prey for seduction by the Devil; but Nider also describes numerous exemplary women who conformed with his reformist ideal.[10] The cases Nider describes have nothing to do with the newly invented witches' sect but are reports of individual trials of women in which charges of sorcery also played a role. Neither in the Formicarius nor in any other of Nider's works can he be said to focus witchcraft crimes on women.[11]

Nider's gender-neutral notion of this new diabolical sect was consistent with that of other 15th century theologians. Pierre Mamor(is), a

Illustration 5.1 The baptism of a male witch as envisaged by the persecutors. With this ritual the candidate became apostate from God, joined the ranks of the unfaithful and professed his belief in the cause of evil. In the background, other men and women are waiting to receive the rites and join the ranks of the Devil's army. Guazzo's work was published in Italy but based on the observations and experiences he made in Central Europe (Woodcut from: Francesco Maria Guazzo, *Compendium Maleficarum*, Milan 1626.)

French Professor of Theology at the University of Poitiers saw 'homines et mulieres',[12] that is 'men and women' in this diabolical sect. The same was true of the Inquisitor Nicolas Jacquier, who operated in northern France, but like Johannes Nider participated in the Council of Basle, and who saw this group as consisting of both genders, and described their fall from the Catholic faith, the Devil's pact formed by both men and women. In Jacquier's work, however, there is no mistaking the close relationship between heresy and witchcraft; indeed he equates the two:

> Not only women attend the sect or synagogue of the witches; men also frequent them, and worse [still] clerics and religious men. They stand and can be discerned communicating with the demons...by

> renouncing God, the Catholic faith and the mysteries of the faith, whom the demons promise protection and support...[13]

Clergy who read Nider's work experienced enlightenment and were inspired to rethink their ideas on witches.[14] Within the church, belief in harm induced by magic began to grow. The 'Formicarius' intensified the perception of alleged witchcraft as a crime and the reception of cumulative demonologies in learned Catholic discussion. Nider's treatise appeared in five editions between 1480 and 1692, and was appended to 'The Witches' Hammer' which first appeared in 1486.

The struggle of the 'womanish era': *The Witches' Hammer* (1486)

In 1445, at the age of 15, the most likely sole author of *The Witches' Hammer*, Heinrich Kramer, also known by his latinized name, Heinrich Institor(is)[15], joined a Dominican monastery. In 1479 the Pope appointed him Inquisitor for southern Germany, but the witch trials he initiated in Innsbruck failed. In 1486 his *Malleus maleficarum, The Witches' Hammer* appeared.[16] There seems to be a general consensus in international research that the German Professor of Theology, Jakob Sprenger – long thought to have been a co-author of this work – was, in fact not involved. By naming another authority, Institor(is) was evidently trying to immunize his work against criticism.

The Witches' Hammer is based on theological traditions and is a collage-style compilation of important statements by church authorities. Institor(is) tries by the way he selects and places the citations to account for the reality of comtemporary witchcraft crimes and rejects the fictional concept of traditional Mediaeval magic. *The Witches' Hammer* describes at various points maleficium, the Devil's pact, sexual relations with the Devil, but only rare cases of the Sabbat and there is neither a detailed nor a compact description in *the Witches' Hammer* of this latter pattern and the consequences it had for inquisitional practice.

The title of the work is itself in the feminine form Malleus Malefic*a*rum, thus revealing the prime tendency of the work to denote witchcraft a female offence. This is in contrast to the usage of other 15th century authors such as Jacquier who included the male sex by using the masculine plural form in his title 'Flagellum malefic*o*rum'. Institor(is) used the same term when designating the newly discovered and alleged witchcraft crimes an aspect of the heretical movement and classifying them as 'heresis malefic*o*rum'.[17] For Institor(is) this heresy movement was of a new calibre, since the structure of its membership differed from previous heretical groups in that, as he saw it, it was now largely in female hands and commanded immense and new powers, given the support these groups had from the Devil.

The Witches' Hammer portrays the entire female sex – with the exception of women such as Mary or other female saints, who are characterized as asexual – as a potential partner of evil. The relevant passages in the text are, admittedly, well known but should, nonetheless, be cited here once more:

> Woman, therefore, is evil as a result of nature because she doubts more quickly in the Faith. She also denies the Faith more quickly, this being the base for acts of sorcery.... Indeed, just as the result of the first defect, that of intelligence, is that they commit the renunciation of the Faith more easily than do men, so too the result of the second, namely irregular desires and passions, is that they seek, think up and inflict various acts of vengeance, whether through acts of sorcery or other means, Hence, it is no wonder that such a large number exists in this category ... Conclusion: Everything is governed by carnal lusting, which is insatiable in them.... and for this reason they even cavort with demons to satisfy their lust ... Hence, and consequently, it should be called the Heresy not of the Sorcerers but of Sorceresses, to name it after the predominant element. Blessed be the Highest One, Who has, down to the present day, preserved the male kind from such a disgraceful behaviour, and clearly made man privileged since He wished to be born and suffer on our behalf in the guise of a man[18]

Institor(is) did actually concede that women only represent the majority (and not the entirety) of the Devil's followers: '... while women are sorcerers in greater numbers than men ...',[19] thus seeming to relativize the axiom whereby this new crime is attributed on principle to women. These remain, however, hollow words and serve only as protection against potential allegations of one-sidedness. Men do not, Institor(is) continued, pass down to their children the ability to perform witchcraft or the desire to form a pact with evil forces; the disposition towards such evil acts is bequeathed strictly matrilinearly.[20] His belief that men are little disposed to witchcraft is illustrated by his mention of intercourse with the Devil to which men are not drawn '... since the natural strength of reason by which men surpass women leads men to shrink from such things to a greater degree.'[21]

Yet Institor(is) did not entirely deny the existence of male witches. Unlike the carriers of magical notes securing protection from war injuries, who are of little relevance, these male witches enter into a pact with the Devil and thus become male agents of evil. They are able to enchant weapons and are also known as the archer-sorcerers whose deathly skills induced various princes to employ them as mercenaries:

> The final (for the present time) kind of sorcery is that in which men are tainted.... First, the severity of the crime as manifested in archer sorcerers should be noted with reference to seven different horrible crimes ... they shoot at the most holy image of the Crucifix with an arrow during the solemn rites of the Mass as if shooting at a target. What cruelty and insult for the Savior! ... they must enter into an agreement with the demon to commit apostasy by word in addition to apostasy by work ... they will be able to kill the same number of men on a given day ...[22]

Institor(is), then, sees military conflict as being the chief area in which men are able to become actively involved in witchcraft on a par with women.

Not only does Institor(is) categorize witchcraft as a primarily female crime but he goes one step further; he characterizes his own era as 'womanly time',[23] thus decrying it as less worthy than past ages in which the world was not yet full of evil. Mackay translates the Latin adjective 'muliebre' as 'womanly'; perhaps 'womanish' or a more explicit expression such as 'womanly lightness' gives a better indication of the deprecatory nature of this term.

In this era, Institor(is) argues, feminine characteristics encroach on men and apostasy in men brings about the downfall of humanity. His is a society in which '... effeminate men who have no Zeal for the Faith leave such crimes unpunished ...'.[24] Here, he attributes one of the hegemonial contemporary concepts of women to men; the gender concept for this type of men is not diametrically opposed to that of women.

In order to support his arguments and to underline the feminine character of witchcraft, Institor(is) goes as far as to make slight alterations to borrowings from earlier demonological works. Another Dominican brother, Johannes Nider, reports trials of male and female defendants in the 15th century. *In the Witches' Hammer,* however, the names of the accused men are omitted; Institor(is) copies the facts almost word for word from Nider but names only women as alleged evil-doers. Where, in the *Formicarius* it says unmistakably 'malefici utriusque sexus infantes vorant', that is 'witches of both sexes eat children', *the Witches' Hammer* reads: 'malefice infantes devorare solent', that is '[female] witches have the habit of devouring babies'.[25] Nider also describes early witch trials in Savoy and in regions of today's Switzerland, which tell of 'malefici' (the gender-neutral term for witches) who were burnt at the stake. In relaying this information, Institor(is), however, speaks exclusively of women as the alleged offenders.[26] Institor(is) thus feminizes 'intellectual borrowings' and historical sources by eliminating men from the reports of those persecuted, and ascribing the alleged crimes to women.

Whereas older research credits *the Witches' Hammer* virtually with canonical respect, assuming it to have had a broadly positive reception[27], more recent studies assume that the work did not have such a great impact, despite its 29 editions.[28] This debate might gain from differentiating between the different historical periods; in the 16th century before the publication of other demonological works the impact of *the Witches' Hammer* was certainly greater than in the 17th century. Witchcraft research has also shown that in larger territories such as the Prince-Bishopric of Mainz, Franche-Comté and in the Austrian hereditary territories the 'Malleus' had little practical effect on the development of the persecution of witches, indicating that the reception of the treatise differed from one region to another.[29] The Spanish Inquisition at any rate did not recognize the authority of the 'Malleus'.[30] In all these areas the number of men persecuted was above average. This again poses the question as to whether the theory of witch persecution followed the practice, rather than the other way around.

'The Protestant Pope': Martin Luther (1526)

> Likewise the witches, who are the Devil's whores and steal milk, raise storms, ride on goats or broomsticks or fly through the air on their mantles, shoot, lame or maim people, martyr babies in their cradles, cast spells to hinder men in their conjugal relations ... and force people into love and immorality and many other works of the Devil.[31]

The 'Protestant Pope' seems here to be placing himself in the tradition of the elaborated concept of witchcraft which had developed in learned Catholic discourse towards the end of the 15th century. However, the citation proves to be a definition of the prevailing contemporary view of witches rather than a representation of Luther's own position on the reality or otherwise of witchcraft. Luther's true concept of witchcraft can only be gleaned from the many scattered mentions throughout all his works, for there is no compact work available on this matter. In principle, Luther thought it possible to practise maleficium by means of magical aggression, thus supporting the idea of the Devil's pact and sexual relations with the Devil which lay behind it, but he distinctly rejected the reality of the witches' flight. The concept of witchcraft as a collective crime is not found in his works.[32]

With the exception of his recurrent call for the death penalty for sorcery,[33] Luther's witchcraft concept, then, can be classified as complying with contemporary Catholic discourse in the tradition of the 'Canon Episcopi'. To call Luther an opponent of the 'witch craze', as some historians have tried to do,[34] is an attempt to retrieve his honour but does not do justice to his position. As regards the persecution of witches, Luther remained silent, a fact which can only be interpreted as acceptance of the way secular justice dealt with alleged witches. In 1540, witches were burnt at the stake in Wittenberg, the town where Luther lived and worked for much of his life; Luther was aware of this, as indeed he was of witch trials in other Protestant-ruled towns and territories. Admittedly, he died before the first major witch-hunts took place around 1560, but in his lifetime there was an unmistakable increase in the number of burnings in Lutheran Thuringia, Osnabrück, Pomerania and other regions. Even taking into account the communication difficulties of the early modern era, it can be assumed that it was possible to be aware of these executions, the more so since they clearly represented more than isolated individual cases. Luther remained silent.

Before assessing Luther's opinion on the gender issue in witchcraft crimes, the nature and value of the sources often used to cite him should be closely scrutinized. When citing Luther's statements, researchers have frequently used sources not authorized by Luther himself, such as the printed versions, available in large numbers after 1566, of his so-called 'Table Talk'. This work was put together largely from notes made restrospectively or even from transcripts of these notes. The value of these tertiary sources is limited in comparison with surviving works written by Luther himself. For the reception of Luther's ideas, however, the Table Talk is of considerable relevance as here Luther's ideas were reduced to a clear presentation of the basic theses; furthermore, they provided a good and authoritative citation. In order to differentiate between reception and original statement, I will for the present use primary sources here.

In the theological works dealing with his principal theories, Luther assumes sorcery or witchcraft crimes to be gender neutral.[35] He says that the passive quest for help from 'male witches and female witches' as well as the practice of magic '...that magic has been practised...that a pact with the Devil has been made'[36] contravene the First Commandment. In the more popular works, however, he turns away from these more abstract evaluations and unequivocally denotes witchcraft a female crime, whereby he is speaking of witchcraft as it is understood by his contemporaries and not as it was used historically or as he described it to have been used historically.

> Of the [female] witch....Why does the law name here women more than men, although men also violate it? Because women more than men are vulnerable to the incantations and adjurations of the Devil. Like Eve....They shall be put to death....It is an extremely just law which lays down that the [female] witches shall be put to death, for they cause much harm, such as hitherto has been ignored...This law relating to female witches must be seen in the light of the harm they cause to body and soul; they administer potions and incantations to stir up hatred, love, storms, all manner of destruction havoc in the home and on the farmlands....Where Satan does not appear, his female abettor, a [female] witch does. [Female] witches should be put to death for they are thieves, adulteresses, robbers, murderers...'[37]

Men do not figure here any longer and Luther does not use the male form of witch at all in this detailed statement on witchcraft. At another place in the text in an analogy with *the Witches' Hammer*, Luther describes men as tending only to weapon magic.[38] It is true that Luther uses the same proportion of feminine and masculine grammatical forms to refer to people imputed to have magical skills[39] but there is a difference in the quality of the activities described. Female witchcraft crimes are committed in association with the Devil:

> First he [the Devil] attacks humans where they are the weakest, namely in the female person, Eve not Adam. All his challenges are directed towards temptation where we are weak and susceptible, where he had attacked Adam...Paul said, Adam was not seduced but Eve, the woman, was; she did not have as much understanding as Adam....His intellect was greater, she was bad and simple-minded. She did not perceive Satan's ploy.[40]

Unlike in *the Witches' Hammer* where women's susceptibility is taken to be the consequence of female hypersexuality, Luther sees their susceptibility as arising from weakness of character and lack of intellectual ability in the tradition of Eve. The male sex, then, can hardly serve as the Devil's gateway to mankind. Magic as practised by men is at the most natural magic, with no evil connections,[41] for Luther argues, 'a man is endowed with more and greater understanding, courage and stability'.[42] Luther was not only derogatory about women, he also redefined their role. As in the past, he saw them as subordinate to their husbands but he taught that the relationship between man and wife should be based on mutual respect, support and love. In his view, woman as the ideal housewife represents a necessary counterpart to man with an independent role and rights.[43]

Even if Luther envisaged women as God's creatures and ideally as pious marriage partners, his view of the world was based on the gender hierarchy and it was this which influenced his conception that witchcraft was gender-related. For Luther witchcraft emanated from women:

> August 25th in the year 1538, there was much talk of [female] witches and sorceresses who stole eggs from hens' nests, and milk and butter: we should show them [the female witches and sorceresses] no mercy. I would burn them myself for one reads in the law that the priests began to stone the offenders...[44]

Strict Calvinists: L. Daneau (1573) and H. Bullinger (1586)

Lambert Daneau was born into an aristocratic tax collector family. Although orphaned young, he was able to study Law and Theology in Orléans, Bourges and Geneva. After the events of St Bartholomew's Day 1572 Daneau, a Huguenot, emigrated to Geneva where he taught theology at the university, later moving on to the Universities of Leiden and Gent, where he was accused of intolerance. Daneau wrote 27 works, most of them moral-theological writings and in 1573, now a well-known protagonist of Calvinism, published a work on the persecution of witches, which also appeared in French the same year. In 1575 it was published in German and in 1586 in English.[45] This second-generation reformer died in 1595.

Considering that there was – and is – no such legal entity as a reformed church, Daneau can be viewed as a representative of a particular line in Calvinism. Two other Calvinist opponents of the persecutions, the Reformist pastor from Hesse, Anton Prätorius, and the Heidelberg theologian Herman Witekind, also wrote Calvinist interpretations of witchcraft. The very title of Daneau's work equates witchcraft crimes with heresy for the word 'eriges', no longer used in modern French, means 'heretic'.[46] He considers maleficium and the Devil's pact self-evident realities which require no further explanation. The maleficents, he says, were perpetrators of harm to both humans and animals, chiefly by means of poison; they met irregularly at the Sabbat where they renewed their pact with the evil one and procured the poison they needed for their evil deeds[47]; Daneau does not, however, mention intercourse with the Devil.[48] Anyone convicted of a witchcraft crime should be given the death sentence – without exception. Daneau sums his arguments thus:

> In short, I uphold that all [male and female] witches are deserving of public and universal hatred and thus of death for they are enemies of the human race, apostates from the Christian faith, they are guilty of lese-majesty, both human and divine, they are traitors, they revolt against and desert God.... A [male and female] witch is a diabolical poisoner and murderer.[49]

This quote shows that Daneau was not at all interested in the gender specificity of witchcraft crimes. In the 1573 and 1579 editions he is almost consistent in his use of the semantically generic term 'sorcier'. Only rarely does he use the gendered terms 'sorciers et sorcières' and 'eriges et sorcières'[50] although he does remark, more or less by the way, that 'fearful and soft or weak'[51] women were particularly susceptible to the Devil's courtship. In his work he refers to actual trials in France, one of which was the trial of a male peasant, another of a male aristocrat.[52] Daneau adds two detailed protocols of trials held in the year 1574 to the end of his work. The confessions made in the course of these trials derived from two women and a man; the latter was implicated in the trial through denunciations and he was attested to have played a major role in spreading the witches' sect.[53]

So both his theoretical arguments and his examples go to underline Daneau's notion that witchcraft crimes were not gender related but could be committed equally by women and men.

Little is known about the reception of Daneau's work. However, his works were known to a Lutheran village parson by the name of Meiger, who lived in Holstein; they were also quoted by the Saxon jurist Carpzov and even by a high-ranking church official in Riga, Latvia.[54] It is certain that Daneau's thoughts were echoed in the French-speaking areas of the empire. Surprisingly, though, the leading Calvinist power, the Electorate of Palatinate, did not follow his suggestions and the Reformist authorities here suppressed almost all the requests of the population to hold trials. The Electorate of Palatinate thus became a persecution-free zone within the Holy Roman Empire.[55]

A similar, though modified and not so generalized, concept of witchcraft was expressed by Heinrich Bullinger of Zurich, Zwingli's successor as leader of the Protestant church in northern Switzerland. His comprehensive correspondence influenced the development of the Reformation throughout Europe. In 1571 he published a short work in which he declared that he considered maleficium, the Devil's pact and intercourse with the Devil to be real[56]; this work was intended as assistance for the clergy rather than for laypeople.[57] At much the same time, a true witch hysteria erupted in Geneva in connection with an outbreak of the plague, and Zürich and other places in Switzerland also saw an increase in the number of witchcraft trials from about 1570 onwards. Bullinger noted that '...amongst women there are some who are called sorceresses and witches....They renounce God and the true faith and pledge themselves to the Devil....' The Devil approaches these women, wins them over, and he sustains the pact by holding 'wedding, repast and dance; he cohabits with them and commits many abominations with them....'[58]

Yet Bullinger also knows men who

> are sorcerers and in their main activities are much akin to the [female] witches so that they are known as male witches and make a pact and come to an understanding with the Devil, to whom they commit themselves...

In using the two grammatical forms 'malefici and maleficae',[59] Bullinger attributes magical aggression to both sexes, although he considers women to show a greater tendency to join with the Devil for, he stresses, 'You shall not allow the sorceress to live.'[60]

The Danish reformer: Niels Hemmingsen (1576)

In 1553, Hemmingsen, a pupil of the highly regarded Protestant theologian Melanchthon, was appointed Professor at the University of Copenhagen and soon became a decisive authority of the second generation of reformers in the Danish Lutheran church. In 1575 he published a work on the witch persecutions; he had previously been attacked for his Calvinist opinions and for this reason the Danish king finally relieved him of his teaching duties in 1579.[61] The work on witches appeared in Latin and in Danish in 1575/6 and, in order to reach a wider audience, in 1586 also in German.[62]

As this is the only complete work written by a Reformer and dealing with Danish witch persecutions to appear in Denmark, it retained its decisive influence even after Hemmingsen's dismissal from his post; it remained particularly relevant for the training of clergy who also came from the north of Germany, largely from Holstein.

In keeping with Protestant tradition, Hemmingsen was particularly interested in combatting folkloristic superstition since, in his eyes, anyone who believed in the effectiveness of magical powers or made use of others' magical activities must be an apostate from God.[63] Hemmingsen taught in the tradition of Christian demonology that only a pact with the Devil makes it possible to perform magic deeds, for humans beings are not able to develop magic powers of their own accord.[64] Magical harm to livestock, humans and crops as well as – clearly for many male theologians of the time an inevitable feature – male virility, though at times imagined was frequently real and thus punishable by death. 'Maleficium' is at the centre of his arguments[65]; however, he categorically denies the existence of the witches' Sabbat:

> Accordingly we must ask whether the female witches, having assumed other forms, meet at a certain place by night to feast and drink with one another? This should be considered a deception which derives from the demons....The female witches consider it to be reality. But in truth it is only a deception by the Devil.[66]

This gives a clear view of Hemmingsen's witchcraft image: witches are of the female sex, for the Devil derives his 'strength from the [female] witches'.[67] Men were able to relate closely to God, and rarely does Hemmingsen use the male form 'zeuberer'[male witch].[68] In the Danish edition of 1576 he speaks consistently of 'troldkvinde' and 'troldkone'[69] – both feminine noun forms – as agents of the Devil. In Hemmingsen's view it is not the alleged carnal lust of the Witches' Hammer which drives women into the fangs of the Devil but the fact that they are less able than men to commit themselves to the faith. This, he expresses in Lutheran tradition as follows:

> For the Devil takes objection to his secrets being divulged as he does not wish for people of good understanding to become aware of his evil tricks or for his arts to fall into contempt. Thus he prefers to use women rather than male persons for his deeds, for women, like Eve, can more easily be deceived.[70]

The effects of Hemmingsen's teachings were felt in the Danish-speaking world into the 17th century. Attempts by the Danish bishop Brochmand in the middle of the 17th century to assert the reality of the Witches' Sabbat, in contradiction of Hemmingsen's ideas, fell on deaf ears in theological circles; the foundations laid by Hemmingsen went too deep.[71] At the centre of Danish demonology was the notion of maleficium based on the Devil's pact; other elements such as the Witches' Sabbat, a combined product of early modern French-German demonology, were not received with any degree of passion and had no significant impact in the Kingdom of Denmark.

The Catholic political theorist: Jean Bodin (1580)

After completing his studies, Jean Bodin was appointed Professor of Law at the University of Toulouse and in 1584 he became Public Prosecutor in Laôn, where he died 12 years later. In his chief work *Six livres de la République* he developed the concept of a state which, though absolute, was bound by divine and natural law; in a later work he also demanded tolerance between the various Christian denominations.

In *De la Démonomanie Des Sorciers*, printed in 1580, he ascribed the state an active role in the fight against evil in the form of magical activities for these, he argued, constituted an offence against God and natural law. Bodin also applied the call for the assertion of order by the sovereign princes to the realm of evil, at the centre of which he saw the so-called Witches' Sabbat.[72] This was both the real and the symbolic manifestation of disorder, the antithesis to the newly designed 'res publica' of absolutism.[73] Bodin's demonology, then, was 'political demonology'.[74]

Bodin begins his work with a comprehensive definition in which he discusses and condemns all those people who cooperate with either good or bad demons. He does not, however, categorize them gender-wise:

> A [male witch or female] witch [*'sorcier'*] is a person who consciously tries to accomplish something by diabolical means.[75]

Bodin uses the term 'sorcier' as a gender-neutral category for people who practise witchcraft, i.e. both male and female witches. In a more detailed definition of the crime of witchcraft he leaves no doubt as to the fact that he sees both sexes as being, in principle, capable of the crime:

> But one should also note that the word 'sorcier' [male witch or female witch] is not only used of those who cast the die to determine

> whether good or evil will come to pass (which is tantamount to magic) but principally of those [both men and women are implied here by the masculine and feminine demonstrative pronouns 'ceux' and 'celles', R.S.] who strew or bury harmful powders on the paths or under the thresholds of stables to bring death upon those who pass there.[76]

The term 'sorciers' is used throughout all four books of this work for even once it has been worked, harmful magic cannot be gendered. Bodin names several forms of magical aggression:

> This is why the [male and female] witches are forced by Satan to do evil, to poison men and beasts[77]

Subsequently, he underlines his argument with numerous examples from confessions made in French witchcraft trials. In Souillac a man admitted to weather magic, in Poitiers a man caused the death of livestock, in the Auvergne horses, in Alençon people were said to have been killed. Women allegedly spread diseases by means of powders in Senlis; in Soissons they confessed to using magic powers to split open girls' heads, in Laôn they damaged crops in the fields.[78]

Bodin also considered the basis of witchcraft, the voluntary pact with the Devil including possible subsequent copulation with the Devil, as something which could be undertaken by both sexes:

> All the more, the contracts, agreements, sacrifices, worship and detestable copulations of the [male and female] witches are not only voluntary but take place of their own free and spontaneous will...[79]

This French jurist reports in his treatise on many witch trials in the course of which the accused admitted to the pact with evil. Male and female witches in Paris, Toulouse, Maine and Poitou had made this criminal pact; and other persons of both sexes had gone one step further and also had sexual intercourse with the Devil.[80]

In his description of the witches' Sabbat,[81] the core element of Bodin's demonology, men's participation in witchcraft crimes becomes even clearer. Bodin does not give a cohesive analysis of this aspect of witchcraft, nor does he provide any specific arguments on this point, he simply relates the accounts of various people who had admitted taking part in the meeting of the witches' sects and who reported that numerous persons of both sexes had attended there. He recounts the statement of one alleged male witch thus:

> The man, finding himself in the company of a large number of [male and female] witches unknown to him and hideous devils with human countenances, began to say, 'My God, where are we?'...[82]
>
> When they saw each other at the gathering, his wife took him [her husband] aside to watch the mysterious spectacle until she showed her respect to the leader of the assembly who was pompously dressed as a prince and accompanied by *a great multitude of men and women* who paid homage to their master.[83]

These descriptions are complemented by further reports of the witches' Sabbat in trials, some of women, some of men and women, from the regions of Ribemont, Blois, Châteauroux, Châtellerault and Laval in France, and from Savoy (at that time not yet a part of France).[84] Bodin also gives a more detailed description of the lives and alleged crimes of a number of male witches. A male witch by the name of 'Trois-Eschelles' plays a special role for he appears repeatedly throughout the various books of this work. Around 1570 in the region of Poitou, 'Trois-Eschelles Manseau' confessed to having used a magic powder to kill people and animals and to destroy the harvest; his male accomplices, like women, bore the Devil's mark as the witches' stigma on their bodies; he partook in the witches' Sabbat, where he mentioned that both men and women were present, and even whilst under arrest he gave proof of his magical skills.[85] Bodin viewed witchcraft as a primarily gender-unspecific crime; he considered it identical with heresy and thus as the apostasy of a large group of people from God, state and all forms of order.[86] This organized group contained, thus Bodin, members of all social classes, from princes to their subjects, and of different generations, from parents to their children.[87]

Misogynist views, such as Bodin expressed in earlier works, do not appear in the *Démonomanie des Sorciers*[88] until the chapter in which he expresses his reaction to the arguments of the opponent of persecution, Johannes Weyer. In this chapter, which was added to the other four volumes at a later date, Bodin argues that women are more likely to become witches by reason of their 'bestial needs', their moral weakness and the smaller size of their heads.[89] Women, who Bodin places on a par with snakes and flies, infect men, and eventually also children with their diabolical tendencies. The character of the male sex in Bodin's view is such that for the greater part men are not initiators of, but accomplices in, magical-demonic activities:

> Satan addressed himself first and foremost to the woman, by whom man was seduced. Further, I contend that God wished to secure order and to weaken Satan by giving him power primarily over the less esteemed creatures such as serpents, flies and other beasts which the law of God calls unclean; and then over other brutal beasts and over the human race: and over humans rather more than over the others. I add that Satan, by women's means, draws the husbands and the children to his leash...[90]

Bodin's frequently cited statement that there is one male witch to 50 female witches is, in fact, in the original work[91] a repetition of the opinion of other, for the most part ancient, authors. The reference to this proportion is intended to indicate the fact that, of those who tend towards magical aggression, women are in the majority; but the numbers are by no means meant to be taken literally.

Bodin's *Démonomanie* appeared in 26 editions and in French, Latin, Italian and German. In 1596 the Pope placed the work on the Index of prohibited books, arguing that it relied too heavily on Jewish sources; this did not, however, have any impact on the popularity of the books.[92] Bodin's works met with widespread approval[93] – although jurists formed a large proportion of his readership.[94] However, in considering the impact of his work, the influence of particular arguments on the various regional persecutions should also be taken into account. The systematic development of thought in the *Démonomanie* bolstered contemporary demonology in that it appeared to be based on a stable foundation.

The satirical translator: Johann Fischart (1581)

Bodin's *Démonomanie* first appeared in German translation in 1581 and so became accessible to those readers unable to understand French or Latin.[95] It was translated by Johann Fischart; born in Alsace, Fischer was a Protestant jurist at the Imperial Chamber Court in Speyer and later a local magistrate in Lorraine, and had published a number of satirical works. On close scrutiny, it becomes apparent that Fischart did not render an exact translation of Bodin's work; by using satirical puns and twisting words he altered the language and linguistic form of the work. The 'sabbat des sorciers', for instance, became the 'Witches' Imperial Diet', an allusion to the

Imperial Diet which comprised the estates of the Holy Roman Empire. In order to give a correct rendering of the feminine form 'sorcière' and to distinguish it in German from the masculine 'sorcier', he used the typical German feminine suffix '-in' and developed a new word 'Hexin'.[96] This he then used as an additional feminine form alongside the gender-neutral term 'Hexe'. Witches' marks were to be found, not as in Bodin 'on the thighs' but 'on the arse cheeks'.[97] Despite this satirical undertone, Fischer identifies with Bodin's teachings and expands on the latter's work with linguistic modifications and his own contextual additions, which might have been significant for its reception in the empire.

As Bodin, Fischart expresses the view that the female sex is the more vulnerable one, intensifying Bodin's misogynist remarks by an addition of his own:

(Translation of Bodin's sentence)

> The poets suggested, for they wrote that Pallas, the Goddess of Wisdom was born from the brain of Zeus and could not show herself to have a mother, that wisdom does not come from women, for they are by nature more akin to animals. (Fischart's addition)... and both adage and experience show that if a regiment of women were to be commissioned it would not endure beyond sunset: And that it is said women have long dresses and weak minds.[98]

Fischart nevertheless follows Bodin's principle that both sexes are capable of entering into the pact with the Devil and the consequences which ensue. Bodin's term 'sorcier' is regularly translated as 'male witches and female witches' ('Hexenmeister und Hexe') so that the semantically neutral French noun is expressed in the German title in distinct masculine and feminine grammatical forms. In 1581 Fischart translated 'Démonomanie des sorciers' true to the original meaning and use of words, as 'Daemonomania, concerning the wild and furious host of demons, all manner of magicians, female witches and male witches'. This latter pair (male and female witches) appears repeatedly together with other combinations (such as sorcerer and sorceress, 'Zauberer und Zauberin' – here Fischart added the feminine suffix '-in' to the masculine word 'Zauberer' – as well as other formulations[99]) in the titles of 11 of 27 chapters, something which could not have been overlooked even by inexperienced readers. The titles are as follows:

'On the description or definition of female witches and male witches ['*Hexen und Hexenmeister*']'[100]

'On the rapture and extasy of the male witches and female witches ['*Zauberer und Hexen*'] and their manner of associating and copulating with the evil spirits'[101]
'Whether the male witches and female witches ['*Zauberer und Zauberin*'] maintain their carnal relationships with the evil spirits'[102]
'Whether the male witches and female witches ['*Zauberer und Zauberin*'] have the power to create and disseminate illness, infertility, hail and storms, and to kill humans and animals'[103]
'Whether the male witches and female witches ['*Zauberer und Unholden*'] help the sick to the best of treatments and health'[104]
'Whether the male witches and female witches ['*Zauberer und Unholden*'] through their witchcraft can bring people beauty, dignity, honour, riches and skills, and can cause and pass on fertility'[105]
'Whether the sorcerers and sorceresses ['*Zauberer und Unholden*'] can do more harm than any other'[106]
'How to investigate and take legal proceedings against the female witches and male witches ['*Hexen und Hexenmeister*'].'[107]
'On the confessions and avowals of the female witches and male witches exacted with and without torture ['*Unholden and Zauberer*'].'[108]
'On suspicions and speculations with regard to the male witches and female witches ['*Zauberer und Unholden*']'[109]
'On the punishments that the male witches and female witches ['*Zauberer und Unholden*'] should receive.'[110]

Fischart – as Bodin – then states that '...countless sorcerers and witches in Germany...'[111] are not only capable of apostasy from God and alliances with Satan but have even admitted to and practised the Devil's pact. These people make up the 'host of demons'.

Fischart's translation must have been in considerable demand as new editions appeared in 1586 and 1591. It is not yet known whether or how the reception of the work varied from one region to another.

Lutheran orthodoxy: Johannes Godelmann (1584)

Godelmann (sometimes spelt Goedelmann), a Lutheran jurist, came originally from Württemberg, studied law in Wittenberg, Rostock and Basle and in 1583 became Professor for Roman Law at the University of Rostock and was appointed court counsellor by the Prince Electorate of Saxony. His witchcraft lectures appeared in print five times between 1584 and 1676.[112]

Godelmann accepted in principle that maleficium could be practised on people, animals and plants, but rejected the idea of weather magic as fiction.[113] He also accepted the Devil's pact as the cause of this magical aggression, but classed both intercourse with the Devil[114] and the pattern of the witches' Sabbat as products of the imagination which he attributed to delusions due to phases of impaired consciousness.[115]

Whether made with or without torture, he considered denunciations to be of little significance. The naming of accomplices – male and female – was only to lead to prosecution if family members were involved; Godelmann was an ardent supporter of the family theory in witchcraft.[116]

He argued in favour of graduated penalties, a pattern that today can be considered typical of Lutheran orthodoxy:[117] witchcraft was only to be punished by burning when it was coupled with a pact with the Devil. Godelmann did not foresee the death penalty for phantasized witchcraft or Devil's pacts from which no harm arose.

For Godelmann, witchcraft was unequivocally sex-specific. Admittedly, he does occassionally see men as possible sources of maleficium[118] but women are for him the typical source of magical aggression. Whereas men are able to resist the influence of the Devil by wont of their reason and physical constitution, women's weak and revengeful nature, their credulity and lower level of intelligence coupled with a sense of mistrust make them more likely to enter a pact with the Devil:

> Why women are found most among this species [all witches] is obvious. For the weaker the nature of a person is, the more the soul seeks revenge and such is mostly the nature of women. And whoever is of such disposition can be persuaded by the Devil to change their minds from one course to another, pulled from good to bad, and even seduced, duped and deceived ...[119]

Because men, unlike women, do not produce the fatal moisture from their bodies, thus Godelmann, they are less susceptible to the Devil and his pacts.[120] This is fully in keeping with classical western theory, the so-called medical theory of the juices, which he uses here, as did the authors of the Witches' Hammer, to support his reasoning that women were largely responsible for witchcraft crimes.

Having thus vented his opinions on women, Godelmann returns to men: if men, despite their physical and intellectual superiority, nonetheless submit to the Devil, then:

> A mild sentence should be passed upon those whom we trust by reason of the weakness of their sex that they will not subject themselves

to such a thing. The men must be punished more severely the more it is their due to rule women with their example.[121]

Whoever, then, was endowed by dint of their birth with better means of resisting Satan's advances but nonetheless yielded to the power of evil and no longer set the example expected of him as a man must, according to this Protestant jurist, reckon with more severe punishment.

Godelmann's work made a distinctive mark. Because of his position as legal advisor on practical matters of witch persecution in northern Germany and thanks also to his printed works, his emphasis on the element of 'maleficium' in the witch paradigm, his rejection of the idea of the witches' Sabbat and of special legal procedure for cases of alleged magic made a decisive impression on Protestant demonology.[122] Little importance was ascribed to denunciations of other persons not involved in the trial itself. Although Godelmann was sceptical of the excesses of the witch-hunts which arose from the dynamics of an escalating witch trial, he remained a supporter of witch trials as such, although these, he argued, should be treated according to normal legal procedure and not be subjected to more severe judicial procedures.

Moderate authors: the *Theatrum de veneficis* (1586)

In 1586 Abraham Sawr, a Protestant jurist from Marburg edited a collection of essays on witchcraft written by various authors, some of whom had already written on the subject prior to the publication of this *Theatrum de veneficis*.[123]

Three authors, Jacob Vallick, Johann Ewich and Abraham Sawr, held similar viewpoints, and their position on the gender specificity of witchcraft will be presented here. Jacob Vallick was a local parson in a small parish near the western border of the Duchy of Cleves, and saw himself in the old Catholic tradition but also as committed to the reform of the Council of Trent. His essay first appeared in Dutch in 1559.[124] Johann Ewich studied medicine in Italy, practised as a doctor in Duisburg and later Bremen where he also taught at the town's renowned grammar school. He was a Protestant and a friend of Johannes Weyer, also a doctor and opponent of the witch-hunts. Ewich's essay of 1586 had previously been published in two editions.[125] Abraham Sawr studied at the Protestant universities of Wittenberg and Marburg and, in addition to the *Theatrum de veneficis*, compiled several legal manuals.[126]

These three authors believe in the reality of maleficium through the agency of the Devil, either as a pact or a so-called relationship, but caution against overestimating the importance of the crime of witchcraft.[127] They all reject the Sabbat paradigm, claiming this is only a product of the imagination and thus fiction.[128] Sawr writes:

> ...that poor people talk themselves into believing that they have been together at dances, have copulated with the Devil, have begotten his children; this I can and will not truly believe.[129]

Even though all three authors are fundamentally in favour of the death penalty for witchcraft crimes, they advocate mild penalties for those who confess.[130] They are also in agreement on the gendering of magic. Admittedly, Ewich thinks it possible in theory that men might be 'inflicted with this pestilence'[131] but otherwise sees only women as making Devil's confederates:

> There now follows in our description that witchcraft generally originates from the female sex. For although men are sometimes to blame, it is mostly women who are guilty. This is because of the weakness of their disposition and nature, and often also the debility of old age or the inexperience of youth, or bad upbringing or inattentiveness to the word of God...[132]

Ewich, then, sees factors ranging from the female constitution to socialization deficits in early modern society as responsible for witchcraft.

Vallick has an allegedly bewitched woman ask, 'Dear, how does it come to pass that more women become sorceresses than men?'[133] His reply indicates that he considers men believe more deeply in God and are better able to deal with personal conflicts and accept modest financial circumstances than women. Conversely, women 'believe less', 'want to know and experience everything' and are 'vindictive as soon as they want for something'.[134]

All three authors also call for moderation in the persecution of witches, reject the witches' Sabbat in their demonology and present a clear image of witches, the contours of which are clearly female. The theological foundations of Vallick's standpoint incidentally are not in line with Catholic demonology in that he does not use the Old Testament to support his arguments.[135]

Nothing is known about the reception of the *Theatrum de veneficis*. However, the fact that a village parson, Samuel Meiger in Holstein, refers to this book after completing his studies,[136] would indicate that it had more than regional impact.

The village parson in Holstein: Samuel Meiger (1587)

The son of a clergyman, Samuel Meiger studied theology in Copenhagen and in 1556, at the age of 24, took up an appointment as parson of Nortorf in Holstein, which he held until his death in 1610. In 1587 he published his writings on witchcraft in Low German. This book is one of the few contributions to demonology from the northern German region and is a good example of the way a Lutheran minister in Holstein would have thought. The title *Panurgia Lamiarum* (On the Deceitfulness of Witches) and the fact that it was written in Low German are good indications of his intended readership. Meiger wanted to step outside the learned debate and convey the problematic of witchcraft to those who were confronted with alleged magic deeds in their everyday lives. As there had been a considerable increase in the degree of literacy in the Protestant regions since 1550, Meiger could have expected his teachings to reach the various local authorities, such as the squires, the town councillors and the local magistrates in the service of the king and dukes. This Lutheran work was intended as counsel and support in their daily work.[137]

Meiger refers to numerous demonological works; he is familiar with the thoughts of St Augustine and Albertus Magnus, the works of the Calvinist Danaeus, the Catholics Bodin and Olaus Magnus as well as the Lutherans Hemmingsen or Hocker. He also cites Luther's Table Talks, and is not unfamiliar with the works of Weyer, an opponent of persecution. Even long after the completion of his university studies, Meiger refers to the 'current research status', and though only published one year earlier, included the 'Theatrum de veneficis' in his arguments. It would seem certain then that this was an author who was extremely interested in witchcraft and witch persecution.

For Meiger the deeds of witche are real: they use magic – though rarely weather magic – to inflict harm on humans and animals.[138] Like the Lutheran Godelmann, he doubts the existence of weather magic and neither here nor in many other places in his works, is he able to bring himself to believe in such a concept of maleficium.[139] He has no doubt as to the reality of the Devil's pact, the underlying element of all witchcraft, or of intercourse with the Devil.[140] However, he views the pattern of the witches' Sabbat critically; he reports statements '... about witches' Imperial Diets and annual gatherings on the Blocksberg ...',[141] cites opponents and proponents of this view and was unable to come to a final decision of his own on the matter. Faced with this dichotomy, he advises the authorities to regularly inspect all potential witches' meeting places to determine the truth in the debate as to the existence or non-existence of these witch conventions. As regards 'south German witches', he has heard reports of a 'meeting place in the Black Forest'[142] but has nothing explicit to report of Sabbats in Holstein. Nothing but the death penalty can in Meiger's view be considered suitable punishment for witchcraft; torture, however, should not be put to excessive use to extort confessions.[143]

Meiger leaves no doubt as to the sex of the perpetrators of 'tovereye' (Low German for 'sorcery'): he uses the word 'Hexe' ('female witch'), which was not in common usage in the courts of Schleswig-Holstein until 1630, but not the word 'Hexenmeister' (male witch).[144] He does, however, use the term 'Zauberer' (sorcerer) and he describes the case of a man who was accused – but, according to Meiger presumably not proven guilty – of using magic, was protected and supported by his family but finally died a tragic death in a confessional.[145] He does not mention a connection between men and witchcraft. The very structure of the book makes it evident that Meiger ascribes witchcraft offences solely to women. In the titles of the 24 chapters of the first and second books, women are given 15 times as the alleged perpetrators of crime; men not once. In the first book Meiger deals with the reality of witchcraft crimes. Having rejected the fictional concept of magic and providing much evidence both from his own observations and from references to theological authorities, he proceeds to the question of the perpetrators, male and female. He formulates the following titles for these chapters:

> 9. That the Devil works magic through the female witches, contrary to the opinion of many scholars. 10. That the female witches can cause damage both to pious Christians and to the unbelieving and evil. 12. If the female witches can use magic to cause storms, tempests, wind, hail, lightning and thunder. 14. How the Devil rewards his servants such as female witches.[146]

In a second book Meiger continues by giving reasons for the special quality of this new crime by these servants of hell. His choice of terminology reflects his opinion that the source of magical aggression is to be found in the female sex alone. He connects the crime of witchcraft with a contravention of the Ten Commandments, the substance of which he then deals with individually. He attributes all infringements here to female witches and not to the sorcerers who he occassionally mentions:

1. How the female witches ['*Hexen*'] sin against the holy commandments of God and how they act in contravention of the first commandment.

2. On the sins of the female witches ['*Hexen*'] against the second commandment.
3. On the female witches ['*Hexen*'] abuse of and sins against the third commandment.
4. On the sins of the female witches ['*Töversche*'] against the fourth commandment.
5. On the sins of the female witches ['*Töversche*'] against the fifth commandment.
6. On the sins of the female witches ['*Hexen*'] against the sixth commandment and whether the witches join flesh with the Devil.
7. On the sins of the female witches ['*Töversche*'] against the seventh commandment.
8. How the female witches ['*Hexen*'] transgress the eighth commandment.
9. On the sins of the female witches ['*Hexen*'] against the last commandment[147]

This unmistakably denotes the sex-specific nature of witchcraft in Meiger's work. This is also mirrored in his title in which the Devil's confederates are described by the feminine form of the Latin genitive: 'Panurgia lami*arum,* Sag*arum,* Strigum ac venefic*arum*...'. The masculine genitive form 'maleficorum' from 'maleficus', i.e. male witch is not used here – in contrast, for example to the usage of the Catholic demonologist, Binsfeld. The term 'strix', a synonym for witch, which Meiger also uses, is also feminine. Though in theory the existence of male witches could not be conclusively excluded, in practice Meiger has no doubt that witchcraft offences originated from women – as the following passage illustrates:

> Because the sorcerer and the sorceress kill man and beast and destroy their health, it is right to punish them as *murderesses* with death. It is my conviction that the witches practise their magic with a good deal of poison.[148]

Whereas in the first lines Meiger assumes the possibility that both sexes are potential Devil's confederates, the remarks which immediately follow speak only of women – as 'murderesses' or 'witches'.

Although Meiger represented moderate positions, his knowledge of demonological works in combination with his plea in favour of the burning of allegedly proven witches show that this Protestant minister was seriously committed to the witch persecutions.

His knowledge of the Bible, however, was not as good as that of the demonological works: he consistently confused the Old Testament books Deuteronomy and Exodus.

The death-dealing suffragan Bishop Petrus Binsfeld (1589)

Although Binsfeld was born of a peasant family from the Eifel region he was able to study theology, thanks to the patronage of an abbot. In 1580 he was appointed suffragan to the Catholic Archbishop of Trier and subsequently Dean of the University of Trier.[149] His *Tractatus de confessionibus Maleficorum et Sagarum* ('Treatise on Confusions of Male and Female Witches') first appeared in Trier in 1589. This work, in which he expressed his opinions on the witch persecutions, was reprinted four times and appeared in German translation in 1590, 1591 and 1592.[150] The later editions became rather inflated by the addition of large amounts of material, largely examples of witchcraft cases. For Binsfeld, witchcraft was a specific type of crime involving a wide range of maleficium, for

> The [male and female] witches [*'malefici'*] with the help of the Devil can impede the birth-giving force between married couples and other persons ... cause illness and ruin and kill man and beast ..., weather summoning, rain, thunder, hail ..., bring about infertility and a dearth of all things which support human life ...[151]

Even the types of magic generally ascribed to women, love and weather magic, can in his view be practised equally by male witches.

Binsfeld had no doubt as to the reality of the Devil's pact, whether tacitly or expressly and voluntarily concluded, nor did he doubt the existence of sexual relations with the Devil, although he did concede that this may be a product of the imagination[152]: Men and women sealed these relations with a Devil's pact, as Binsfeld makes quite clear,

> [Male witches and female] witches [*'malefici'*] perform their unchaste deeds with the Devil.[153]

This intercourse, however, consitutes a relationship in which the Devil wields his power over his confederates; Binsfeld does not follow the arguments in the 'Witches' Hammer', which speak of a lustful sexual relationship beween witches and the Devil, and in his arguments there is no longer any sign of anything approaching an equal relationship between the Devil's agents – male or female – and Satan himself. Witches and male witches are characterized by their dependence.

Binsfeld did not question the idea that female witches and their male equivalents took part in the witches' Sabbat. Unlike Bodin, he did not go into the details of these nocturnal gatherings, but instead tried to prove their existence by citing excerpts from confessions. To him, the Sabbat was a reality and was attended by members of both sexes:

> Many of both sexes – men, women, boys and girls confirm the truth of it.[154]
>
> The 'witches' sect' met at night to implement '... their evil suggestions which they discuss in their gatherings ...'[155]

Binsfeld, then, believed in the image of the witches' Sabbat, basing his arguments on Bodin and the confessions of accused persons.

The title of Binsfeld's work already shows that the group acting under the leadership of the Devil – who, incidentally, were designated 'traitors to their country' – [156] was composed of members of both sexes: 'Tractatus de confessionibus Malefic*orum* et Sag*arum*',[157] i.e. male witches and female witches. At many points in the work he says both implicitly and explicitly in descriptions of the various elements of the witch paradigm that the Devil's covenanters were not restricted to one or the other sex.

He explains the susceptibility of many people to these pacts by their 'lasciviousness and carnal lust'. Unlike the author of *The Witches' Hammer* he also applies this to men, for, 'Wine and women beguile those who are endowed with understanding and make them apostates'[158]; clearly a reference to men.

By reason of the 'weakness of their understanding' and the 'stupidity of their sex'[159] but also of their tendency to faintheartedness and sadness when lacking male protection,[160] women are particularly predestined to becoming members of Satan's anti-society. Men are equally threatened when they are lacking in inner stability, for this makes them unable to resist the permanent temptations of the Devil.[161]

Considering the importance Binsfeld attaches to the pattern of the witches' Sabbat in his witch image, it is logical that the statements of interrogated male and female witches should be highly relevant in legal terms and justify the use of torture. Binsfeld is responsible for numerous burnings in the region of Trier towards the end of the 16th century – a suffragan bishop who dealt in death.

Illustration 5.2 One male and one female witch are sitting at each of the tables and are being served by underdevils or demons: illustration of the rituals at a witches' gathering as imagined by the persecutors. The scene at the table in the bottom left-hand corner illustrates the dependency of the sect members or the sexual relationships involved: both devils are holding the man and the woman tightly with their claws (Woodcut from: Francesco Maria Guazzo, *Compendium Maleficarum*, Milan 1626.)

The works of this Catholic theologian were highly respected, particularly in the Electorate of Trier, but also in other regions, especially the Rhinelands and Luxembourg,[162] territories in which the proportion of men persecuted as witches was not low. His teachings influenced leading Catholic theologians and were instrumental in rigidifying Catholic standpoints on witch persecutions throughout the Holy Roman Empire. In Bavaria, an important Counter-Reformation force, Binsfeld's thought formed the theoretical basis for strict witchcraft laws.[163]

The public prosecutor: Nicolas Rémy (1595)

Rémy, the son of a jurist, grew up in Lorraine, studied law in France and in 1575 took up a position as Secretary to the Duke in Nancy, advancing to the post of General State Prosecutor for Lorraine in 1591. In 1595 he published a work on the witch persecutions in Latin. This *Daemonolatreiae* appeared in a total of eight editions, two of which were in German. Rémy held office for 15 years and in his function as state prosecutor intervened in the practice of witch persecutions.[164]

He reports of many types of maleficium from his practical experience. The initiators of this magic were 'sagae' or 'veneficae' (i.e. female witches) and also 'malefici' (male and female witches) or 'sortilegi' (sorcerers). Rémy refers to numerous examples of magical aggression by women, but also by men, and goes into some detail: Claudius Morelius (Claude Morel) from a village in Lorraine was proven to have used magic to cause the sickness of another man, Joannes Carmaeus (Jean Charmes) caused storm and heavy rain, Petronius Armentorius (Pierre Arment) murdered his own son, and Benedictus Drigens (Benoît Drigé) poisoned 150 sheep.[165] Rémy goes on to list other men who had made pacts with the Devil, and had thus caused diverse damage in Lorraine. He gives the names of the following men tried in locations throughout the territory: Jacques Agathe from Leyr, Mathieu Amant from Houécourt, Ysatz Auguel, Balial Basle from Dombsale, Jean Boursier from Dombat, Jean Bulme from Amance, Erric Carmouche from Pange, Dominique Fallué from Rupt-les-Mourons, Claude und François Fellé from Mazerulles, Didier Finance, Didier Gandon from Saulxures, Gaspard Haffner from Morhange, Hazelot from Saint-Epvre, Errik Hennezel from Vergaville, Jacquot Jacobin from Mirecourt, Jean de Ville from Lorquin, Brice Merg from Forbach, Jean Pécheur from Gerbéviller, Dominque Pétron from Gironcourt, Pierre from Delme, Claude Simonet, Antoine Welsch from Guermange and Quérive Xallé from Blainville.[166] Some of the accused men, Rémy reported, committed these evil deeds in cooperation with their wives. As public prosecutor he was clearly familiar with these cases and fully in keeping with contemporary demonology considered them to originate from the Devil's pact. However, he no longer saw male witches and female witches as equal partners of Satan. Both sexes had been degraded and were now Satan's subjects; however, they still had to agree to the crimes committed. Rémy dedicates an entire chapter entitled On the reasons why the Devil often covets the consensus and the will of the [male and female] witches [*'malefici'*] when he wishes to lure someone to destruction' to explaining his reasoning, and refers in the title specifically to both sexes.[167]

This Catholic jurist, however, shows greater interest in the act of intercourse with the Devil. In his view, the Devil seals his pact with women – and with men – by sexual intercourse, felt by the people concerned to be unnatural. The Devil signifies death, and thus he is cold; this applies to male and female witches alike. Rémy sums up,

> But all those who have reported to us of such works, whether man or woman, who enter into a liaison of the flesh with demons, avow unanimously that nothing colder nor less amiable than this is conceivable.'[168]

Rémy presents the case of Petronius Armentarius (Pierre Arment) in detail, for this man alleged that his demonic lover regularly made him freeze almost to death during intercourse. Ericus Hennezelius (Errick Hennezel) from the village of Vergaville reports that he felt 'himself to be in a cold hole full of cold water' during copulation. The two alleged male witches name their succubi as 'Abrahelem' and 'Scuatzeberg', respectively – word creations which indicate that torture may have played a role here.[169]

Rémy pays particular attention in several chapters to the reality of the witches' flight and the Sabbat, referring to authorities in the theological discussion, but more frequently to the knowledge gained from experience, a method particularly in keeping with the Renaissance concept of science. He cites descriptions taken from the confessions of a large number of accused.[170] From these we can infer that numerous people flew at night to the witches' Sabbat, among them many men. Franciscus Fellaeus (François Fellé) was proven to have smeared a magic ointment on his fork so as to be able to fly on it. Joannes de Villa (Jean de Ville) regularly set out two hours before midnight, Albertus Mandreus (Albert Mandrou or Mandreu) mentions the presence of many wealthy people, and Dominicus Petronius (Dominique Pétron) was impressed by the abundance of food served at the gathering.[171]

Rémy also reports that the Devil's confederates of both sexes met at the Sabbat, witches coaxed music out of 'shepherds' crooks', male witches beat the tact with 'heavy clubs', both were, in military manner, under the charge of an officer. This ritual, it was said, was of particular significance for the event, as it enhanced the aggressive atmosphere.[172]

Having presented many individual acts of witchcraft committed by both male and female witches, Rémy felt it necessary to add a few qualifying remarks for the benefit of his readers:

> So, I personally am of the opinion that more women than men are guilty of this. And it is not without cause that there are more

> women among this debauched rabble, for there we find witches, soothsayers ... etc. of the female sex.[173]

He proceeds to prove woman's greater tendency to witchcraft by referring to two ancient authors, Fabius and Plinius, repeating brief remarks to this effect at several other points in the text.[174] These remarks indicate that men are fundamentally less likely to enter a pact with the Devil, but are not immune. Wives, he argues, frequently draw their husbands into the ban of misanthropic, destructive witchcraft.

Rémy also developed a kinship theory of witchcraft which admitted the possibility that such tendencies could be inherited by children of both sexes, from both mother and father. Any attempt to win these children – whether boys or girls – back to God were, in his view, futile.[175]

Rémy, the public prosecutor, demanded the death penalty for all 'malefici' (all male and female witches).[176] He prided himself on the allegedly glorious deed of having brought 800 people to be burnt at the stake in Lorraine; however, this figure is rightfully disputed today.[177]

The books of this jurist were widely read in the Holy Roman Empire, and their influence is estimated to have been even greater than that of *The Witches' Hammer.*[178] Evidence of this success can be found way beyond the boundaries of Lorraine in the entire southwest of the empire[179]. His thoughts are also echoed in contemporary writings which did not stem from demonological sources: the well-known German satirist Grimmelshausen refers in his description of a witches' Sabbat specifically to Rémy as chief witness of such occurrences.[180]

The encyclopaedist of magic: Martín Del Rio (1599/1600)

Del Rio came from an aristocratic family in the Spanish Netherlands, studied philosophy and law, became Vice-Chancellor of Brabant in 1578, joined the Jesuits in 1580 and taught theology in Liège, Graz and Salamanca. He wrote more than 20 philosophical and theological works, of which one was devoted to witchcraft, the *Disquisitionum magicarum* written in 1599/1600.[181] Del Rio's work should not be considered as one among many, but as a comprehensive demonological compendium, and with its six volumes can indeed be regarded as an Encyclopaedia of Magic. For Del Rio, a Catholic theologian, witchcraft was one of the gravest and most abominable crimes[182] and to be punished with the greatest severity, that is by the death penalty. He saw absolutely no alternative.

He deals in detail with maleficium and its variants, pointing out from the beginning that magical aggression did not only stem from women:

> Very often they [workers of harmful magic] harm small children...The reason is that they destroy those who are plainly innocent and harmless both in body and soul, and this is especially so if these workers of magic kill their own children....Undoubtedly when they use natural poisons they can, with God's permission, harm both good and bad people...[183]

Maxwell-Stuart solved the awkward problem of how to render the term witch by translating the gender-neutral 'malefici' as 'workers of harmful magic'. This reasoning is easy to follow as these people are described in the Latin version in the singular as 'maleficus' and in the plural as 'malefici', thus, semantically, the words characterize female and male witches.

Del Rio had no doubt that both sexes carry out destructive activities because they are apostates from God and thus, indirectly, because they have entered into a pact with the Devil:

> Workers of harmful magic, or witches (*lamiae*), however, withdraw from God by an express denial of God and of the faith. This is apostasy, properly called a type of infidelity...[184]

Both sexes engage in intercourse with the Devil, who appears either as incubus, that is 'the one lying above', or as succubus, 'the one lying beneath'. The two terms were synonyms for the Devil who slept with the witches in the form of a man or a woman:

> Axiom I: It is common for workers of harmful magic (*malefici*) and witches (*lamiae*) to perform the sexual act with evil spirits. The former do it with succubae, the latter with incubi[185]

Del Rio does not only assume the theoretical possibility that both sexes can commit witchcraft offences; he gives concrete examples of individual male witches from actual trials. He gives details of the trial of one Jean del Vaux of Stavelot in present-day Belgium, but also describes trials of women.[186] The latter do not appear in any great numbers, however, until Del Rio's description of the Sabbat, where he writes,

> The evil spirit attached to each of these workers of harmful magic (*malefici*) sits near him: sometimes on one side of him, sometimes opposite...sometimes they take part in this feast with their face

> covered by a mask, a linen cloth, or some other veil or facial representation.... After the feast, each evil spirit takes by the hand the disciple of whom he has charge, and so that they may do everything with the most absurd kind of ritual, each person bends over backwards, joins hands in a circle, and tosses his head as frenzied fanatics do. Then they begin to dance... Then their demon-lovers copulate with them in the most repulsive fashion.... Finally we are told, each person gives an account of the wicked deeds he had done since the last meeting. The more serious these are and the more detestable, the more they are praised with ever greater fulsomeness. But if they have done nothing, or the deeds are not dreadful enough, the sluggish witches are given an appalling beating by the evil spirit or by some senior worker of harmful magic *(maleficus)*...[187]

This description clearly illustrates that the recruits of the witches' Sabbat were both men and women. As Del Rio sees it, the members of this diabolical circle were subjected to a ritual reminiscent of the military in which each person had to recount his or her deeds of harmful magic, and in some cases to go into greater detail. If any of the – male or female – witches failed to achieve their planned quota, they were subjected to rigorous penalties. In Del Rio's Latin version the 'maleficus senior', one of the elder of the many male witches present, gives a thorough beating to any male or female witches who may not have fulfilled their goal and were thus in the eyes of the Devil not sufficiently destructive. In the Devil's hierarchical military-like organisation, he is assisted in the lower ranks by male witches who occupy important positions of command which permit them as the Devil's representatives to punish the ordinary witches and male witches.

Gender specificity does not, then, appear to play a major role in Del Rio's witch image; his concern is to combat and analyze what he has detected as the organized crimes of his, early modern, times.

His thought processes are not, however, always consistent. At times, gender-specific terms penetrate the otherwise apparently self-evident gender-neutral descriptions of witchcraft crimes. In the evidence he purports to provide of the reality of night flights, he gives only female examples. It is the 'sagae', the female witches, whose ability to fly he wishes to prove.[188] In his fourth book, the author deals with witch trials. In a chapter on the credibility of witnesses in witch trials, but not in a general discussion of male and female behavioural patterns and without raising the issue of the Devil's pact, Del Rio distinguishes typical female and male characteristics. Women as witnesses are, he maintains, liable to manipulation by demons on account of their fickleness, lasciviousness, instability, talkativeness, strong need to win approval, their 'damp and sticky nature', intellectual weakness and tendency to react emotionally.[189] In summarizing, Del Rio chooses words which demonstrate clearly his depreciation of the female sex, for women 'defile and dishonour the mind' more than men:

> Thus, women can more easily imagine things, but men promote such imagination with less pertinacity: they [the women] are less able to apply their intellect, indeed they possess less intelligence. It is easier for a demon to dupe them openly with false similarity [better: false analogies].[190]

Because these are the characteristics of women, Del Rio believed, in the logic of this gender-polarized thought, that men possessed the opposite characteristics and hence made the better witnesses. Del Rio considered men to be endowed with emotional stability and greater intellectual capacity and less delicate biological constitution. However, he only regards these in terms of qualities with which to appraise the credibility of evidence in witch trials; he does not list these characteristics as a reason for greater criminal (in the sense of witchcraft crimes) tendencies in women.

With the exception of these three lines – in a 1,070 page work – Del Rio does not explicitly broach the issue of sex specificity.[191]

The title of the books *Disquisitionum magicarum*[192] cannot be interpreted as evidence that Del Rio viewed women as the perpetrators of witchcraft crimes; 'magicarum' with its feminine ending -arum is not a noun but an adjective in the genitive, made to agree with the feminine noun 'disquisito'. Admittedly, it is not unusual for Latin nouns to be nominalized ('bonus' can mean both 'good' and 'the good man', for example); however, had such an excellent Latin scholar as Del Rio intended a misogynist interpretation, he would have chosen a title such as *Disquisitionum maleficarum*.

Del Rio's books appeared 26 times, thus reaching a number of editions similar to *The Witches' Hammer*. Historical research has ascribed the work great impact in the witch persecutions and described it as the most well-known and most authoritative demonological work.[193]

The werewolf finder: Henri Boguet (1602)

Boguet grew up in a small village in Franche-Comté in very modest surroundings. After studying law he was appointed senior judge of the monasterial district of St Claude, where he conducted a large number of witchcraft trials. In addition to edifying Catholic literature, he wrote his *Discourse execreable* on witchcraft in 1602, which appeared in a total of 11 editions. He died in 1619 shortly after his appointment to the Parliamentary Council.[194]

Boguet was involved in the practical side of the witch persecutions; his written work comprised theoretical reflections on his experiences in witchcraft trials which he wished to relay to other people. Time and again, in his questioning of witnesses and accused, he came across contradictions of contemporary learned thought, which he attempted to resolve in the sense of current Catholic doctrine or prevailing demonological theories. While in office in St Claude he conducted numerous trials of people who allegedly bore the characteristics of werewolves. When the accused actually began to behave like animals and to run around the courtroom before him on all fours, Boguet began to doubt the validity of the majority Catholic position which had always declared transmutations to animals impossible.[195] However, in this intellectual dichotomy and growing scepticism with regard to classical Catholic doctrine, the theologian in Boguet prevailed over the werewolf finder. He declared these phenomena illusions which the Devil had deceived humans into believing, and, quoting the laws on witchcraft, condemned the accused to death.

Contradictions are also apparent in Boguet's genderization of witchcraft crimes. In his descriptions of the witch-hunts in St Claude he frequently describes men as male witches and integrates them and their function into the witch paradigm: in order to perform harmful magic, men and women enter a contractual relationship with evil through the Devil's pact and intercourse with the Devil.[196] In 31 chapters of the work he deals with witches and in 28 of them he uses the generic term 'sorciers':

> Chapter XXII: Whether the [male and female] witches [*'sorciers'*] cause hail
>
> Chapter XXIII: On the poisonous powder of the [male and female] witches [*'sorciers'*][197]

Only in Chapter 11 does he split the neutral term into both possible grammatical forms, 'sorcier' and 'sorcière':

> Chapter XI: On the Devil's copulation with the male witch and the female witch [*'sorciers et sorcières'*][198]

Boguet, the senior judge of a monasterial territory, also ascribes types of maleficium to male witches which many demonologists had determined to be typical female offences. He even attributes weather magic to the male domain.[199]

As regards intercourse with the Devil, however, he remarks that women in general are more likely to yield to the Devil because their sexual needs are greater[200]:

> It happens that Satan has intercourse with them all; he uses them because he knows women so enjoy the pleasures of the flesh that such titillation will keep them obedient to him.... And as the male witch is no less inclined to this pleasure than the female witch, this is why he also takes on the form of a woman, to please him.

In Boguet's view, then, men join ranks with the Devil by reason of their hypersexuality and for the same reason practise their destructive potential on others. Thus, for Boguet, the male witch is a sex offender. This is similar to the description of the female sex in the 'Witches' Hammer' – with the exception that Boguet only applied it to one group of his own sex, the male witch.

Boguet gives a precise and tangible description of the witches' Sabbat in which the presence of a large number of men assumes the presence of an equally large number of women. In his account of the meetings, not only do these multitudes of male and female witches have intercourse with their incubi and succubi but they are also often involved in incestuous relationships:

> The dances over, the [male and female] witches [*'sorciers'*] begin to copulate: the son does not spare the mother, the brother the sister, nor the father the daughters, incest is common...I leave it to the imagination to decide whether all possible kinds of lewdness are practised there or not, but what is even more strange is that Satan takes on the form of an incubus for the women and a succubus for the men.[201]

Boguet devotes nine chapters to the pattern of the witches' Sabbat,[202] the core element of his demonology. He also formulates a kinship theory for witchcraft along patriarchal lines: this major crime is transmitted via the father of the house to all members of the extended family such as wife, daughters, sons, nephews and nieces:

> The father witch normally makes of his son; the mother of the daughter; the brotherof the sister; the aunt of the niece or the nephew

a male or female witch, and they commit their wicked deeds and abominations by night and in secret.[203]

Having set down in writing these experiences from his own persecution practice, Boguet attempts – as he did with his evaluation of werewolves – to smooth out any possible discrepancies with differing theological viewpoints: in 1602, 1606 and 1610 he presented numerous male witches and analyzed their deeds and motives. In the 1610 edition of his treatise he added a remark to the effect that most of those who entered a pact with the Devil were women[204]; he did not, however, make any changes to his descriptions of the trials of male Devil's agents.

In France, Boguet's work became a bestseller though it was only published in French in Lyon, Paris and Rouen, that is not within the Holy Roman Empire. Thus, it is hard to assess how it was received in the empire, although the fact that this 'Discours execrable' appeared in 11 editions indicates that it was widely known, particularly in the French-speaking parts.[205]

The zealot: David Meder (1605)

Meder studied theology in Leipzig, became general inspector in the county of Hohenlohe in Württemberg (southwest Germany). In 1595 he returned to central Germany to become a preacher in the town of Naumburg in the Electorate of Saxony and later in the nearby small town of Nebra. In addition to his regular sermons, he also had his witchcraft sermons printed.[206]

Meder made passionate attacks on all opponents of the witch-hunts, likening them to male witches or female witches ['*Hexenmann und Hexenweib*'] themselves, for the sceptic '...is either a fool or is gravely lacking in prudence or is a male witch or a female witch'.[207] Meder persists throughout his witch sermons with this belief in an offence which could be perpetrated by both sexes. Early in the work he expressly states that the Biblical references to witchcraft and punishment by death for this crime relate to both men and women.[208] He subsumes these 'male witches and female witches'[209] under the term 'witchpeople' or 'witchpersons' ['*Hexenleute and Hexenmenschen*'][210] and sees numerous cases of material harm as stemming from their magic deeds in connection with their apostasy and pacts with the Devil.[211] As Boguet, Meder considers that both sexes become dependent, there is then no longer a difference between the sexes:

> To summarize, we should know that no sooner has a person become a male or female witch ['*Hexenmann und Hexenweib*'] do they become the poisoners and the ruin of the good creatures of God, for the Devil leaves them no peace, they are obliged to cause harm ...[212]

Meder also considers the witches' Sabbat, where there was much feasting and dancing, a reality. The sexual orgies and ecstatic states described by other Catholic demonologists are, however, lacking in this Protestant preacher's account of an alleged witch convention. He views the function of this gathering of witches and male witches as one of planning:

> First of all, they all ..., whether man or woman, vow that they can fly in the air from one place to another, especially by night to their feasts, dances and celebrations where they then consult as to where, when and how they will work harm on other people.[213]

Meder does not provide any further details of the Sabbat and admits that confessions of witches' flights and Sabbat participation might be a product of the imagination of the accused. The collective element of the witchcraft offence which was manifested in the idea of nocturnal gatherings, was not of central importance to him. Having zealously and extensively described the crimes of witches and sorcerers and earned himself the title 'bloodthirsty',[214] he speaks out against consistently severe punishment for delinquents.

People who have succumbed to the Devil could possibly be won back to God, Meder argues, and thus all those who had entered a pact with the Devil but not committed any harm as a result, should only be required to do penance. It is noteworthy that in so arguing, this former zealot contradicts the 1572 constitution of the Electorate of Saxony which had been drafted by Lutheran jurists and which foresaw the death penalty for such crimes. In his discussion of the correct type of punishment for witchcraft, the Protestant minister. Meder follows the widespread Lutheran-orthodox line. He rejects the idea that the death penalty should be passed on principle for allegedly proven witchcraft, and only under certain conditions does he accept confessions made under torture.[215]

Meder does not find it problematic first to refer to the Catholic Bodin in his depiction of the witches' Sabbat, but then to follow the arguments

Illustration 5.3 Two male witches and one female witch are dancing with devils – a musician sitting up in a tree is accompanying them on a viola: Illustration showing the course of events at the witches' Sabbat (Woodcut from: Francesco Maria Guazzo, *Compendium Maleficarum*, Milan 1626.)

of the German Protestant Brenz in his ideas on punishment for witchcraft offences. In his sermons he attempts to synthesize both channels.

In Meder's view, a person was more likely to become a witch if he or she led a sinful life. He lists all breaches of rigid church norms, from intoxication and gluttony to a growing disbelief, as a kind of primary infection. In the final stage, such individuals, he says, lose all their inhibitions and commit the vilest of all offences, the major crime of witchcraft.

In contrast to the view presented in *The 'Witches' Hammer'*, Meder sees men as particularly in danger of becoming ensnared by the Devil when he appears to them in the guise of an attractive woman. Women, however, commit themselves to evil for different reasons: '... the female sex is especially revengeful and cannot easily be reconciled.'[216]

Nothing is known about the reception of Meder's work. The fact that his sermons were printed a second time in the same place, Leipzig, would indicate that his influence remained fairly regional. Later Protestant authors barely referred to him. The Protestant provost of Livland, Samson, referred to Meder in his 1626 witchcraft sermons, but simply cited an example and not any core elements of Meder's witchcraft teachings.[217] He would appear, then, not to have been a decisive opinion-shaping figure in the overall Protestant witch debate.

The authority from the north: Hermann Samson (1626)

Samson read theology in Rostock and Wittenberg, took up a post as a Protestant minister in Riga in 1608, where he became provost in 1622 and Professor of Theology in 1631. He rejected offers of posts as principal minister at the universities of Rostock, Hamburg and Danzig. He was a convinced Lutheran, dealt intensively with Catholic and reformed theology and was respected as an authority not only in the Baltic-Scandinavian region but throughout northern Germany.[218] He published collections of exemplary sermons,[219] which were widely read in Lutheran circles, and in 1626 he had his witchcraft sermons printed.

He did not dispute the effectiveness of witchcraft; both black and white magic could only be worked through a Devil's pact and presupposed apostasy from God. As late as 1626, Samson contradicted the arguments of Weyer, an opponent of the witch-hunts, from the mid-16th century.[220] Samson did not accept the idea of intercourse with the Devil and apodictically declared, 'The Devil has no flesh and thus he cannot copulate.'[221] He replaced this element of demonology by a ritual lacking in sexual connotations, in which a so-called Devil's baptism was performed either by Satan himself or by a female representative, that is a woman or a witch.[222] In contrast to the ideas of the Catholics Boguet and Del Rio who saw men in key executive functions, women fulfilled central roles in Samson's teachings.

Not all witchcraft, Samson believed, should be punished with the death penalty; only the Devil's pact with ensuing maleficium was, without exception, punishable by burning at the stake. In other cases, he considered a 'salutary admonition' to be a feasible punishment. He also emphasized that Lutherans, unlike Catholics and Calvinists, did not kill heretics. Any confession made under torture could only be conditionally accepted or might even be declared invalid.[223]

Samson had a clearly delineated witch image; there was no doubt in his mind that women committed witchcraft crimes, and he mentioned this fact in the very first of his nine sermons[224]:

> Firstly, God's teachings wish to show us that the female sex is a weak receptacle and in greater danger of succumbing to to the devious approaches of the Devil than men. For the Hebrews have a proverb: Quò plures mulieres, eò plures maleficae. The more women, the more [female] witches. The game the Devil began with Eve and how he conquered her is evident. In sum, where the fence is lowest, the nobleman Satan will willingly climb over it.[225]

Men, whom he designates as the 'strong sex'[226] are thus more immune to the proposals of the Devil. They are able to fight out and solve their disputes openly. Conversely, women would for reasons of revenge cause harm to '...people and livestock, fields and crops etc. through their sorcery and poisonous ointments and weather magic...'[227] – with the help of the Devil.

'There are so many sorceresses...' Samson proclaimed in Riga Cathedral[228] and listed concrete cases of witchcraft in which almost exclusively women were the culprits.[229] Samson does, however, round this picture off by giving examples of male witches from what he considers to be a prominent group of Devil's confederates:

> Popes are witches ['*Zauberer*']...Thence experience shows that many more of these people were found among the Popes than elsewhere.[230]

He attributed the term male witch to five historical popes. The popes Sylvester II, Benedict IX, John XX and XXI and Gregory VII were all, in his opinion, male witches. Other Catholics, too, were to be considered as having entered pacts with the Devil; Jesuits, Samson maintained, were particularly prone to witchcraft offences.[231] Samson's image of male witches was restricted to clearly delineated groups of clerics. These statements must, however, be seen against the background of the denominational disputes in Livland (present-day Latvia) at that time. Samson himself published anti-Jesuit pamphlets and thus earned himself the reputation of an 'anti-Christ'.

Samson is very wary in his discussion of the existence of a witches' Sabbat. He reports on the positions of the Catholic Bodin, of Luther and other authorities in the witch debate. Over several pages of his treatise he fails to make a clear statement, frequently using the subjunctive mode as an expression of possibility or uncertainty, but finally brings himself to present a thesis. Witches' Sabbats were, he said, occasionally possible for the well-being of the witches, but were mostly only products of women's imagination.[232] For Samson, the witches' gatherings have become social events rather than a central crime-planning and organizing entity. He gives one example in which he points out that women, but not men, flew to such meetings.[233] A witches' sect did, then, exist for him although he tries to play down the significnce of such a sect by using a diminutive form of the noun. The Devil's agency described in detail and as a threat by other demonologists is made several times by the Lutheran Samson to sound harmless through the use of the German diminutive ending '-lein': 'Zaubergesindlein' and 'Satans- und Drachengesindlein', which might be rendered approximately as sorcerers' little riffraff and Satan's and dragons' little riffraff, respectively.[234]

The witch commissioner: Hinrich von Schultheiß (1634)

Hinrich von Schultheiß came from a family of magistrates and well-to-do farmers, and studied law at the Catholic universities of Cologne and Würzburg. After working as a public official at the High Court of the Prince-Archbishopric of Cologne, the sovereign Ferdinand of Bavaria appointed him Councillor to the Prince Elector of Cologne. Schultheiß had already been active in witchcraft trials since 1613 but as specially appointed 'witch commissioner' he led numerous charges against alleged witches and male witches in Westphalia, and was ennobled in 1633.[235]

In 1634 Schultheiß, a Catholic and consistent advocate of the witch-hunts, published a work on witch trials, written in the form of a dialogue beween an aristocrat and a witch commissioner, which was intended as a guideline for the exemplary conduct of a witchcraft case. Thus it was not a treatise on witchcraft but a legal tract which dealt in ten chapters with guilt and innocence, correct circumstantial evidence and interrogation methods, and the correct confessions needed to convict Devil's confederates.[236] Even a work of this nature, however, allows some conclusions to be drawn regarding the gendering of witchcraft crime.

Schultheiß classifies witchcraft offences as particularly severe crimes, far worse than those of robbery or murder[237] because the culprits had entered a pact with the Devil and thus sworn an alliance against contemporary society. These people, he said, had institutionalized their organization in the form of the 'Devils' and witches' gathering'.[238] Schultheiß thus unites all the elements of the witch paradigm in a cumulative unit.

Schultheiß does not explicitly mention the gendering of witchcraft offences. However, in his various discourses, it became apparent what his tendencies were with regard to the practical side of witch- hunting and thus his witch image, too, is discernible.

As witch commissioner Schultheiß' first move in a witchcraft indictment was to seek further delinquents in the family circle, suspecting primarily the witches' parents, husbands and children of the same offence.[239] This concept that witchcraft was spread through consanguinity meant that men were, in principle, also potentially capable of performing magic deeds.

In a fictive trial written down for demonstration purposes Schultheiß presents an accused woman by the name of 'Gretha' who, after initial resistance, finally pleads guilty to harmful magic and attending the Sabbat.[240] Schultheiß, however, is not satisfied with this confession and presses the allegedly proven witch to name further accomplices. He continues the interrogation with the suggestive question: 'And did you have a [male] associate or several [male] associates?'[241]

In this question he uses the masculine Latin noun 'socius' and not the feminine form 'socia', thus asking her if she had a (male) accomplice. The accused witch names a male accomplice who she calls 'Thonnis' who, she says, attended the Sabbat with her. Thonnis, after being subjected to thumb- and legscrews, admits to the pact with the Devil:

Doctor: Now it is time for you, Thonnis, to save your soul, for the Devil wants to deceive you and presumes you will not confess without torture, you shall first be tormented. Now, deceive the Devil and confess without torment, your limbs shall then not be torn asunder, show respect to God and tell me who taught you?

Thonnis: Oh Jesus, oh Jesus. Oh Jesus. Alas, alas, desist, desist, M. Jürgen....

Doctor: Thonnis, spare your limbs, you are for God's mercy not the first, nor the last who learned the devilish arts, if you will only tell me without torture who taught you, I assure you I will show you as much mercy as I can justify before God and his Highness the Prince Electorate, the councillors, tell me, in the name of Jesus, who taught you?

Thonnis: Oh Jesus. Oh Jesus, desist, desist, I will tell you, I will confess all.

Doctor: Le ave off, M. Jürgen. Now, tell me Thonnis, who taught you?

Thonnis: It was N.N....[242]

Here Schultheiß demonstrates how he can bring an alleged male witch to an indirect confession to the Devil's pact and thus to the crime of witchcraft by making him name his so-called master. One of the commissioner's methods of interrogation is to give the accused hope of a less excruciating death. To carry this cynicism to the extreme, Schultheiß has Thonnis thank his torturers for their help in making him confess:

> ...the Devil has deceived me long enough, he shall deceive me no longer. Thank God that it is off my mind, that I have said it.[243]

Men like Thonnis appear frequently in Schultheiß' works, some as musicians at the witches' Sabbat, but also as men accused, independently of women, of being male witches, that is as fully recognized and legitimized agents of the Devil. However, there are relatively few examples of trials of women from Schultheiß' own practice.[244]

Schultheiß assumes that in principle 'male and female witches' [*'Zauberer und Hexen'*],[245] that is persons of both sexes, can be accused of witchcraft. Men, however, as we can deduce from his model trial, counted for the witch commissioner as secondary delinquents. They were accomplices, and only as a result of denunciations was their function as male witches revealed. Nor did they cause any major harm with their magical aggression. Whereas Schultheiß confronts his protagonist 'Gretha' with numerous questions pertaining to her harmful magic, including her intercourse with the Devil, he spends comparatively little time on her male accomplice. 'Thonnis' has only to admit to the Devil's pact and not to all the details of the entire crime. In Schultheiß' view, men are, however, more immune to interrogation practices which do not include torture: 'Gretha' admits her guilt after a fairly lengthy verbal interrogation, whereas 'Thonnis' only confesses after torture has been used.

Other than the critical reponse of the University of Cologne[246] nothing is known about the reception of Schultheiß' work, though it is known that he continued to conduct witch trials after the publication of the book and until shortly before his death. The persecution practice laid out in his treatise was continued, clearly with the support of the territorial sovereign.

The Protestant jurist: Benedict Carpzov (1635)

Carpzov came from a family of Saxon scholars, studied law, and at the age of 25 became assessor at the high court in Leipzig. In 1645 he was appointed professor at Leipzig and with his teachings laid the groundstone for independent German penology, was considered an outstanding legal authority of his time and proved to be one of the main exponents of a theocratic-absolutist concept of state and law.[247]

In his work Practicae Novae[248] of 1635 the Protestant Carpzov dealt in three comprehensive chapters with sorcery crimes and legal proceedings in witchcraft trials. He considered witchcraft the worst and most abominable of all felonies and, above all else, a 'crimen laesae majestatis divinae', i.e. lese-majesty. Thus, he argued, witchcraft cases should be tried outside of ordinary court procedures.[249] To a certain extent, he proved to be a practical jurist anxious to ensure that justice was dispensed in accordance with the rule of law and sharply critical both of the misuse of torture and of the hitherto existing teachings on circumstantial evidence which did not meet his requirements in terms of rationality. Even though the legal procedures he strove for were repressive, Carpzov was not one of the fanatical witch-hunters of his time; in practice he showed himself to be not the dreaded jurist, but rather the reverse.[250]

In his view, harmful magic could be worked by both sexes – as he indicated in his first chapter on the topic of witchcraft:

> It is above all important to teach and it will be necessary to show that the male witch and female witch ['*venefici et* [illegible]n cause various illnesses.[251]

The Devil's pact forms the core of his demonology, and this, too, he presents as a crime committed by both sexes:

> ...One cannot deny that male witches and female witches ['*magi et sagae*'] have a pact with the Devil in which they renounce the alliance formed with God through baptism. Yet they renounce God by having this pact with the Devil.[252]

Carpzov is inconsistent in his descriptions: at times he sees only female handmaids of the Devil at work; at other times he speaks of Satan's pacts with both sexes:

> Hence the male witches and female witches ['*malefici et maleficae*'] have sexual intercourse with the demon when they have made the pact with him.[253]

This intercourse alone is, in Carpzov's view, sufficient legal basis for death by burning[254] and in so thinking he went beyond the valid legal practice of the empire which only foresaw punishment for maleficium in combination with the Devil's pact. With respect to intercourse with the Devil as an element of the witch paradigm, Carpzov also appeared to disavow his original statement on the gender neutrality of the crime, since in his later statements he speaks exclusively of women.[255] In his evaluation of the witches' Sabbat, Carpzov clearly finds it difficult to commit himself. He refers to statements by Luther and other Protestant theologians, cites in detail both proponents and opponents of this concept, such as Rémy, Bodin and Del Rio and attempts to find an acceptable compromise for himself:

> However much I do not deny that the female witches' [*'sagae et lamiae'*] participation in diabolical gatherings, copulations and choirs seems often to be only in their imagination.... The female witches [*'sagae'*] somehow take part, sometimes in sleep, and sometimes in body, in the meetings.[256]

Otherwise a precise author with a clear eye for detail, Carpzov resorts in his uncertainty here to noncommittal statements such as 'somehow', 'sometimes in sleep' and 'sometimes in body'. Rarely, according to Carpzov, is the witches' Sabbat real, and in most cases it is a problem of delusions resulting from a loss of the ability to think in realistic terms. These night gatherings ... of all witches of both sexes [*'striges et malefici'*]'[257] do not, however, play such a major role for this Lutheran author as for Catholic authors. In his final, generalizing summary there are many descriptions of crimes, but the witches' Sabbat is not found here as a concept in its own right.[258] Neither does it appear as a search term in its own right in the subject index of the work; it is merely given as a sub-category, surely indicating that these gatherings did not play any great role in Carpzov's mind.

He no longer restricts the witch stereotype to women; indeed, in his theoretical debate with the opponent of persecution, Weyer, he stresses that men and women commit this crime, calling them 'malefici sexus utriusque', witches of both sexes.[259] In the sections which follow these fundamental observations, however, Carpzov no longer seems to see this gender-unspecific side of the witch trials; the intuitive image of women as culprits which was hitherto in the background, now comes to the fore again.

Carpzov's works were published nine times in Latin and four times in an abridged German version and received much attention in both Catholic and Protestant territories.[260] The Practicae novae became a standard legal work but nevertheless remained controversial. Protestant jurists took little notice of the demonological part of Carpzov's juristic work.[261] To what extent this demonology was in a position to make any wide impact is debatable, as the witch persecutions in many Protestant territories of the empire had already reached their zenith (in terms of numbers) by the time the Practicae Novae appeared.

The founder of modern psychiatry: Johann Weyer (1563)

Johann Weyer (also given as Johannes Wier, Wierus or Weier) was born of a merchant's family in Brabant, read medicine in Paris and Orléans and was a pupil of the well-known humanist scholar Cornelius Agrippa of Nettelsheim, who had defended witches in court. In addition to various medical works, Weyer published, in 1563, a treatise on the witch persecutions entitled *De praestigiis daemonum* (On the tricks of the Devil)[262] which later appeared in six Latin, one French and two German editions. In 1550 he was appointed personal physician to the Duke of Jülich-Cleves, a position he held until his retirement; he died a natural death in 1588.[263]

Weyer is considered a very religious Lutheran. He contested the reality of witchcraft crimes and attributed alleged maleficium to fantasies arising from suggestions made by the Devil. The Devil, Weyer argued, acted only within the limits of God's commandments and did not need any agents, male or female, for his destructive deeds. Weyer attributed the relationships with the Devil, to which numerous accused witches admitted, to a natural illness which he described as 'melancholia' and which in modern psychology would be termed psychopathology; in the terms of depth psychology this is identical to a hysterical perception disorder. Weyer rejects all elements of the witch paradigm as unreal and advocates that they be treated medically rather than punished by death,[264] and it is for this reason that he is considered the founder of modern psychology.[265]

In Weyer's opinion, the male sex is immune to the fantasies of 'melancholy' for men can, by virtue of their biology, accommodate the impressions of the senses in a more realistic way; it is this which protects them against witchcraft fantasies:

> Males see no ghosts.... Such phenomena appear to children, women, the insane, the foolish and the sick, who are driven by perpetual fear and intense dreams.[266]

Weyer discusses the gender-specific one-sidedness of the witch-hunts in the 16th century but does not seek their causes in a psychopathological fixation of persecution:

> That the talk here is of female witches and not also of male witches is not due to the fact that men, when they work magic, are spared here or that not a hair on their head is harmed. But because the female sex can by reason of their inborn simple-mindedness be more easily duped by the tricks of the Devil.[267]

The concentration of death penalties among women, then, is due to the psychological disorders of the victims themselves. Their tendency towards 'melancholia' is also determined by their nature, so that maleficium, Devil's pacts and witches' flights take place in their fantasy but are experienced by them as reality. However, Weyer explains, these fantasies do not correspond to any reality. Women develop such disorders because, in contrast to men, they are 'fickle, gullible and not masters of their own selves', are 'driven by perpetual fear and intense dreams', 'lacking in circumspection', 'without understanding' or simply 'foolish'.[268] Men, then, are distinguished from women by their understanding, their independence and their slight propensity to verbalization.[269] Women, on the other hand, have a natural disposition to develop these harmless neuroses which, unable to relate to reality, they then describe in the confessions of witch trials, as diabolical experiences.

Weyer bases his arguments, in which female witches have become defenceless and helpless victims and are no longer aggressive offenders, on an image of women which is, in fact, almost identical with that of the proponents of persecution. It has been pointed out in historical research that Weyer criticized the fixation of witch persecution on women by alluding to the dangerous but unpunishable deeds of male sorcerers.[270] This requires some further explanation. Weyer advocated more protection for women but did not attempt to secure any relief through the persecution of more men in the witch-hunts. He distinguished beween 'malefici' and 'magi' as male witches. Whereas the former, he argued, correspond to mentally ill female witches, the latter belong to the category of the traditional, learned sorcerer. With the help of spirits, 'magi' were able to evoke illusory images and should, thus, be punished; they were not, however, identical to witches[271] but should be seen as second class sorcerers and not as real Devil's confederates.[272] Without the aid of a pact, these sorcerers activated diabolical powers and generated phantasms which bore no relation to reality.

Weyer observes that this is 'trickery'. Weyer's 'protection of women' was not, then, a 'man-hunt', although the possibility that it might have been understood as such cannot be excluded.

Even though Weyer's work is considered unimportant for the persecution period itself,[273] he changed thought structures[274] and influenced other authors; the Protestant jurist, Godelmann, for example, borrowed some important ideas[275] in his call for more moderate persecution.

The critic of witchcraft trials: Friedrich Spee (1631)

Spee entered the Jesuit order in 1610, taught moral theology in Speyer, Worms, Paderborn and Cologne and was active in the Counter Reformation in northwestern Germany as a missionary among the people. In his work he was frequently confronted with witch persecutions, and in 1631 he published, anonymously and without the permission of his order, his book Cautio criminalis (directly translated as 'A Warning on Criminal Justice, or a Book on Witch Trials'),[276] whereupon he was sent by the leader of his order to Trier – where he died four years later.

In 51 chapters, Spee questioned the reality of the entire paradigm of witchcraft offences, but concentrated on and confined himself to a criticism of the legal procedures and specific aspects of witch trials.[277] Despite his struggle against this legal practice he cannot be counted as one of the forerunners of the philosophy of the Enlightenment.[278]

Spee, the Jesuit, left no doubt as to whom he viewed as the victims of the witch-hunts. Not only in the title did he name the 'sagae', the female witches, but throughout the work, including his description of the fictive trial victims 'Gaja' and 'Titia', the persecution of women was a central theme.[279] Nor was the importance of this theme relativized by other statements such as, 'Usually trials are conducted against women',[280] or by his mentions of alleged 'sorcerers' in the sense of 'male witches'.[281]

Hence, Spee discussed the supposed natural characteristics only of women, and not of men or male witches. As weak creatures and because of their frailty, weakness and gossipy nature, women were in need of special protection, particularly during witchcraft trials; under the pressure of torture any manner of confession could be extracted from them: 'Indeed, if men, even pious ones, as we have said above, are so weak in spirit that they would prefer death to torture, what are we to presume of that fragile sex?'[282]

Spee's concept of femininity is here similar to that of the proponents of persecution,[283] although Spee draws completely different conclusions. He uses pedagogical means to explain the large number of female confessions in the witch trials: he attempts to rouse the pity of his male readers by reversing the roles in his fictive examples. He presents a fictitious man by the name of 'Titius' who, like many female witches has recanted a confession made under torture and is now in a desperate situation. Spee expresses his arguments through the use of questions:

> What do you want Titius to do? To make a timely retraction before the judges and to be led back to be tortured? To steadfastly hold out against them by persisting in his retraction.... But this is futile. He already knows his weakness, he knows for certain what is going to happen now, that he will not endure the interrogation, just as he was unable to endure it earlier.[284]

Spee also attempts to expose the unjust gender-specific procedures in witch trials by demonstrating the different way in which circumstantial evidence was evaluated in trials of men accused of serious felony and a woman accused of witchcraft.[285] Spee also uses this change of perspective in another section where he argues that the use of torture is a cause of the particularly prevalent persecution of women.[286]

Spee's 'Cautio criminalis' is not only about ending the witch persecutions but in particular about the gender-specific selection which occurred in the trials,[287] although the author does not explicitly present new 'wanted' images or direct the trials onto a new, i.e. male-specific, course.

Recent historical research has been able to correct the impression that Spee's arguments had relatively little impact on the witch persecutions. Indeed, his 'Cautio criminalis' was widely read by contemporary jurists and mobilized more than simply the outright sceptics of the persecution practice, despite its theological orientation, its unclear denominational alignment and the fact that it was published anonymously.[288] It is also certain that the work was known in areas[289] where the proportion of men in 17th century witch-hunts was disproportionately high. It is, however, not certain whether this was due to the work of Spee himself or to that of Weyer. Both these persecution opponents stressed the female-specific aspect of the witch trials without arguing for greater gender balance. They may, however, have been understood in this way, and might thus unintentionally have contributed to the destruction of the female witch stereotype, although as yet no empirical analysis has been conducted which indicates that this was the case.

Summary

A close look at the demonological and theological literature of the 15th to 17th centuries shows that there was considerable latitude in the gendering of witchcraft offences.

Some chronological phases can be identified. Learned discourse in the late Middle Ages saw in women a greater affinity to magical aggression, but still held with the idea that in principle both sexes were capable of witchcraft. In the 15th century, the Dominican Nider, the university professor, Mamoris, and the inquisitor Jacquier all still stressed the extensive involvement of men in these newly invented offences.

With *The Witches' Hammer* the alleged crime of witchcraft was clearly attributed to women. Although he did not explicitly exclude men, the author substantiated this position by his arguments and his train of thought. The French political theorist Bodin explicitly corrected this evaluation almost 100 years after the publication of the 'Witches' Hammer' and re-introduced both sexes to the witch image – despite the extremely misogynistic remarks of his final chapter. This reasoning was followed by well-known advocates of persecution such as Binsfeld and Del Rio and genuine practitioners such as Rémy, Boguet and Schultheiß.

Whereas *The Witches' Hammer* associated the entire female sex with witchcraft, these latter authors were concerned with proportions. They gave reasons for their arguments that men were less inclined than women to make pacts with evil. The issue of gender-specificity had become one of quantity rather than quality. Witchcraft was, then, not considered a crime specific to women, although many writers of the early modern era had no doubt as to the fact that far more women than men were allegedly involved in witchcraft.

Contrary to widespread opinion, the perpetrators of witchcraft were, not only in practice but also in learned demonology, more heterogeneous than the British historian Clark maintains. The argument that men were 'literally unthinkable' as witches or that contemporary demonology 'lacks any sustained concern for the gender issue' can definitely not be confirmed.[290] A list of the frequency of gendered language in demonological texts supports this: in early modern studies – with the exception of *The Witches' Hammer* – there are a greater number of references to male than to female witches.

In his treatise, Bodin makes 820 and 399, and Binsfeld 157 and 47 references to male and female maleficents, respectively.[291] Methodological caution is, however, required when making such quantifications. Firstly, the dative and ablative plurals of the feminine 'maleficae' and the masculine 'malefici' are identical, meaning that in certain contexts it is not possible to make clear grammatical distinctions between the two genders. Secondly, some works are full of inconsistencies. Institor(is), for example, alternates in the description of one person within the same text section from one gender to the other or constantly oscillates between the two.[292] It is not surprising that his writings are full of formal and logical errors, given the speed and haste with which he wrote. He believed that the end of the world was so close that his work had to be printed without delay; by eradicating evil he believed he would be able to prevent the apocalypse.

One paradox in the debate mentioned above is that the fixation of the witch stereotype on women tended to be a consistent position of Protestant rather than Catholic authors. With the exception of *The Witches' Hammer* – of which the extreme statements on the gender issue represented only a minority opinion in Catholic demonology – it was mainly Protestant-Lutheran scholars who, almost to the point of denominational orthodoxy, excluded men as potential Devil's confederates and held fast to the female witch stereotype. Beginning with the definitive authority, Martin Luther, and in the following decades clearly followed by reformers such as Hemmingsen, the village pastor Meiger, the general inspector Samson, the jurist Godelmann and the doctor Ewich, Lutherans viewed witches as women, though, unlike the Witches' Hammer, they did not view women as witches. Nor did they resort to the enraged and misogynist language of the infamous author of this work; instead, they justified their position by alluding to the first woman to be seduced by the Devil, the biblical Eve. It was not until the 17th century that some Protestant authors, such as Meder and Carpzov, began to include more men in their function as male witches in the persecution paradigm.

Reformed theology did not develop a homogeneous witch image. Daneau, a Calvinist theologian with considerable influence in the French-speaking territories, assumed that witchcraft was not gendered, whereas the Zwinglian Bullinger was more reserved on this point.

In general, then, it can be assumed that learned discourse was relatively heterogeneous as regards the gender profile of the workers of magic. Concepts of femininity were very clearly described in demonology. Whereas the Dominican monk Institor(is)is still saw in women sexualized, demonic and aggressive beings, the view of the female sex changed, particularly among Protestant authors, from bad to weak. Women in their view had character deficits and biological deficiencies without any sexual connotations. Conversely – *and this is the principal focus of this study* – the concept of masculinity was less frequently verbalized in learned discourse. Men were primarily considered the 'strong sex', as the Protestant provost Samson stressed. They were characterized by special intellectual ability – as shown by the size of their heads – thus the Catholic Bodin – or by characteristics such as independence and faith in God. This, Luther felt obliged to remark upon. The concept of the male sex was founded in demonological discourse on the antonyms of the female attributes. Men possesed what women did not have or represent. The world of men consisted of a series of negations of womanly characteristics. He was largely – and the word 'largely' is important here – what she did not personify: generally speaking, not a sex offender, but in the Witches' Hammer a dangerous warrior; for Bodin a creator and designer of civilization; for Hemmingsen endowed with great faculties to enable him to relate to God and intense, unshakable faith; for Godelmann men were of complex mental constitution and holy; for Ewich and Valick forgiving, tolerant and conciliatory; for Binsfeld men were characterized by their understanding; in Samson's view they were composed, discreet and 'strong receptacles'; for Del Rio emotionally stable and self-controlled, and not psychopathological to the extent that older women were perceived by Weyer and Spee.

Whereas women were considered morally, mentally and physically deficient, the learned men and practitioners of demonological discourse valued the rationality, logic, steadfastness, religiousness and the autonomy of men. These personal characteristics stood in the tradition which equipped men with intellect and understanding, and women with body, weakness and irrationality. However, again with the exception of the infamous Witches' Hammer, misogynist statements were of no great significance in witchcraft literature; the reason for this relative abstinence was not the self-evidence of women's tendency to witchcraft but – at least in the Catholic camp – the ambivalence of the witch image.

All the above-mentioned positively charged male characteristics afforded resistance but not immunity to the challenges of the Devil and the potential defection to the actively destructive camp of evil. The Catholic jurist Boguet, for example, believed that men joined forces with evil because of their hypersexuality and that they performed their magic aggressive acts on the basis of this pact. The male witch was for him as much a sex offender as the woman in the Witches' Hammer whose actions were determined by her sexual needs, except that for Boguet this only applied to some of his own sex. The suffragan Bishop

Binsfeld of Trier wrote that men developed a disposition to witchcraft through alcohol and sexual desire, so that the only men who were always in a position to resist tendencies to practise witchcraft were the counter-reformationist, ascetic priests of the new era. Some demonologists contended that men were not as liable as women to become Devil's confederates, although they confirmed their disposition towards such crimes and the real existence of male Devil's agents. Men could be won over as future male witches to the services of the anti-world through kinship 'infection'. The same personality profiles applied to the 'fallen' men, the male witches, as to female witches. They were feminized, not because of their appearance or their sexual orientation, but because their personality features were considered feminine.[293] And because, as some authors taught, they had little natural inclination to witchcraft, they had to be more severely punished than women.

Despite the concept, which spanned all denominations, of the gender polarity in the character profiles, learned demonological discourse did not think only in female categories. The dualistic concept of gender characteristics gradually levelled out in the discourse. The concept of masculinity and femininity became more differentiated, though not really pluralistic. The ambivalent witch pattern in Catholic and, to an extent, Reformed discourse could be upated, accessed and adapted to current persecution requirements, for demonology theoretically allowed the prosecution of both sexes in witch trials.

The views of the majority of Protestant scholars, however, did not on the whole permit such a large degree of ambivalence. In many Lutheran territories, changes in the witch image of certain authors only really became established after the peak of the persecution period. The greater degree of openness in theological matters which arose from the structure of the Protestant church, had little impact on the witchcraft debate. A definite witch stereotype survived above all in the Protestant camp.

The issue of gendering in the elite discussion did not end in the debate on the characteristics of the prototype Devil's confederate. Some authors also entered the discussion on another social plane. They saw the reason for the increase in magical aggression in the dissolution of patriarchal, God-given circumstances essential to the existence of mankind. His was a 'womanly light' period, Institor(is) claimed, and spoke of 'womanish men who no longer have any religious zeal'. The religious foundation of society, as represented and continuously regenerated by men, appears to him to have been shaken by the increasingly immoral and abnormal behaviour of men. This is a threat not only to individuals but to society as a whole.

The gendering of the witch concept was particularly ambivalent amongst those theologians and demonologists who expressly integrated the collective element, the witches' Sabbat into their witch paradigm. This cumulative image which contained the four elements: maleficium, the Devil's pact, sexual relations with the Devil and the witches' dance and flight was a product of Catholic and reformist teachings, whereas the majority of Lutherans were sceptical of the existence of nightly gatherings as a collective activity organized by a secret coalition.[294] Persecution practice in Protestant territories did not, however, always follow this theoretical scepticism.[295]

Male witches performed a wide spectrum of harmful magic – both the Catholic and the reformed authors were in agreement on this point: weather magic and the resulting damage to harvests, causing sickness to animals, human afflictions, even murder through poisoning, all these were commonly described in the literature as types of male witchcraft. Few demonologists ascribe either infanticide (before or after birth) or love magic to the male domain; only Nider describes one case of infanticide. Which type of magic had male, and which, female connotations was only partially determined by roles universally ascribed to men and women.

Not surprisingly, almost all Catholic authors had alleged male witches – as female witches – forming a pact with the Devil. Similarly, they assumed that this pact was consolidated by intercourse between the two parties.[296] These men slept with female demons, the so-called 'succubi' who appeared to them in the guise of attractive women. These men were considered heterosexual, but as men with female character traits.

Many demonological theories saw aggressive magical acts performed by individual male witches as persons in their own right. However, these men only developed their main activities in the large organized and depersonalized group of inhuman Devil's agents (who were both male and female) which formed a threatening anti-society to the Christian community. Male witches also attained significant positions in the witches' Sabbat, construed as part of the collective crime of witchcraft. Some demonologists assumed that this event, described variously as a feast, dance or orgy,[297] was preceded by collective sexual intercourse among not an equal, but a similar, number of people of both sexes; this constituted the establishment of the devil's sect. In Del Rio's work the male witches had a commanding function within this large confederacy. The men present at these Sabbats were far more than insignificant attendants or musicians on the margins of this dramatic event. Nevertheless, in the descriptions of the trials, they were not infrequently identified as 'secondary' maleficent persons in the testimonies of female 'primary witches'. The denunciations made in witch trials were an essential and indispensable means of discovering alleged male witches.

Authors from all three Christian religions followed the idea of the family or kinship nature of witchcraft. Whereas the author of *The Witches' Hammer* in his fixation on women could only conceive of a matrilinear transmission of witchcraft, most other authors assumed that either spouse could infect the other or their own children. Boguet even saw men as 'fathers of the house' as playing a dominant role in this process. This framework of suspicion cast on a family meant that men could, both theoretically and in practice, also be accused in witch trials.

Weyer, an opponent of persecution, used a similar image of the respective gender characteristics as the advocates of the witch-hunts, but drew different consequences and rejected the idea of witch trials. Although writing as early as the 16th century, he focussed on the persecution of women and rejected the idea of maleficium as fiction – even Spee only indirectly criticized the concept of the reality of maleficium, though he stressed the need to protect women. Neither Weyer nor Spee used the argument of gender-specific inequality in the witch persecutions to iron out this inequality by securing more accusations of men; on the contrary, their criticism aimed at limiting the number of persecutions in general – or even at abolishing them altogether. It is possible, however, that local officials may, in the light of growing doubts as to whether it was right to restrict persecution to women, have interpreted and implemented their arguments in this way. The ambivalent witch image in Catholic and later parts of Protestant demonology could have legitimized such a change in the gendering of persecution. Men could now increasingly become the focus of suspicion and, as alleged agents of the Devil, the target of the learned jurists who, in the trials of the 17th century, replaced the executioners of earlier years. This idea is bound up with an account of the reception of the *Cautio criminalis* and can only be suggested here as a hypothesis; further research is needed if it is to be verified.

It can be argued against this hypothesis that the numbers of male persecution victims in the witch trials had increased even before the publication of the *Cautio Criminalis* and that the reception of Spee's work resulted, at the most, in an intensification of an already existent trend.

There were regional differences in the reception of demonological works. *The Witches' Hammer* with its emphasis on women as the sex guilty of witchcraft played a comparatively insignificant role in parts of the Holy Roman Empire such as the Austrian hereditary lands, Lorraine and Franche-Comté. It has been proven that persecution in these territories was aimed increasingly, and at an above-average rate, at men, and there were numerous trials of alleged male witches. To this extent, it is possible to agree with the criticism, which came originally from British and American historical research, that the impact and the quasi-canonical validity of *The Witches' Hammer* has been overestimated. The majority of Catholic authors did not follow its focus on women. Indeed, demonologists such as Del Rio and Binsfeld and, to a slightly lesser extent, Rémy played an extremely important role in Catholic witch persecution discourse and practice – and the witch concept they developed was a more gender-neutral one.

Exodus 22/18

When the Catholic suffragan bishop of Trier had his treatise on the witch persecutions printed in 1589, it seemed to him that a Bible reference would be the most impressive legitimization of the title. A passage from the Old Testament selected from the Book of Exodus, Chapter 22, Verse 18 was to be clearly visible on the front page:

> Maleficos non patieris vivere super terram

A possible translation of this into English would be,

> You shall not permit sorcerers or sorceresses/male or female witches to live.[298]

In the German edition of Binsfeld's treatise this sentence, attributed to Moses, was translated literally, using the masculine form:

> You shall not permit sorcerers ['*Zauberer*'] to live.[299]

This statement targets the persecution of male sorcerers and is found not only in Binsfeld but in almost all Catholic advocates of persecution, and even an opponent such as Spee complies with this translation. In 1487 Institor(is) refers to this place in the Bible[300] and renders it in masculine form, though revealingly not in the chapter in which he deals with the female disposition towards witchcraft. He cites this Old Testament verse when dealing with the problem of why God allows the Devil's activities and not when debating the gendering of this newly invented crime; obviously this Bible quote does not easily fit into his witchcraft concept. Both Del Rio and Schultheiß used the grammatical masculine form.[301] French authors such as Boguet use the masculine generic form anyway, as this corresponds to the usage in their own language:

> You will by no means permit the sorcerers/male and female witches to live[302]

It is possible in Latin, French and German to use feminine terms. Catholic authors did not, however, make use of this possibility in their translation of this sentence, although they used the feminine gender at other points in their texts, which shows that the choice of terms cannot be reduced to a linguistic or translation problem. Reformist authorities translate this sentence variously. The Calvinist Daneau uses the Catholic translation:

> Moses condemned them ['*sorciers*'] through the condemnation of God, in Exodus, Chapt. 22.[303]

The Zwinglian Bullinger uses a feminine noun[304] for this citation from the Book of Exodus 22, Verse 18, as do all Lutheran authorities:

> You shall not permit sorceresses/female witches to live.[305]

All contemporary demonologists and theologians of whatever denomination refer to this Old Testament sentence as a legitimization of witch persecution and as central evidence of God's law and command.[306] Exodus 22, 18 is not, then, just any reference but is a statement of great relevance, also for persecution practice.

For Catholics, the translation of this supposed injunction of God's was alone sufficient to warrant that witchcraft could not be thought of in purely female terms – though there are also other passages in the Old Testament which would have permitted a moderate attitude towards persecution. At the least, the participation of men in this major crime had to be accepted, for the Holy Scriptures did not permit that the witch image be restricted to women.

Protestants, however, were bound to the 'Sola scriptura' principle of Luther's; in 1534 Luther had translated this sentence from the Scriptures into German using the feminine gender, and according to the 'Sola scriptura' principle, the Holy Scripture alone was the place where norms and truth were to be found. Reformed theology developed as a result of the study of writings and, in reflecting on the Bible, theologians took its word literally and as a God-given norm. The Lutheran version of Exodus 22, 18[307] was not, then, simply a guideline, but a precise maxim. For Lutheran demonologists and jurists this Bible verse alone was sufficient to cast in a female mould their conception of evil on earth as the contemporary agency of destruction: for them, as precise commentators on the Bible, witchcraft stemmed from women. Reformist theologians assumed a position in the centre and were not uniform in their argumentation.

There is no doubt that the Hebrew word 'mekhaššefāh' in the Old Testament is feminine and can only be translated as 'sorceress'.[308] Here, however, it is not the linguistic precision but the contemporary interpretation which is important.

As early as the 16th century, the persecution opponent, Weyer, pointed to the consequences of incorrect translations, maintaining that the verse in question was impossible to translate. He alluded here to the different semantic reference of language and expounded on the problems of the Hebrew word which he viewed as taken out of context. In his view, the correct translation was 'Giftmischerin', 'female poisoner' – thus a real crime – and not to be confused with the word 'sorceress', since at the time of the Old Testament the much-discussed modern concept of witchcraft did not exist.[309] Weyer's main point here, however, was to combat all ideas of witches and not to discuss the gendering of persecution practice.

The different denominational interpretations of Exodus 22, 18 persisted; the reasons for these differences are at least in part to be found in the history of Bible translation. Catholic authors referred to the Council of Trent (1546–63) and the Bible version recognized there as authentic, the Vulgate. The Church Father Hieronymus who lived in Palestine and Rome, had created a translation in the 4th century from original Hebrew, Aramaic and Greek texts which had asserted itself since the end of the Middle Ages as the commonly used edition, the 'editio vulgata'. He translated the Exodus verse in male terms,[310] in reference to the Greek version. The resolutions of the tridentine council emphasized the importance of both tradition *and* the Holy Scriptures as the basis of counter-reformation belief, with the result that the ancient translation by Hieronymus was accepted as the correct one. There was no full German translation of the *Vulgata,* but there were partial translations, such as that of Luther's opponent, Eck,[311] and a French version of 1500/1600[312] aimed to help local persecution officials who were not familiar with Latin to base their actions on the exact word of the Bible. In France, however, the translations were considered unauthorized and were sharply criticized as corruptions of God's thought, condemned by theologians, and it was forbidden to print them.[313] The Latin *Vulgata* remained the decisive authority in the Catholic church; it was canonized and thus declared binding.

The version recognized by the Protestants was translated by Luther from Hebrew texts only, and thus related the Exodus verse in question to women, as the grammatical gender in the Hebrew text was unmistakably feminine. Other reformists followed this translation, thus also Bugenhagen who adopted Luther's version in his Low German edition of the Bible:

> Die Toverschen schaltu nicht leven lassen.[314] In English: You shall not allow sorceresses/female witches to live.

Such formulations in the High and the Low German translation written for the north German region were important for Protestants; their conformity to and belief in the literal had been attacked by the theologian and representative of the rebels in the Peasants' War, Thomas Müntzer. As early as 1537/1550 a translation which was closely oriented on Luther's version had appeared for the Danish-speaking regions.[315]

In the reformed church, Johannes Piscator's translation of the Bible became the accepted version. By order of the reformist sovereign of Hesse-Dillenburg, Piscator, a theologian and rector of the reformist university in Herborn, translated the Bible from original Hebrew and Greek texts at the beginning of the 17th century. This so-called 'Herborn Bible' reflects – whether consciously or not must remain open at this stage – the persecution practice in certain reformist territories. In Waadtland in Switzerland the proportion of men persecuted for witchcraft remained at an almost constant 35 per cent, in the Calvinist counties such as Lipper and Nassau it did not fall below 10 per cent. Admittedly, Piscator renders the Old Testament verse in the feminine, but in the appended comment does his best to reactivate the statement, which he wishes to relate to the male sex as well:

> You shall not permit a sorceress to live... Sorceress: Suchlike, also a sorcerer and all those who have pacted with the Devil and with his help deal in superstition and diabolical arts.... Here, however, he

> addresses the sorceresses, for the Devil preys most on the female sex as the weakest sex ...[316]

The Herborn Bible only became predominant in the reformist northern areas of Switzerland and in the Lower Rhine area; the Geneva Calvinists and the Lutherans considered Piscator's version unacceptable.[317]

Reactions to Bible versions and translations and their acceptance by theologians are by no means unrelated to societal influences, nor are they developments determined by purely philological standards. In the High Middle Ages, before persecution had become significant, commentators interpreted sorcery according to Exodus 22, 18 as a call for excommunication rather than in terms of burnings and death sentences.[318] The various translations used by the different denominations certainly did not play a major role in the orientation of persecution practices in the individual territories, but they were more than just a mirror of a circumstance which existed outside of theological discourse, the predetermined gendering of witchcraft prosecutions.

The 'witch heresy' or the legacy of heretical persecution

Both Catholic and reformist authors saw witchcraft as more than a continuation of the tradition of heresy.[319] To them it presented a new variant of heretical activities which they blended together with the traditional forms to create a hitherto unknown supercrime which was distinguished in its destructive potential from any other kind of heresy. The author of the Witches' Hammer derived this new heretical current with its huge potential for harm from apostasy:

> First let it be noted that this heresy of witches differs from other heresies, ... It also differs from every harmful and superstitious art in that, in a way that surpasses all the varieties of divination, this heresy of witches reaches the highest level of evil, since it even takes its designation from evil-doing ('maleficere') or having an evil opinion ('male sentire') ...[320]

Other important demonologists also see witchcraft as connected with heresy, even if they differ on the arguments of Institor(is). Thus, Binsfeld in 1590, more than 100 years after the appearance of *The Witches' Hammer*:

> The witches and foes are heretics or their deeds are intermingled with heresy. Whoever denies this defies experience. To deny God, enter a

> pact with the Devil, worship the Devil, revile Mary, the mother of God, abuse the mysteries of our salvation ... to commit other dreadful sins against God and the saints too abominable to mention. All these together are Godless heresy or indeed they smack of it[321]

Del Rio, writing at the beginning of the 17th century, concurs with this, and the debate on heresy takes up a good deal of space in his work. In his Encyclopaedia of Magic he gives the following authoritative, apodictic and brief summary:

> ... Witches are always suspect of heresy and rarely is this suspicion wrong, for the things they do smack of manifest heresy.[322]

The influential Archbishop of Mainz, Hrabanus Maurus, writing in the 9th century saw the Exodus verse 'Maleficos non patieris vivere' as referring not to sorcerers or witches but to heretics, and rendered the word 'maleficos' (masculine plural) as 'heretics' and the word 'maleficium' as 'heresy'. In the standard work *Directorium inquisitorum* of the Inquisition, that of the Dominican Nicolaus Eymericus written in 1376 the author attempted to connect certain types of heresy with witchcraft and argued that the two offences were closely related. In his arguments, Eymericus, who had been appointed General Inquisitor by the Pope, used the term 'maleficus',[323] named several male culprits and declared them confederates of the Devil. Catholic theology did not question this Bible commentary until the Late Middle Ages when it was reinterpreted by Jean Gerson. Gerson was Chancellor of the University of Paris and known as 'doctor christianissimus' (the most Christian scholar) and a stern opponent of Jan Hus, a man burnt for heresy; it was Gerson who, in a written communication in 1402, made the connection between this Bible passage and forbidden sorcery.[324] During the second half of the 15th century the two concepts of heresy and sorcery, previously generally considered separate entities in theological discourse, merged into one against the background of the persecutions of the Waldenses in the western Alps. The author of a chronicle which appeared in Lucerne around 1450, for instance, made an explicit connection between the concepts of witchcraft and heresy.[325]

The merging of these two spheres was made particularly clear in a correspondence of Pope Alexander VI to an Austrian provost in 1500 in which the Pope described the newly defined apostates as 'haeretici malefici', which can be translated as both 'heretical sorcerers/witches' and 'sorcerous/witchish heretics' and distinctly articulates the new synthesis of the two concepts: ... wherever there is an opportunity or a safe place offers itself ... you shall proceed ... against the scholars and patrons of the heretical sorcerers/witches [or: sorcerous/witchish heretics][326]

One of the most obvious traditional connections made between heresy and the witch paradigm was the concept of the witches' Sabbat, which included details of heretical gatherings. The link between the two concepts was the charge that heretics met by night under the leadership of the Devil and performed cult-like rituals. In the persecution of the Waldenses in the 14th century the Inquisitors established far more detailed and concrete information about this alleged heretical Sabbat. In their reports they maintained that these gatherings, which they called 'Synagoga Satanae', took place once or twice a month led by the Devil. At these gatherings, the participants underwent special rituals to deny and scorn the Christian faith and form instead pacts with the Devil. Obscene acts, it was said, which went as far as collectively practised intercourse with the Devil, sealed this pact.[327] In the 15th century Swiss chronicle mentioned above, the author, Johannes Fründ, described the followers of this movement as men and women[328], thus expressing the dual-gender nature of the Vaudois movement.

Pope Innocence VIII confirmed the idea that both men and women could become members of a new apostate community in his well-known Bull of 1484, where he noted the existence of 'very many persons of both sexes, forgetful of their own souls and in apostasy from the Catholic faith'. He also proclaimed that followers both male and female:

> perform abuse with the demons who mix with them as men and women, and with their enchantments, songs and incantations and with other detestable superstitions and magical transgressions, vices and crimes ruin, suffocate and kill people, women, the animals, livestock ... and also the vineyards, orchards, meadows, pastures, cereals, corn and other crops ...[329]

The heretical cumulative offence in which heretical men even have sexual intercourse with the Devil was thus described; the only thing missing to complete the picture of the witches' Sabbat was the pattern of the heretics' or witches' convention.

In a miniature by Johannes Tinctor(is)[330] – one of the oldest picture documents painted in the transition phase from heretics' to witches' sabbats in the middle of the 15th century – a large number of heretical Waldenses can be seen praying to the Devil in the form of a ram, paying tribute to him with flickering candles and, as a sign of submission and homage, preparing to kiss his posterior. At the centre of the scene men, and one woman, can be discerned. Other men and women are traversing the night sky, flying on animals and broomsticks towards the scene of the cult so as to take part in this preliminary form of the witches' Sabbat. Contemporary thought as portrayed here had, then, a majority of men, but also some women, attending the heretics' Sabbat. This construct is later conveyed to the fantasies on the witches' Sabbat.

In the early modern era this synthesis was given a legal framework in territories such as Franche-Comté; proven attendance of the Sabbat was in itself – even without a case of maleficium – sufficient to warrant punishment for this crime of faith. In the mid-14th century the words 'vaudoisie', 'vauderie' and others related to them meant as much as 'heresy' in the west Swiss/Burgundian region; by the middle of the 15th century they meant 'witchcraft'. Originally, 'vaudoisie' meant nothing more than 'coming from the Vaudois'. The word 'vaudois', the old term for the Waldensians, remained in use until the 17th century, in both witch trials and in demonology, for men and women accused of witchcraft. Henri Boguet, the chief judge in the monasterial district of St Claude in Franche-Comté whose demonological works were reprinted 11 times, used this term exclusively to describe accused witches,[331] thus establishing a close relationship between male and female followers of the Vaudois movement and the new witches and male witches. The presence of men was greater in this collective image of the witches' convention than in any other elements of either the Catholic or the reformist witch paradigm.

Neither in theory nor in practice were heretical activities and gatherings associated with one particular sex. The Inquisition arrested and executed numerous women, but associated hereticism in general primarily with the male sex. Dominicans such as Anonymus from Passau and Bernard Gui left no doubt as to their opinion that men were at the fore of these Mediaeval movements. The Inquisitor Petrus Zwicker, known for his severe and brutal activities from northern Germany to Austria in the 14th and 15th centuries, called men, but not women, enemies of and deviants from the faith.[332] In the actual persecutions, men made up the majority of those suspected and executed.[333]

People previously classed as heretics who thereby became servants of the Devil were now in the reverse role and were considered heretics because they had become the Devil's servants. The parallelism of the increased persecution of male witches in Catholic and, to an extent, in reformist territories with the idea of male participants in heretics' and witches' Sabbats is evident and must be viewed as causal. Here, the heretic image and the heretic trial lived on in the secularized realm of criminal justice. The roots of the charges against alleged male witches are to be found in the tradition of the persecution of heretics in the High and Late Middle Ages; the legacy was also apparent in the gender-specific perception of the new dissenters from the faith, the witches, amongst whom a number of men were still presumed.[334]

The influence of theoretical heretic images on certain aspects of the witch persecutions and their impact on the gender profile of the accused should not, however, be overestimated: demonology attempted to legitimize the witch trials by pointing to the fact that, compared with past offences against the faith, witchcraft threatened new dimensions of harm.[335]

A completely new threat appeared to have developed. In the eyes of their persecutors, however, men no longer formed the majority of those responsible for this 'supercrime' against Christian society; in many regions they became a minority of the accused, but never were their numbers so small that they could be ignored.

6
Magic and Gender in Popular Culture

> Hans Schütte of Kellinghusen accused Jacob Gronemann of sorcery, but proved nothing, fined one thaler
>
> (Verdict of a low court in Holstein, 1683)

This chapter uses original source material from popular culture, or literature which describes such material, to look into the witch image and its gender-specific characteristics in popular discourse.

The so-called magical folk-belief

The analytical distinction between the two spheres of learned and popular culture has led to fruitful discussions among historians, in particular in witchcraft research. This distinction – just as that between 'religion' and 'magic' – remains analytical, however, since both 'cultures' continuously influenced one another. The belief in witchcraft spanned both learned and popular culture and was only able to develop its fatal dynamics because it provided both scholars and illiterate villagers and townsfolk with explanations in and for their daily lives.[1] So-called popular belief encompasses everything that the majority of a population imagines to be true of a world beyond the realm of their everyday experience. It includes religious belief in a modern sense, as well as belief in the effectiveness of magic. This is necessarily a diffuse concept because it describes heterogeneous phenomena, but it differs from the widely used term 'superstition', for popular belief in the early modern period embraced far more than the church's official concept of what constituted deviation from Christian beliefs. There is no sharp delineation between magic and religion, and any assertions to the contrary misjudge the realities of both mediaeval and early modern religious practices; clerics, too, believed in what they were fighting against: the power of magic.

There are methodological problems involved in reconstructing the magical folk-belief of the persecution and pre-persecution eras. For the High and Late Middle Ages the only sources available are the extant writings of chroniclists from learned culture. For the early modern period, the documents on witch trials often, although not exclusively, represent the thought patterns and fantasies of the persecutors – themselves also representatives of learned culture – but not of the persecuted. Statements regarding magical ideas and fantasies were made in response to the courts' question lists, and most answers were thus highly predictable. Such sources must as a result be subjected to close scrutiny. Some researchers hence argue that attempts to use statements made in witch trials to demonstrate popular belief are speculative, since numerous extant ecclesiastical expressions of alleged popular belief are, in fact, stereotyped and persisting reiterations of ideas prevalent in late antiquity. This, it is argued, makes such sources unsuitable for the reconstruction of cultural reality, for they simply describe fictions.[2] Other historians consider such ecclesiastical sources nevertheless to be very valuable; thanks to the diversification of the sources since the Late Middle Ages and obvious digressions from established patterns, it is possible to infer something about the reality of past thought.[3] This school focuses on the manuals of confession and their proximity to pastoral reality.

There is consensus among historians that although popular and demonological beliefs constantly interacted with one another, they were only in part identical. Nor is it disputed that magic was worked in all sections of society in an attempt to force luck and escape from life's hardships.

The image of magic in popular culture, however, was fundamentally ambivalent in that it presumed a unity of 'black' and 'white magic', for if someone was able to work a cure, he or she was also able to work harm. The key elements of this image were maleficium worked – without the assistance of the Devil – against individuals, and the personal qualities of the perpetrator of magic. From the late Middle Ages onwards, however, the diabolic component became increasingly central to the demonological notion of witchcraft, with the result that any kind of magic was interpreted as an effluent of satanic agents on earth. It is certain that beliefs of popular culture were masked, reinterpreted or even 'contaminated'. Representatives of all Christian denominations criminalized, discriminated or diabolized magic beliefs deemed positive in popular belief, such as incantations, soothsaying and healing. Although the Devil had only a marginal place in the witch notion of popular culture, the population made use of the opportunity to exclude and persecute alleged sorcerers and sorceresses who they regarded as the originators of harm.[4]

Magic and gender: Burchard von Worms revisited

Popular sermons, canon laws passed at bishops' synods and the confessional literature of the High and Late Middle Ages have been criticized with respect to their value as historical sources reflecting popular magic-belief, and this criticism must be taken seriously. Basing an analysis of magic and gender on such sources does not automatically produce reliable results.

Research to date reflects this problem. Whereas some studies point to the involvement of both sexes in magic activities in popular culture,[5] others using different types of sources come to opposite conclusions, and see magic as a primarily female domain.[6]

Mediaeval penitential canons, however, probably best mirror the mentality of popular culture. Priests used them and the lists of questions they contained as guidelines for confessions because they stipulated the penances to be given. These canons were copied over and over again, brought up to date and adapted to regional conditions to accommodate the everyday life and religious practice of the people making the confessions. This meant that they were not simply monotonous repetitions of ecclesiastical-literary traditions but had to relate to popular ways of thought and interpretations of the world, for they would otherwise have had no practical value for the priests using them. The well-known penitential canon, the 'corrector', written in the 11th century by Burchard of Worms is particularly revealing. In the Catholic tradition of his time the Bishop of Worms rigorously rejected the effectiveness of any kind of magic ritual. He listed those rituals with which he was familiar, thus composing a canon of questions in the form of a confession manual following the tradition of the penitential canons of the Early Middle Ages.

The 'corrector' is of particular relevance in witchcraft research because of its discussion of a woman named Hulda who rode the night skies; this description is evidence that the idea of the witches' flight was already known. In popular belief, night flight and people who practised it were viewed in a positive, as well as a negative, light, but this was reinterpreted in Christian demonology – as were many beliefs considered to be heathen.[7]

The 'corrector' is not only of interest because it mentions elements of the later elite witchcraft concept but also because it provides us with information about the people who worked magic in the High Middle Ages. It mentions the magical activities of women who used magic spells and incantations to restore damaged pieces of weaving, as in counter-magic, or who were able to perform positive love-magic.[8] The author also mentioned magic worked by men whom he called 'magi', who were invited into homes and households either to perform magical incantations or, by observing the birds, to foresee the future. Anyone who accepted the help of these sorcerers should, according to Burchard, be severely punished:

> Have you asked the help of sorcerers and invited them into your house to investigate evil intrigues...or following the customs of the heathens? [Have you sought out] soothsayers so that you will know the future as of a prophet, or those who throw lots, or hope to be able to divine the future from the lots or those who devote their time to consulting the birds or to incantations? Have you invited them? If you have done so, two years' orderly fasting as your penance.[9]

Burchard of Worms also named herdsmen as the group of men who played a major role in all magic rituals:

> Have you made ligatures and incantations and all those various magic practices worked by godless people, swineherds and cattleherds and occasionally hunters by pronouncing devilish utterances on the bread and the herbs ... ?[10]

These herdsmen practised countermagic and were reponsible for protecting the livestock. Burchard described them as 'homines nefarii', godless people whom he would like to exclude from the Christian community.

The 'corrector' shows that in the High Middle Ages both men and women actively performed supportive, protective and healing magic. The penitential canon does not permit us to infer the proportions of men and women involved; magic in popular culture does not seem – at least as perceived in Burchard von Worms' canon – to have been generally recognized as gender-specific. The ability to work magic was considered gender-neutral. Variants of magic, however, do seem to have been attributed more readily to one or the other sex: love magic clearly did not belong in the male domain.

Slander charges, allegations of magic and gender

A wide variety of magic was practised in early modern life. This we know from extant church records but also from secular texts such as legal statutes, poetry and literature as well as magic charms and spells.

Many records still exist to provide us with extensive information on popular culture in Schleswig, Holstein and Saxony-Lauenburg, and it is for this reason that I deal with this region in greater detail here. Historical sources tell us of animal skulls nailed to stable doors to ward off ominous powers. Charms made of paper and animals' claws were thought to keep danger away. Villagers would drive their livestock through a fire lit out in the open in order to protect them from disease. Dead animals were buried near sick animals so that the spirit causing any lingering illness would be tranferred to the dead bodies and good health would return to the sick.[11] In difficult cases, professional forces were consulted; first and foremost, these people attempted to heal animals, although they sometimes worked their magic for humans. It seems, then, that a good deal of magic was practised although it is not known exactly how widespread or intense these activities were. Some may have tried to practise magic on a large scale, others less so: it is hard to assess the general importance of such individual or collective practices in everyday life. In the many records of magic activities to which people confessed without the use of force, the main reason given for employing magic is either to secure someone's subsistence or to secure them advantages – and not to cause harm to others. Pastors frequently report on rituals and behavioural patterns which testify to the deeply rooted nature of magic thought. These reports should, however, be read with care, for the Protestant clergy showed a tendency to dramatize the situation when dealing with the so-called superstitious customs. This is illustrated by a case in southern Holstein; this record seems credible because it gives a compact description of rituals which, though frequently mentioned elsewhere, are only described in isolation from one another in other records.

A clergyman described an event in 1639 in the village of Siek when a large number of the inhabitants roamed the village naked by night, carrying the hook of a cooking pot; they drew a circle around the village along which they lay pieces of bread, wanting thus to protect the village from diseases. This pot fixture, an iron bar from the hearth, on which the pot used for cooking food in the respective household was hung, was passed down from one generation to the next and was imagined by the villagers to be magically charged. Its magical power could be used to ward off danger. The cult-like removal of all clothing was seen as intensifying the effect of the hook, as was the fact that this all took place at night. The circle, as a closed geometrical shape, represented a figure which could ban all wrongs. The bread was intended as food to appease the imagined demons of disease.[12]

Yet, maleficium – harm allegedly caused to other people – was not insignificant either. In the context of gender and magic it is remarkable that the proportion of men accused of magical aggression was relatively high on the village level.[13] The focus of the witch concept in popular culture does not appear to have been as much on women as it was in the 'Witches' Hammer' of learned demonology.

The sources which provide us with the best insight into the gendering of the witch image in popular culture are those which have not been subjected to the influence of the authorities or legal structures or to observations by learned culture. Of such sources, slander cases best meet these requirements, since the material gives a direct rendering of the conflicts as they were argued out among the ordinary people. Records of these cases provide a solid and reliable source of information on popular imagination and fantasies.

In the territories Holstein and Saxony-Lauenburg in the north of the empire as well as in Schleswig, slander cases filed for prior accusations of witchcraft[14] were the responsibility of the lower courts. Such cases were generally filed when an accused person considered their reputation to have been damaged. As honour was considered to be a person's 'symbolical capital' and any infringement on a person's honour had severe negative impact on their status in early modern society, claims related to magic in particular, were frequently made in retrospect.

The frequency of slander cases filed by both men and women in the period under investigation shows that the parties concerned often chose to take the offensive and attempt to achieve rehabilitation in court rather than to adopt defensive behaviour outside the court. Aggressive reactions prevailed when people were suspected or accused of magic; when, for example a woman and her daughter were accused of magic, a man broke into the house of the accuser, dragged her out of bed by the hair and beat her with his fists, causing her considerable bodily harm.[15] Other slander cases related to accusations of witchcraft were even dealt with by the highest court in the empire, the Imperial Chamber Court.[16] It seems that it was less common for people to react passively and avoid conflict by keeping silent,[17] since court cases were filed even for minor insinuations. What is more, it was common knowledge that the lower courts would convict the complainants if the original accusations could not be proven – and this was, of course, difficult. Court cases, then, were very likely to be successful. People did not want to imply their guilt by behaving evasively.

The verdicts and protocols of the lower courts are found in the penal records and reach back to the mid-16th century, that is to a period for which there is little other source material for the region under discussion. Depending on the scribe, the protocols – written in low German – contain greater or lesser detail on the offence recorded; frequently, though, there are only a few lines. It is nearly always possible to determine the sex of the complainant and the defendant and the reason for the dispute; pure abuse cannot, however, be distinguished from specific allegations. The lower courts in the localities were made up of farmers under the leadership of a local magistrate, in the manorial districts they also included landowning peasants and the lord of the manor, in the towns they were made up of citizens and the town's reeve. In most cases they imposed fines.

In the period 1580 to 1730 a total of 510 slander cases (for accusations of magic) involving 615 people were filed in Schleswig, Holstein and Saxony-Lauenburg.[18] Despite the gaps in the material and all the reservations with respect to quantitative methods already noted in Chapter 3, I have chosen to apply these methods here.

A wide range of terms was used to describe alleged workers of magic. There are records of Drache [dragon], Hexe [female witch], Hexenmann [male witch], Teufel [devil], Teufelin [she-devil], Werwolf [werewolf], Wicker and Wickerin [male and female cunning folk], Zauberer and Zauberin [sorcerer and sorceress] all in the orthographical variants of the time. The term 'Drache', for example was used in connection with unlawful enrichment. The word 'Zauberin' [sorceress] was replaced abruptly after 1640 by 'Hexe' [female witch], whereas the masculine 'Zauberer' remained the male equivalent for 'Hexe' for some time after this.[19]

Men appear charged with slander in the first extant court accounts, which date back to the late 16th century. In 1592, the court scribe in the district of Dithmarschen entered the following in the penal records:

> Hans Schwarz versus Johann Rode, because he [Rode] described him [Schwarz] as a sorcerer. Johann Rode to pay a fine of one Mark.'[20]

Johann Rode had, as we can see, accused Hans Schwarz of working magic and insulted him by calling him a sorcerer. The latter had defended himself, and as Rode had been unable to prove his allegation before the court, he was obliged to withdraw his accusation and to pay a fine of one 'lübsch' Mark (i.e. one Mark in the currency of the Hanseatic town of Lübeck which was in common use in northern Germany), for unduly insulting Schwarz.

The term witch (Hexe) is predominant in the penal records, appearing 104 times as against 17 mentions of the term male witch (Hexenmeister); this is probably due to the fact that the traditional concept 'sorcerer' co-existed for a long time with the newer term 'male witch'.

In 1615, Claus Bornholdt of the district of Steinburg successfully filed charges because he had been verbally abused as an 'olde toverer', Low German for old sorcerer. In 1623, a woman by the name of Pawel Kuel from the parish of Jevenstedt called Jochim Brueß a sorcerer; in 1625 Claus Heesch suspected Hans Gosch of sorcery; in 1649 Aßmus Stubbegk abused Thomas Fries of Apenrade as 'a he-witch' (Hexen-Mann). In Eutin, a herdsman pressed charges against someone who had 'proclaimed him and his family sorcerers'. In 1681, a low court in Cismar punished Henning Rüßow because he had 'abused Jacob Bliesemer, calling him a sorcerer'. The same court convicted a woman for slander, the court scribe entering the following in the protocol: 'The wife of Joachim Brandt of Dahme abused Marx Flöker and his family, calling them sorcerer, she must pay a fine – 2 imperial thalers.' In 1689, a Hans Könke of Pinneberg paid a lesser fine (one imperial thaler) for a similar insult: he had 'abused old Jochim Könke as an old male witch'. Towards the end of the 17th century the term 'male witch' (Hexenmeister) became more frequent, gradually replacing the 'sorcerer'. Two peasants disputing in 1704 no longer used the traditional terms previously used in the court record; one of the two, a Jochim Spethmann, paid eight imperial thalers for 'insulting Claes Wensien as a male witch and not being able to prove anything'. A low court in the district of Ratzeburg passed the following sentence on a man and wife taken into custody in 1729 for accusing another person of maleficium:

> The woman accused of slander must go to prison with her husband and remain there until she can prove to the complainant that he is a male witch.[21]

In contrast to other German-speaking regions, the cumulative, learned demonology did not catch on in large sections of Holstein and Schleswig's rural population. Magic aggression was widely understood to be merely individual maleficium.[22] The explicit notion of Devil's pacts and Sabbat meetings of witches and male witches is not in evidence in the majority of the slander cases. The image here is of the spell-casting vindictive, ill-wishing neighbour known personally to the complainants; these were not the agents of the Devil endowed with special powers. In order to find out who was responsible for a theft, the inhabitants of a village in Holstein asked the Devil for help for he was supposed to have a well-known magic search instrument, the 'sieve'.[23] The Devil appears here, then, not as an embodiment of destructiveness but as a figure who, though uncanny, is not entirely negative, and can be asked for support – without the seekers of help incurring any obligation to reciprocate.

The few references which indicate an influence of learned demonology show that the uneducated people of this region had only a very vague and indistinct idea of what it involved. Seldom was anyone – man or woman – alleged to have done more than been present at 'the magic dance' (Zauberdanze) or 'on the Blocksberg' (the mythical mountain where witches' gatherings took place'). For instance, a peasant was told in strife to 'go to the Wartenberg [a local hill] and dance with the witches', a woman was called a 'Blocksberger' and told, 'May the Devil fetch you'. Accusations which testify to the influence of learned demonology such as the case of the old man who had allegedly spent a long time as a trumpeter on the Blocksberg – and it was 'this which gave him his crooked mouth' – remained almost unique.[24]

In the 510 slander cases, such elements – variously developed – of the concept of a witches' Sabbat appeared in only twelve cases. It was maleficium which was the focus of the popular witch belief.

The evaluation of slander cases brought against 615 people between 1580 and 1750s, and in which the sex of the accused was evident in 608 cases, showed that 70 per cent of those accused or maligned as workers of magic were women and 30 per cent men. Despite all reservations regarding the representative value of these figures, it is plain that magic offences were primarily associated with women, but that the proportion of men affected is by no means negligible (Figure 6.1).

Popular belief in the region and period under consideration did little to confirm the perspective of learned – and in particular Protestant demonology – and its gendering of witchcraft. There were only minor changes in the gender correlations in the course of the 17th century Figure 6.2 which presents absolute numbers of charges chronologically from 1580 to 1750 demonstrates that women were consistently more frequently affected than men.

Figure 6.3 places the spotlight on the relative numbers of men and women involved in accusations of magic. Whereas women were the objects of 70 per cent to 80 per cent of such accusations between 1580

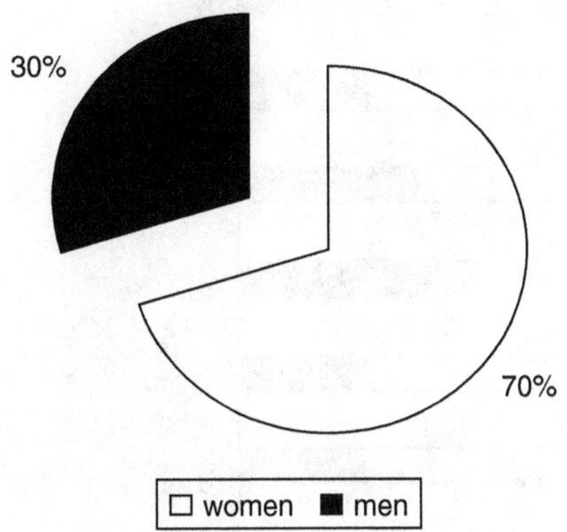

Figure 6.1 Proportions of people suspected of magic – Schleswig and Holstein: men and women, 1580–1750

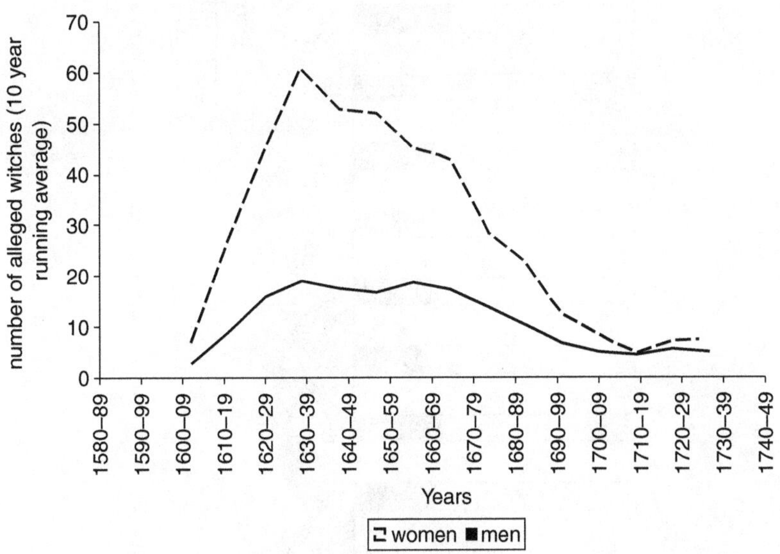

Figure 6.2 Schleswig and Holstein: accusations of magic in slander cases – proportion of men and women, 1580–1750

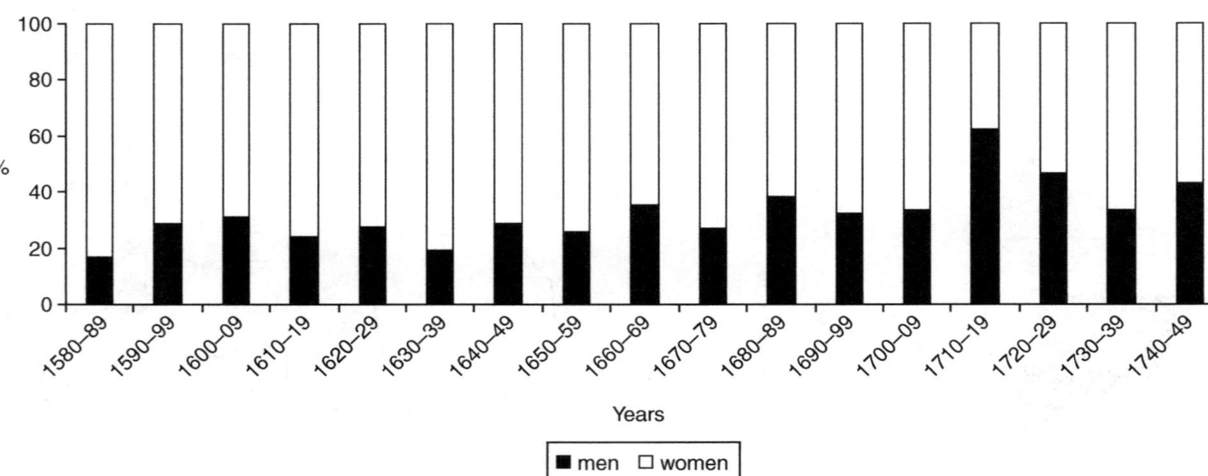

Figure 6.3 Schleswig and Holstein: accusations of magic in slander cases % of men and women, 1580–1750

and 1650, the relations changed somewhat after this date, with the numbers of men increasing.

From around 1640, but more markedly from about 1660 to 1700 the proportion of men accused of being male witches or similar was about 30 per cent. It rose to over 60 per cent at its peak in the early 18th century but it must be remembered that the absolute total fell considerably in this period. The differences in the gender profile of people maligned as witches became slightly but not significantly less marked in the 17th century, with women still representing the central figures in about two-thirds of all cases of magic-related maleficium cases in this rural region. This interpretation of the world was largely of male origin, for 69 per cent of those who accused or maligned other men and women were men. 31 per cent of those who accused women were themselves women – a proportion of some significance. From 1730 onwards, charges of magical aggression became rare as an allegation was no longer generally considered threatening.

The penal records show a wide spectrum of possible harmful magic activities which might range from curses which caused distress at sea to the theft of bees, to the disappearance – by magical means – of a labour-intensive piece of woven flax. In only about a quarter of cases is it possible to reconstruct the reasons for the legal action, as the records of charges and sentences often followed a strict scheme. In the majority of cases, the court scribe noted such general statements as, for example,

> 'Peter Brake accused Gretche Schaprogeneß of working magic.'[25]

Whilst such information does not permit us to reconstruct an actual case, there are 122 trials recorded from which the type of maleficium and the background to the charge can be deduced. Actual damage was attributed to the magical activities of certain persons, as the following typical example shows:

> 'Iver Thies is charged with having accused Peter Jacob Ovens of using sorcery to kill his wife.'[26]

In this case, a male complainant attempted to clear himself of the charge of causing death by unnatural means. For the period in question, harm to livestock and the eliciting of disease were the most frequently imagined magical offences; only in a few cases was damage to crops connected with magical destruction. The question as to whether there were gender-typical areas of magic in popular beliefs raises methodological problems: for men, in particular, the number of cases in which the type of magic offence is actually named is only 35, and thus statistically too small to make any truly reliable statements. The results of a quantitative analysis, however, do point to significant differences with respect to the types of magic attributed to men and women!

98 per cent of milk and butter magic offences, 97 per cent of offences in which harm was dealt to livestock and 92 per cent of offences involving death caused by unnatural means were attributed to women. Dishonest enrichment was attributed almost exclusively to men, 72 per cent of werewolf cases and 60 per cent of cases in which horses suffered magical harm were thought to have been committed by men. The female spheres, then, were the causing of sickness and disease and the enchantment of livestock; male domains were harm caused to horses and possessions acquired by magical, and thus unlawful, means (see Figure 6.4).

This evaluation shows that in popular belief specific offences were attributed to one or the other sex. This must, however, be viewed in the light of the roles men and women played in working life of the early modern period. In this traditional agrarian society specific fields of work were assigned to either men or women. Women's work included caring for livestock and the dairy work – at least at a subsistence level – as well as caring for the sick, and the preparation of meals. The division of labour went so far that milking was considered strictly taboo for men. The principal male domains were caring for the draught animals, such as the horses.[27] There was a tendency for this division

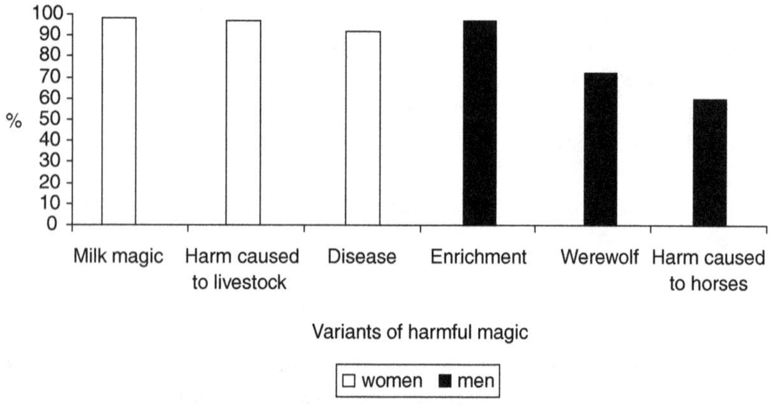

Figure 6.4 Schleswig and Holstein: classification of harmful magic in slander cases – % of men and women, 1530–1780

of labour to become less stringent in market-oriented agrarian sectors where, as in Holstein and Schleswig, new professions were arising as a result of the commercialization of dairy and livestock raising; men then broke away from traditional roles in practising their new jobs as milkers. Nevertheless, the traditional clearly defined division of labour remained in the self-supporting peasant households.[28]

As keeping horses was an extremely costly business in early modern society and horses required one and a half times the amount of food required by cows, there were not many to be found on peasant farms; indeed, oxen were used as draught animals in Holstein up into the 19th century. These facts alone mean that this male domain on the farm could not become a target for a high level of magical activities. This would indicate that the position of women in the production and reproduction process in Schleswig and Holstein played an important role in the development of magic accusations in popular belief.[29]

Slander cases give some indication of the gendering of harmful magic, which was primarily ascribed to women, but clearly also to men. However, they provide less information on its counterpart, positive or so-called 'white magic' such as protective, defensive or countermagic. The criminalization of such practices can also be tracked in Schleswig, Holstein and Saxony-Lauenburg. Activities which the authorities considered to be based on superstition, such as the so-called incantations or 'blessings' of humans, animals or crops, had been forbidden since the 16th century and anyone who practised or enlisted the help of such activities was strictly contravening legal norms. The practising of defensive magic and the seeking out of (male or female) countermagic specialists was a statutory offence liable to public prosecution; this affected both men and women. Healing magic was primarily, though by no means exclusively a female domain. The sources report avid consultations with female and male 'cunning folk'.[30]

The extant records from Schleswig and Holstein show that neither were men associated more frequently than women with 'white magic', nor, conversely, were women considered more frequent perpetrators of black magic than men. Such an ideal division between the two poles of magic fails to recognize the ambivalent character of magical potentials. Even men who were locally active as healers could easily be accused of practising magic if their protective magic had negative consequences[31] – whether or not a simple allegation would develop into a formal witch trial was at this point still undecided.

7
The Persecution of Male Witches in Holstein

> I became suspected of witchcraft and was taken to task by the authorities because I am able to invoke evil spirits to heal sicknesses
>
> (Hans Broecker, a healer, after his arrest as a male witch, June 1645)

> But I only gave my horses a potion that you can buy from the apothecary
>
> (Peter Goldbeck, a smith, after his arrest for witchcraft in November 1652)

One in four witches was male. Such a figure, however, reveals very little about the personal profiles of the individual men accused as male witches: This chapter looks behind the pure statistics to describe the persecution of men from a more human perspective, focussing on the individual fates and the conflict constellations which gave rise to the trials.

In order to portray certain characters and personalities individually the following takes a close look at the witch trials in one specific region. Taking Holstein (including Saxony-Lauenburg and Lübeck) as an example, personal profiles of accused male witches are brought to life and, most importantly, the reasons for the low proportion of males among the persecuted are discussed.

The chapter also discusses the extent to which male witches may have been drawn into witchcraft trials as subsidiary persons on account of their close relation to female witches. Finally, the chapter investigates whether male witches were brought before the courts for different offences than female witches.

Peter Steffens, a herdsman and male witch

In June 1689 Peter Steffens, a 50-year-old cowherd was arrested in the district of Ratzeburg. Several witnesses had accused him of 'Segen-Sprechen' and 'Böt[h]en',[1] that is to say of chanting magic spells and incantations, and invoking evil spirits to heal sicknesses. These witnesses (both men and women) finally admitted, after exhaustive questioning, to themselves having sought Steffen's help. As a result, the officiating local magistrate was able to determine all those who had belonged to the clientele of this man, clearly a specialized practitioner. The witness Paul Stötke from Talkau, even recounted that Steffens had wanted to teach him the art of magic and sworn him to secrecy. On the way to the trial, Steffens jumped into Ratzeburg Lake in an attempt to drown himself, but was pulled out of the water again by his escorts. This prompted the court to use torture in the trials, for in the eyes of the judge attempted suicide was tantamount to a confession of guilt. Steffens was subjected to 'a fair degree of torture which he suffered almost motionless'. This his questioners found inexplicable, looked for new circumstantial evidence and ordered torture to be applied again. Under the agonies of renewed torture Steffens still did not confess, but subsequently admitted that he 'had made a pact with Satan and given him his body and soul. A she-devil by the name of Aria had then joined him and promised to nourish him. With her help he was to continue to use his incantations to heal the sick. He had often had intercourse and committed shameful deeds with this devil'.[2] Finally, he confessed to even more: it was true that he had killed people and animals, but the Devil's pact had also meant he had been able to help many people. A certain Johann Beuthin, for example, had had trouble with his loin, that is he had probably had back pain or sciatica, and Steffens had succeeded in healing him of his affliction. He had, however, mostly employed his art in saving animals from death.

At this point in his confession the role of the she-devil changed – originally an object of lust, she became the dominant element in the relationship. Steffens reports that she had him in her grip and even beat him if he tried to desist from his evil deeds; one day when he had been going to receive the Lord's Supper again after a long period of abstinence, she had maltreated him so 'that blood kept flowing from him'.[3] On hearing this, the court decided to send the files to an – unnamed – university and to ask for legal assistance. The reply was that this was a proven case of witchcraft to be punished by burning at the stake. The high court of the principality mitigated the sentence, and this herdsman and cunning man was executed by strangling and his body subsequently burnt.[4]

This was a classic witch trial in which the court in Saxony-Lauenburg wrested from the accused a confession of all the features of the learned witch concept: maleficium worked on humans and animals, the pact and the intercourse with a devil. The only element not to appear in Steffens' confession or, indeed, in the court's questions is the witches' Sabbat, which would appear thus not to have been of interest.

Steffens – at 50, an old man in early modern terms – was one of the still widespread and popular so-called cunning folk who purported to be able to use the special skills attributed to them to heal physical and mental ailments. For the authorities, this supportive and healing magic was not white magic and thus untainted and distinct from witchcraft; on the contrary, it was associated with the deeds of the Devil as embodied on earth. In the Ratzeburg trial, the judges apportioned all forms of positive magic to the so-called black and maleficent magic. They went on to secure a confirmation of this interpretation through a confession obtained under torture. Despite his confession, Steffens attempted to save himself by presenting himself as a victim. As an object, not a subject of the events he had been forcibly prevented by the agent of evil from ending the devil's pact, for how else can we interpret his description of how he tried to go to church to receive the sacrament and hence return to the Christian community? That Steffens had internalized the moral norms of his time can be seen in the fact that he described intercourse with the she-devil as 'shameful', hoping that by conforming to what he assumed the court and establishment expected of him, he, the repentant sinner, would be able to escape the death sentence.

In stressing the passive and dependent part he played in his pact with the Devil, Steffens assumed a role frequently played by female victims of the witch-hunts. Neither the roles in which the accused were cast nor their acceptance of roles in the witch trials matched the established views on typical male and female characteristics.

In Steffens' case, neither his emphasis of his role as victim, nor his repentance, and certainly not his positive acts of healing as confirmed by the witnesses, sufficed to save the old herdsman. His confession to the Devil's pact left no doubt in the judges' minds that such connections with evil could only be punished by death.

The witch, or more appropriately male witch trial of Peter Steffens was one of many in Holstein, Lauenburg and Lübeck. Further cases will be presented later in this chapter, but first it is expedient to draw a picture of the geographical, historical and legal background to the witch persecutions in this region.

Location, the law and sources

The analysis for the period 1540–1730 is restricted to the area of present-day Holstein; unlike Schleswig to the north, this area – which consisted of the Duchy of Holstein, the Duchy of Saxony-Lauenburg, several other smaller territories,[5] and the Imperial City of Lübeck – belonged to the Holy Roman Empire of German Nations. These territories belonged to the Lower Saxon Circle in which imperial law ruled. The Duchy of Schleswig remained a Danish fief and was thus not part of the empire.

The history of Holstein cannot, however, be detached from the combined history of Schleswig and Holstein, particularly when analyzing topics such as the witch persecutions which often developed across boundaries and regions. In 1460, the joint estates of the two duchies had been given an assurance by the territorial sovereign that they would not be separated and ruled by different sovereigns. Externally, this remained true but ruptures began to appear in internal unity in the 16th century. From 1581, both the King of Denmark and the Duke of Gottorf ruled the territories but the lands each sovereign held were strewn throughout Schleswig and Holstein, making it impossible to form a pattern of enclosed territories. However, the districts ruled jointly by the sovereigns of Schleswig and Holstein, the common high court and the common recognition of the Protestant church acted like a bracket drawing the two together. This is in evidence in the witch persecutions, where jurisdiction relating to the trials was passed by the same institution for both Schleswig and Holstein. The small Duchy of Saxony-Lauenburg was unaffected by these developments, being a territory in its own right and only becoming part of the Principality of Lüneburg in 1705.

The question of sovereignty in Lübeck and surroundings was a complicated one; it is, however, necessary to outline the situation here in order to understand local witch trials. After the Reformation, members of the nobility prevented the dissolution of the Prince-Bishopric of Lübeck and elected Protestant Prince-Bishops who henceforth ruled a large territory around the town of Lübeck, where they also dispensed justice. The monasteries located within the town walls also possessed a large number of villages outside the city where they were also responsible for the dispensation of justice. As other towns of a similar size such as Metz, Nuremberg and Ulm, the Hanseatic town of Lübeck had also acquired sizeable posessions outside the town walls, where they were responsible for the jurisdiction. A few Lübeck patricians also owned manors in Holstein and administered the law on their lands.

Other than Kiel and Lübeck, no towns in Holstein or Lauenburg had been granted autonomy. In theory, the respective town councillors in these non-autonomous towns had the jurisdiction, but in practice the royal and ducal magistrates always intervened.

Holstein was the most heavily populated of these regions in the 16th and 17th centuries, with a population of 210,000 to 240,000. In the same period, the population of Saxony Lauenburg, a region with many lakes and forests, fluctuated between 20,000 and 22,000, whilst Lübeck's population ranged between 25,000 and 31,000.[6]

In the districts of Holstein and Lauenburg traditional law, passed down verbally from one generation to the next, had been in force since the High Middle Ages; this Holstein and Saxon law included the offence of sorcery which it declared punishable by death at the stake. From the mid-16th century the influence of CharlesV's central law, the Carolina, was increasingly felt. The local sovereigns modified this legal framework for their possessions in the Duchy of Holstein, introducing their own witchcraft laws. In 1567, 1572 and 1591, for example, they ordered the pronouncement of the death penalty for proven maleficium performed on the basis of a Devil's pact. For so-called 'Wickerei' (divining and counter-magic), and 'Segnerei' (healing by chanting incantations), the penalty was milder; there was still a distinction between harmful and non-harmful magic. The Danish King Frederick II added the injunctions of the 'Kalundborg Recess' to the imperial code for his lands in Holstein; these stipulated that death sentences pronounced by local courts had to be confirmed by higher judicial authorities. In practice, however, these injunctions were not always implemented. The other territorial sovereigns all tightened up their witchcraft laws at the end of the 16th and beginning of the 17th century in that sorcery offences were classified as inevitably bound up with the Devil's pact.[7] The line between white and black magic began, even at the highest levels, to fade into a universe of magic; early modern demonology had thus become established in the territorial laws of Holstein, Schleswig and Lauenburg which now exceeded in severity the provisions of imperial law in the Carolina, although they were less harsh than the cruel terms of the edicts enacted by other Lutheran territories such as the Electorate of Saxony or Württemberg.

The laws and ordinances themselves must be distinguished from the practical administration of justice. Here, too, the situation was complex and varied. In the 16th century districts of Holstein and Lauenburg, justice was administered by the so-called popular courts which were made up of a group of the more well-to-do landowning peasants, the so-called 'Hufner', who were supervised by an official nominated by the sovereign. On the large manorial estates, however, the nobles were more or less autonomous in their dispensation of justice, as were the elected councillors in the towns.[8]

During the period of the witch persecutions there were changes in the distribution of power in the various courts. Towards the end of the 16th century, the influence of the state increased markedly and was clearly reflected in the practice of the witch trials: magistrates were informed of persons suspected of witchcraft, carried out their own investigations of subjects, questioned suspects before the court convened, authorized arrests, made arrests based on charges placed by private individuals, devised the questions to be asked of suspects and witnesses in the trials, ordered households to be searched and collected evidence such as water samples. A disempowerment of the popular courts by officials appointed by the territorial sovereigns and the increasing intervention of professional jurists in the chambers and universities were, then, the chief characteristics of the peak persecution period.

This development is illustrated by the following example: the provost of the monastery in the market town of Preetz had a similar position to that accorded to the duke's and prince's magistrates and presided over the court. In 1620, he refused to recognize a sentence passed by the local popular court and sought legal support from jurists at the University of Rostock. He described the court members as 'simple and witless peasants'; the law faculty expressly condoned his viewpoint and procedure. The advisors in Rostock described the decision made by the popular court as 'barbarically opposed to all reason'. The provost was able to simply ignore the court verdict.[9]

The entire analysis of this study area is based on records to be found in the state archives (Landesarchiv) of Schleswig-Holstein and criminal court records in a number of town and city archives, which either document witch trials – in varying degrees of detail – or in which there are indirect references to persecutions. Further data came from contemporary chronicles or legal dissertations and collections of verdicts from the 17th century. The verdict books from the law faculties at the universities of Rostock and Greifswald[10] provided additional information. These different sources should be seen as complementary to one another, making it possible to document numerous witch trials.

The impact of witch trials often extended even further, particularly because the executions were major and spectacular events experienced by a large number of people, and because news of witch-hunts was recorded in various sources. The court documents usually end with the verdict, but in the cases where the executions are described, all sources mention large crowds of people who came together on such occasions. Even though the present study is based on a wide spectrum of sources – trial documents, penal records, court accounts and university verdict books – it does not pretend to have covered all witchcraft trials. For a quantitative survey, however, which aims to show tendencies, these sources are sufficient.

Trials and surges

The first verifiable witch trial took place in Kiel in 1530 when two women were charged with love magic and with causing sickness, for which they were condemned to death.[11] By 1580 at the latest the territories between the North and Baltic Seas were feeling the pressure that was driving the persecutions throughout Europe, from Scandinavia down to Italy. The number of witch trials rose steadily, reaching a climax between 1610 and 1630. In these decades, persecution of alleged servants of the Devil also increased in areas of the duchies otherwise characterized by a low level of persecution, as, for example, Dithmarschen. A third wave of persecution built up from about 1660, ebbing away in the decade after 1680. As in the rest of Europe, persecution in Holstein came in waves, that is, it was notably concentrated in certain periods. In this northern region, though, the waves did not come as sharply distinctive surges followed by marked periods of abatement; here there was more of a cumulative effect in which persecution surged, with minor abatements, to reach its height in the early 17th century. The principal phase of witch persecution was concentrated in the first half of the 17th century; of all witches accused in these territories, one in two were charged between 1600 and 1640, one in four in a period of only 20 years, between 1610 and 1630.

It was a long time before the witch-hunts really came to an end. The last classic trial to lead to an execution took place in Lauenburg in 1689; this was the trial of the herdsman Peter Steffens described at the beginning of this chapter. In 1724, a court in Rendsburg also pronounced a death sentence, but this time the trial had already shed the features of a conventional witch trial: a soldier accused of having made a pact with the Devil was beheaded according to martial law.[12] In their early stages the witch-hunts in Holstein had targeted women but they ended with the execution of men.

For the period 1530–1735, there are records of trials involving 439 people in Holstein, Lauenburg and Lübeck.[13] 317 people, that is 72 per cent, were executed, most of them by burning, 6 per cent were banished from the country and 6 per cent were acquitted; the verdicts on the rest are unknown.

There were major regional differences in the persecution structure. In the Hanseatic town of Lübeck and its territories, records survive for the period 1530–1735 of 35 trials, resulting in the execution of ten (29 per cent) people. The city councillors acquitted almost one third of all those accused, and banished approximately another third.[14] In one year – 1637 – only was there a major trial in which ten women were accused. Persecution practice in Lübeck, then, was similar to the low-level practice of other early modern large towns and cities.

The majority of all witch trials in Holstein and Saxony-Lauenburg targeted individuals, 51 per cent of the 194 trials for which records are extant. In 41 per cent of trials between two and five people were accused, in 6 per cent between six and ten, and there were only four trials in which more than ten people were charged. Holstein was as such a region of low-scale panics, in which even small chains of trials were few in number. This pattern remained typical even during the persecution surges of the early 17th century. The large-scale trials, which nonetheless took place on some estates,[15] occurred mainly (with the exception of the island of Fehmarn) outside of the more intense persecution periods. Consequently, Holstein rarely experienced any of the major chains of inter-related witch-hunts and remained a country in which even the so-called 'small panics' were in the minority.

All in all, the witch persecutions in Holstein present an ambivalent picture. On the one hand, the relatively low number of trials points to a low level of persecution; on the other hand, the high execution rates, that is the frequency with which an accusation led to the pronouncement of a death sentence, demonstrate – though these meagre words can most certainly not sufficiently describe the tragic nature of these events – how severely this alleged crime was punished. With its population of between 260,000 and 290,000, approximately 450 verifiable trials and over 70 per cent death sentences, Holstein should be categorized as a territory with a medium persecution rate. Despite the absence of mass trials and organized witch-hunting committees in the villages, the large number of individual trials – the majority of which were requested and initiated 'from below',[16] and approved and conducted by the various responsible authorities – attest to the high tension potential in early modern Holstein society and to the way this tension was released in the persecution processs.

The crime of witchcraft

Male and female witches were Devil's confederates – all persecutors in Holstein were in agreement on this point. From 1570 onwards the Devil's pact became the most decisive feature of this new crime; once it had been determined whether harm had been caused, the trials focused on the cause of the crime, i.e. the pact with the Devil. The use of magic to harm animals or cause sickness in humans had become an issue in Holstein; weather magic played a totally subordinate role here. Unlike the southern and western regions of Germany and the Austrian territories where weather magic and the damage caused to the vineyards and other crops was of prime importance, hail and thunderstorms, which occurred comparatively infrequently in the north, were evidently viewed as less threatening, and certainly not interpreted as the work of witches. The extent to which such imagined damage is a function of the geographical locality and the different values attached to the resources of this locality is illustrated in particular by the rare forms of damage imagined to have been caused by witchcraft. The magic 'sinking of ships' and destruction of fish stocks, occurred only in the immediate vicinity of the coast. Werewolf charges, that is allegations that a person had transformed him or herself into an aggressive animal, rarely cropped up in Schleswig-Holstein, an area which even in this period no longer had much dense forest cover; if such accusations were made at all, then it was in the more wooded hilly areas to the east, and certainly not in the low-lying coastal regions.[17]

The image of the witches' Sabbat as the witches' cult centre and a hatchery of all manner of harm is by no means universal in the confessions made by alleged witches in Holstein. Of the trial records which contain qualified statements on the offences, no more than one in two notes this element of collective witchcraft practice.[18]

If we assume that the witches' Sabbat pattern as it presents itself in the confessions is also a reflection on the questions or question catalogues used by the judges or the 'Fiskal' (an early form of public prosecutor), then we can also assume that the collective witchcraft image was also of minor significance to the persecutors. When, in 1682, an accused woman was asked, under torture, if she '... had been on the Blocksberg [mountain]' she answered in the negative, and the Latin 'Negat' was noted down in the records. In the course of the trial she did, however, mention a single meeting with one other woman, 'Other than this woman nobody was there, they had had nothing to eat or drink, had seen Satan, she had only danced once with Jochim Marten's wife.'[19] The court did not ask for any further names, so was obviously not interested in hearing any more denunciations: the focus of their interest was individual maleficium and not the collective deed, with the result that the case did not escalate, and ended with a sentence on two women.

Witches' gatherings sometimes consisted of only two people, the accused and the Devil.[20] The Devil's confederates did not meet, as customary, on mountains but in farmhouses and without being noticed by the inhabitants.[21] One accused woman mentioned a black mass, without being able to go into any detail about the rituals. Carstine Colscheen admitted that 'she once went to the (black) church on the same mountain'. More developed patterns came to light in a few trials, such as a trial in Pinneberg in 1611, where a woman admitted joining with others to 'fly across the [River] Elbe on wings' and serving as a 'dish-washer' at the dance.[22] Such indications that a hierarchical structure may have existed at the witches' Sabbat were rare in Holstein, as was the imagined militaristic organization of the Devil's sect. In one of the few trials where such matters arose, and which was held in 1613 on a manorial estate near Lübeck, there was talk of membership in Devil's companies.[23] When, as a result of torture, the accused in a trial in 1677 actually gave further details of the doings at the witches' Sabbat and in a continuation of the trial implicated 20 other alleged attendees, the outcome was not – as might have been expected elsewhere – mass executions, but two banishments and the burning of the principal accused.[24] The various authorities showed certain reservations in their investigations of the alleged gatherings of witches and male witches, recorded denunciations of accomplices but did not fully accept them. In 1595, the magistrate of Neumünster refused, with the support of the Duke, to allow a public proclamation of the names of people who had been denounced subsequent to a trial.[25] After a series of denunciations in trials in the district of Eutin the Prince Bishop ordered in 1668 that 'anybody accusing other people of unproven witchcraft would be subject to a fine of 30 imperial thalers'.[26] The magistrate for Bergedorf also laid down a penalty for any subject who further accused or took action against people denounced in a witchchraft trial.[27]

The law faculties at the Protestant universities of Rostock and Greifwald supported these endeavours and refused to acknowledge any relevance of such denunciations for criminal proceedings. In particular, they rejected the use of torture for these persons.[28] The jurists from these two universities dealt with about a third of all witchcraft trials between 1580 and 1630 and thus had considerable influence on the legal practice of witchcraft persecution in Holstein.

In many trials there were either no denunciations or these were restricted to a small circle of people. The largest number of people denounced in one trial was 26, in the monastic district of Preetz.[29] This is in stark contrast to single trials in other regions such as the Bishopric of Eichstätt where 484 people were denounced, the county of Baden Baden where there were 150 denunciations in 1628, the Prince-Bishopric of Bamberg with 126 denunciations or the Electorate of Trier with 150 people denounced; such figures were unknown in Holstein.[30]

The prototype trial began with alleged maleficium and ended with a confession to the Devil's pact; this applied to almost half the cases in Holstein. Maleficium, and not alleged membership of a secret coalition of Devil's agents, was the focus of attention. The witches' Sabbat as a '...powerful collective image of early modern society which so agitated the fantasy of learned theologians and the simple people alike that countless people fell victim to it'[31] found little echo in either elite or popular culture in Holstein. The tradition of the mediaeval concept of magic persisted and was basically only extended in the early modern era to include the Devil's pact and, in some cases, intercourse with the Devil. The collective witchcraft offence, the organized crime of the early modern age, remained on the periphery. In those cases in which witchcraft was interpreted as the contemplated and coordinated act of an organized group, this related to small and not large groups. These small groups were defined by family ties and not by an anonymous military organization founded solely for the purpose of practising witchcraft.

Witches: male and female

The proportion of male victims in the witch persecutions of Holstein and Saxony-Lauenburg was 12 per cent, 52 men and 387 women. This was well below the average for the entire empire. Other statistics further confirm the gender specificity in this region: Whereas 74 per cent of women tried for witchcraft were executed, the corresponding figure for men was 62 per cent, and while 25 per cent of men indicted for witchcraft were acquitted, only 10 per cent of women were released. The courts, then, were not only more avid in charging women but they also judged them more severely. Not only did men stand a greater chance of surviving a witchchraft trial, they also had a better chance of complete acquittal.

The type of maleficium of which men and women were accused also showed gender-specific tendencies.[32] 59 per cent of accused women had allegedly caused sickness or death by working magic, and 47 per cent had caused harm to cattle; in 39 per cent of cases men were accused of harming livestock, followed by magic spells cast on horses at 33 per cent. Love magic had barely any significance in Holstein, but was not considered to be monopolized by women since there are records of a man accused of this offence.

The data presented here confirm the theory that the various types of maleficium were not ascribed uniformly to men and women and that this gender-specificity was dependent on the different fields in which men and women worked and operated. Suspicions of witchcraft were related to the respective positions of men and women in the production and reproduction processes of early modern agrarian societies. However, the accusations of slander made in the context of popular culture did not entirely resemble accusations made at witchcraft trial level. The courts partially accepted these accusations, filtering them in the course of the witch trials, with the result that previously clearly distinct gender-specific patterns now became blurred.

Other gender-specific accusations were added in the course of the trials under the influence of learned legal culture: alleged male witches, for example, were never accused of so-called 'host desecration', this crime was ascribed purely to their female counterparts. Women accused of this offence allegedly failed to swallow the Eucharist – the symbol of Christ's body – at the Lord's supper, and instead removed it from their mouths to then misuse it for magic purposes. The Witches' Hammer of 1487 had already advised that women be closely observed when receiving Communion and should be told to accept the host with their mouths open and their tongues out. According to Institoris, any other usage of the host constituted 'the greatest ignominy for the Creator'.[33] Desecration of the Eucharist sealed both the pact with the Devil and apostasy from God, and further represented a ritual and symbolic mockery of the Holy Trinity, constituting a case of lese-majesty. Host desecration qualified and optimized the pact with the Devil. Men, even male witches, were not considered capable of committing such crimes, for in the eyes of the courts the male pact with the Devil did not achieve the degree of perfection and irreversibility reached by the pact that women entered with Satan.

Another area of witchcraft accusations in which different gender concepts are conspicuous is that of intercourse with the Devil. Based on the fundamental assumption that the confessions of the accused in the trials largely mirrored the ideas and fantasies of their inquisitors, it is obvious why women admitted to the sexual components of the Devil's pact. 58 per cent of the female suspects admitted having had intercourse with the Devil one or more times.[34] Only 11 per cent of men, however, admitted to this crime in the course of their trials; they admitted to pacting with the Devil and could thus be exposed as male witches, but they were far less frequently coerced into confessing to intercourse with the Devil.

An analysis of trials in which denunciations were made shows that when the initially accused men and women named potential accomplices (both male and female), the courts filtered this information and only followed up certain leads. When, in 1577, Anneke Rehben was told in a witch trial in eastern Holstein to give the name of her teacher (whereby the judge specifically used the feminine form'Lehrmeisterin'), she named a man. The manor court, presided over by the lord of the manor, however, ignored her denunciation, and convicted four women.[35] In 1593, Lene Stubbeke from the town of Rendsburg accused two women and a man, Claus Grewe, of being her accomplices. The judges summoned and questioned Grewe, but he insisted on his innocence. The case against him was dropped; the two women, however, were arrested and burnt the same month.[36] Anneke Pape from the village of Herzhorn in the Elbmarsch district was repeatedly accused of witchcraft and finally admitted having attended the witches' dance on the Brocken mountain. She maintained that she had flown with a group of people across the River Elbe on wings. She went on to name four men and four women as her accomplices, thus incriminating an equal number of people of either sex in this crime. She was even able to name the respective succubi and incubi present on the Blocksberg for this group of people and to describe the different types of maleficium they had performed or planned. The county court, however, quashed the evidence pointing to the men and confronted the accused with two of the women she had denounced; the three women were then executed.[37] In a further case in 1618, Telse Maß, a widow from Meldorf in Dithmarschen admitted to the offences of which she was accused, saying she had committed them together with one man and one other woman. Whereas there is no mention in the sources of the man being persecuted, the execution of the two women is on record.[38] In 1619, a woman, whose name is not given, was arrested in Rendsburg and denounced several 'socios', that is male accomplices (the term 'socias' in the feminine was not used). The Law Faculty at the University of Rostock, having examined the records, advised the court to close the case.[39] In 1622 the

Rendsburg town council indicted Anke Holings and her two children. Although mother and daughter were arrested, there is no further mention of the son as the case progresses. Nor does his name appear in the verdict passed by the jurists in Rostock one year after the commencement of the trial. The local court pressed the charges against the two women, but this time the legal expertise provided by the University of Rostock intervened in favour of members of the female sex, thus restricting the persecuting zeal of the lower judicial organs.[40]

This tendency to exclude men from further charges after denunciation in a witchcraft trial was particularly marked in the mid-17th century persecution practice of the monastery of Preetz. The sources provide more detail here for the monastic court recorded a large number of names obtained from the accused under torture. The accused Silke Mundes, for example, described in 1643, in one of few such cases in Holstein, precise details of the witches' Sabbat, admitted to being a member of a 'Rotte', a company or sub-division of the witches' sect, which, she said, consisted of seven persons, including her own mother, 'Erneke Lampe, a drummer, his wife Anneke Lampen ... Hans Lage and his wife Wolber ...'.[41] Only two women were condemned to death. In a later trial the accused Elsche Vollbiers was forced to provide the court with the longest list of denunciations hitherto found in research of this region; the list comprised 4 men and 22 women. A named female cowherd was executed, but no action taken to arrest the alleged men.[42]

In Gremsmühlen in eastern Holstein a woman named Anna Krüger was accused of witchcraft in 1650. After being subjected to torture she described the nocturnal gathering as resembling a peasants' feast with fried chicken, boiled pike, and cheese, followed by dancing. One of the attendees she named was a man, who was consequently questioned by the court, but denied the charges made against him. After a confrontation in court with Anna Krüger, the accused, Hinrich Wöben, finally admitted to intercourse with the Devil. In the terms of learned demonology, this presumed a prior pact with the Devil. Wöben, however, refused to admit to having practised maleficium. There is no further information available as to his fate, but it is certain that Anna Krüger, the primary accused, was burnt in 1650.[43] The trial in 1667 of Gretje Offen, a woman from the Stormarn region took a similar course; this woman described a man from the vicinity of her village as her master, a grave accusation. This man, Heinrich Wicht, she said, had procured her contact with the Devil,[44] so that she was then able to enter into the pact necessary for the practice of witchcraft. The court condemned Gretje

Offen to death by burning; it is not known what happened to the man, but it is possible that he died early on in the trial.[45]

Finally, in 1689 when a woman on an estate in the Duchy of Saxony-Lauenburg denounced several men and women as witches, the authorities took the matter in hand and completely forbade any further denunciations. The court councillors at Lauenburg proclaimed that the following was to be read from the pulpit of every church in the land:

> In the name of his Highness, his Eminence, our gracious prince and master, each and every inhabitant and subject of this duchy, whoever he may be, will be subject to a fine or corporal punishment should he, either now or at any later time, lend any belief to, or allude to the accusations made by the woman who has been flogged. Heed these words if you wish to avoid the afore-mentioned punishment...[46]

This was an indication that the era of the witch persecutions in Holstein was coming to an end. The same year, 1689, saw the last classic witch trial to end in an execution. The authorities no longer accepted denunciations, and most certainly not denunciations of men.

The selection process, in which the courts excluded certain groups of people, can also be observed in witchcraft trials in which men were involved but were not officially charged by the court. When, in 1603, a woman called Mettke Jarr was accused of pyromagic, infanticide and intercourse with her stepfather and eventually also confessed to intercourse with the Devil, the court pronounced her and one other woman guilty of proven witchcraft, and condemned them both to death. The stepfather, however, was not interrogated because of any magic he might have worked, although this would have been the obvious accusation given his close relationship to the accused, but was charged with deviating from sexual norms. He was executed – not for witchcraft but for fornication.[47] In a similar case in the county of Pinneberg a few years earlier, in 1599, the alleged witch Sielke Reder denounced five other women as guilty of witchcraft, and her husband whom she accused of a property offence. The judges appeared to think her statements sufficient and did not press any sorcery charges against the husband, despite his close relationship to the accused. They did, however, act on the denunciations of the women, with the result that eight years later they were all dead – executed by burning.[48]

The Lutheran magistrates, the town councillors, the provosts in the monasteries and the lords of the manor, whose position became increasingly important in the course of the witch persecutions, employed a gender-specific selection procedure in the trials. The pivot of their attention was the Protestant female witch stereotype. Without doubt, there were more men denounced under torture than were later convicted.

In the section on popular culture it was shown that this culture had no regular stereotypes and that the connection between gender and witchcraft was considerably less pronounced than in elite culture. In the *slander trials almost a third of those accused of sorcery and witchcraft were men,* in the *witch trials only one tenth were men.*

This gender-specific selection procedure is expressed plainly in the call made in 1587 by Samuel Meiger, a parson from a village in Holstein. In the Low German vernacular he appealed to the authorities to take a stronger stance, '... that the authorities may pass the correct judgements on the activities of the *sorceresses* and not show any outdated mercy toward them'.[49] In this appeal, Meiger excluded the possibility of any connection between witchcraft and the male sex; there was no doubt in his mind that there was an affinity between magic aggression and women.

Primary male witches

What, then, was the personal and social profile of those men who were not filtered out in this selective process prior to and during the trials, and ended up actually being accused as male witches?

Two groups can be distinguished here: the 'primary' and the 'secondary' male witches. The former were charged at the beginning of a trial series or in an individual trial, whereas the latter were the victims of a denunciation in a current trial and were drawn into the process as a result. This distinction can be made for Holstein, but not for other territories. In the serial trials which took place, for example, in Bamberg and Würzburg it is not possible to identify an initial trial or, thus, the 'primary witch' or 'primary male witch' who triggered off the chain of prosecutions.

As only a small number of men were indicted as male witches in Holstein and Saxony-Lauenburg it is possible to look more closely at the persecution of individuals.

When, in 1544, the daughter of a parson in Travemünde fell ill and died shortly afterwards, Lübeck's town council had two women arrested who were suspected of having used magic to bring about her death. But even under the agony of torture, the two women refused to confess, and, in accordance with the laws of the Carolina, they were released. The attention then turned to one Cornelius van Dorne, the man who had originally aroused suspicion of the two women. Possibly under commission from someone else, though this is not certain, van Dorne had used his magic crystal ball – a device for detecting otherwise hidden associations – to reveal the illness of the parson's daughter as resulting from magic aggression. The council ordered van Dorne's arrest and, after questioning, he admitted to using magic and so having violated the first of the Ten Commandments; he was released on an oath to refrain from vengeance.[50]

People such as van Dorne were to be found frequently in 16th century Holstein. A few years after this case, an executioner beheaded a 'Toverer mit einer Cristallen', a diviner or soothsayer with a (magic) glass ball which he used as a horoscope. He had been tampering with his firearm and had shot a woman by mistake. The town councillors of Oldenburg condemned this man, Melchior von Wurtzenberg (possibly an imaginary name) to be beheaded, the usual penalty for manslaughter. The records of the town scribe, however, indicate that manslaughter was not the verdict: the council had granted him a reprieve of his original sentence, allowing him an honourable execution by the sword, although the verdict of burning at the stake had been passed on the grounds of his supposed magic activities.[51]

In 1558, two mariners, Hans Schomaker and Hans Steneke also made an oath to refrain from vengeance. They were 'suspected of the dire crime of magic' because they 'tried to use many profane and unnatural means'.[52] The council had them both arrested, and tried unsuccessfully to press charges. They were unable to prove that harm had been caused – indeed this may well not even have been the mariners' intention. The two mariners had obviously hoped to ward off the threat of danger by pronouncing a magic blessing or incantation. In the light of their jobs, it is quite feasible that they might have performed such a ritual to prevent a storm at sea. The council released both men after they had sworn an oath recognizing their arrest as legitimate. These trials demonstrate the reactions of people in Lübeck to such occurrences: person and problem were banished, disposed of to the outside world. This pattern did not change in the ensuing years of the witch persecutions; Lübeck remained a town with few persecutions. In cases of widespread suspicion, the council simply banished the accused from the city after they had been obliged to swear an oath to refrain from vengeance subsequent to their release.

In 1588 a Claus Martensen was denounced as an accomplice by several women in the monastic district of Preetz. Under torture he confessed to the crimes of which he was accused. Among other things, he admitted flying to the Blocksberg mountain 'on a beer barrel'.[53] At this point, the provost of the monastery intervened in the trial with the assistance of the Protestant jurists from the Law Faculty in Rostock and began, in contrast to the trials of the two women, to discuss the role torture had played in Martensen's confession. The provost spoke persuasively to Martensen, now already condemned as a male witch, and the following is written in the court records:

> After the verdict had been pronounced, he professed when pressed hard by Provost Diederich Blome that he had only contrived everything under the pain of the torture or had repeated what had been said to him. This statement induced the provost to take the case to the Law Faculty at Rostock. They then decided that he was to be released from custody under oath to refrain from vengeance – although the farmers had convicted him.[54]

Some years later, in 1612 and in Mölln, a town on Lübeck's territory, Gorries Egge, a self-confessed witch-doctor, speaker of healing blessings and incantations (Segner), and invoker of evil spirits (Böter) described himself as the pupil of a woman burnt for witchcraft and of her son. This time the authorities in Lübeck no longer dispensed with this problem in a brief inquiry followed by a release; instead they initiated a true inquisition trial. As the main incriminating witness, Egge had made a statement against a woman charged with witchcraft and as a result became a suspect himself. The Lübeck council dropped the charge against the woman when it became known that another inhabitant of Mölln had encouraged Egge to make his statement, indeed had even paid him to do so. Egge was subjected to a public whipping and then banished from the town.

Witch-doctors who denounced other people – primarily women – as witches often found themselves at the start of a long chain of trials. As the Egge case shows, the magical expert became a witch, himself banned from his homeland. Here, no mass trial ensued since such a development was prevented by Lübeck's policy of banishing workers of magic from its territory.[55]

Lübeck continued to pursue this policy in the 17th century, although not always consistently, as the following case from 1645 shows. Hans Broeker, known as the 'Böter', the man who invoked evil spirits as a means of healing, had fled from the estate of his lord to Lübeck where he had publicly offered his services as a worker of protective or supportive magic. Not surprisingly, he was suspected of magic himself, but when questioned by the officials of the town, his replies were obviously not quite what they had expected. The two mayors ordered his arrest and closed the case traditionally by having him swear the oath to refrain from vengeance[56] and banishing him from Lübeck, without a formal witch trial ever being held.

In 1604, the Lübeck Cathedral Chapter made a decision to pass a death sentence. In the cathedral's marriage register, there is the following succinct entry: 'a "houseman", a male witch has been burnt'.[57] In the towns, the term 'houseman' was used to describe either a male house servant or a tower look-out, a public servant who had to warn of any fires they might see from their look-out posts in the town's towers.[58] The tower look-outs were classified as belonging to a dishonourable trade and, despite an imperial law passed in 1578, were not organized in guilds. They were generally considered 'disreputable'.[59] as we are told by the first German universal encyclopaedia of 1743. It is not possible to tell, however, whether this particular condemned male witch was a servant of a Lübeck citizen or one of those who belonged to the unintegrated and reputedly disreputable section of society.

Another trial of a male witch ended in the death sentence. In 1613, according to a communication composed by a notary after the event, there arose in Trenthorst, an estate near Lübeck, 'a dreadful uproar against Laurens Nuppenow...that he had made superstitious prophecies, cast magic spells and invoked evil spirits for the peasants, though all this was strictly forbidden by imperial law'. When the accused actually admitted this to the parson after listening to his 'grim sermons on repentance', Joachim Wettken, the gentleman owner of the estate, intervened and opened a formal witchcraft trial.[60] He had Nuppenow arrested and questioned again until he admitted to practising as a so-called 'Wicker', a cunning man, and also denounced six local women for similar offences. When confronted with Nuppenow before the court, they disputed his claims. Wettken applied torture, whereupon Nuppenow confessed that he had 'encountered the Devil in person in the shape of a comely man in black and holding a red apple in his hand. He told him that he would teach him a better art so that he would fare better.'[61] This testimony of Nuppenow's espoused the Biblical image of the apple and Eve's seduction. In his case, however, it was a man and a diviner who the Devil won over with the Biblical fruit – an indication that some persecutors at least considered certain members of the male sex unable to resist the seductive powers of the Devil. In agreeing to this offer of the Devil's, Nuppenow admitted having made a pact with evil and was thus a proven male witch. However, this confession also shows that he considered his work as a diviner, portrayed here as an art of lesser importance, to be a harmless offence unconnected with the Devil. In his dual role as lord of the manor and judge, Wettken used the 40-question strong catalogue to try and find further evidence of magic practices. Laurentz Nuppenow admitted to having had sexual intercourse with a woman who had been burnt some time previously as a witch, and also with a cow, and thus to sodomy. He also admitted practising extensive maleficium, admitting attempted murder – or the causing of sickness by magical means – of Thomas Wetken's wife, other local landlords and even of the magistrate of the nearby district of Trittau.

Having confessed to responsibility for the death of cows, hens and horses he finally also admitted to attending the witches' Sabbat. A jurist present at the trial noted:

> And then they gathered at their Blocksberg near Schlamersdorf (a nearby village) and at this place he, Nuppenow, had intercourse with the Devil and pledged himself to him. He vowed to renounce the name of God and no longer be faithful to Him. While forming this alliance they had drunk pure wine and handed each other the glasses over their shoulders.... At this alliance the following were present: Annette Gottkers of Poggensee, she who had first proposed that he should become acquainted with these devilish arts; also Anneke Hagemans of Poggensee whose mother had been burnt six or seven years previously; then he declared that Cathrine Wollnus of Siebenbäumen, old Wybcke from Reinfelde, old Lene Spirings and old Kohlersche of Bockfelde had held their Blocksbergs in the Schuckenburg Heath (wasteland near the estate R.S.).[62]

Three of the women he named were subsequently arrested, and confessed under torture to having committed these offences together. In their confessions they repeat – sometimes word for word – the statements made by Nuppenow, which would imply that the confessions were extorted from them under torture. The landlord even wrenched a confession out of one of the accused, at one time Nuppenow's employer, to the effect that she had acted as his teacher. Another woman admitted to destructive practices as a werewolf. On the basis of these confessions, the three women and Nuppenow himself were burnt at the stake.[63] This trial differed from many others in that here the focus was on a male witch who, through his extorted confession, had incriminated the women who were subsequently accused of the same offence. According to the information he himself gave, Nuppenow had been the servant of an artisan in Kiel and later of a widow on a farm near Trenthorst, and as such he belonged to the lowest strata of early modern society.

In another case which took place in Rendsburg in 1613 a man was also accused and sentenced to death. One Heinrich Plön was accused of pyromagic and it was reported in a chronicle '... that he caused a fire larger than had been heard of for a long time'.[64] The town's council had him executed.

When, in 1620, a court in Preetz accused a man by the name of Klaus Klindt of witchcraft and sentenced him to torture, the monastery authorities came to his aid. The provost refused to accept the decision of the court and appealed to the jurists in Rostock. The latter were unable to find sufficient evidence for a charge and, as the higher court, ordered this alleged male witch to be released,[65] an intervention and decision which was not seen in comparable trials of women.[66]

In 1635, Jochim Emecke, cowherd of the town of Plön was suspected of witchcraft. He had for a long time been known locally as a healer, and had often been asked for help when both people and livestock fell ill.[67] The herdsman was not a member of the indigenous population, had worked as a servant in other places and had attracted attention in Plön principally because he had challenged the omnipotence of God. Other than healing, he had also been known as a 'witch finder'. In this role, in the spring of 1635 he ascribed a livestock epidemic to magic aggression and accused a woman by the name of Engel Wulf, of whom he had long been suspicious, of having caused it. Before the court, a witness reported the following conversation which had taken place after his cow had become ill and Emecke had been called:

> 'As for his wife', the witness says, 'the cowherd told her there were many evil people in the world and had she anything to do with them? She replied she hoped not and knew not that she had anything to do with such a person. The cowherd then asked if the cow had approached anyone. She answered that the cow had moved onto the canvas that was spread on the ground and seemed comfortable. The cowherd asked who the canvas belonged to and she answered that it was Wulf's, whereupon he replied immediately that he now had enough.'[68]

In this conversation the cowherd had clearly found the evidence he was seeking as a 'witch-finder'; he interpreted the cow's behaviour as indirectly pointing to the person responsible for the animal's illness. In the course of his examinations of sicknesses he had repeatedly alluded to the magic works of Engel Wulf.[69] This time he expressed his suspicions in public and the authorities in Plön felt obliged to react, albeit cautiously. Both the accused and the accuser were subjected to the ducking test. When this turned out positive for them both, the town council decided to employ torture and interrogation. Wulf admitted to maleficium and the Devil's pact it involved, Emecke only 'Wicken' and 'Böten', divining and invoking evil spirits to heal the sicknesses they had caused. During the trial he also gave a more precise description of his previous deeds: he had healed a potter by the magic ritual of cutting his fingernails during the night and throwing them into a river. Emecke also admitted, however, having disputed God's rule over the world. He attempted to play down his statement and deny that it was meant seriously: 'A person who can work magic sends out his spirit. That God no longer rules the world, that was just something he had said without meaning it.'[70]

This can only be understood in the context of the cowherd's life and work. He did not interpret circumstances in a theological sense; to discuss the omnipotence of God and the function of the Devil was alien to him. On the contrary, he as a witch-finder interpreted events and damage from the perspective of popular magic. As nature was endowed with countless spirits which could also cause harm and which worked on behalf of supposed witches, a balance in the form of protective countermagic had to be created. He obviously considered that part of dispelling any evil magic included tracking down the supposed cause of the evil spell, as well as the banishing of any magical aggresion itself. It was for this reason that he collected evidence against Wulf, who tried frantically to defend herself. The witch-finder, then, saw himself in the role of an investigator working to assist the indecisive authorities. In popular culture he worked as a 'witch-doctor'. It is not difficult to interpret his actions as forms of analogical magic; for example, in removing the fingernail clippings, seen as parts of the entity body, he was attempting to cause the illness itself to disappear. In this function, Emecke was a healer. In cases where the illness was interpreted as the result of a spell, the witch-banner became a witch-finder. Doubtless, he also played the role of a private witch-hunter, denounced fellow human beings, in this case, a woman, and because of his accusations and the magic procedures he employed in his investigations, himself fell under suspicion.

Wulf and Emecke were executed after the trial, which lasted less than a week and a half. The woman was burnt as a witch and the man, who had not admitted to maleficium, was beheaded for blasphemy stemming from his divining and the other magic rituals he employed, in which he had abused the name of God. In the verdict, the Plön town councillors quoted Article 106 of the Caroline Code, although this article allowed the judges to use their discretion as to whether the death penalty should be imposed or not. The court, however, adhered to the death penalty, although they did not equate divining and witch banning with witchcraft – beheading, unlike death by burning to which Wulf was subjected, was considered an honourable punishment.

In the summer of 1652, Claus Wegner, a subject of the duke, complained of the death of his horses, naming a smith, Peter Goldbeck of Tremsbüttel, as the possible cause. He had asked him to help heal one horse, but by late summer an epidemic had spread through the region.[71] An official who had for many years suspected Goldbeck of working harmful magic, but had until this occurrence had no tangible reason to indict him,[72] saw in this denunciation a reason to attack. Goldbeck, who was 36 years old and had moved to the district 20 years previously, was arrested and interrogated. Other witnesses further incriminated him as using magic incantations and invoking evil spirits as a means of healing. He denied any guilt and declared, 'he had only given his horses a potion to drink which could be obtained from the apothecary', obviously trying to describe the resources he had used as natural medications available to anyone. The local magistrate decided to use torture, and the smith confessed that he had given his own livestock a magic blessing and communicated with the Devil such that he had 'surrendered to him'. In the minds of his persecutors this revealed him to be a male witch. Goldbeck denounced nobody, and was not asked to do so; the trial was not extended to include other people. The duke's councillors in Gottorf commuted the sentence of burning to one of beheading. In so doing, they supported the proposal of the official in Tremsbüttel who favoured this coup de grace because Goldbeck 'has several well-behaved children'.[73]

In 1654 Marcus Schneekloth was denounced by 'all the inhabitants'[74] and subsequently arrested for alleged witchcraft in Stakendorf, a village belonging to the monastery of Preetz. Schneekloth was an old man[75] and stated that he had 'not learnt a trade'. In the source material he appears as a broken, almost weak-minded character. He soon confessed under interrogation to the crimes of which he was accused. Whether or not torture was employed cannot be discerned from the brief trial record, although the presence of an executioner would indicate that he had been subjected to such agonies. Schneekloth admitted to maleficium, saying that he had killed cows and foals in his neighbourhood

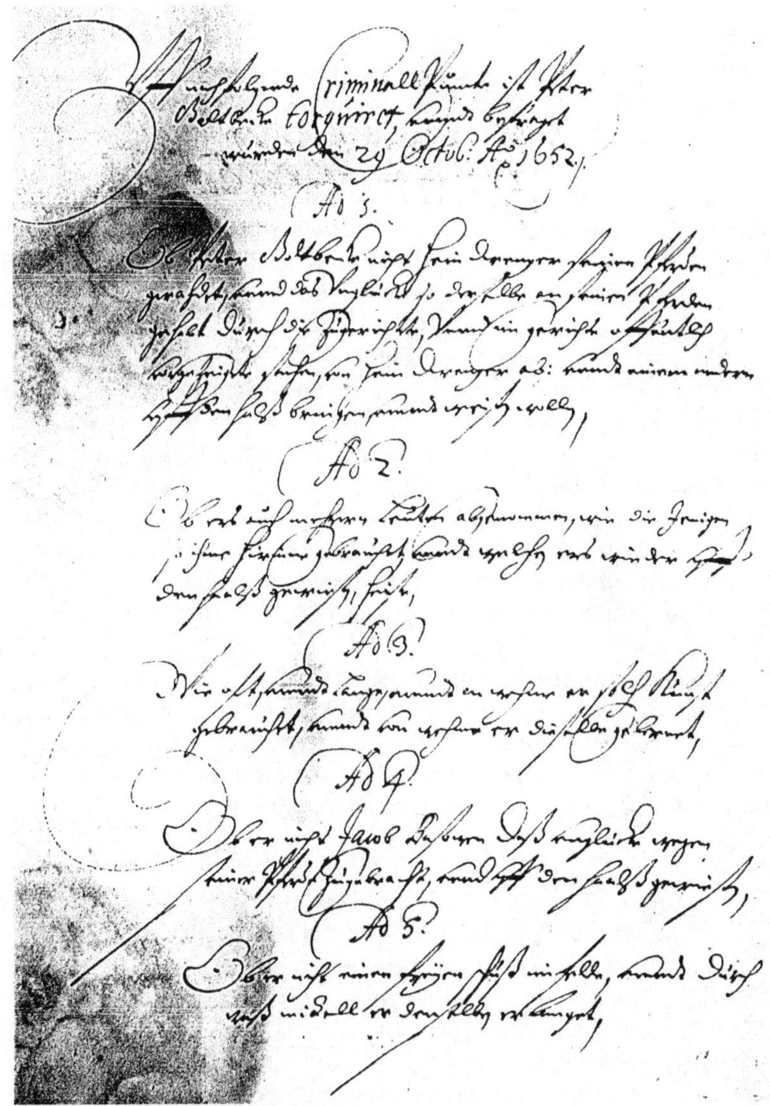

Illustration 7.1 Record of the torture of a male witch: the blacksmith Peter Goldbeck from Holstein confesses here to practising professional counter-magic to heal horses, and to having made a pact with the Devil (Records of 1652, Landesarchiv Schleswig-Holstein 7/1758)

and in the village. As considered typical of male magic aggression in Holstein, horses were his primary target. In the court's view he had either killed them or cast a spell on them to make them kick out in aggression. At the end of the trial the old man was in a state of mental turmoil. He begged to be put to death for 'he could not be saved before his death was ordered'.[76] He named his dead mother as his teacher; she had, he said, procured him a devil, a servant, to help him survive. He gave the devil's name as 'Quadfas' and this Quadfas, he said, had demanded a permanent alliance with the realm of evil in the form of a baptism bond. The name 'Quadfas' is derived from the Middle High German 'Qu[a]ad', i.e. 'bad' or 'evil' and 'fas', i.e. he or she speaks,[77] and Schneekloth thus denoted the Devil as someone who spreads evil. Since he had confessed to working maleficium on horses, Schneekloth was condemned to death and executed. As in the Goldbeck case, no further accomplices were named, although this time other trials – of women[78] – did follow in the same district a month later, so that Schneekloth's trial must be seen as one of a wave of trials in the Preetz district.

In 1668 there was again a trial involving herdsmen. Marx Dankers and Klaus Grundt from the vicinity of Segeberg were brought before the court as alleged male witches. Dankers accused his colleague Grundt of being the initiator of their common pact with the Devil:

> Whereupon in the first night a spirit had come to him in the form of a woman and by the name of Earl Wolmer who promised to help them. They had conspired with this spirit and had intercourse for four years. In this time they had caused great harm to horses, pigs and cows using black seed and black grease which they had been given by the Devil.[79]

With this testimony he confessed to sealing a pact with the Devil, to intercourse with the Devil and to the resultant maleficium. His confession was also a severe incrimination of his colleague Grundt. After his arrest, the latter confessed to the same offences and to having slept not only with the succubus but also with his cattle 'driven on by his demon', thus also admitting sodomy, a crime punishable by death. His neighbour's daughter alleged that she had witnessed this crime.[80] Grundt's reasons for agreeing to this satanic bond were that his livestock were always escaping and the Devil had promised to use his supernatural powers to prevent such catastrophes. Unlike other witchcraft cases, however, the herdsman was not the master of this relationship: he was delivered up to the fangs of evil and completely at the mercy of the

Devil, for 'had he also seduced Marx Dankers, this would also have been against his will, all the more so as the Devil pretty much compelled him to do it'.[81] Both men confessed to attending the Sabbat, and denounced their own wives, Grundt also his 14-year-old daughter. Grundt himself died while under arrest; Grundt's wife and Marx Danckers and his wife were executed, while Grundt's daughter was placed in the care of the church and threatened with burning should she repeat the offence.

It was quite a different type of maleficium of which the monastic court in Preetz accused the 40-year-old shoemaker and widower Andreas Brehmer in 1681. Shoemakers were occasionally ostracized, were thought of as infamous and having a bad reputation.[82] A woman accused Brehmer of 'having fastened a lock at her wedding' so that intercourse caused her such great pain that it was impossible for her husband to 'have carnal knowledge of her'.[83] The responsible public prosecutor opened an official investigation of this denunciation, found several witnesses and ordered a physical examination of the complainant, Magdalena König. The three women who conducted the examination found her to be 'in the same condition as any other woman of her years', i.e. she seemed to have no physical abnormalities. This was sufficient evidence for the court to decide to interrogate Brehmer to determine whether he had worked harmful love magic. He did indeed admit to having brought a lock with him to the wedding ceremony, but denied maleficium. The love magic the court assumed to have taken place belonged in the category of analogue rituals; a ritual was assumed by its similarity to a counterpart to be able to cause a certain occurrence or event. In this case, it was based on the idea that at the moment of marriage a knot was tied to make the bridegroom impotent or, in the analogies of magic thinking, to close the vagina and thus prevent further sexual intercourse. This love magic only worked fully if the lock was made permanently inaccessible and, for example, thrown into the water. In Brehmer's case the court sent the files to the Law Faculty at the University of Kiel, which had been established in 1665, asking for an expert opinion. The jurists in Kiel decided in favour of allowing the use of torture to determine the truth of the matter, and Brehmer was subjected to third degree torture by means of some of the most horrific instruments: the executioner used thumbscrews, a Spanish boot and finally the rack on which the victim's body was pulled asunder.[84] Brehmer still did not confess. At this point in the trial, a defence lawyer commissioned by Brehmer, presented an expertise written by two doctors in Kiel who certified that from a medical point of view a 'redress by natural means was possible'[85] in this case, and thus a reversal of the evil seemed feasible. The court in Preetz condemned the shoemaker although he had not confessed, but mitigated the sentence as he had not worked the magic to the full: it had, of course, not been possible to prove that he had disposed of the lock and thus the power of the maleficium only reached half its potential, that is, it was reversible. Brehmer had to swear an oath to refrain from vengeance, was publicly whipped and banished from the country.[86]

Brehmer's trial shows that the practice of love magic was not considered an exclusively female activity. It did, however, require extraordinary magic skills, and in all other witchcraft trials in which it played a role was specified by witnesses to have been practised by professional cunning men.[87] This would indicate that Brehmer either worked as a cunning man or was reputed to do so.

Joachim Krohn, an 88-year-old man who lived alone, was denounced as a magical expert. The ecclesiastical court at Lauenburg, a court which was empowered to order a secular court to prosecute, took up the case. In the course of these investigations, however, Krohn produced letters in which the witnesses for the prosecution retracted their statements. Krohn admitted being able to heal, but, he argued, he had only used natural means and occasionally phrases from Christian prayers. The more specific description of his arts, however, showed that in a sick case, for example, he worked with rituals which his contemporaries could not sanctify as Christian. The pastor investigating the case noted down without further comment the following healing ritual used by Krohn:

> Magnus Zimmermann's servant also came to him with a burning belly, as he called it. He first advised him to have a drink of some water in which someone had drowned. Then he was to collect his urine in a jug and to pour a little of it over a sword, axe, hatchet etc. into a fire and wait for it to burn. The rest he was to spoon over the roof...[88]

Yet even this disclosure of healing procedures, in which it is easy to recognize the analogue notion of countermagic was not to Krohn's detriment.[89] In 1681, after this report had been made, the Protestant consistory closed the case. Now, at the end of the 17th century and in the perception of this court, divining and witchcraft began to be seen again as two separate issues.

In the trial of the cowherd Peter Steffens in Ratzeburg in 1689, however, this view was not yet apparent. In addition to practising as a cunning man, he admitted to the Devil's pact and intercourse with the

Devil and, in the last classic witchcraft trial in the region, was consequently sentenced to death and executed.[90]

The scepticism which was emerging at the end of the 17th century by no means implied that the entire witch paradigm suffered a radical loss of plausibility. Indeed, into the early 18th century it continued to be applied in Holstein to a specific male profession: to soldiers. In Glückstadt in 1714 the 18-year-old soldier and sailor Johann Nagel made a treaty with the Devil which he wrote with his own blood and in which he described Satan as 'Brother Devil'. Nagel's commitment to the Devil did not long remain a secret, and once discovered he was placed under arrest. He justified his Devil's pact with the harsh treatment and beatings he suffered in the Danish army. After an extensive trial, the officer responsible decided not to plead for a witchcraft trial to be opened; instead he gave the young soldier over to the Protestant pastor in Glückstadt because, he argued, Nagel was not known as a blasphemer and thus this was not a severe case or offence.[91] The witchcraft pattern had here already been reduced to a combination of a Devil's pact with magic aimed at securing personal gain and no longer with maleficium, and for this reason it was not difficult for the Danish officer to reject the idea of convening a witchcraft trial.

In 1721 Johann von Acken formed a pact with the Devil, so that the latter would procure him a discharge from the army which his father had forced him to join because of his insubordinate behaviour. A military court charged the 17-year-old soldier with forming a Devil's pact and sentenced him to run the gauntlet 24 times. Such sentences could result in death and were on a par with executions. The responsible pastor eventually begged 'Christ with all his heart to accept this lost sheep'. The judge certainly took these words to heart and the accused was sentenced to a typical disciplinary measure; this shows that by this time it was of far greater consequence and merit to win sinners back to the Christian fold than it had been during the period of the classic witch-hunts.[92] The same soldier appears, however, to have formed another pact with the Devil. A chronicle of the year 1724 written by an anonymous citizen of Rendsburg reports of a new Devil's pact in the Rendsburg garrison. This was also discovered and it is possible, though not certain, that the military court found the young soldier from Rostock guilty of a repeat offence and thus sentenced him to death under martial law. After he had been publicly beheaded and the pact burnt for all to see, the town preacher was obliged by royal order to hold a cautionary sermon pointing out the soldier's sinfulness.[93]

By the time of these trials, the persecution of witches, or rather of male witches, and the crime of witchcraft were no longer taken in the administration of justice to be an offence liable to public prosecution; persecution now only occurred in certain areas of society and under special conditions. The source cited above refers specifically to the court martial. The soldiers' pacts with the Devil may be interpreted as a reaction to a disciplinary offensive in absolutist armies which were known not to be fully operative due to the large number of desertions. It was in this context that, in the middle of the Great Northern War, plans had been implemented to reorganize the Danish army through the deployment of new units and large-scale campaigns in Mecklenburg to attract men to join up.

Herdsmen, blacksmiths and even a pirate

The core group of primary male witches in Holstein's early modern society was to be found among the cunning folk. These people practised a wide spectrum of magically connotated incantations, astrology and also herbal medicine for the benefit of their customers.[94] This was not their main occupation however; they practised their healing arts as a secondary profession or trade. The fact that they were persecuted has to do with the fading of the distinction between 'divining' and 'witchcraft', a distinction which was no longer accepted by Holstein authorities in the 17th century. After tolerating them for many years, both secular and non-secular authorities began in the 16th century to lay down punishments for the widespread practice of offering help or personal advantage by means of incantations or rituals. As early modern demonology gained in acceptance, the tarnish of the Devil's pact cast its shadow over popular practices. In the opinion of the Holstein authorities, the wide spectrum of magic practices bore the characteristics of witchcraft, and witchcraft was inextricably bound up with the renunciation of God and with a subversive aggression which targeted the Christian community.

Numerous herdsmen counted among these magic folk; as early as the 11th century, Burchard of Worms had associated herdsmen with the art of magic and ascribed the practice of healing magic and incantations to them. He also castigated their clientele, evidence that the supposed skills of these herdsmen found wide recognition and custom.

The trade of the herdsman was one of the lowest that early modern society had to offer in terms of work, remuneration and esteem. Since the 14th century the trades of herdsman, executioner, grave digger, knacker and miller had been considered dishonourable; they were socially marginalized, refused the rights of citizenship and excluded from the guilds. Villagers and townspeople alike avoided these people and – in the cases where they were given permission to marry – their families. Frequently, the only social contacts available to them were their colleagues out in the pastures beyond the settlements. Such discrimination did not originate with the authorities; indeed, attempts were even made to counter such non-integration, as evidenced by explicit imperial laws passed in 1548 and again in 1577. The fact that the decrees were repeated shows that the attempt at a formal reintegration of these groups met with resistance, the stigma attached to these professions being so firmly and deeply anchored in the minds of the population. The children of herdsmen were excluded from guilds as late as the mid-18th century so that it remained impossible for them to follow any other than the profession of their fathers or grandfathers.[95] It was not only the loss of honour, which also entailed the loss of companionship, but also the permanent threat to their material existence incurred by the seasonal nature of their work which forced herdsmen into a position on the edge of society.[96]

Yet, villagers in particular often sought contact with herdsmen on a certain level. Through their permanent dealings with animals, their lives and work close to nature, families built up rich knowledge of weather and medicinal and healing practices which was passed down through the generations; what is more, the services of the herdsmen were to be had cheaply – thanks to their status as a group not integrated into the estates of early modern society. In 1735 the first 'Universal Encyclopaedia' to appear in German wrote that herdsmen 'are said to know a good deal about the treatment of sick animals'.[97] Clearly, then, there was a connection between the perceived ability of herdsmen to heal humans and animals and their social position and work. Their help was often sought clandestinely, since to be caught as a customer of a despised outsider meant a loss of honour and reputation. In this sense, those seeking help were equally as averse to the herdsmen as they were hopeful of the efficacy of their skills. The contradictory nature of the herdsmen's position – socially and morally they were outsiders, but as healers they were useful and commanded a certain respect – meant that they were generally treated with a mixture of disgust and awe.[98] Considering the healing work they practised as well as their relative mobility, the lack of social control arising from the solitariness of their work and their near-exclusion from the communication webs of the villages and towns, it is not surprising that people began to fantasize about the lives and skills of the herdsmen. Successful healing cases and the herdsmen's singular means of existence became pervaded with ideas of magic and exaggerated; they became uncanny figures. The rural population had long begun to fear them because the witchcraft discourse had augmented their suspicion that the magic skills the herdsmen doubtless employed could be turned against their customers. They began to be accredited with a certain role, as seen in the Holstein cases: in the sense of a self-fulfilling prophecy, they began to accommodate this role in their own behaviour. In Holstein, as in other regions, herdsmen formed a specific target group in witchcraft charges[99] and the percentage of this profession among the males accused was disproportionately high.[100]

In addition to the herdsmen, the smiths also practised in a medical function[101] and were renowned as excellent healers. In Holstein, however, their competence was considered to be strictly limited to the healing of horses. Like the herdsmen, they played the role of magic and countermagic specialists and ascribed sicknesses of horses to human magical aggression.[102]

A second group consisted of people who were of fixed abode but who belonged to marginal social groups and as such were stigmatized and excluded from the estates of early modern society. Some of these overlapped with the group of the cunning folk, their classification as 'dishonourable' being the issue they had in common.

Anyone classed as 'dishonourable' was socially blemished, was avoided to the point where people shirked physical contact with them, and on the whole thoroughly despised. Members of this group were denied the chance to fulfil the norms of social decency: they lived 'indecently' and in cases of conflict they were often suspected of dishonest motives, including magic.

Formal criteria can be used to describe one further group among the 'primary' male witches: people who were either criminal or who were accused of being so, as the following case illustrates.

In 1593, a number of pirates imprisoned (and later executed) in Copenhagen denounced the citizen of Lübeck, Roloff Janeke, as an accomplice of theirs. Janeke's task, they said, had been to win new pirates for the group and to pass on messages and information. It was not until ten years later that Lübeck's town council considered evidence against him to have been substantiated, and had him arrested. Janeke, however, denied any connection with piracy. The authorities then accused him of additional offences, for he had committed 'all manner of despicable and forbidden devilish arts'. He was accused of having used a special magic ointment to magically charge his own weapons and make them particularly effective; of inexplicably managing to avoid an earlier arrest; of using his connections with the Devil to find hidden treasures and open doors without keys to commit major thefts. Finally, he was accused of 'persuading women to commit unchaste deeds'.[103] The spectrum of offences, then, ranged from criminal offences to disregard of sexual norms to witchcraft crimes. Without delay, the authorities in Lübeck decided to employ torture; Janeke was subjected to torture twice, but admitted nothing. The council debated whether to apply this painful procedure once more, but at this point in the trial it seems that Janeke's relatives intervened. Clearly they were not without fortune and standing, and Janeke himself was not merely an inhabitant of Lübeck but enjoyed the rights of a citizen of the town. The relatives demanded that jurists at a university be consulted for legal advice.[104] The senators refused and applied, for reasons which can no longer be determined, to the Imperial Chamber Court, an institution which could be consulted in the case of a breach of formal law. It is to be supposed that the motive behind this decision was that the councillors wanted to avoid being accused of breaking the law after they had ordered a prisoner to be tortured more than once. In March 1604, the messenger from the Imperial Chamber court arrived in Lübeck and handed over to the councillors a detailed letter acknowledging the legality of their appeal and the lawfulness of their procedure in the case of Janeke. As the prisoner had not made a confession and as he had 'previously demonstrated his humility'[105] the lawyers in Speyer ordered Janeke's release, for he had not been proven to be a pirate or to have used magic. At the same time, he was sentenced to pay the costs of the trial to the amount of only ten Imperial thalers. Janeke was then free.

This was the only trial in the entire study area in which a person was suspected of the weapon magic described by the authors of the Hammer of Witches as a typical male crime. Janeke, the alleged pirate and male witch, was saved by his social status because, prompted by the influence of his relatives, the highest court prevented this criminal case from being transformed into a witchcraft trial. After the original charge had been placed, the court in Lübeck had obviously intended to do just this for they had interpreted the offences as magic actions and as such in contemporary thought only realizable in connection with a Devil's pact.

In 1612, 70-year-old Jochim Witte, a member of the lower class, was abused by the district reeve as a sorcerer and thief. Witte took this accusation before the court in an attempt to free himself of suspicion. Once in court in Bergedorf (a place ruled collectively by the Hanseatic towns of Hamburg and Lübeck), however, the roles of complainant and

Illustration 7.2 The male witch and common criminal: a leaflet from 1666 shows a male witch signing the Devil's pact in an open field. In his confession he claimed to have used witchcraft to paralyze children so that they were no longer able to walk and had to crawl around, and to have gone on to commit other crimes such as attempted manslaughter (top right) in southeast Germany. (In: Stadtmuseum Munich, Grafiksammlung M I/320.)

accused were reversed. The reeve proved that Witte had not previously complained about similar accusations made in the past and quoted witnesses who accused Witte himself of theft or indeed reported of previous convictions for theft. In this way, the reeve was able to place Witte in the role of a petty criminal. The case for witchcraft gained in momentum, the court had him arrested and after hearing further witnesses who did no more than repeat the statements of third parties, ordered torture to be applied. Witte confessed after a short time to having enchanted animals; all in all, his torturers forced him to admit to having practised witchcraft on 37 cows, 20 horses, 24 pigs and 7 calves. He said he had killed these 88 animals by pouring 'in the name of the Devil' a mixture of blood and water over the animals' bodies, a magic means of causing their death. With this admission, he confessed to maleficium and the Devil's pact, and in the course of the trial he also named three alleged female accomplices from nearby villages. At this point, however, the responsible authorities intervened and criticized the early use of torture. Witte remained under arrest, but the accused women were set free. When this decision became public, a large number of peasants armed with forks, pikes and pitchforks gathered and stormed the court building which they occupied for two days and nights. They clamoured for the body of Witte, who had died, a broken man, the night before, to be burnt, for they were convinced that he had been proven to be male witch. They also demanded that the women be subjected anew to more severe torture. The authorities in Lübeck did not, however, allow themselves to be misled by this riot; after the mob had withdrawn they acted quickly. Witte was given a Christian burial, for in the opinion of the council his guilt had not been proven. The alleged witches were also allowed to return to their villages and the rebellious peasants were sentenced to heavy fines. The councillors of both Hamburg and Lübeck adhered to their legal standpoint in Witte's trial and showed that they would not accept any insurgency in their jurisdiction even if it might arise from suspicions of witchcraft, and most certainly not if it came from any popular would-be witch persecutors.[106]

This intervention by the authorities in Lübeck was in line with their general attitude towards persecution of witches; this was characterized on the one hand by moderation and on the other by their policy of banishing people who had come under suspicion (as described above).

The development into a witch trial of a trial which set out as a petty criminal case can also be seen in other instances. In 1589, for example, several landlords together accused a certain Heinrich Fruchtenichts and his wife of theft, but it was not long before they complemented this with an accusation of witchcraft.[107] When a local court in East Holstein began to investigate the case of Andreas Termis, originally accused of fraud, he soon also became suspected of witchcraft. When asked for legal advice, the jurists of Rostock University, after examining the evidence and the witnesses' statements, agreed to the use of torture to secure the conviction of Termis, the supposed offender. It is not known how the case ended, but as the use of torture generally resulted in a confession, it can be assumed that Termis was convicted as a male witch.[108] The case against a husband and wife by the name of Timmermann in 1625 demonstrates that men tended to be accused of crimes where magic was not involved, but that such cases could, though by no means did necessarily, mutate into witchcraft cases. The couple were accused of arson on the Ahrensburg estate: whereas the wife was accused and convicted of pyromagic and subsequently burnt as a witch, her husband was charged (for the same deed) simply with arson, without use of magic. Notwithstanding the different charge, he was also executed.[109]

There is one case which remains unique in terms of the course it took and the motives for which it was conducted. In 1646, Hanß Struck, an elderly farmer from the district of Eutin accused himself of sodomy with cows and of extramarital sexual intercourse.[110] The court clearly suspected him of having committed further offences and ordered torture to be applied during an interrogation, whereupon Struck added to his list of crimes, committed by reason of a Devil's pact, magic aggression towards his own and other horses as well as working magic to make his neighbour ill. In total, he admitted to 26 cases of maleficium; the only thing he did not confess to was intercourse with the Devil. As in other male witch trials, this was replaced by sodomy. He further incriminated his wife as an accomplice, but later withdrew his statement. At the end of the protracted torture session, the scribe recorded of the accused that he 'did not know what to say'.[111] Struck, it seems, was unable to conjure up any more crimes he might have committed. On the initiative of the prince-bishop's court Struck's self-confession to a violation of sexual norms had been turned into a witchcraft trial. Struck also stated that he had lent large sums of money to the entire village. The sum he had lent amounted to 106 imperial thalers, the contemporary equivalent of the price of 13 cows.[112] Whether his figures were correct or not can no longer be proven, but Struck was executed on the grounds of the Devil's pact and maleficium; the costs of the trial were covered by consfiscation of his property. His fortune was assessed at 543 Marks in Lübeck's currency. Only two farmers made small claims on this estate, saying they had lent Struck money. This confirms that at the time of his execution Struck was not a debtor.[113] Anna Struck, his wife, tried to assert claims on the property, but when she appeared before the local magistrate, he simply banished her from the land, although in the terms of contemporary justice she had cleared herself of any accusations of witchcraft in a negative ducking test.[114]

In contrast to other imperial territories, the Prince Bishopric of Lübeck, to which Eutin belonged, did not have a confiscation order for witchcraft trials; or at least there is no record of the existence of such regulations regarding the appropriation of material assets. Thus it can be assumed that the people responsible themselves benefited materially from the estate of Hanß Struck, who as a landowning peasant was comparatively well-to-do. The costs of the trial would certainly have been lower than the monetary value of the confiscated lands, particularly since there were no large bills outstanding and no demands made by third parties. University expertise had not been requested; between 5 and 8 thalers was the usual rate at Rostock University in such cases. If, however, Struck's description of his extensive money-lending activities was accurate, then this trial shows similarities with the persecution of Jews in the Middle Ages, which were also motivated by the violent and brutal amortization of credit sums. The authorities exploited for their own self-interests the original situation in which this well-to-do farmer had made a self-accusation and developed the case into a witchcraft trial. On the other hand, the self-accusation at the beginning of the trial played an important role, as Struck was clearly unable to assimilate in his personality the contradiction between recently established norms, particularly sexual norms, and his own behaviour. By making his feelings of guilt known to the authorities he became caught up in the mills of witch persecutions.

Secondary male witches

The 'secondary' male witches formed a far more heterogeneous group and comprised about 40 per cent of all the men persecuted.

The group was heterogeneous particularly with respect to age and professions. The men accused ranged in age from 22 to 60, and professionally the range was as follows: 14 peasants tied to an estate – the majority of the accused – two peasant reeves, an innkeeper, a herdsman and ex-smith; the occupations of the others are unknown. With two exceptions, all the accused had one thing in common: as completely dependent peasants tied to the estates of their masters they all belonged to the lowest social classes, although the status of the indivduals within this class varied. Fewer than half these 'secondary' male witches came under suspicion via a woman who had been denounced as a witch or because they were related to such a woman.

Hinrich Slesvick was burnt in 1551 because he and his wife had become involved in a dispute with neighbours and thence been accused of maleficium. In the confessions made by the couple, he appeared as the perpetrator of the magic aggression which originated from his wife. Slesvick's wife made an exhaustive confession covering several pages of the court records, admitting to using magical means to cause sickness, harm to cattle and to sour the milk as well as to a kind of love magic. Following this, Hinrich Slesvick only added a general declaration as an accessory to the crimes. After each of his wife's admissions, the court scribe noted as a description of Hinrich's role: 'Hinrich Slesvick confirmed and confessed all this of his free will and [stated] that he had advised that these deeds be carried out and he [too] performed them.'[115] The court did not ask to know more; after the hearing had been recorded in writing they dealt primarily with the wife and her maleficium. Through her statements Slesvick became a secondary suspect and his maleficium potential also slipped into second position behind that of the 'primary witch'.

In 1600, Hans Lüders played a similar role; he was regarded as a witness and accomplice of the maleficium performed by his mother and interrogated under torture on the matter.[116] In 1574 Tönnies Nickel also became suspected of witchcraft as a result of accusations against his wife; she was sentenced to execution and he to banishment.[117]

In 1615, a court indicted Hans Klindt, a reasonably wealthy citizen of Eutin, on the basis of a denunciation made by a sister of his who had been burnt as a witch. Despite torture, Klindt made no confession, but by this time an early modern variety of a citizens' action group had been formed to demand his execution. In a public meeting, ten citizens declared that they 'would lay down their bodies, property and blood'[118] to see Klindt convicted and executed. The town council refused to give in to their demands. In the meantime, Klindt had admitted to witchcraft crimes, only to recant his confession again the following day. Upon this, the council released him from prison on condition that he swear an oath to refrain from vengeance. After the trial Hans Klindt tried to continue living in Eutin but later became the victim of a lynching in which he was struck dead.[119]

In 1676, Hinrich Busch was also implicated in a witchcraft trial on the basis of statements made by a female relative. Suspicions of his role had grown during the preliminary investigations as a result of a witches' mark found on him by the executioner from Kiel. Busch experienced no pain during the pricking test to which he was subjected, neither did the wound bleed.[120] Busch confessed voluntarily, was then subjected to torture in order to obtain a full confession. From his statement it is clear that he must have been a very old man for he speaks of a master who, 50 years previously, had persuaded him to denounce God. Busch admitted to making a pact with the Devil, to having 'received seed and powder from him with which he had harmed and killed humans and animals'[121] He confessed to intercourse with the Devil, describing an unusual form that this had taken. In his words, the Devil 'had appeared to him in the form of a man on Bruhnsrade [a large field in the north of Kiel] and wished him good morning. The Devil then persuaded him to renounce God and surrender to him; theafter he made a pact with him and had intercourse with him.'[122] Busch had thus conceded to having a homosexual relationship with the Devil, for there was no mention here of the usual succubi. Together with his daughter, Busch was convicted of proven witchcraft, condemned to death by the Kiel council and burnt. Busch, as many alleged male witches, was a herdsman. In 1673 he had come to Kiel as a smith[123] and had there taken up the lowest of jobs: he became a town herdsman. This victim represents two professions, both of which were reputed to be familiar with magic workings.

These cases show that a decisive reason for placing charges against men was often suspicion of the entire family. Under certain conditions the gender-specific focus dissolved, and the mechanisms which tended to protect men more than women from prosecution no longer functioned as well in the case of disreputable families. The mere fact that family members were on trial meant that men, too, could be accused of witchcraft. The case of the man was closely dependent on that of his relative (often his wife), and a few testimonies from witnesses were sufficient to place charges against him.

Two years later, in 1678, the owner of an estate called Depenau, which lay to the south of Kiel, accused four people of witchcraft. None of them survived the trial. It is not possible to reconstruct from the fragments of the remaining trial records whether the two men involved were secondary accused or whether they were implicated from the start. One of the men, Ove Freßen, was burnt with the two women, but the other, Claus Lille, died in prison before the sentence could be enforced.[124] The confessions bear the stamp of the manor court of a nobleman, Joachim von Brockdorff; this court seemed determined to prove one of the male accused to be a witch. Under torture this man had not made a clear confession, but was nonetheless condemned to death. He explained the witches' mark found on his body as a skin flaw. Finally he had admitted to witchcraft, but was unable to define it. Whereas, on the one hand, he admitted to killing horses and calves and saw this in connection with a Devil's pact, on the other hand he denied being apostate from God. This was nevertheless enough for the court to pronounce the death sentence, which was enforced in 1678, the same year.[125]

In Depenau there was also a fierce conflict at the beginning of the 18th century between peasant serfs and the lord of the manor. The same nobleman who had led the earlier trials now repeatedly insulted his subjects as 'witches, devils and rebels'.[126] This time, however, the allegations did not lead to a witchcraft trial but to social conflict. In this dispute over the demands he was making with respect to improving the effectivity of his operations on the estate the landlord used the terminology of witchcraft accusations. The conflict in Depenau culminated in the shooting of some of the peasant serfs, for which the lord of the manor, Joachim von Brockdorff, was sentenced before a higher court. The trials he had initiated in earlier years clearly marked the beginnnings of his attempts to discipline his subjects[127] concealed beneath allegations of witchcraft.

Large-scale trials in Holstein did not necessarily mean that a higher proportion of men were implicated. In 1666 a court on the lands of the monastery in Preetz condemned 14 people to death for witchcraft. All of them came from the same part of the monastery's lands and had made self-confessions, although at the same time implicating other people as accomplices. Among the executed, all of whom were still young, was one Heinrich Stoltenbergh who stated that he had killed a horse and calf belonging to his father.[128] When informed of the mass confessions in the village, the monasterial authorities were first somewhat uncertain how to react, but when the villagers became active, the authorities were quick to respond. Urged on by the villagers, the self-confessors had named more and more alleged accomplices so that the number of people under suspicion had escalated. The populace was obviously thus trying to find a common cause for a number of adversities and finally to find the people personally responsible. In the end, the people of one of the villages demanded – in writing – that the people they assumed to be guilty be executed.[129] In the light of this communication, which was no less than a request for mass extermination, the provost forbade any further unauthorized interrogations, and had this instruction read out in the Sunday sermons. Finally, he decided to instigate a formal witchcraft trial of an unknown number of accused. The accused comprised men and women of various ages, as the legal consultant, Mauritius of Kiel University, recorded in his report.[130] Asked for legal advice, the faculty in Kiel confirmed the provost's viewpoint that the trial and the denunciations must be controlled.[131] Given the way the accusations were originally made and the way the matter developed, it seems justified to speak of hysteria in the village communities. At the end of the trial before the court, 13 women and one man had been sentenced to death, although the records show that this proportion does not reflect the respective proportion of men and women involved in the trial. What is more, Heinrich Stoltenbergh, the only male accused of a Devil's pact was classified as less dangerous because he had only practised maleficium but had not won over (male or female) accomplices to aid him in his deeds. And, unlike his female counterparts, Stoltenbergh was beheaded and not burnt.[132]

In another trial which, by Holstein's standards, was also conducted on a large scale, the proportion of men accused was small: in 1664, the lord of a manor in East Holstein ordered the burning of ten people from his various estates. He had acted on the accusations made by some of his peasant serfs, encouraged by Protestant pastors to deal rigorously with the matter. The trial began with the arrest of two women who, under torture, denounced other women as accomplices. In the course of the trial the lord condemned ten women and only one man to death for alleged witchcraft.[133] Other than the name, N. Dahle nothing is known about this man or his status, although it is apparent that this persecution was generally directed at the wives of well-to-do, landowning peasants on the estates, rather than at those even lower in social rank.

The same applied to Clauß Kohler, condemned and burnt as a male witch in a village belonging to the Cathedral Chapter of Lübeck in 1669. He had been denounced by a woman and was executed together with four women. At the time of his execution he was no longer young; in 1654 he had remarried after the death of his wife;[134] he left behind a considerable fortune, the sum of which clearly shows that he was not a member of the sub-peasant class,[135] although it was not sufficient to cover the costs of the trial. These allegedly amounted to over 100 imperial thalers and were ultimately paid by a brother-in-law. Considering how high this claim was, it can be assumed that, as in the case of the Prince-Bishop's subject, Hans Struck in 1646, the authorities in Lübeck themselves benefited financially from the case. Such high costs had to this date not been incurred in any of the Holstein trials, and the expert report requested here from the University of Greifswald would have cost between 4 and 8 imperial thalers.[136] This indicates that there was indeed a substantial difference between the probable actual costs and the sum claimed from the family.

One of Holstein's largest trials, which took place on two estates, saw the breakdown of hitherto upheld gender-specific barriers.[137]

On the Schmoel estate in the north of Holstein close to the Baltic coast several people had died of an unknown illness, and the wife of a scribe accused a cottager by the name of Mette Schlan of being the originator of the epidemic. When the woman who had accused Schlan herself fell ill, her husband intensified the accusations. At this point, the landlord, Earl Christoph von Rantzau, intervened and had Mette Schlan arrested and interrogated. Under torture she admitted to magical aggression and implicated six other people as accomplices, two of them men: the peasants' reeve, Claus Stötterogge and her own father, Hans Lütke. All six were arrested, interrogated under torture and themselves denounced further people as guilty of witchcraft. Lütke listed ten people (eight known women and two men) in his 'Rotte', his company of the witches' sect, who had allegedly attended the Sabbat. He also declared that he himself had been a werewolf. Stötterogge named four women; after the interrogation he was able to escape from the prison but was later found and in the course of his re-arrest injured one of the farm labourers who tried to apprehend him. Two days after several people had made confessions, Christoph von Rantzau condemned four of the accused – Mette Schlan, her father Hans Lütke, and two other women – to death.

When, on April 27th of the same year a number of local farmers accused more people of maleficium, blaming them for causing damage to cows, horses, pigs and, unusually for Holstein, corn, Rantzau ordered new arrests. Seven women and three men were taken to the cellars of the manor house at Schmoel, already suffering from the brutal and bloody treatment they had experienced when they were seized. At the house they were subjected to brutal interrogations. Trine Möller gave a detailed description of the procedure at a witches' Sabbat: she depicted how, together with her 'company', she had flown on foxtails, black dogs and cats to the Blocksberg where they had eaten black fish and black meat. She denounced six women and four men as further attendees. The cottager Hinrich Steffen confessed to having gone to the Sabbat together with a red cock, six women and three men and acted there as a lieutenant. He even admitted to having desecrated the host at the Lord's Supper, a crime to which men rarely confessed in witchcraft trials. The accused, Claus Möller, allegedly floated to a witches' dance with a calf and saw his own role at the Sabbat as that of a captain. Finally, he denounced eleven women and four men as alleged accomplices.

The denunciations were largely identical and the result of specifically directed questions asked during the interrogation. Rantzau suggested certain names during the questioning and expected the accused only to confirm these – under torture:

> ... 10. Are you not aware that Asmus Sehmer, who drowned himself here in the ditch, was able to work witchcraft, and did he not belong to your company? What company did he otherwise keep? ... 18. Were not Mette Schlan, Hanß Lütke, Silcke Nippen and Engel Otten who have been burnt, and also Claus Stötterogge, who is still alive, witches and sorcerers? 19. Are not Siecke Sehmers, Decke Büntzen, Engel Stötteroggen, Abel Möllers, Claus Möller, Peter Möller and Hinrich Steffen able to use witchcraft? And also old Abel Schönings and Barg Schöning's wife from Matzwitz?[138]

Preliminary suspicions were then simply confirmed under the pressure of torture. In his prepared questions he included the names of both men and women, in accordance with his own witchcraft notion. He was made angry by the statements of some of the accused and in such cases had the torture procedure repeated – even in the case of a pregnant woman of whose condition he was aware.[139] At the beginning of May, Rantzau condemned eleven of the accused (seven women and four men) to death and they were burnt in public the same month. Not enough of this, he pursued his persecutions further.

When, at the end of May 1686, on one of his other estates in Övelgönne 'all the landowning peasants and cottagers' and all the former's 'labourers from the Övelgönne estate' accused a man and a woman from the village of witchcraft, Rantzau had them both arrested. Under interrogation and torture the woman, Lene Paschen, denounced the accused man, Hinrich Markmann. The latter, however, refused to confess either under regular interrogation or under torture. He testified that 'he was unable to work magic' but that 'about 22 years previously when he was still unmarried, he had had intercourse with a horse, committed immoral deeds and sodomy. He had done this about five times, but later when he was married he had done it about three times with a cow and committed sodomy'.[140] Lene Paschen also incriminated Markmann as a member of her 'company' in the witches' flight, to which other men and women had also belonged. At the end of June 1686, Rantzau condemned her and another woman to death by burning for proven witchcraft; Markmann was also executed – for intercourse with animals.

The contours of the witches' Sabbat, an element of the witch paradigm, emerged very clearly in these confessions. At these alleged witches' gatherings, men represented a diabolical elite in the form of officers (a captain and a lieutenant were mentioned in Schmoel), whereas women were active in more subordinate roles. The portrayal of the Sabbat was a reflection of this world in the afterworld. The colours are particularly significant: black, the colour of death and evil dominated in sharp contrast to white, the symbol of Christianity and purity. The questions Rantzau posed as judge regarding attendance at these Sabbats were taken from a prepared catalogue and were both systematic and suggestive. They also allowed for the denunciation of men. In these trials, Rantzau, attempted to identify from his position of power the members of a witches' sect and to eliminate them. 'Devil's vermin'[141] was his term for the condemned, and he called for their extermination if the world was not to perish. His motive was to fight this threatening and sorcerous secret coalition. The motive of the peasants serfs was the struggle against what they supposed to be the maleficium which had been afflicting them and their families for months and which they thought to have originated in the doings of certain neighbours. The investigations in Schmoel concentrated on two so-called 'witch families' to which almost all the people executed belonged.[142] The Schmoel trials demonstrate how these similar interests combined and worked together in accusing and charging alleged witches and male witches.

The witch stereotype collapsed in these, by Holstein's standards, large-scale trials; the proportion of men executed was 33 per cent of the total number of people executed. Rantzau, as an earl of the empire who had converted to Catholicism, tended in his trials to use the arguments of Catholic-influenced demonology with its emphasis on the witches' Sabbat element and an image which did not fundamentally exclude men from suspicion of witchcraft. Rantzau had converted to Catholicism in 1650 and had since actively propagated the spread of the Catholic faith in Lutheran northern Germany.[143] His witchcraft notion shaped Holstein's largest trial to the extent that the gender-specific filter which up until that point had always been employed, was no longer effective.

Healers and criminals as male witches?

Many of those who belonged to the group of primary male witches had certain things in common: they either belonged to the cunning folk or were alleged criminals who had become involved in witchcraft trials as a result of charges for other offences:

The cunning-men represented about a third of all men accused at the beginning of a surge of trials, clearly a significant proportion. In most cases this was not their main occupation – many were also herdsmen and all lived and worked as magical experts in an intermediate zone between life and death. It was believed that these specialists possessed skills which permitted them to perform both beneficent and maleficent magic, for anyone able to sustain life might also be able to destroy it.

Male healers were, then, comparatively frequently accused; the specification male (and not female) healers, incidentally, is intentional here, so as not to be seen to be confirming the cliché of the witch as a herbalist and midwife!

Another statistically interesting group is the men who became involved in witchcraft cases by way of other criminal charges or accusations. They represented about a quarter of the men persecuted and were often initially accused by complainants and witnesses of severely deviant or norm-violating behaviour. Subsequent accusations of witchcraft were initially on a par with other accusations and often only gained in their life-threatening significance as the trial progressed. The courts in Holstein tended to charge men more often with criminal offences not involving the use of magic. Women, on the other hand, when charged with criminal offences were generally seen to have commited these offences through maleficium.

Healers and criminals as male witches? Herdsmen, blacksmiths, cunning-men and alleged criminals represented more than half the male primary suspects in Holstein's witchcraft trials; logically, this means that an almost equal proportion did not fit these categories.

Objective characteristics are barely apparent for the group of secondary male witches. The roles they played in society and their consequent susceptibility to involvement in conflicts were of less importance than their proximity to cases of harmful magic or to the alleged female worker of this magic. Denunciations in witchcraft trials spread the seed of suspicion and expanded the circle of possible suspects beyond any witch stereotypes. Fewer than half these secondary male witches were verifiably closely related to the female primary witch or were involved in family-related trials. The expansion potential of witch trials and their escalation dynamics meant that, provided the denunciations appeared theologically plausible, accusations could affect groups of people who would not normally have been suspected within the primary group. The low numbers of 'secondary male witches' in Holstein is due to the fact that the witches' Sabbat component was not of central importance in the regional witch image; as this element of the paradigm did not figure at all in many trials, the number of denunciations remained comparatively low, as did, thus, the number of subsequent connected trials. Few of the accused men, however, were charged with the extremely periphery role of the so-called Sabbat-attendee; they more often took a secondary and thus subordinate position in the trials. The witch image of Lutheran theology was firmly female, and this was generally the reason for the low proportion of men who became victims of the persecutions in Holstein as well as for a gender-specific selection process which resulted in comparatively few men actually being charged as alleged male witches.

8
Carinthia. Wanted: Beggar, Male

> I am prepared to bear all agonies to show my innocence, for whatever happens, I must die some time.
>
> (Christian Wucher, charged as a male witch, 14 February 1721)

Two-thirds of the people accused as witches in Carinthia (in present-day Austria) were male. As for Holstein in the previous chapter, this chapter investigates the personal profiles of these male witches and describes the conflict situations from which the witch trials arose. Carinthia, however, has to be approached from a different perspective: What were the issues driving the persecution practice of this territory in which men represented the majority of the accused?

Hans of Veitsberg, a vagrant

In the spring of 1658 a beggar and vagrant from the village of Veitsberg, by the name of Hans, was arrested for alleged witchcraft. The judge in St Veit handed the case over to the regional court in Paternion, where the accused confessed, without torture, to the following: a Hans Singer from Villach, a man condemned of witchcraft some time previously, had coaxed him by means of a magic ointment into practising witchcraft. Together with six other men, almost all of whom were also vagrants, and one woman, he had rubbed this ointment on his skin, whereupon his feet and hands had transformed into wings and he had been able to fly. A large black dog had tried to scratch a mark on him with its claws but he had managed to prevent this. He and his fellow witches were able to change the weather by mixing and pounding stones, sand, human and animal hair together and then boiling it all with a child's body in a large cauldron. From the resulting mass they formed balls which they shot up into the clouds; this brought about the desired weather change.

His motive, he told the judge, was to satisfy some Carinthian peasants who had asked him to help them with good weather. He also gave revenge as one of his motives, for some of the farmers had refused his request for alms. Uncertain of the credibility of these statements, the court then decided to apply torture as a means of verification; the judge was recorded in the minutes as having said that the man appeared 'simple-minded' and possibly 'corrupt'.

A catalogue of 20 questions was prepared for this interrogation under torture.[1] This included questions about the type of weather magic, e.g. 'heavy showers, downpours, snow and frost', about the names and abodes of his accomplices, his 'Genossen' ('male comrades') and later 'Genossinnen' (female comrades). The judge also wanted to know whether the accused had 'committed himself to somebody else', i.e. was apostate from God. Hans repeated the statements he had made earlier, gave specific details of the weather magic, describing his ability to summon rain during dry periods. He also described the so-called 'gatherings' of the witches: pipers and drummers had struck up for the dancing, and numerous witches, together with several devils, were in attendance. They took seat at 'five tables' which had been put up for them. Hans named two other male witches, one so-called 'Krumphendl' and one 'Schittenkopf', both of whom had probably already been executed as a result of a prior arrest, by the time of the trial.[2] When the court called upon the beggar to pray, his voice seems to have failed him, for the minutes of the trial record that he only twitched 'because there was something wrong with his tongue'. The court records end at this point, but there seems little doubt that in view of his extensive confession, confirmed by torture, the sentence can only have been death: Hans of Veitsberg died at the stake in 1658.

This mid-17th century trial in Carinthia targeted one man in an individual witch trial, and in the investigations which ensued from this trial it was primarily men who were suspected, although one woman called 'Liendlin' played a special role. The judges at the court in Paternion had no legal or ideological doubts with respect to the principle of applying the four main elements of demonology to the male sex. The accused confessed to maleficium, to a Devil's pact in the form of apostasy (although this was only implied by his statement and his inability to pray), to attending the witches' Sabbat and to the witches' flight. He described the feasting and dancing which took place at these secret gatherings, but did not mention any sexual aspects. There was no mention in this trial of intercourse with the Devil.

The accused was a vagrant, and denounced others in the same position as himself as members of witches' sects. It is not clear from the court records whether this was a result of the court's strategy or whether this was an unsolicited testimony.

The persecution described here can be considered typical for the Carinthia region, for the majority of trials here were not aimed at women. In this part of the Austrian hereditary lands men stood out as primary witches. Frequently, they were the first to be accused in a chain of trials and it was they who denounced other alleged agents, both male and female: The witch paradigm was reversed, for here it was men who drew women into the trials. The authorities and courts had a new target and concentrated their investigations on the male sex.

The territory and the law

Carinthia had belonged to the House of Habsburg since 1335, and in the 16th century, together with the Archduchy of Austria, Styria and Carniola, it formed a coherent area in the southern Alps. As a part of so-called Inner Austria, Carinthia was subordinate to the government in Graz which administered the territory through a governor, a representative of the sovereign. The population of Carinthia in the 17th century was ca. 180,000 and in the mid-18th century ca. 250,000.[3]

The Archduke Ferdinand of Styria, a man of Jesuit upbringing later to become Holy Roman Emperor, initiated and carried out within the space of a few decades a ruthless re-Catholicization process against the resistance of the Protestant estates. By 1620 at the latest, the estates had been disempowered and absolutism had made its breakthrough.[4]

The Carolina and the Carinthian legal system of 1577 formed the legal basis for charges against male and female witches, but it was not until the so-called 'Ferdinandea', Emperor Ferdinand II's Court Regulations of 1656, that all elements of the complete and elaborated witchcraft teachings and demonology were carried over into the witch persecutions.[5] In the Constitutio Theresia of 1758, witchcraft was still theoretically defined as a criminal act but the regulations narrowed down the definition of the word and demanded rigorous evidence before sentences could be passed.

The centralization of authority from the first third of the 17th century onwards, had a considerable influence on the course of witch trials and the sentences passed. The governor, as representative of the regent, had far-reaching jurisdictive powers in criminal cases[6] for the numerous regional, town and market courts were not permitted to pass sentences independently, and had to refer to the higher courts to determine their verdicts. These higher instances consisted of 'travelling courts' which had been granted the competences to deal with these cases by the territorial sovereign, and travelled from place to place to return verdicts. The tribunals consisted of a prosecutor, a scribe, an executioner and a counsel for the defence. The lower courts in the rural districts were permitted to raise charges and interrogate before the arrival of these 'mobile decision makers', but it was the representatives of the sovereign who, after examining the records, decided how the trial was to continue and whether torture should be applied. This meant that they had the final decision on whether or not a trial should be continued after a confession had been made. If the travelling courts were engaged in other trials or unable to attend for other reasons, the accused were obliged to remain in prison for lengthy periods of time, waiting for the trial to continue; it was quite possible for people to have to wait 3 years.[7]

There were a few exceptions, such as the 'free' regional courts in Paternion and Spittal which were not bound to these regulations; thanks to privileges they had their own senior judge and were able to act more autonomously in witch trials.[8] The localities Wolfsberg, Villach and St Leonhard formed an enclave of the Frankish Prince-Bishopric of Bamberg within Carinthia and were thus ruled from German Bamberg. Two other localities, Friesach and Maria Saal, belonged to the Prince-Archbishopric of Salzburg, under whose jurisdiction they fell. The larger part of Carinthia, then, formed a coherent territory, but there were a few exceptions which reflected the colourful political map of the early modern Holy Roman Empire. The struggle for competences which arose from this medley of responsibilities shared between Habsburg and non-Habsburg institutions continued throughout the 17th century and was not legally solved until some time later.[9]

Trials and persecution surges

The first known witch trial in Carinthia took place in 1465. In 1492, the idea of a Devil's pact appeared for the first time in a confession, in which the accused spoke of an alliance with the Devil while plotting a crime.[10] In both trials, the accused were women, and the trials are exemplary of a very long period in which witchcraft trials were few and sporadic. In the second half of the 17th century, circumstances changed: The number of trials escalated, peaking in surges between

1650 and 1670 and 1680 and 1690. The courts pronounced a large number of death sentences, although 'only' one in two of the accused (of a total of 256 for whom records are still extant)[11] were executed. Compared with the intense persecutions in southwest Germany or Franconia, Carinthia suffered a low level of persecution, and saw only a few persecution surges or mass trials. From about 1650–1660 onwards the courts inquired regularly into possible Sabbat attendance, as a component of the witch paradigm, and frequently asked for the names of accomplices, but were often satisfied after a certain number of names had been given and inquired no further. Nevertheless, the dominant pattern in Carinthia was one of 'small panics', that is trials with up to five accused; only three trials exceeded this figure. In 1686 and 1687 a total of 57 people were investigated, in 1705 and 1706 in Wolfsberg ten people and again in 1714–1715, 23 people.[12] As breaches of regulations in trials became apparent, the inner-Austrian government in Graz began to control the witch trials more stringently. The last known trial based on the notion of the Devil's pact took place in St. Leonhard[13] when the court in Bamberg condemned the male accused, Paul Schäfer, to death in 1726. The witch persecutions continued until 1772, but the death sentence was no longer passed, and the opinion of the court no longer included any demonological elements. As in Holstein, women were the prime targets of the early witch-hunts, but as time went on, more men were charged. Persecutions began late in Carinthia compared with other imperial territories – not until the mid-17th century and after the end of the Counter Reformation in Inner Austria. Most of the condemned were not burnt at the stake but beheaded, and their bodies subsequently burnt. Again, by comparison with other territories persecution ended extremely late, with witch trials still taking place in the first half of the 18th century.

New on the wanted list: men

Thanks to a provision made in 1656 by the Inner Austrian government which stipulated that precise details of all persons involved in witchcraft trials be recorded, it is easier to reconstruct the gender and personal profiles of victims in Carithia than in other territories. About 68 per cent of all such trials targeted male witches. Earlier sources are much less detailed or reliable but as far as it is possible to tell, the majority of people charged for witchcraft before 1610 were women. As Figure 8.1. clearly shows, a period of almost 30 years followed, in which persecution virtually stopped, only to be resumed again with a new gender focus.

From 1630 onwards the witch stereotype seems to have been reversed: the crime of witchcraft was attributed to men in 80–90 per cent of the cases brought before the courts. During Carinthia's peak persecution period between 1650 and 1680 this new male witch stereotype again began to recede but not to change fundamentally, for numbers never fell below 60 per cent. In the early 18th century, men again consistently represented over three quarters of the accused. The trial of Hans of Veitsberg mentioned above fell in the peak persecution period in which men remained the primary targets.

This study of Carinthia is based on files from the regional archives in Klagenfurt which contain the collected records of witchcraft trials for the entire region. Other data are taken from local and regional historical research, which has repeatedly shown an interest in the witch-hunts from the last third of the 19th century to the present day. For the purposes of a quantitative evaluation aiming to show tendencies, the sources can be classified as good to satisfactory, but again it must be stressed that this study does not pretend to comprise all witchcraft trials.

Figures 8.1 and 8.2 show the persecution cycles and the gender-specific bias of the witch-hunts in Carinthia in both absolute and relative figures.[14]

The combination of a Devil's pact and weather magic was typical for Carinthia, occurring in almost 40 per cent of confessions made in trials.[15] Whereas women were often accused of milk magic,[16] this was very rarely the case for men. By far the most common crime of which male witches were accused between 1630 and 1720 was weather magic.[17]

The 76-year-old beggar Stefan N. from Trägenwinkel maintained in the summer of 1666 that he could cause it to rain by bathing in one of Carinthia's lakes. Members of the rural population had asked him for help, but the shower he had summoned had unintentionally turned out to be so heavy that a mill had been flooded and destroyed by the water masses.[18] In 1653, the 18-year-old farm servant and beggar, Kaspar Haintz, declared in an interrogation that the 'magic rain-makers' brewed the weather up in a kettle, in which they formed 'old pieces of shoe leather, flax refuse, wild boar fur, birch leaves and old shoe laces' into balls which they shot up in to the clouds. At the request of certain farmers he had created downpours to cause injury to their fellow farmers. Heat also seems to have belonged to their repertoire, for Haintz confessed not only to creating rainshowers, the time and place of which he was able to specify, but also to generating heat waves by burning a skull.[19]

Weather magic was not only viewed as beneficent white magic but also perceived as a threat: someone who could have a positive influence

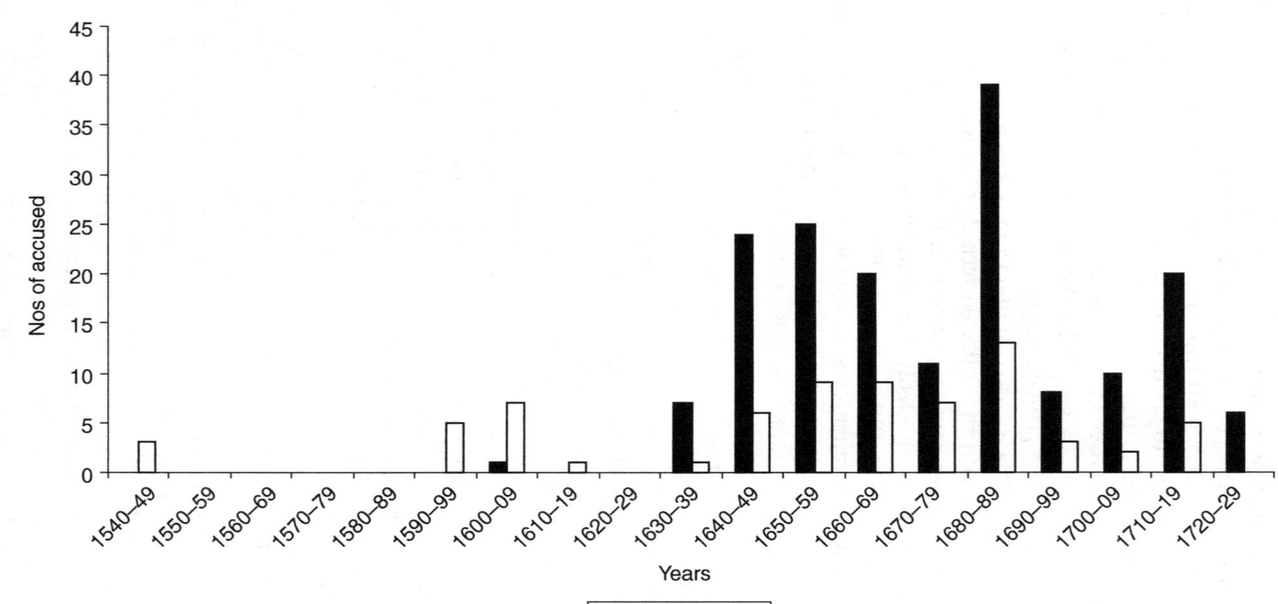

Figure 8.1 Duchy of Carinthia: witchcraft persecutions – numbers of men and women, 1540–1729

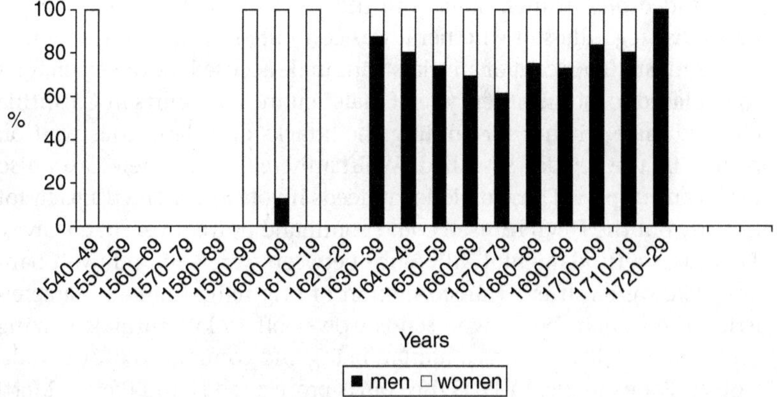

Figure 8.2 Duchy of Carinthia: witchcraft persecutions by sex – % of men and women, 1540–1729

on the weather could also have a negative influence. For many contemporaries, witchcraft with its two intrinsically connected aspects was an ambivalent issue. In 1687, witnesses and the court itself gave a number of witches the blame for a hailshower which had destroyed the entire grape harvest.[20] Similarly, in 1664, the beggar Peter Trattner was accused of having worked magic to induce sub-zero temperatures, a deed to which he finally admitted.[21] The farmer Peter Enzi confirmed after enduring five hours of torture that he had caused snow and hail to fall, which he had previously 'carried and sent in little sacks'.[22] Hans Preisöchsl declared under torture in Straßburg in 1646 that he stirred together 'wool, human hair, pigs' droppings and blood from his hands'[23] to create showers. Simon Holdenacher claimed as his speciality the creation of frost, and Sebastian Praitbrenner stated that to provoke heavy rainfall he threw bugs out of his coat onto an anthill.[24]

Hail in particular was thought of as a product of magic aggression. Hail occurred (or occurs) very locally, thus sparing some farmers but destroying much of the harvest, and thus the livelihood, of the stricken farmers for the following year. Such disparate consequences of hail, and also heavy local rainshowers, confirmed suspicions that these phenomena might be the result of maleficium. The persecutors in Carinthia as followers of classic demonology were convinced that the Devil's pact always underlay weather magic, and anyone charged with this offence had no choice but to admit to the pact in court, often under torture. This variant of maleficium typical for the region was not considered to be founded on harmless sorcery in the sense of the traditional 'magia naturalis', regardless of whether it was commited by men or women.

In almost 20 per cent of all trials with male accused, however, charges were placed for some other type of maleficium. The courts in Carinthia charged male witches for guiding the attacks of a dangerous wolf on people in the region, so-called 'Wolfbannerei' or in a few cases also for lycanthropy.[25] These maleficent deeds involved the Devil's pact, for nobody but the Devil himself could command power over such wolves. There was a fundamental difference between werewolf and 'wolf banner'. The werewolf is a transformation of originally human characteristics; the human being who sends wolves off to kill animals grazing on farmers' fields remains a human being and commands only certain wolves. For example, in 1705 the courts prosecuted Hanßl Pfeifer, Mertl Greß, Anderl Herzog and 'black' Lippi for guiding and instructing a wolf to the detriment of other members of the population. The judges showed no mercy and all four mountain herdsmen were executed.[26] According to the statement made by the accused Peter Perwolf in 1701, every cattleherd must possess magical powers over wolves. Presumably, he meant by this that good herdsmen should be in a position to protect their herds from wolf attacks. For the complainants as for the court, however, such a statement implied a confession to possessing the skill to perform maleficium and, possibly, to use it in practice: reason enough for farmers not only to mistrust the man and his colleagues but in the event of any damage occurring, to accuse them of witchcraft. So it was on the initiative of the local farmers that Perwolf was executed.[27] There were a considerable number of cases in which accusations of weather magic and wolf instruction were made, the large majority of which targeted men from the lowest strata of the lowest social class, the herdsmen. These were people who tended the animals on the mountain pastures during the summer months, thus isolated from the inhabitants of the settlements in the valleys, apart from the few occasions where circumstances required contact. In the winter, these people eked out a living as beggars travelling from place to place. Nevertheless, 'wolfbannerei' was a crime of which not only men were accused.[28]

The Devil's pact – which had to exist to reveal a person as an agent of the Devil – as described by one Bartelmä Droscheter, took the form of a written contract under a new name. Under the most gruesome torture, in which he was hoisted up in the strappado with weights attached to his body, 50-year-old Klement Reibeis maintained that it could also be a verbal contract in which the person committed his or her soul to the Devil. The Devil also threatened violence and coerced the victims, as the accused Hans Träxler stated during his trial.[29] In 1715, Peter Enzi claimed that he had used his own blood to sign such a pact, and had received money for his signature.[30] In the case of a 13-year-old beggar, the Devil had scratched his mark on the boy's head as a sign of the pact.[31] This mark could also be made, as in the case of a Gregor Rade, accused in Weissenegg, on the left hand and foot.[32]

Intercourse with the Devil receded as a symbol of apostasy and evidence of the Devil's pact for men in Carinthian trials, but did not disappear entirely. According to Stefan N., the Devil had 'twice ... lain with him as a woman'[33] and Georg Eder saw the Devil transformed into a woman who had 'made show of her interest in him'.[34] The Devil in the shape of an attractive woman, known as succubus, was not the only way male Devil's confederates were seduced, for the Devil could appear 'at night in all kinds of shapes, also as a woman'.[35]

For the persecutors, the question of copulation with the Devil was of less significance than attendance at the witches' Sabbat, for the crime of witchcraft was considered in Carinthia to be a collective crime. In the trial of the beggar Hanßl Sachs in Spittal in 1630 the judge specifically inquired after his 'company'.[36] Another vagrant stressed that he had become acquainted with many 'Gevattersleute', that is other men, at the gatherings.[37] A company, or group, of witches was said, in a confession made by Blasius Kofler, executed in 1653, to consist of ten people; a statement made by one Lorenz Perauer gave up to 100, and Bartlmä Droscheter 400 people.[38] The focus of these night gatherings, which mostly took place on the 'Saualpe', a mountain to the east of Klagenfurt, was common maleficium. Christian Wucher, a vagrant arrested in Maria Saal in 1720 gave further details, first denouncing 28 men and only 3 women, then extending this list to a total of 54 names, among whom men again formed the majority.[39] Perauer stressed that he and others as simple farm servants had only been given 'a little to drink' at the meetings, whereas others had enjoyed large quantities of wine, for like Wucher, Perauer belonged to the lower strata of the witches' society and functioned merely as a servant.

Witchcraft was experienced as a collective threat, expressed in the belief in the existence of the witches' Sabbat as the hub where magic crimes were planned and organized. The Sabbat was often described as the 'witches' meal' in Carinthian trials and indeed the alleged delinquents often depicted it as similar to a peasants' feast to which the participants flew on oven forks or wooden sticks. In the trial of the beggar Hans of Veitsberg the court, having determined the precise type of magical aggression they were dealing with, went straight on to ask for the names of the accused's accomplices. This further demonstrates that Hans' alleged crimes were not viewed as the product of an individual person. It was such trial strategies that initiated the chains of trials in this region; these strategies, exemplified by the questions quoted below, were barely to be found in the northern German witch trials discussed in the previous chapter:

1. Did he remember his statement repeated three times and not made under torture and did he confess to it?
2. In what form and why did Hans take to the art of weathermaking? And how long did he practise this art?
3. Who were his accomplices and did he not teach any of them the art of witchcraft? What are their names and where are they to be found?
4. Did he travel with them on a plank or a wooden bowl or on a beam from the hayloft, and did he go first, or last, how often, and how far? ...[40]

Women also attended the witches' gatherings: Christoph N., charged in Leonstein in 1663, declared that he had seen there 'beautiful women, like countesses',[41] and in Althofen in 1721 Simon Puntz mentioned the presence of 'noblewomen'.[42] The beggarwoman Regina Paumann named after her arrest three men, all of them farmers, and five women, among whom were 'two brides, dairymaids by the names of Bärbl and Margareth' as her 'accomplices in witchcraft'.[43] Women were also apparent as teachers, as for example, those known as 'Liendlin' or 'Kohlrouschin'.[44] On the whole, however, men of varying social status were named as masters or teachers. Bartelmä Droscheter mentioned day-labourers, Simon Punz an innkeeper, Bartl Strasser – in 1631 – a tramp, and Hans Winkler a vagrant as teachers of magic skills.[45] After an interrogation pertaining to his alleged Devil's pact and membership of a witches' sect, the beggar Simon Punz is recorded as saying:

> He finally admitted that about three years ago when he was begging on the Lorenzberg mountain, near Micheldorf in the court district of Althofen, a man of medium height and dressed in black approached him; he spoke to him and said he should travel with him up into the clouds, for a long time he refused to do so.... But then he allowed himself to be persuaded, whereupon the man rubbed an ointment onto his skin around his middle; two grey he-goats then appeared, on which they sat and rode through a storm over the mountains. They descended on a mountain.... Yes, he believed there were five

> of them, two gentlemen and three gentlewomen. [On further questioning, he continued]....There were no doubt more, farmers and beggars among them who he did not know. He had often heard say that Pämbhäckl of Weindorf and the wheat farmer from Krappfeld were also witches...on his first ride through the clouds he had seen Waitzbauer stirring the shower with a shovel...[46]

This description is typical for Carinthia in that it combines weather magic and a belief in an aggressive magic sect in which many men were involved.

Approximately half of all people accused were charged at the beginning of a trial series and informed the courts of further accomplices, some but not all under the pressures of torture. Men, of course, also named large numbers of women as fellow witches, and vice versa, but on the whole the courts mostly followed up the denunciations of males. Gender-specific selection processes also took place here; however, between 1630 and 1725 (with a slight upward trend in the numbers of women persecuted from 1670 to 1680) women were generally considered to be less susceptible to witchcraft, and men were the prime focus of the persecutions.

Beggars and vagrants persecuted for witchcraft

Blasius Kofler, a vagrant arrested for witchcraft, gave a more homogeneous picture of the social status and gender of his accomplices. Under torture he made the following statement,

> ...Simon from Pressenberg, Jörg of Pressental, a beggar in the Katsch valley, Kropf [Goitre] Paul, who was staying around Gmünd, a certain 'Stopf' who has red hair and beard and who carries salt about, Stangl Adam, a beggarwoman from Villach, another beggarwoman near Greifenburg by the name of Katharina, a beggar with a fierce dog, the beggar Simon from Villach, a beggar by the name of Jakl, a peasant-woman from Lind..., a young beardless man from Greifenburg called Bartl, the beggar Lipp from Mautendorf in Lungau, a woman named Ursl, Hans Schittenkopf who is imprisoned in Himmelsberg.[47]

Based on the assumption that statements made in interrogations, particularly when made under torture, generally reflected what the investigator expected of them, and that confessions reveal more about the fantasies of the accuser than the accused, these denunciations give a picture of the type of people the judiciary were targeting: the beggars who roamed the lands were considered to be particularly prone to magical aggression, and judges did what they could to make sure certain names were given in the trials. 'Cross-eyed Blasy' alone named eight people who all belonged to this marginal group.

An analysis of the Carinthian witch trials shows clearly that both witnesses and courts perceived witchcraft as the collective crime of a witches' society of predominantly masculine character. This society as reflected in the confessions of the accused was analogous to the estates of the early modern era, with members of the nobility at the top of the hierarchy and their subjects serving them in the lowest strata.

This depiction of a destructive and secret devil's sect spanning all estates contrasts with the social profile of the people accused and executed in the witch trials. Of 128 people of known social status who were charged with witchcraft, almost half belonged to the lowest and most marginal estate of society.[48] Among this marginal group were four gypsies, accused in a rare case in the Holy Roman Empire.[49]

It cannot be said that the judiciary suppressed statements incriminating integrated members of society and the first estates; this would have been in contradiction to the new legal norms relating to inquisitional trials, as well as the obligation to record all aspects of court procedure in writing. What did happen, however, was that accusations of people from these higher social groups were not followed up with charges. For example, within a short space of time the courts exonerated four pastors suspected of witchcraft[50] and did not follow up accusations made against members of the upper bourgeoisie or the nobility. In court in 1603, a beggar by the name of Hans Träxler named as his teacher of witchcraft Anna Neumann of Wasserleonburg, the daughter of a wealthy merchant in Villach who had just married into the Carinthian nobility. She, he maintained, had promised him money if he would 'do a dreadful thing'. Under torture, however, he retracted his statement.[51] The influential woman in question was accused several times, but was never interrogated.[52] In Paternion in 1662, even accusations made against fully integrated farmers were not further pursued. When the accused, Regina Pauman denounced a considerable number of farmers these suspicions were not followed up and in the end the only people to actually be persecuted as a result of her denunciations were the vagrants Leonhard, Bärtl and Toni.[53] In 1705 the judge von Weisenegg released a farmer suspected of having made a pact with the Devil and instead prosecuted a group of 6 vagrants. When torture was ordered, it was only a question of time before they all confessed and were consequently

Illustration 8.1 A male witch in action, commiting some of his alleged crimes. Centre: damaging hail magic intended as a revenge on neighbours and landlord. Top right: sacrilege – the host as the symbol of the body of Christ is trampled on and then thrown to a dog to eat. Top left: A traveller is assaulted: a 'normal' crime not involving magic. (Leaflet from 1666, in: Stadtmuseum Munich, Grafiksammlung MI/320.)

sentenced to death.[54] Allegations which targeted people outside of the lowest social classes generally appeared implausible to the courts and were of no consequence in any further investigations. The courts had a clear image of likely suspects, and this image consisted largely of beggars and vagrants. Carinthian courts, then, pursued suspicions and denunciations on the basis of social strata and not, as in other territories of the empire, on family relations.

The personal information provided by many of these beggars and vagrants reveals the most harrowing circumstances, although it should be borne in mind that not all this information is necessarily entirely correct.

Beggars generally came from families of beggars.[55] The accused Hans Träxler, whose parents were also beggars, came from Lungau in the Prince-Archbishopric of Salzburg, moved from place to place, covering considerable distances. He named places where he had been in Styria and Salzburg and said that he had worked on occasion, but had not always been paid for his labours.[56] The same applied to 26-year-old

Simon N., who also came from the Salzburg region and travelled across the high Tauern mountain range and around Carinthia.[57] Both these two stories are typical of beggars' lives prior to the Thirty Years War.

The proportion of children and adolescents among the beggars and vagabonds in Carinthia was high. The tendency to prosecute young people became apparent in the southern Alps even before the so-called 'Zauberbuben' (boy witch) mass trials of 1675 to 1681. Bartl Schneider was just 15 years old when he was arrested for witchcraft in 1658. He told the court that he had had to roam the lands from an early age as his parents had been burnt as witches in Slovenia.[58] Kaspar Haintz who was arrested in 1653 had been roaming the countryside with other beggars since his thirteenth year and lived from odd jobs, for example as a swineherd.[59] The beggarboy Kholi was arrested in 1652 at the age of 16, a boy called Michael in 1664 at only eleven.[60] A boy known as Gregor did not know his own age but must have been between twelve and fourteen at the time of his arrest; Hans Winkler was 17 when a court had him arrested in 1631.[61] The witchcraft trial of 13-year-old Thomas N. in 1676[62] was connected with the Sorcerer Jack trials in which numerous young vagrants were accused of witchcraft in Salzburg.

At the other end of the scale, the Carinthian authorities also charged old vagrants. Stefan of Trägenwinkel, for example, was 76 and Lorenz Perauer 53[63] when they were brought before the court – in an early modern context, both old. Pankraz Sumer was unable to estimate his own age, no longer knew his mother and father, but both parents had abandoned him alone in a village as an adolescent boy. Since then he had been a beggar and had had occasional work 'weighing children' and 'caring for cattle'.[64] When Zacharias Feichter was told to pray in front of the court in Althofen in 1646 in order to prove his capacity to believe, all he managed to bring out was an 'Amen'[65]; it seems this, the closing word of a prayer, was all he associated with Christianity. In another trial in 1688, Thomas Schmaudl, born in Tirol, described his childhood as a beggarboy, his intermmitent work as a herdsman and his release from the army where he had served as a soldier. As Rumbl, another beggar and occasional herdsman, he had spent his subsequent life roaming from place to place.[66]

The physical disabilities of many of these vagrants are also much in evidence. The beggarboy Kholi had only one eye and so was no longer able to see in three dimensions; Blasius Kofler was also visually impaired, hence his nickname 'cross-eyed Blasy'; the old man, Lorenz Perauer was completely blind when he was arrested. The names of the beggars 'Kropf Paul' and 'Kropf Jakl' indicate that they had a thyroid condition fairly common in regions with a low level of iodine which causes swollen necks known as goitres or 'Kropf', resulting in severe breathing difficulties under exertion. The terms 'krummer [crooked] Vastl'and 'krummer Veidl' indicate that the such-named vagrants were hunchbacks, a condition often resulting from rickets or tuberculosis. The name 'Krumpfhändl', the one with the crooked hand, speaks for itself.[67] The judges noted that 40-year-old Simon Punz was partially paralyzed and unable to walk normally. He himself described his life as follows:

> When he was, as far as he knew, in his fourteenth year and still lived with his father, he was out on a road ... his whole body had suddenly buckled up and he was seized so badly that he had been obliged to spend almost a year bed-ridden in his father's house. On the advice of some good people, his father had carried him on his back a half-hour's journey from his house and set him down on an anthill in the hope that this would cure him, but it had not helped.... When his father died ten years ago and his mother was no longer alive he became a servant to his godfather but had not stayed long because of his crippled feet; since then had been a beggar.[68]

There is no reason to doubt this statement on the causes of Punz's plight. The description of his paralysis points to either polio or, more probably, a severe rheumatic complaint and it is highly plausible that the death of his parents robbed him of any social security, making him dependent on outside help. Begging was ultimately his only resort.

In summary, then, the vagrants suspected of witchcraft included not only people with physical disabilities but people who for other reasons were not fully employable in early modern agrarian society. In some cases, the replies given in the trials indicate that some of these people were mentally retarded. Even judges used terms such as 'einfältig' (simple-minded) or possibly mentally weak or at least backward, and not only when referring to the young accused. Leonhard, a vagrant described as old, was only able to communicate by means of signs, and the name 'verrückter Peter' (mad Peter), speaks for itself.[69]

Changed perception of charity and the crisis of the 17th century

Historical research has shown that the persecution of witches and beggars is synchronous in various parts of the Austrian hereditary lands.[70]

There are various opinions on the reasons for this coincidence: some authors see them in the persistent population increase in the Austrian regions in the 17th century; unlike other territories of the empire, Inner Austria did not suffer great losses in the Thirty Years War and the lower ranks of society increased in numbers due to the many soldiers released from service after 1648. This section of the lower estate often suffered a lack of material resources which forced them into vagrancy, marginalized them and finally, in the thinking of the sovereign authorities, criminalized them.[71] Other authors, however, explain the synchrony of these persecution processes in terms of a reevaluation of the status of poverty, which led to a change in the way vagrants were perceived and a growing lack of compassion. This was reflected in new far more restrained alms-giving practices on the part of the authorities, which ultimately developed into repressions and the growth of an active 'witch justice': By declaring beggars as witches they did away with the paternalistic poor policy, of which beggars had been the figurehead.'[72]

The following gives an outline of the social and economic developments which need to be elucidated before these theses can be discussed. The long-term economic depression which marked the 17th century came late, but all the more intensively, to the southeastern parts of the empire; one of its consequences was an increase in the marginilization of and pauperism among the lower classes in the region. This, combined with the fact that the Austrian population nearly doubled in the period 1527–1754, from 1.5 million to 2.7 million (the Carinthian population grew from ca. 150,000 to 250,000), was reason enough for an increase in the proportion of unemployed marginal groups in the lowest echelons of society to rise to 20 per cent.[73] In Carinthia, however, the economic development was experienced as a stagnation of the economy and not, as in other Austrian hereditary lands, as a tangible economic slump. Even mining was not as severely affected in Carinthia as in the rest of Inner Austria.[74]

The absolutist-minded authorities in many parts of the Holy Roman Empire reacted to the growing mass impoverishment with disciplinary strategies which reflected the rulers' universal claim to order. From 1620 onwards we can assume that absolutism had made its breakthrough in Carinthia.[75] Under a crisis ideology with a keynote which decreed that merit and achievement resulted from hardship and fear,[76] the tendency already apparent in the late Middle Ages to take action against vagrants was reinforced. In the numerous new classes of beggars laid down by government order, the authorities attempted to distinguish between socially acceptable and unacceptable marginal groups; to do this they introduced categories which included such terminology as 'honest' and 'self-inflicted poverty'.

In the Middle Ages beggars were more closely integrated in society and were able to rely on the alms which indeed were central to their salvation. By the 16th century, the process of marginalization and exclusion had further developed, as the view that work and poverty were of equal status disappeared. The work ethos upheld by Reformation and Counter-Reformation alike brought with it a moral deprecation of the status of poverty and enhanced the status of work. Idleness came to be perceived as a sin and a crime against the state. The conscientious and conformist subject became the positive antipode to the work-shy stigmatized beggarman or – woman, epitomized in the most negatively charged of all groups, the vagrant nomad and stranger.[77] Thus a process took place throughout large parts of Europe in which stigmatization turned into criminalization:

> Offenders were arrested and punished not because of their actions, but because of their marginal position in society. The implication was that vagrants were not ordinary criminals, they were regarded as a major threat to society.[78]

In 17th century Austria this social disciplining was a fundamental process manifested in the form of police regulations. In the new police regulations or 'Polizeyordnungen' punishment was threatened for perpetrating the following crimes: spontaneous blasphemous utterances, gluttony, adultery, swearing, gambling and, in particular illegal begging. For the betterment of the population the various authorities ordered that these regulations be read out regularly each month on the market squares and in the churches. They even went as far as to employ secret agents whose job it was to ensure compliance with the directives.[79] This goal was further to be achieved by a decentralization of poor relief, whereby these endeavours were directed in particular at the homeless and at those whose allegedly lunchaste lives did not conform with the new norms. One consequence of this reevaluation process was that the Inner Austrian government undertook large-scale deportations of vagrants in the first half of the 18th century. Beggars were detained and collectively transported to the border, where they were released onto the territories of neighbouring lands in which the bureaucratic administration of vagrants was not yet as advanced.[80] In 1683, Vienna alone transported 7000 beggars outside of the city boundaries.[81]

The survival chances and existence of vagrants in Carinthia also changed accordingly in the course of the 17th century. Due to the reduction of available resources resulting from the economic downturn and the erosion of traditional Christian charity, the people on the streets began to fight more offensively for their subsistence. Pleas for help became more aggressive in nature: beggars resorted to threats which they underpinned by references to their alleged magic skills and witchcraft powers. The vagrant Träxler threatened to employ weather magic in 1663 because a farmer 'had given him bad food both in the morning and the afternoon'.[82] Another vagrant admitted to having summoned a thunderstorm in which two farmers were killed by lightning because they had 'not paid him a wage'.[83] In 1630, Hans Sachs reacted similarly because the farmers in the area had treated him well in some cases, but had also done him ill.[84] Stefan of Trägenwinkel threatened to 'take a bite of' (that is, to kill, R.S.) the pigs in a farmyard 'because a farmer had not given him a cake to eat'.[85] Lorenz Perauer, an old man, admitted summoning frost to the detriment of the inhabitants of rural regions 'where the gruff people live who are not willing to give shelter or food'.[86] Other vagrants who also reported threats made to peasants out of revenge were: Hans of Veitsberg who disclosed that he had not received alms,[87] Augustin Felsberger, and in 1653 or 1676, a 13-year-old beggar boy by the name of Thomas N.[88] Another vagrant showed his gratitude to the rural population for their material support by purporting to use magic means to summon good weather to their farms. Upon his arrest, however, he attested frankly that he did not believe in such witchcraft and was totally incapable of committing this crime, and had only used such ploys to secure his own subsistence:

> What he had said he had heard from beggars, there were so many of them together in the shelter and they had spoken of witchcraft – things. He himself could do none of it, and most certainly had never actually performed anything...an injustice was being done to him...he had only repeated what the others had claimed, that is, that he was able to pronounce counter-spells to banish the weather magic. That is why the people thought he must be able to work magic. The reason why he made such suspicious statements about himself was that he hoped thus to be given more alms by the peasants and peasant women[89]

Beggars did not only use the threat of weather magic and consequent crop damage as a means of intimidation or revenge, but also attempted

derin sie jn wolten zu kleinen stucken hauwen / So hat der hencker die pulferseckh genumen / vnnd hats weit vnder das Volckh geworffen/ Also hat darnach der hencker dz holtz angezündt/hat aber das holtz nit prinen wellen/ denn der Teuffel mit dem pfarrer geredt hat / vnd zu im gesagt/er wol jn auß der pein helffen/wenn er sein wil sein/dz hat aber der Pfarrer nit thuen wellen/ darnach ist der Teuffel wider verschwunden/darnach hat das holtz angefangen zu prinen/vnd seint also veprunnen/man hat sy aber in ainer stund noch hören leben/Solches ist nun geschehen im 1575. jar den 18. Martij.

Illustration 8.2 The execution of a reputable male witch in March 1575 in Mittersill, present-day Austria. A court accused the parson, Ruprecht Ramsauer, a man over 70, and his housekeeper of having worked for decades together with the Devil to produce hail and weather magic. The coloured drawing to be found in the contemporary chronicle of Johann Jacob Wick, was not the work of an eye witness and thus, like many other illustrations, does not have the value of original source material. However, it is highly probable that it was drawn by a witness of other contemporary witch burnings. In the top left corner, the Devil can be seen offering to support the pastor in his hour of need if he will only commit himself to evil once more. A crowd of people can be seen in the background watching the execution. (In: Zentralbibliothek Zurich, Ms. F 24, 56.)

to use it strategically as a way of improving their position in short-term, verbal work agreements. Should their employers, mostly landowning farmers fully integrated into their estate in society, not honour these agreements, the vagrants had no means of ensuring that the terms of the contract be fulfilled. Aggressive threats, then, were part of a defensive strategy with which the beggars attempted to avoid being cheated out of their wages for the many seasonal jobs they undertook. The Carinthian sources provide no evidence of the 'lazy vagabond'; on the contrary, it seems the vagrants used every opportunity to take up work to ensure their own subsistence. Numerous statements made by witnesses, as well as the biographies, show that they took on a large number of tasks. Individual explanations for the increase in beggary are out of place here since structural reasons were the cause of this mass poverty. Wars, a long-term economic depression followed by a series of epidemics, and the way material resources and opportunity were distributed, brought about the mass impoverishment of this territory.

Vagrants were portrayed as antisocial deviants who lived off the community as a whole. But they were also a prime means of exemplifying norm deviations in other fields. In 1723, the well-known Italian archivist and Catholic priest, Ludvico Muratori, described the travelling folk in his work 'Della carità christiana' as 'malicious, devious, idle, work-shy and lustful beggars'.[90] He associated the lives of vagrants with dissolute sexual practice, the background to such fantasies being the fact that beggar couples were forced by the marriage restrictions which required a couple to possess certain financial means, to live in extramarital relationships, which the church, in turn, no longer tolerated. Muratori here equated the term 'extramarital' with sexual deviance. In the Carinthian witchcraft trials, these ideas in combination with alleged maleficium rapidly turned into the familiar image of a sexual liaison with the Devil; this assumed evidence of sexual perversion was then seen to fortify the image of the accused as the negative antithesis to the newly established sexual norms. Muratori's work appeared in the German language in Vienna in the second half of the 18th century, thus lending further moral authority to the policy hitherto applied.

The social control and regulative policy practised in absolutist states explain the persecution of deviant behaviour, but not the way this was criminalized in the witchcraft trials. Carinthia was not alone in pronouncing mandates against beggars. The sovereign of Brunswick-Lüneburg passed 18 decrees between 1650 and 1698,[91] 48 mandates were issued in Upper Lusatia between 1590 and 1797,[92] all without an ensuing increase in the number of witch trials. Neither was the population increase between 1500 and 1750 peculiar to Inner Austria.[93]

The reasons for the particular direction taken by the witch persecutions in Carinthia must be sought rather in the mental reevaluation process of the time than in the social and economic developments which, without doubt, took place in this period. At a time when the disfunctionality of witch persecutions was becoming apparent in other parts of the empire, the slow east-west shift meant that the witch paradigm was relatively late in reaching Inner Austria. As late as 1569 a council in Salzburg, which was responsible for Carinthia, dismissed witchcraft in true mediaeval Catholic tradition as a product of the imagination. This council decreed that in cases of witchcraft accusations the illusory nature of witchcraft should be pointed out and the sinners, whether male or female, be given religious instruction so as to enable them to return to the Christian community. Only intractable persons should be reported to the higher church authorities.[94] These arguments, which were fully in line with the traditions of the High Middle Ages, were still being proponed at a time when major witch-hunts were taking place in more westerly territories such as the Catholic Electorate of Trier and the Catholic Duchy of Lorraine. The theologians in Salzburg still viewed the belief in maleficium and the witches' flight as punishable crimes and contested the feasability of witchcraft.

However, the pattern of witchcraft teachings as received at this late date in this eastern region was one which was no longer controversial (either as an entity or in its individual elements) in demonology discourse, for at the latest since the appearance of Bodin's works, Catholic demonology had regarded witchcraft as a collective crime. Correspondingly, the courts applied a specific pattern to outsiders who were not an integral part of the social estates and who were reputed to pose a threat. The Assembly of the Estates in Styria, a neighbour of Carinthia's, had already construed a connection between vagrants and witchcraft crimes in 1580, when it declared:

> ...that it is not only the travelling agricultural labourers but also other deleterious persons who steal dishonourably and work magic or commit similar deeds and who have given themselves up entirely to a life of idleness, who occasionally roam the land[95]

It was this association of serious crime, such as witchcraft, with marginal social groups which, against the background of the economic crisis of the 17th century, was then revived and brought up to date, paving the way for an interpretation of witchcraft as a collective crime.

Contrary to the assumptions of certain interest groups, beggar groups were loosely organized since they would otherwise have undermined their own subsistence; this is documented by the question catalogues and the judges' interrogation strategies in the witchcraft trials. They did not strive to lead a collective form of life and certainly did not set up formal communication channels or structures[96] but rather formed informal, heterogeneous, spontaneous groups without any long-term contacts.

It is apparent, however, from the records of the Carinthian witchcraft trials that the authorities stylized vagrants as a formal, highly cohesive, and instrumentally rationalized and organized group. The courts were quick to ask about the members of the respective 'teams' or 'Rotten' ('companies') who the judges assumed to have taken part in the collective conspiracy; the goal was to obtain, under torture, as many names of known vagrants as possible; these people would then be accused of a common conspiracy.

The Inner Austrian government with its absolutist tendencies was able to assert its focus on this social element against the local authorities which were not yet partners to this policy. For instance, in 1671 a local court acquitted the 20-year-old beggar Hans Schlegele of witchcraft (and even granted him alms upon his release) on the grounds that there was no circumstantial evidence and because he was clearly mentally retarded. However, the Inner Austrian government to which Carinthia was subordinate, reacted with the harsh instruction 'the more so because such simpletons are easily and most often infected with witchcraft, this subtle matter'[97] that Schlegele be re-arrested and a witchcraft trial opened. Ten years earlier the councillors of Graz had ordered that the sermons on three consecutive Sundays should point out the connection between witchcraft and begging. In this mandate they declared that beggars were the principal perpetrators of 'the vice of witchcraft' and that witchcraft aroused the wrath of God with a multitude of negative consequences for harvest and health.[98] The communication, which was certainly sent to all Styrian – if not also to other – pastors, thus called for the exterminition of all vagrants according to the Christian policy of order, and placed all such people under general and collective suspicion. Clearly, the authorities could not have been motivated by the expectation of any personal gain from these paupers, for the costs of the trials were generally borne by the keepers of the courts and not the alleged delinquents.[99]

The social order policy of the Counter-Reformation joined forces, then, with the witch persecutions but was also supported by the integrated estates of the population, as expressed in a report on the Carinthian farmers, who in 1691 called upon an official, himself not unwilling to persecute, to actually make an arrest:

> My noble, gracious and highly esteemed lord! Upon my visit to the church festivities in Weitschach a fortnight ago, I was sought out in the courthouse by Christian Pämber ... and many of his neighbours, who asked whether I might not arrest and confine the beggar Anderl, for he had made suspicious speeches on the Monday after the first church fair. Thereupon I took a large number of peasants to task, who not only confirmed the above but added that it was high time this man be removed, for there was nothing useful about him. Yet they were unable to put forward any true evidence against him. To find a motive for this and to relieve the parish of its scruples, I have been looking out for this man for many years.[100]

In this case a vagrant, later charged as a male witch, was decried as useless to society. This example shows how an integration ideology was able to unite the authorities with the populace in the struggle against male and female witches. However, the low number of persecutions in Carinthia shows that this identity of interests was not pronounced in this region, and witch persecutions or denunciations were not as intensive on either side as they were in other territories.

The reason for the focus on men in Carinthia's witch persecutions is to be found in the structure of early modern vagrant groups. The representatives of both central and local state poor relief considered that men were mobile and more easily able to procure their own subsistence than women; this meant they were not entitled to receive alms on an organized basis. Thus, the wandering groups of impoverished people consisted largely of men, whereas the non-vagrant beggars were mostly female.[101] This was certainly the profile of vagrants in Carinthia. In order to secure themselves some means of remaining alive in a period when charitableness was on the decrease, beggars tended to appear in small groups, thus improving their potential to make threats. It is not, then, surprising that under interrogation male beggars named their travelling comrades and other beggars of their acquaintance, so that the courts ultimately drew entire circles of such vagrants into the witch trials. The authorities had so assimilated the image of the witches' Sabbat that the courts were able to sift out the identified target group of male persons and to ignore any other – for example, female – suspects.

The witch persecutions in Carinthia stand for a typical process of social labelling: economic crises meant certain people were deprived of the chance to work legally, were thus driven out of integrated society, refused the traditional means of poor relief, were discriminated against and were collectively accused of criminal acts. The outsiders came to be regarded as delinquents and ultimately began to act accordingly. Yet this explanation alone does not do justice to the complex reality of the situation. The vagrants reacted with aggression to this crisis in Christian charity and demanded what they believed they were entitled to – if necessary using their alleged magic omnipotence as a means of blackmail.

In the imagination of some of these beggars this alleged competence took on a kind of reality. In 1671, for example, Hans Schlegele admitted voluntarily to having worked disastrous weather magic, to being able to fly, and to having posed a threat by planning crimes at the witches' gatherings.[102] Gregor N., only a little over ten years old, described in an interrogation without torture, how he had flown to the clouds and how rainfall had ensued.[103] Zacharias Feichter, a beggarboy, also declared without being tortured that he was able to fly.[104] In 1666, the elderly vagrant, Stefan, also claimed to be able to summon rain – again, in an interrogation where torture was not applied.[105] Eighteen-year-old Caspar Haintz boasted of maleficium in a pre-trial investigation where no threats had been uttered on the part of the court.[106] In 1676, the young beggar, Thomas also admitted voluntarily to being a witch and to being able to use an ointment to cause showers to fall.[107] In another trial without torture Paul Schäfer depicted himself as the master of a wolf-like dog which attacked and killed cattle at his command. When the court investigated this alleged damage, it was found to be untrue, invented by the accused.[108] These accused male witches and 'Zauberbuben' ('sorcerer lads') transformed the accusations with which they were confronted into self-accusations – even though such a self-accusation was often a justification for the pronouncement of a death sentence.

Marked from early childhood by social exclusion, with no chance of developing any self-assurance or esteem, beggars began to fantasize that they possessed a capacity for magic, and this they ultimately perceived as their reality. The witch trials provided these ostracized and humiliated people with a stage on which they might receive the attention they had so long foregone and perhaps find some gratification. By identifying themselves with evil, they were attempting to procure themselves some

Illustration 8.3 Taken bare-chested to their public execution: the male witches Paul, Gumprecht and Jacob Pappenheimer (and the only woman, the wife and mother, Anna Pappenheimer), the farm labourer Ulrich Schmälzl and the tailor Georg Schölz all admitted to fire and weather magic and harm of cattle, as well as to manslaughter. All were tied and taken thus to the stake (Leaflet from 1600 in: Stadtmuseum Munich, Grafiksammlung M I/532.)

last social standing and to compensate for their many years of powerlessness. The phenomenon by which a person uses the omnipotence of fantasies to flee from their impotence in real life has been described in detail in youth psychology as a typical depravation or development phenomenon[109] and interpreted as a cry for help and recognition.

In the second half of the 17th and the first half of the 18th century the stigmas that these vagrants thus inflicted on themselves ultimately led to the death sentences and beheadings. The witch trials were also able to develop in this way because their victims, most of whom were men, largely accepted the roles ascribed to them. These male victims could, however, only be considered role players in the witch persecutions because majority opinion in Catholic demonology did not exclude men from participation in witchcraft crimes; indeed, it specifically named men as suitable candidates as agents in secret diabolical societies.

Mediaeval inquisition and male heretics

In the Austrian hereditary lands, the persecution of alleged, and primarily male, members of secret societies was rooted in tradition. From the

13th century onwards numerous Waldensian communities had settled in Lower and Upper Austria, and despite waves of persecution had remained, among other places, in Carinthia into the 15th century.[110] Travelling preachers were the connection between the various Waldensian groups, celebrating with them their masses according to Waldensian rites. As the grasp of the Inquisition became felt, the official church began to assert itself more powerfully and renewed the massive attacks on this self-assured community. Records dating from 1436 onwards report a bitter extirpation process, which also reached Carinthia and Styria. The Waldensian bishop, Stefan Neumeister, who was burnt in Wien-Himberg in 1467, gave the number of his followers in Austria as 80,000. The Inquisitors, outraged at the degree of hereticism rampant in many a region,[111] spread the notion of a Waldensian devil's cult which was manifested in secret night gatherings, the 'heretics' Sabbat', hence creating imageries which could later be recalled and rejuvenated. The anti-heretic traditions became felt again towards the end of the 15th century, but more strongly from 1630 onwards. The idea of an extensive conspiracy could easily be applied theologically to new heretical groups. In Upper Austria, the region where there had been so many heretics in the Middle Ages, it was primarily men who became the victims of the witch-hunts of the 16th to 18th centuries, and in Carinthia with its many mediaeval Waldensian communities[112] the proportion of men accused was also above average. By contrast, there were fewer trials of alleged male than of female witches in the neighbouring county of Tirol, in which only few heretic trials (the primary targets of which were men) were conducted by the Inquisition in the Middle Ages.

Traditions of persecution, social conflicts and the witch

The main Carinthian male witch type comes from the lowest class of vagrants and beggars, a group which overlapped with that of the cattleherds. Neither of these groups was integrated, and both represented people living on the verge of starvation, in conflict with the fully integrated population of the estates. Most of these people were accused of weather magic, a variant of maleficium which was ascribed to women in other regions of Europe.

In comparison with the rest of Europe, the witch persecutions began late in Carinthia, at a time when the female witch stereotype was already outdated. Yet, the fact that the numbers of trials did not peak until the late 17th century is not sufficient to explain the high proportion of men accused. Factors such as the beginnings of social disciplining, which in

Carinthia was directed by way of witchcraft accusations at the vagrants in the population, also played an important role. A further determining factor was the extension, or continuity, of the persecution of male heretics which had begun in this region in the Middle Ages, although both the authorities and the non-vagrant population now accused not heretics but a newly arisen group of apparently destructive persons. The persecution traditions formed, or at least influenced, the image of the gender of this allegedly aggressive group. The fantasies of the heretics' Sabbat or the Devil's cult, were transferred to its variant, the witches' Sabbat. This collective component of the witchcraft concept played a major role in Carinthia's witch trials, although it cannot be said to have set mass trials in motion.

In less than half the cases were the accused primary male witches, in all other cases they became involved in the trials as a result of denunciations. Nonetheless, neither the accused, nor the accusor nor the witnesses viewed the roles of these secondary male witches as ancillary: This means that men were not just drawn into witch trials as boy-witches, Sabbat-attendees or as relatives of accused women, but as primary suspects – in other words, as suspects themselves accused of witchcraft in their own right.

9
Male Witches, Feminized Men or Shamans?

> We know that, after the flight, the accused, like all other witchfolk, had a particular kind of demon at the gatherings, the men had a bride, and the women a bridegroom.
>
> (Reason given by the judge for a sentence passed in a witch trial near Regensburg 1689)

> (There are) ... effeminate men who have no Zeal for the Faith ...
>
> (Heinrich Institoris 1486)

> I removed the heart and the liver of a pike, these I smoked to intoxicate the possessed people; I then pulled apart a pitch-black hen and laid it on their heads ... to expel the evil spirits ...
>
> (Christoph Gostner, a healer in South Tyrol, 1595)

Two unequivocal conclusions can be drawn from the systematic analysis of witch trials in Holstein, Carinthia and Franche-Comté:

First, the courts charged large numbers of men independently of women and in their own right. Their identification as alleged witches was neither a by-product of trials of female witches, nor can it be seen as collateral damage. Side by side with and on the same level as the female witch there stood a male witch, who was by no means a scaled-down or dwarf version of the majority type. Notwithstanding these general conclusions, any analysis of gender distribution must take account of regional context and popular as well as learned witch images, for the dynamics of the witch-hunts produced absolute majorities of female witches just as they occasionally also produced only a minority.

Secondly, there is no clearly defined type of male witch; the personal and structural features of the accused varied considerably. As far as marital status was concerned, the majority of male witches in Holstein were married, in contrast to the Austrian beggars, who tended to be single and have no permanent relationships. In Franche-Comté about half of the men accused as werewolves appear to have been married. Neither was there any homogeneity in terms of age; the witch beggars of Carinthia consisted of old as well as very young vagrants. The ages of the male suspects in Holstein and Franche-Comté varied, but the majority in the early modern period appear to have been old or middle-aged. The types of magic ascribed to male witches also varied from region to region: whereas in Carinthia, men were accused of weather magic, in the west of the empire, this type of magic was ascribed mainly to women.

Despite these differences, large groups of accused male witches in the three territories were in fact distinguishable from other sections of society by reason of their social status.

A person's position in early modern society, unlike in the class society of the 19th century, depended not only on property and financial assets, but on social capital, the 'social capital of honour' (Bourdieu). In the three territories investigated here, a high proportion of male witches counted among those who, according to both economic and symbolical criteria, either had no place in, or were precariously situated on the periphery of, the estates of Central European society. A statistically relevant number, particularly of the primary male witches, experienced social disadvantages which excluded them to a greater or lesser extent from social life, although their individual circumstances varied greatly.

In other territories such as Bamberg or Trier[1] substantial numbers of men from the middle estates, and a few from the upper estates were accused as male witches. This number should not, however, be overestimated: the men persecuted in the first panics in Bamberg came primarily from the lowest social groups, and even in the principal major hunts of 1626 to 1630 only one in four men arrested for witchcraft came from the higher administrative classes. The victims also included craftsmen such as bakers, butchers, smiths and shoemakers. The large number of innkeepers, wine merchants and coopers is especially noteworthy, for it seems that these people, whose occupations involved handling food and drink, were most likely to be accused of intent to poison. Nevertheless, it should not be forgotten that members of the lowest social classes formed the majority of those denounced as Sabbat-attendees, and that many a servant, day labourer, fisherman, musician or grave-digger was also burnt.[2]

The various hypotheses proposed in research to date each only partially cover the reasons for the male witchcraft trials when based on

Illustration 9.1 This image depicts the alleged male witch, 78-year-old Simon Altseer in Rottenbuch, Bavaria invoking the Devil from a magic circle. When the Devil appears and gives him a magically charged pot, Altseer conjures up a multitude of heavy hail- and thunderstorms – at least according to the confession he made under torture. It was for this weather magic that the court charged the old man with witchcraft. (In: Stadtmuseum Munich, Grafiksammlung M I/320.)

theories which are *exclusive* of other possibilities. There is no mono-causal explanation for the trials of male witches; such historical developments can only be explained by a combination of many different factors. The 'relationship approach', the 'mass-trial approach', the 'difference' approach and the 'heresy approach' when taken alone each only provide partial explanations, are too rigid in their systematization and give incomplete explanations of the realities of early modern Central Europe. Depending on the political and social situation and the historical and cultural influences, one or more of these factors can weigh more heavily than the others.

Were male witches possibly feminized or 'womanish' men? Let us take a look at contemporary discourse: In his widely disseminated work of 1629 the theologian Johann Bergmann discussed typical behaviour of men and women, thus addressing an issue which was once more of major interest during this, the peak persecution phase. The author cites numerous authorities from Antiquity and the Middle Ages and, having made detailed reference to Ancient Greek, Roman and Christian ideas and analyzed and debated the issue, draws his conclusions as to the typical features of the two sexes. Women, he wrote, are characterized by their 'inconstancy, frivolity, wrath and impatience', men by their 'prudence, greatness of mind, discretion, forgivingness and steadfastness in the face of misfortune'.[3] With this description, Bergmann drew up and validated a concept of femininity and masculinity which was based on a construct of opposites. However, in attempting to present this very distinct message and rigid catalogue of characteristics to his contemporaries as exemplary, traditional and proven, the theologian Bergmann proved to be ahead of his time. Historical research has shown that such polarities were not generally existent as social constructs at this time, and the possible spectrum of gender-related attributes and identities was wider than Bergmann allowed. The discussion of typical gender-specific characteristics was not complete and a glance at various ways of life in the early modern period shows that masculinity was also lived in a way which did not correspond to this classic duality of the sexes. Bergmann must, thus, be viewed as representative of an intellectual movement whose goal it was to establish a definitive hegemonic pattern. It was not, however, until the Enlightenment that the 'gender profile patterns' became thus restricted – in theory as in practice.[4]

The analysis of demonology in chapter 5 shows that many attributes ascribed to women were also applicable to men. In the context of the predominant contemporary theological world view and at a time when patriarchal rule, hitherto viewed as a vital element of existence, was seen to be on the brink of collapse, the 'feminized' men, the author of the Witches' Hammer stressed, acquired genuine characteristics of the opposite sex. From these men the male witches were recruited[5] who, by reason of their potential proximity to witchcraft crime broke through the dichotomous pattern of gender differences both in theoretical discussion and in terms of their very real persecution. These men were indirectly feminized, yet they were most clearly not regarded as women – they remained men.[6]

This raises the question as to whether, ultimately, these men were not in fact also victim to a narrower and more restrictive social view of gender profiles. In other words: Did the witch-hunts not serve, directly or indirectly, as a means of establishing new norms of gender ideals and asserting and publicizing these norms via the inclusion of men in witch trials? This question is too complex to be answered within the confines of this study; it is, however, certain that the gender-specific structure of the witch-hunts was not a reflection of the rigid gender polarity asserted in contemporary debate on typical male and female characteristics. The British historian Larner's definition of the persecutions as 'sex-related, not sex-specific', does not apply across the board for all periods and all regions in which witches were sent to the stake.

The developments towards binary role allocation during the study period which ascribed moral offences predominantly to women, also permeated the persecution of male witches. Neither the demonologies nor persecution practice accused men – to put it cautiously – to the same degree as women of sexual deviance. Male witches did not copulate as frequently with the Devil as their female counterparts; their ambivalence in their faith was the reason why they allegedly turned to the Devil. Male witches were associated with the typically male category, intellect, whereas women were reduced to the level of their bodies and sexuality.

The fundamental openness of the witch pattern can be seen in the lexical development, in the terminology used to describe the phenomenon witchcraft, for this was not uniform throughout the empire. In demonological literature and in regions where there was a high proportion of male persecution, a new term developed, the 'Hexin'. Contemporary German used the suffix '-in' to designate a person as female, but the noun 'Hexe' (witch) to which this suffix was added was grammatically already unambiguously feminine. The jurist and translator from Lorraine, Johann Fischart, for example, used this term repeatedly, and in direct contrast to the male witch:

> When the man saw a large number of male witches and *female witches* [*'Hexinne'*] roaming and swarming around, many of them known to him, he exclaimed in amazement, 'Oh my God, where are we?'[7]

It could be argued that Fischart's intention was to give a correct rendering of the French nouns 'sorcier/sorcière'; however, the terms used by this southern German satirist are also found in other sources. 'Hexin' was also used in conflict situations which might have given rise to an accusation or charge of witchcraft; i.e. it had already found its way into colloquial usage. In 1629, a male citizen of the town of Miltenberg on the River Main described a woman as follows:

> 'You [female] witch [*'Hexin'*], should also be burnt.'

Then, turning to her son, he said,

> 'You [male] witch [*'Hexenmann'*], you thief, you should be burnt just like your mother'.[8]

Mother and son died at the stake the same year, following a series of denunciations for alleged witchcraft by the inhabitants of the town.

This newly developed term is in fact linguistically redundant, containing as it does two features describing grammatical genus, where only one is necessary. In cases where the term 'Hexin' was used, then, the original word 'Hexe' was differentiated, generalized and used to mean both men and women. On a lexic level, it was still feminine, when designating a person, however, it was neutralized and had no clear genus. Semantically, the term 'Hexe' had also changed, for it had lost some of its female characteristics and was sometimes used as a generic term. Alongside this term 'Hexe' with its tendency to non-gender-specific meaning, the clearly gender-specific terms *'Hexin and Hexenmann'* (male witch) were used.

The new name for female witches appears at times of crisis in many areas of the empire in connection with extensive charges of magic. *'Hexin'* is found in southern and central but also in eastern and northern parts, as well as in German-speaking regions outside the empire.[9]

The word 'Hexe' was found in word formations which, because grammatically neutral, referred to both genders. This occurred in particular through the formation of certain plurals. A list of the people executed in a town with a high level of persecution was no longer called a 'Hexenliste' (list of witches) but

> 'Lists of the *witch-folk* [*'Hexen-Leute',* men and women, R.S.] beheaded and burnt in Würzburg'[10]

and in the reasoning of the court in an extensive trial:

> Whereupon court was held beneath the town hall and ... the *witch-folk* ... were brought before the judge.[11]

This new generic term led to the development of forms in which the word 'Hexe' was used adjectivally to describe a semantically generic noun. An example from another key persecution zone illustrates this usage:

> His wife had told him before his arrest that he was to name many other *witchish persons* [*'hexische Personen'*] ... as his accomplices.[12]

In 1612, the authors of an interrogation catalogue for use in trials in Mainz sought to avoid the problem which had arisen from the ambiguity of various terms for the witchraft phenomenon by reverting to unmistakable wording. The sub-title of their work clearly dilineated who they were referring to:

> Questions to be put to *magical male and female persons* ['*zauberische Mann- und Weibs-Personen*'] while under arrrest.[13]

Linguistic developments can also be observed for the category persecuted men, and these should be viewed in the context of persecution practice. For example, the following is recorded for a man from the Electorate of Mainz whose mother had been burnt as a witch,

> This Jörg Schlader was now publicly considered to be a *male witch* ['*Hexenmann*']. It no longer pleases anybody to see his face, and he is fearful for he does not know where to stay.[14]

This passage describes the uprooting and distress of a stigmatized person who was unable to defend himself in the face of accusations against a relative. It clearly expresses this man's fear and the threat he faced of being seen as a male witch without any subaltern functions.

In addition to 'Hexenmann', the term 'Hexenmeister' (literally: witch-master) was in common use. Semantically, this term had a double function, meaning not only simply a male witch but also a witch with a leading or special position within the witches' sect. When, in 1663, a man accused in Esslingen of witchcraft denounced a female witness as a 'Hexenmann', she fiercely rejected the idea, but finally admitted to having 'learnt witchcraft from a now deceased *Hexenmeister*'.[15]

In this sense, then, a 'Hexenmeister' was someone who, in the imagined contemporary world, held a leading position and passed on his knowledge. In the demonologies, these 'Hexenmeister' held higher military ranks, as, for example, portrayed by Del Rio, and punished witches who did not fulfil their destruction potential. The concept 'Hexenmeister' in the sense of witch-master again shows that the power structures of the witches' Sabbat in the other world bore similarity to those of this world. In this of all spheres, the inverted world of these gatherings, the cult centre of witchcraft, assumed the gender hierarchy structures of early modern society, for here, as the sovereigns their territories the Devil ruled his world supported by his male dignitaries.

The concept of what constituted a male witch thus remained ambivalent for men accused of witchcraft crimes. On the one hand, they were often ascribed female tasks, space and roles, but on the other – particularly

Illustration 9.2 Torture of the 60-year-old farmer and town councillor Holger Lirtz. The leg screws are applied and the alleged male witch groans with pain. Lirtz had been denounced by a woman in an earlier interrogation; his good reputation was obviously not sufficient in the eyes of the witch commissioner Buirmann to spare him these agonies. After many hours of interrogation during which the pricking test was carried out almost 30 times on supposed Devil's marks on the body of the old man, Lirtz confessed – and was executed. The background shows a victim being hoisted up, his hands tied together behind his back and weights attached to his legs. (From: Hermann Löher, *Most Melancholy Complaint*, 1676, pp. 35–39, in: Alte Bibliothek, St Michael's Grammar School, Bad Münstereifel.)

in Catholic demonology – some performed leadership functions in the hierarchy of the Devil's sect. They punished for deviant behaviour in the anti-world women whom they did not consider to be sufficiently evil and aggressive. The Devil's cosmos, it is true, was one of inverted (or reversed) order, but for male theoreticians this did not apply to male–female relationships!

And yet, men were burnt as alleged members of the Devil's sect who, in their own understanding, aspired to recognize witchcraft and counter its harmfulness, that is to fight against this anonymous organization. Did the Christian rulers and authorities misinterpret the doings of these counter-magic specialists, suspecting them of witchcraft and maleficium, and is this why they began their process of eradication? It is argued that the 'witch-doctors' who popular culture viewed in a positive light, were also accused of witchcraft because Christian demonology saw magic and counter-magic as identical activities.[16] Were these healers and soothsayers possibly the European version of shamans, the very antipodes of evil spirits and hence, logically, also of witches?

Although the activities and distinctive features of shamans vary from one society to another, certain fundamental elements are common to all:[17] Shamans are, in most cases, male persons who have access to the spirits and souls of the deceased. They play a mediating and ritual role between the natural and the other world, for they are able to cross the boundary between the two. From this cosmologically privileged position developed the tasks of healing, divining and warding off misfortune. In order to enter the invisible world and to communicate with the spirits, shamans combine special techniques, rituals and equipment in dramatic performances. To be able to make this contact with the immaterial world the shaman has to enter an altered state of consciousness. The rituals are performed in public, and shamans use music, singing or, in some societies, drumming to place themselves in the necessary physical and mental states. Shamans frequently, but not always, undertake an extrabodily journey, usually accompanied by spiritual helpers, to wrest the soul of the sick person away from the evil spirits. The soul can then return to the body, the alien spirit lets go and the sick person recovers. Here, the greatest workload and thus any victory is borne primarily by the spiritual helpers.[18]

The basic thought behind shamanism is the idea that all that occurs on earth is shaped by spiritual powers. In the states in which the soul leaves the body or is occupied by the spirits so that it is able to contend with them, counter-magic specialists counter the attacks of aggressive forces in what might be termed a battle of spirits.

Shamans and witches, then, represent opposite poles in human societies. Shamans can, admittedly, also be destructive – indeed, in some societies they could even be killed for their destructive works – but their principal function was one of protecting from and healing sickness.

However, since counter-magic specialists or cunning-folk were only one group among the male victims of the witch persecutions, the fact that magic specialists and shamans were treated as equivalents is only a partial explanation for the presence of men among the accused. Among the variants of shamanism were also those in settled peasant societies in which there were many cases where women took on the role of the shaman.[19] Female cunning-folk, whether self-professed or thus designated by others, constituted only a small proportion of the female majority before the European courts of justice. Quantitative reasons alone, then, show that shamanism is not a sufficient explanation for the numbers of men accused of witchcraft.[20]

Similarities are not the same as analogies, and parallelisms are not causalities. It is true that male witches in Central Europe practised ritual magic, as shamans do, but hardly any mentions of dramatic performances, altered states of consciousness or even extrabodily journeys are to be found in the sources, and those notations that do exist are fragmentary and inconsistent; see for example, the cases of Conrad Stoeckhlin in Bavaria[21] and possibly some accused from the Jura mountains of France. In the case of other cunning men such as Christoph Gostner or Mathias Perger in Tirol these alleged shamanic aspects were either no longer recognizable or had never existed.[22] Analogies can only be assumed for an extremely small percentage of the men designated as male witches. Cunning-men did not work in the open,[23] and ritual equipment such as drums, were indeed used at the witches' Sabbat meetings, but there is no record of them being used in therapeutic seances. According to reports (including those few reports which were made without the influence of torture) of the phenomenon which comes closest to the extrabodily journey, the witches' flight, help and healing were rarely expected of these gatherings. Neither did the collective drama of the witches' gatherings correspond to the individual struggles of the shamans.[24] In view of the fact that witch persecutions in Central Europe were initiated by sections of the population, the question arises as to why the very people who had allegedly suffered at the hands of witches should turn to shamans, people who believed invisible spirits and not real, identifiable persons, i.e. witches, to be the cause of evil in the world.

Similarities can at best be discerned when shamanism is stripped of its core elements, the special relationship with, or control over, spirits, dissociation of body and soul, and its disturbing seances, as discussed in ethnological research.[25] Such a constricted version of this world view can, however, be linked to all forms of magic, for it implies the loss of shamanism's own specific profile.

The belief in witches – and with it the charges made against men – may possibly have roots in shamanism, but the peculiarities of shamanism appear vary rarely, if at all, in the male trials in the regions studied here. Individual sources describing trials of men in north Sweden and north Norway and possibly also in parts of southeastern Europe, do seem to provide evidence of shamanic practices[26] – but these are not territories of the Holy Roman Empire in Central Europe. The persecutors sought the alleged male witch in other settings and groups; all that was needed was violent staging on the part of the courts to find him there and send him to his death at the stake.

10
The Power of the 'Witch Folk' and the Rulers

> Not all those who dance are merry.
>
> (Christoph Lehmann, town scribe in Speyer, 1570–1638)

By the early modern period witch theory had cast aside the idea that what constituted witchcraft was harm caused by individuals to other individuals; this had been rejected in favour of the concept that witches represented a major attack of organized crime on society as a whole, an attack which involved the use of violence, was planned to take place over an indefinite period of time and was based on power struggles and a division of labour within a hierarchical system.

In contemporary fantasy, witches attacked such basics as life, health, nutrition and fertility, and were thus endowed with an almost unlimited power to destabilize society, destroying its morality and forcing this world – in a reversal of the divine order of things – to bow to Satan's rule. The danger of alleged witches, then, lay in their involvement in the plots and intrigues of a worldwide conspiracy devised by a secret society. Witches were not perceived as people on the periphery of society who openly committed their evil deeds, but rather as people who deliberately worked their destructive powers from within. Sooner or later, their presence would strike at the very heart of a community. Witches were not enemies in the sense of the visible external enemy encountered in a war but opponents who had to be exposed on the domestic front.

This was reflected in the Catholic, and to an extent also in the Protestant demonology of the 16th to 18th centuries, in particular in the portrayal of the witches' Sabbat. Demonologists varied in their fantasies as to the individual facets of this illusory gathering, but they all agreed that the witches' Sabbat was the 'inversion' and antithesis of the Christian world.[1] The concept of the witches' Sabbat as interpreted by learned elite culture presented dramatically negative images which evoked not only the idea of a gathering in which Christian rituals were systematically inverted, but also visions of an anti-society with deviant and aggressive norms. Satan's followers possessed characteristics which should be abhorred by any Christian person, therefore the witch stood at the end of every scale of moral values: the witch image contains parodic symbols, such as the witches' feast as a mirror of conviviality, symbols of perversion such as incest and bestiality, necrophile fantasies such as the boiling up of childrens' bodies, and general ideas of inversion, such as nocturnalism.

This went so far that the Catholic theologian Binsfeld, for example, saw the activities of this satanic organization not only as a threat to Christian society but as a danger to the entire physical existence of humanity. He wrote in 1592:

> The male and female witches (*'malefici'*) associate with the Devil to the detriment of human beings and the destruction of all things that are important for the well-being of body and soul.... For this reason the above-mentioned law calls them enemies of common welfare.... The male and female witches associate with the Devil to ruin the human race.[2]

In this description of these demonic and destructive troops Binsfeld uses the grammatical masculine plural but semantically gender-neutral term witches (*'malefici'*) in order to include both sexes in his statement.

In 1606 the Catholic judge Boguet wrote of the 'countless number [of witches] proliferating by the day'.[3] He compared this Devil's sect with a Hydra whose heads always regrew when cut off, and which in this era of the 'Antichrist' had to be combatted with the greatest severity if the Christian world was to be saved.[4] In another edition of his treatise he estimated the number of witches of both sexes at 1,800,000,[5] all of whom were set to destroy Christian society.

The witch commissioner Schultheiß was of the opinion that the Christian way of life could only be saved by the employment and active deployment of witch persecutors, for the power of the Devil and his agents was so great 'that even if there was an interruption of only a few years in the extirpation process, Christianity would be suppressed'.[6]

The French jurist, Bodin, in particular, was key to divesting the Devil's sect of its anonymity, for he ascribed their destructive works to a wide range of people:

> I have said that Satan has [male] witches of all different qualities: He used to have several popes. He has kings, princes, priests, preachers and in several places judges, doctors, in short he has people of all professions...[7]

This clearly shows that the threat emanating from the Devil's sect is upmost in Bodin's mind; the gender of the Devil's agents was important but not key. The princes play a major role in this power struggle between the divine and satanic worlds, for agents of the Devil are to be found even amongst their number. And it was precisely these people who were leading humanity to a bloodbath. Their activity, in Bodin's mind an indisputable and proven fact, was an indicator of the degree of political and social subversion which had already penetrated Christian society. Their intention, Bodin argued, was to reverse the positive values of the Christian community – where they had not already destroyed them:

> Furthermore, Satan has nothing greater than his appeal to the princes. For since they have become immersed in this, they must do Satan's will, that is they mock all religion and provide their subjects with examples of all manner of lasciviousness, incest, parricide, cruelty, exacting taxes and exciting sedition among their subjects, or [inciting] civil war to see bloodshed...[8]

According to Bodin, sheer numbers – he gives 100,000 to 300,000 as a likely figure – as well as the wide span of the organization's membership are the reasons for its great power.[9]

This perception of magic aggressors, then, is of a secret coalition of downright rebels and executors of the Devil's will who constitute an offensive and powerful anti-society in the cosmic-political struggle against divine and natural law.[10] The background given by the above remarks shows the quality the witches' sect was assumed to have, as well as the allegedly vast numbers of people in the form of female *and* male witches who stood ready to fight as the enemies of Christianity.

This witch image belongs to a dualistic view of the world in which two antagonistic supreme beings stood *vis-à-vis* one another in the struggle for the power over the material world and human souls. Such a notion was in contradiction to the Christian notion of monotheism, in which there was only one God and where the Devil was a function of God, playing only a subordinate role in the doings of the world.[11] Although this dualistic interpretation had been rejected several times in the history of the Catholic church, it re-emerged in later years, particularly after the Council of Trent, and was further disseminated in Counter-Reformation preaching.

Such a witchcraft paradigm structure is a variant of a conspiracy theory[12] which is characterized by the following: irrationality despite a high degree of logical consistency;[13] large numbers of aggressors acting collectively within a given society;[14] a mentality based on radical dualist thinking and antagonistic structures[15] and; a perception of the opponents as depersonalized beings and not as individuals.[16]

All features of the witch image correspond to the typical elements of a conspiracy theory, the function of which it is to simplify perception of complex situations and relations, especially in times of social change. At the same time, such explanations offer some relief from the pressure of reality in an apparently complicated or crisis-prone world. Conspiracy theories also provide material suitable for the projection of one's own ideas and goals onto others, where they can then be combatted. Projections are operations in which the acting subjects misjudge or fail to recognize feelings, desires and fears of their own, which they then relocate, outside of their own persons, in other people. These stigmatized substitutes often reach oversize proportions in people's projections.[17] Such mechanisms mean that conspiracy theories are helpful in providing (apparent) explanations of political, social and economic changes in society which have not been understood or assimilated, and in presenting a definable social group as the originators of this crisis and change.

The integrating power of the witch fantasies lay in the fact that they attributed the structural changes of the early modern era and the distinct economic crises since 1560 to the works of a Devil's sect recruited among both women *and* men. In gender-neutral terms 'evil folk'[18] – as they became known in many regions of the Holy Roman Empire – were at work. It was considered imperative to expose and to remove from the face of the earth as many members of these auxiliary troops as possible, and thus to break the power of evil, for these men *and* women – unlike the unassailable Devil himself – were identifiable.

The belief in the existence of a powerful and threatening Devil's sect was a mirror of contemporary structures and reflected, in particular, fantasies of an inverted hierarchical centralization, although such a process was, in fact, clearly taking place in the real world. In this world, however, it was not the Devil who was taking over and expanding his power, but the secular rulers whose disciplining offensive was beginning to make their powers seem boundless. In the same move, however, such conspiracy theories provided a legitimization for contemporary political and constitutional change: 17th century rulers increasingly came to understand the early modern state as a community whose metaphysical purpose was to achieve the salvation of its subjects. The overriding goal was the creation of an ideal Christian state, not only in Geneva where church and secular community were one. Through a Christianization of the community the new state was to acquire the character of a salvationist community and, by barring all blemish and evil, to avert the wrath of God.[19] Such objectives were particularly in evidence in a number of Catholic territories in which the witch-hunts were characterized by the high proportion of male victims.

In order to safeguard this world in a period characterized by fear and an increasingly gloomy world view, the authorities throughout the empire enforced this policy and lent it moral impetus by passing manifold decrees and laws on their subjects: Faith (both how and what was practised), marital life, clothing for all occasions, care of the poor, economic processes and travelling all began to be regulated from above; what is more, the new norms were formulated and applied by a growing bureaucracy and increasing number of jurists. Sanctions were increasingly applied to behaviour which merely appeared to be deviant and not only to behaviour which was actually deviant in a legal sense.[20] There is no doubt that the whole population gradually became subject to this social change and to the new norms.[21]

Economic crises and the resulting periods of hunger meant that many subjects began to express their desire to expel female *and* male witches from their villages and towns. These economic slumps were followed by regulatory and disciplinatory strategies on the part of the authorities, an expression of a general hardening of people's mentalities.

The charges brought against men – and in some regions against large numbers of men – by the authorities and by members of the public in the context of the witch persecutions between 1530 and 1730 were one aspect of this sustained development. This in no way calls into question the prevalence of women among the persecuted; however, the disparate images of the male and female sex wore off in the idea of the incarnation of evil, embodied by the female *and* the male witch and merged in the concept of 'witch folk' as the agents of evil, with both sexes joining forces as members of the ominous Devil's sect. To the successors of the Biblical Eve a new male partner had now been added who was similar in nature to the image of the easily influenced and religiously weak-willed woman of the early modern period. The trials of the so-called male witches were initiated both 'from below' and 'from above', but were more frequently carried out and approved in territories where the demonology of the ruling faith gave theological backing to persecution.

Within this thought complex the male witch represented a fateful construct in a period permeated by pessimism and fear and characterized by intensive human conflict as a result of severe economic crises, by rulers whose aim it was to make subjects out of their people, and in which Christianity became an ideology.

Notes

Published works are cited in full – with the exception of very long subtitles – at first mention. All subsequent mentions give only author or editor names and publication date.

1 The Trial of Peter Kleikamp or – So Many Questions

1. Records of the trial in 1615 in B. Niehues, *Zur Geschichte des Hexenglaubens und der Hexenprozesse, vornehmlich im ehemaligen Fürstbisthum Münster* (Münster 1875), pp. 77–96.
2. As this study concentrates on the male persecution victims, I do not discuss this issue in detail. For reasons of space I have simply listed the pertinent literature published up to 2007. A general summary of the frequent theoretical approaches can be found in: A. Coudert, *Female Witches* in *EOW II* (2006), pp. 356–358; R. M. Tovio, 'Women at Stake. Interpretations of Women's Role in Witchcraft and Witch Hunts from the Early 20th Century to the Present, in *'ARV'. Nordic Yearbook of Folklore* 62 (2006), pp. 187–205; M. Wiesner-Hanks, *Gender* in *EOW II* (2006), pp. 407–411. Further accounts: S. Brauner, *Fearless Wives and Frightened Shrews. The Construction of the Witch in Early Modern Germany* (Massachusetts 1995), pp. 13–20. R.v. Dülmen, 'Die Dienerin des Bösen. Zum Hexenbild in der frühen Neuzeit', in *Zeitschrift für historische Forschung* 18 (1991), pp. 385–398; C. Opitz, Hexenverfolgung als Frauenverfolgung, in *Der Hexenstreit. Frauen in der frühneuzeitlichen Hexenverfolgung,* (Freiburg 1995), pp. 246–270. The exponents of the most prominent theses are given here in alphabetical order: I. Ahrendt-Schulte, Schadenszauber und Konflikte im Spiegel der Hexenprozesse des 16. Jahrhunderts in der Grafschaft Lippe, in H. Wunder/C. Vanja, (eds), *Wandel der Geschlechtsbeziehungen zu Beginn der Neuzeit* (Frankfurt 1991), pp. 213–15; A.L. Barstow; *The Witchcraze. A New History of European Witch Hunts* (San Francisco 1994); W.d. Blécourt, 'The Making of the Female Witch. Reflections on Witchcraft and Gender in the Early Modern Period', *Gender and History* 12 (2000), pp. 287–309; M. Hester, 'Patriarchal Reconstruction and Witch-hunting', in J. Barry et al. (eds), *Witchcraft in Early Modern Europe* (Cambrige 1996), pp. 288–306; E. Labouvie, *Zauberei und Hexenwerk. Ländlicher Hexenglaube in der frühen Neuzeit* (Frankfurt 1991); E. Pócs, 'Why Witches Are Women', in *Acta Ethnographica Hungarica* 48 (2003), pp. 367–383; L. Roper, *Witch Craze. Terror and Fantasy in Baroque Germany* (New Haven 2004); H. Wunder, *Er ist Sonn, sie ist Mond, Frauen in der Frühen Neuzeit* (München 1992), pp. 192–203.
3. General discussion in B. Levack, *The Witch-Hunt in Early Modern Europe* (London 1987), p. 125. Esp. on this thesis: Wiesner-Hanks (2006) 410; Barstow (1994) 24; G.R. Quaife, *Godly Zeal and Furious Rage: The Witch in Early Modern Europe* (London 1987), pp. 79–90.

4. H.C. Eric Midelfort, *Witch Hunting in Southwestern Germany 1562–1684: The Social and Intellectual Foundations* (Stanford 1972), p. 179.
5. Pócs (2003) 380; E. Labouvie, Männer in Hexenprozeß. Zur Sozialanthropologie eines männlichen 'Verständnisses von Magie und Hexerei', in *Geschichte und Gesellschaft* 16 (1990), pp. 56–78; Wunder (1992) 192–203; Blécourt (2000) 293 rebuts the, spheres' theory, but argues along the lines of different and less malevolent magic.
6. Indications of the connection in: W. Monter, 'Toads and Eucharists: the Male Witches of Normandy, 1564–1660', *French Historical Studies* 20 (1997), pp. 563–595, esp. 592. W. Monter, *Witchcraft in France and Switzerland. The Borderlands during the Reformation* (Ithaca 1976), pp. 22–24. 195.
7. Rolf Schulte, *Hexenmeister. Die Verfolgung von Männern im Rahmen der Hexenverfolgung von 1530–1730 im Alten Reich* (Frankfurt 2000).
8. L. Apps and A. Gow, *Male Witches in Early Modern Europe* (Manchester 2003).
9. W. Monter, *Male witches* in *EOW III* (2006) 711–713.
10. K. Amundsen, 'The Duke's Devil and Doctor Lambe's Darling: a Case Study of the Male Witch in Early Modern England', PSI-SIGMA *Historical Journal (University of Nevada, Las Vegas)*, 2 (2004) (http://www.unlv.edu/student_orgs/psisigma/PAT%20Articles/Amundsen.pdf, (accessed. *October* 10 2006); W. Behringer, *The Shaman of Oberstdorf. Chonrad Stoeckhlin and the Phantoms of the Night* (Charlotteville 1998); R. Briggs, *The Witches of Lorraine* (Oxford 2007), pp. 331–69; B. Fuge, 'Le roi des sorciers. Ein luxemburgischer Hexenporzeß' in H. Eiden and R. Voltmer, *Hexenprozesse und Gerichtspraxis* (Trier 2002) 69–122; M. Gaskill, 'The Devil in the Shape of a Man: Witchcraft, Conflict and Belief in Jacobean England', *Historical Research* 71 (1998), pp. 142–71; R. Hagen, 'Female Witches and Sami Sorceres in the Witch-trials of Artic Norway', in *ARV. Nordic Yearbook of Folklore* 62 (2006); A. Heikinnen and Timo Kervinen, 'Finland: the Male Domination', in B. Ankarloo and G. Henningsen (eds), *Early Modern European Witchcraft. Centres and Peripheries* (Oxford 1990) pp. 319–38; Elizabeth J. Kent, 'Masculinity and Male Witches in Old and New England, 1593–1680', *History Workshop Journal* 60 (2005), pp. 69–92. V. Kivelson, 'Male Witches and Gendered Categories in Seventeenth-century Russia', *Comparative Studies in Society and History* 45 (2003), pp. 606–31; K. Lambrecht, 'Tabu und Tod. Männer als Opfer frühneuzeitlicher Verfolgungswellen', in Ahrendt-Schulte (2002), pp. 193–208, Monter (1997) 563–95; A. Rowlands, *Witchcraft Narratives in Germany: Rothenburg, 1561–1652* (Manchester 2003), pp. 160–72; N. Schindler, *Rebellion, Community and Custom in Early Modern Germany* (Cambridge 2002), pp. 236–92. R. Walinski-Kiehl, 'Males, "Masculine Honour", and Witch Hunting in Seventeenth-Century Germany', *Men and Masculinities* 6 (2004), pp. 254–71.
11. *The Oxford English Dictionary,* 2nd edn, vol. XX (Oxford 1991), p. 437; similar: *Webster's Encyclopedic Unabridged Dictionary of the English Language* (New York 1989), p. 1639.
12. *Oxford Dictionary* (1991), p. 437.
13. W.W. Skeats, *An Etymological Dictionary of the English Language* (Oxford 1888), p. 714. P. Maxwell-Stuart, *Wizards. A History* (Brimscombe 2004), pp. 127–45.

14. P. Maxwell-Stuart in his translation of M. Del Rio, *Investigations into magic* (Manchester 2000), p. 24.
15. *Trésor de la langue française*, 15 (Paris 1992), p. 695.

2 The Persecution of Men as Werewolves in Burgundy

1. H. Boguet, *Discours execrable des sorciers, ensemble leur Procez, faits depuis 2 ans en çà, en divers endroicts de la France* (Rouen 1606), p. 185. Further: pp. 1, 8, 15, 47, 30, 97, 117, 127, 135, 185, 228, 234, 287; 302. Court protocoles in ADD 10 F 10 bzw. ADD 10 F 13.
2. Boguet (1606) 28.
3. To avoid confusion: The judge's name was Boguet, the accused was called Bo*c*quet.
4. ADD 10 F 10, Boguet (1606) 97, 117, 128, 135, 259, 286–7, 331; F. Bavoux, *Les procès inédits de Boguet en matière de sorcellerie dans la grande Judicature de Saint-Claude, XVIe–XVIIe* (Dijon 1958), p. 16.
5. Boguet (1606) 87.
6. See Chapter 5 for a more detailed analysis of Catholic demonology.
7. Boguet (1606) 287.
8. Boguet (1606) 278.
9. Boguet (1606) 15, 29, 58–60, 88, 143, 220, 254, 286, 317, 329, 374.
10. Boguet (1606) 301.
11. Boguet (1606) 284.
12. Boguet (1606) 288.
13. ADD 10 F 42.
14. ADD 10 F 42.
15. Boguet (1606) 92.
16. Boguet (1606) 307–9.
17. Boguet (1606) 322.
18. ADD 2 B 3179/221, Boguet, *Discours execrable* (Lyon 1610) 9, 38.
19. Boguet (1606) 81, 259, 329.
20. '... au pays de Savoye et ses environs, les sorciers y sont si espais, qu'on ne les en peut dénicher, quoyqu'il s'en face une diligence perquisition et encore plus rigoureux justice..., L. Daneau: Deux traictez nouveaux fort utiles pour ce temps, le premier touchant les sorciers...' (Genève 1579), p. 10.
21. M. Senn (ed.), *Die Wickiana*. (Küsnacht/Zürich 1875), pp. 196–198.
22. C. Ginzburg, *Die Benandanti. Feldkultur und Hexenwesen im 16. und 17. Jahrhundert* (Frankfurt 1980). For a criticism of the Ginzburg thesis see primarily: W. de Blécourt, 'Spuren einer Volkskultur oder Dämonisierung? Kritische Anmerkungen zu Ginzburgs "Die Benandanti"' in *Kea, Zeitschrift für Kulturwissenschaften* 5 (1993), pp. 22–4.
23. Behringer (1994) 123.
24. E. Schraut, *Fürstentum Hohenlohe*, in S. Lorenz (ed.), *Wider alle Hexerei und Teufelwerk* (Ostfildern 2004), p. 317. E.M. Lorey, Vom Wolfssegner zum Werwolf in R. Voltmer/G. Gehl (eds), *Alltagsleben und Magie in Hexenprozessen* (Weimar 2003), pp. 65–79. A. Blauert, *Frühe Hexenverfolgungen* (Hamburg 1989), pp. 97–99. W. Nieß, *Hexenprozesse in der Grafschaft Büdingen*

(Büdingen 1982), pp. 153–82; J. Bodin, *De la Démonomanie des Sorciers* (Paris 1586), Book IV, p. 184.

25. K. Morris, *Sorceress or Witch? The Image of Gender in Medieval Iceland and Northern Europe* (Lanham 1991), pp. 97–101, 121–128.
26. 'Audite, fratres, ... Quid sunt ergo opera diaboli, haec sunt ... veneficia, incantationes et sortilegos exquirere, strigas et fictos lupos credere. ... Haec et his similia mala opera sunt diaboli. ... Bonifatius, sermo XV. *"De abrenunciatione in baptismate"'*, in E. Martène/U. Durand (eds), *Veterum Scriptorum et monumenterium Historicorum, Dogmaticorum moralium amplissma collectio,* Vol. IX, (Paris 1733), p. 217, (English transl. according to transl. from Latin by R. Schulte).
27. 'Credisti, quod quidam credere solent ... ut quandocunque ille homo voluerit, in lupum transformari possit quod teutonica Werewulff vocatur, aut in aliam aliquam figuram?' Burchard von Worms, *Corrector sive medicus,* reprinted in H.J. Schmitz (ed.), *Die Bußbücher und das kanonische Bußverfahren* nach *handschriftlichen Quellen,* vol. 2 (Düsseldorf 1898), question 151, p. 442. (transl. R. Schulte/L. Froome).
28. In another copy of the text it says here: '... quod vulgaris stultitia weruvolff vocat', see Schmitz (1898) 442.
29. Burchard von Worms, Corrector, questio 144, p. 440.
30. K. Baumann, *Aberglaube für Laien,* vol.1, (Würzburg 1989), p. 368.
31. F. Kluge, *Etymologisches Wörterbuch* (Berlin/New York 1995), p. 884.
32. W. Hertz, *Der Werwolf. Ein Beitrag zur Sagengeschichte* (Stuttgart 1862), p. 65.
33. M. Bambeck, *Wiesel und Werwolf* (Stuttgart 1990), pp. 57–9.
34. Gervasius von Tilbury, *Otia Imperialia* (ed.: F. Liebknecht) (Hannover 1856), liber III, p. 120.
35. 'Vidimus enim frequenter in Anglia per lunationes homines in lupos mutari, quod hominum genus gerulfos Galli nominant, Anglici vero werewulf dicunt, were enim Anglice virum sonat, wlf lupum'. Gervasius von Tilbury, liber I, 15, p. 4 (transl. R. Schulte and L. Froome).
36. J. Dubois, *Dictionnaire étymologique et historique* (Paris 1993), p. 331.
37. Guillaume d'Auvergne, De Universo in L. Harf-Lancner, 'La métamorphose illusoire: Des théories chrétiennes de la métamorphose aux images médievales du loup-garou', in *Annales E.S.P.* 40 (1985), p. 214.
38. 'Se un homme a tele destinee d'estre leu-warou, c'est fort se son fils s'en tient. Et se filles a et nuiz fils, volentiers sont quauquemaires Les evangiles de Quenouilles', cited in C. Lecouteux, *Fées, Sorcières et Loup-garous au Moyen Age* (Paris 1992), p. 118 (transl. R. Schulte).
39. See as a convenient summary: E.M.Lorey, *Wie der Werwolf unter die Hexen kam,* s. www.elmar-lorey.de/werwolf/genesetext.htm.
40. M. Luther, *Weimarer Ausgabe* (1883 p.), vol.1, p. 406; L. Daneau, *Dialogue tres-utile-necessaire pour ce temps* (Paris 1573), p. 64; N. Hemmingsøn, *En Undervisning aff den hellige skrifft* (København 1576), p. K V d; J. G. Godelmann, *Von Zäuberern, Hexen und Unholden* (Frankfurt 1592), book 2, p. 192; P. Meiger(ius), *De Panurgia Lamiarum* (Hamburg 1587), p. L1; D. Meder, *Acht Hexenpredigten* (Leipzig 1605), p. 80; *H. Samson(ius), Neun außerlesenen und Wohlbegründete Hexen-Predigt* (Riga 1626), p. G II b; B. Carpzov, *Practica Nova,* book I, (Wittenberg 1635/1647), p. 311.
41. Bodin (1586) 94–104.

42. B. Rochelandet, *La répression de la sorcellerie aux XVIe et XVIIe siècle. Contribution à l'analyse du phenomène en Franche-Comté,* tome 1, thèse de doctorat (Besançon 1992), p. 10.
43. Bodin (1580) livre II, 96, 98v.
44. Bodin (1580) livre II, 96v, 97, 98v.
45. E.M. Lorey, *Henrich der Werwolf* (Frankfurt 1997), p. 232.
46. '...principalement les hom[m]es sont plustost tournez en loups...', Bodin (1580), livre II, 103 v.
47. See Boguet (1606) 48, 127, 265; A. Dey, *Histoire de la Sorcellerie au Comté de Bourgogne* (Vesoul 1861/reprint Marseille 1983), p. 28. See also C. Oates, *Metamorphosis and Lycanthropy in Franche-Comté,* 1521–1643, in M. Feher (ed.), *Fragments for a History of the Human Body,* Part One (New York 1989), pp. 305–363. This essay, however, only deals with some of the trials.
48. See ADD, Série 2B/1285; ADD 10 F 54. See also Oates (1989), 335; B. Rochelandet, *Sorcières, Diables et Bûchers en Franche-Comté aux XVIe et XVIIe siècles* (Besançon 1997), p. 146.
49. ADD 10 F 54.
50. Testimony of Ludwig Geizkofler (1573), ADD 10 F 42.
51. J. Courtieu, *Parlement de Dôle. Prétexte du répertoire numérique à la série 2 B 'Parlement de Dôle'* (Besançon 1994), pp. 12–17.
52. Edict of the 'Parlement', 3.9.1573, ADD 10 F 42.
53. ADD 10 F 42.
54. ADD 10 F 42; ADD 2 B 2437/55; This well-known trial is also described in Oates (1989) 338 and Rochelandet (1997) 146. See also a reproduction of a contemporary description in the French National Library, http://gallica.bnf.fr> 'arrest memorable de la Cour du parlement de Dôle' (acc. on March 11, 2008).
55. ADD 10 F 54.
56. Oates (1989) 337. His correct name is Culfin, see ADD 10 F 42.
57. Testimony of Adrienne Joulainn, 31.5.1599, in ADD 2 B 2271.
58. Testimony of Nicole Gilbert, 31.5.1599, ADD 2 B 2271.
59. Testimony of Annette Trouvel, 31.5.1599, ADD 2B 2271.
60. ADD 2 B 2271, 1598–1599. See also Oates (1984) 349–351.
61. ADD 2 B 2547 and ADD 10 F 54. See also Oates (1989) 350.
62. Trial of Guillaume Frarye 1604 and Guillemette Barnard 1605, ADD 2 B 2465/77.
63. Charge placed against Perrenette Glaon from Piedmorain, 1611, ADD 10 F 42.
64. ADD 2 B 2473/94 and ADD 10 F 42.
65. ADD 2 B 2470, 1609–1610.
66. Testimony of Jean Thevenot, ADD 2B 2470, 1609–1610.
67. ADD 2B 2470, 1610.
68. ADHS B 5050.
69. ADHS B 5050.
70. ADD 10 F 42, 1626.
71. For wording of the Edict, see ADD 10 F 42.
72. ADD 2 B 2493.
73. ADD B 15940.
74. ADD 10 F 10. See also Oates (1989) 352–354.
75. ADD 2 B 2516/222–223.
76. ADD 2 B 2515 (1659–1660).

77. ADD 2 B 2519/103–119 and ADD 10 F 76.
78. Evidence o f the servant of C. Vuitton, ADD 2 B 2519/103.
79. Statement of Claude and Mathieu Mathieu 1663, ADD 10 F 76.
80. Letter of the 'Chambre du parlement', ADD 2 B/2519.
81. *Data for this figure are taken from Rochelandet's appendix (1992)*, 2519/103–119 and ADD 10 F 76.
82. B. Rochelandet, *La sorcellerie d'autrefois* (Lyon 1996), p. 90.
83. C. Ginzburg, *Hexensabbat. Entzifferung einer nächtlichen Geschichte* (Berlin 1990), p. 159.
84. Total no. of trials from 1520–1670 was 36.
85. Boguet (1606), pp. 40–42.
86. R. Briggs in K.A. Edwards, *Werewolves, Witches and Wanderings Saints. Traditional Belief and Folklore in Early Modern Europe* (Kirksville 2002), p. 6; P. Dinzelbacher, Lycantrophy, in *EOW III* (2006) 681; Monter (1976) 147.
87. M. Scheutz, Bettler-Werwolf-Galeerensträfling, *Salzburg Archiv* 27 (2001), pp. 221–68; see the list of all known werewolf trials: http://www.elmar-lorey.de/Prozesse.htm (accessed on 8 March 2007).
88. C. Helman, *Körper Mythen. Werwolf, Medusa und das radiologische Auge* (München 1991), p. 104.
89. L. Febvre, *Histoire de Franche-Comté* (Paris 1922), p. 161.
90. Monter (1976) 67, 194.
91. F. Gollut (1590), cited from L. Febvre (1922) 162.
92. Febvre (1922) 163.
93. S. van Bath, *Agriculture in the Vital Revolution*, in E.E. Rich/C.H. Wilson (eds), *The Cambridge Economic History*, vol. V, (Cambridge 1977), p. 90.
94. P. Delsalle, *La Franche-Comté au temps des Archeducs Albert et Isabelle 1598–1633* (Bescançon 2002), pp. 16–20; M. Morineau, *La conjuncture ou les cernes de la croissance*, in E. Le Roy Ladurie/M. Morineau (eds), *Historie Economique et Sociale de la France*, tome 1, De 1450–1660 (Paris 1977), pp. 950–5.
95. Febvre (1922) 194; Delsalle (2002) 16.
96. Febvre (1922) 194.
97. Boguet (1603) 113.
98. 'Quiconque en âage de discrétion sera convaincu d'avoir volontairement esté aux assemblées ou sabbats diaboliques et abominables *des sorciers et sorcières*, ou qui hors d'iceux aura donné quelque maladies à hommes on bestes, ou faict acte de sorcellerie, il sera puny et chastié de la peine de mort', Ordonnance 10.2.1604, reprinted in Delsalle (2002) 138. (Italics by R.S.)
99. It will be for future research to determine whether this thesis applies to the whole of Central Europe. It is, however, certain that Franche-Comté was culturally different from the German-speaking areas. Elmar Lorey's list of all 250 known werewolf trials in West and Central Europe between 1407 and 1725 shows that a third of the accused were female, see http://www.elmar-lorey.de/Prozesse.htm (accessed: 8 March 2007).

3 Male Witches on Trial: An Empirical Approach

1. W. Behringer, *Witches and Witch-Hunts* (Cambridge 2004), p. 150.
2. H.C.E. Midelfort, Alte Fragen und neue Methoden in der Geschichte des Hexenwahns, in Lorenz/Bauer (1995), p. 15.

3. J. Dillinger, Grafschaft Hohenberg, in Lorenz (1994), p. 246.
4. A. Raith, Herzogtum Württemberg, in Lorenz/Schmidt (2004), p. 225.
5. F. Irsigler, Zauberei- und Hexenprozesse in Köln, 15.-17. Jahrhundert, in Franz,/Irsigler (1996), p. 171.
6. R. Schulte: *Hexenverfolgung in Schleswig-Holstein 16.-18. Jahrhundert* (Heide 2001), p. 80.
7. B. Levack, *The Witch-Hunt in Early Modern Europe*, 3rd edn. (London 2006), pp. 33–35.
8. Appeal before and judgement passed by the local court, 1553, in E. Andersen et al. (eds), *De Hansborgske Domme 1545–1578*, vol. 1 (Kopenhagen 1994), pp. 193–194.
9. Claim filed by Johan Muller of Hadersleben/Herzogtum Schleswig in Andersen (1994) 1159.
10. Trial of Catharina Faustes 1640–7, StA Oldesloe: Acta Ac VII C 47.
11. Trial of the Grundt family in 1668, in Mauritius (1669), pp. 346–62.
12. Trial of Gertrud Prüßings und Grete Rieken 1626 on the island of Fehmarn in the Baltic Sea, District Court record book Fehmarn 1626, pp. 118–20.
13. See for example: H. Hundsrucker, Von der Urfehde, in Keller (1989), pp. 217–26.
14. Trial of Elisabeth Fruchtenichts in Kiel/Holstein, LAS 15/2656.
15. Trial of Kay Asmussen 1608, StA Flensburg Sign. A 37e (Zauberei 1607–42)
16. Trial of Gesche Kovahls 1645, StA Mölln Nr. 818 (Kriminalgerichtsprotokolle 1572–63).
17. Trial of Burchart Vaget, LAS 173/155, 1651; Trial of Joerg Schildtknecht 1663, LAS 275/456, 1663.
18. Levack (2006) 23.
19. S. Lorenz (ed.), *Himmlers Hexenkartothek* (Bielefeld 1999).
20. Midelfort (1972). For example for France: R. Muchembled, *Sorcières, justice et société aux 16e et 17e siècles* (Paris 1987), pp. 107–17; for England: J. Sharpe, *Instruments of Darkness. Witchcraft in England 1550–1750* (London 1997), pp. 108–111, 178–79.; for Germany: W. Behringer, *Hexenverfolgung in Bayern, Volksmagie, Glaubenseifer und Staatsräson in der Frühen Neuzeit*, 3rd edn (München 1997), pp. 39–41.
21. Labouvie (1991) 34.
22. U. Schönleitner, *Zauberei- und Hexenprozesse in Österreich* (Wien 1980/81), p. 90.
23. The Book of Daniel 2/37–45.
24. P.K. Hartmann, *Das Heilige Römische Reich deutscher Nation in der Neuzeit 1486–1806* (Stuttgart 2006), pp. 13, 147, 163.
25. Theory and practice, however, often differed: Baden-Baden was Protestant in 1550, became Catholic in 1570, only to become Lutheran again around 1590. The Electorate Palatinate also saw frequent changes in denomination, being Lutheran in 1550, Calvinist in 1560, Lutheran in 1573 and Calvinist again from 1580.
26. I. Mieck, *Europäische Geschichte der Frühen Neuzeit* (Stuttgart 1970), pp. 231–3.
27. W. Schild, *Die Geschichte der Gerichtsbarkeit* (Hamburg 1997), pp. 154–68. E. Schmidt, *Einführung in die Geschichte der Strafrechtspflege* (Göttingen 1965), pp. 93–5.
28. F.-C. Schroeder, *Die peinliche Gerichtsordnung Kaiser Karls V. und des Heiligen Römischen Reichs von 1532* (Stuttgart 2000), § 44, 45–7, 52, 58, 69, 109, 219.
29. P. Oestmann, *Hexenprozesse am Reichskammergericht* (Köln 1997).

30. R. Kieckhefer, *European Witch Trials,* 1300–1500 (London 1976), pp. 108–47.
31. O. Landolt, 'Mit dem Für zu richten und si zuo Bulfer verbrennen Zauberwahn und Hexenverfolgungen im spätmittelalterlichen Schaffhausen', in *Schaffhauser Beiträge zur Geschichte* 78 (2004), p. 171.Transcription und faksimile see http://www.StA-schaffhausen.ch/Schaffhausen-Geschichte/stadtrechnungen_schaffhausen. htm (accessed. 10 April 2007).
32. Behringer (2004), pp. 63–9.
33. M. Ostorero, *'Fôlatrer avec les démons'. Sabbat et chasse aux sorciers à Vevey (1448)* (Lausanne 1995), pp. 105–7.
34. Kieckhefer (1976) graphic p. 11.
35. P. Paravy, *De la Chrétienté romaine à la Réforme en Dauphiné* (Rome 1993), pp. 868–9.
36. C. Tholoson, *Ut magorum et maleficiorum errores in Ostorero et al.* (1999), pp. 362, 374, 378, 404, 414.
37. H. Fründ, 'Rapport sur la chasse aux sorciers et aux sorcières menée dès 1428 dans le diocèse de Sion', in Ostorero (1999) 30, 32, 40.
38. Kieckhefer (1976) 106–74. It is, however, very difficult to quantify the number of accused, as Kieckhefer often does not give numbers for the trials he documents, so that the number of unreported accused is presumably high.
39. Georg Modestin and Kathrin Utz Tremp 'Zur spätmittelalterlichen Hexenverfolgung in der heutigen Westschweiz in', *Zeitenblicke 1* (2002), see http://www.zeitenblicke.historicum.net/2002/01/modestin/modestin.html. (acc. on April 2, 2007) S. Burghartz, Hexenverfolgung als Frauenverfolgung? In Opitz (1995), p. 151. A. Blauert, *Frühe Hexenverfolgungen. Ketzer-, Zauberei- und Hexenprozesse des 15. Jahrhunderts* (Hamburg 1989), pp. 55–7; B. Andermatten and K. Utz Tremp, 'De l'hérésie à la sorcellerie.: L'inquisiteur Ulric de Torrenté OP (vers 1420–1445)', in *Revue d'historie écclestiastique/Zeitschrift für Schweizer Kirchengeschichte* 86 (1992), p. 104.
40. R. Muchembled, 'Les sorcières du Cambrésis', in Dupont-Bouchat et al. (1979), p. 174.
41. Rochelandet (1997) 16–18.
42. Calculated from the Witch Register in the Appendix of Rochelandet (1992) pp. 370–95. In her latest work Rochelandet gives the number of accused as 807, see B. Rochelandet, Destins des femmes en Franche-Comté, (Besançon 2005), p. 155.
43. J.M. Debard, Montbéliard (Montbéliard 1992), p. 25.
44. Rochelandet (1992) 22; (1997) 75–6.
45. E. Biesel, *Hexenjustiz, Volksmagie und soziale Konflikte im lothringischen Raum* (Trier 1997), pp. 49–64, 82–5.
46. Briggs (1989) 67.
47. R. Briggs, 'Women as victims? Witches, judges and community', in *French History* 5 (1991), p. 442.
48. Biesel (1997) 267- 9.
49. Labouvie (1991) 41–52, 70; Labouvie (1990) 69.
50. R. Voltmer, 'St. Maximin, Prince Abbey of', in *EOW IV* (2006) 1082–83; J. Dillinger. *'Böse Leute' Hexenverfolgungen in Schwäbisch-Österreich und Kurtrier im Vergleich* (Trier 1999), pp. 97–100; R. Voltmer and K. Weisenstein (eds), *Das Hexenregister des Claudius Musiel* (Trier 1966). R. Voltmer, 'Einleitung', in Voltmer and Weisenstein (1996) 23. G. Franz, 'Hexenprozesse', in der Stadt

Trier und deren Umgebung. Gerichtsbarkeit in St. Maximum, St. Paulin und St. Matthias, in Franz and Irsigler (1996), p. 343.

51. G. Rummel, *Bauern, Herren und Hexen, Studien zur Sozialgeschichte sponheimischer und kurtrierischer Hexenprozesse 1574–1664* (Göttingen 1991) p. 23; A.R. Baumgarten, *Hexenwahn und Hexenverfolgung im Naheraum* (Frankfurt 1987), p. 355.
52. Calculated from H. Gebhard, *Hexenprozesse im Kurfürstentum Mainz des 17. Jhs.* (Mainz 1989), pp. 64, 233–8.
53. P. Mayer, Statistische Auswertung der Hexenprozeßakten für die Stadt Miltenberg und die Cent Bürgstadt in Keller (1989), pp. 336–8.
54. H. Pohl, *Hexenglaube und Hexenverfolgung im Kurfürstentum Mainz* (Stuttgart 1988), p. 212; Gebhard (1989) 233–8.
55. A. Kettel, *Von Hexen und Unholden in der West- und Zentraleifel* (Prüm 1988), pp. 14–16, 130.
56. Calculated from Kettel's list of victims: in A. Kettel, 'Hexenprozesse in den Grafschaften Blankenheim und Gerolstein', in *Eifeljahrbuch* (1972), pp. 71–5.
57. For a general survey see D. Vanysacker, Netherlands, southern, in *EOW III* (2006) 813–818.
58. R. Voltmer, 'Witch-hunters, Witch-finders and Kings of the Sabbat: The Prominent Role of Men in the Mass Persecutions of Trier, St. Maximin, Luxembourg and the Eifel-territories', in Rowlands and Grundy (2008); R. Voltmer, 'Luxembourg, Duchy of', in *EOW III* (2006) 677–80. The figures given by Dupont-Bouchat, La répression de la sorcellerie dans le Duché du Luxembourg aux XVIe et XVIIe siècles, in Dupont-Bouchat and Frijoff/Muchembled (1978), pp. 127–38 seem to be far too low. Voltmer's research results are soon to be published.
59. Calculated from E. Brouette, 'La sorcellerie dans le comté de Namur au début de l'époque moderne (1509–1546)', in *Annales de la société archéologique de Namur* 42 (1953–54), pp. 388–420.
60. D. Vanysacker (2006) 816. The proportions of women in Brabant and Hainault were high. However, the total numbers are very small and described by the Netherlands expert Hans de Waardt as uncertain; hence they are not used in the calculations.
61. Calculated from R. Muchembled, *Sorcières, justice et société aux 16e et 17e siècles* (Paris 1987), p. 107 Sorcières du Cambrésis in Dupont-Bouchat et al. (1978), pp. 174–8.
62. R. Opsommer and J. Montballyu, 'Flandern-Hexenverfolgung' (acc. on April 3, 2007), in G. Gersmann et al. (eds), *Lexikon der Geschichte der Hexenverfolgung*, see http://www.historicum.net/themen/hexenverfolgung/lexikon. The figures are slightly different from those given in J. Montballyu, Die Hexenprozesse in der Grafschaft Flandern (1495–1692)', in Eiden and Voltmer (2002), p. 287.
63. Midelfort (1972).
64. C. Schneider, *'Die Markgrafschaften Baden-Baden und Baden-Durlach', in Lorenz and Schmidt (2004)* 215- 18; Midelfort gives 31% men here: Midelfort (1972) 181.
65. A. Raith, 'Herzogtum Württemberg', in Lorenz and Schmidt (2004) 225–7.
66. J.M. Schmidt, 'Die Kurpfalz', in Lorenz and Schmidt (2004) 237–52.
67. S. Schleichert, 'Vorderösterreich: Elsaß, Breisgau, Hagenau und Ortenau', in Lorenz/Schmidt (2004) 257–9.

68. M. Tschaikner, 'Vorarlberg', in *EOW IV* (2006) 1174.
69. J. Dillinger, 'Schwäbisch-Österreich', in Lorenz and Schmidt (2004) 284.
70. C. Bumiller, 'Die Grafschaften und Fürstentümer Hohenzollern', in Lorenz and Schmidt (2004) 303.
71. E. Schraut, 'Fürstentum Hohenlohe', in Lorenz and Schmidt (2004) 321–22.
72. W. Mährle, 'Fürstprobstei Ellwangen', in J. Dillinger et al., *Zum Feuer verdammt. Die Hexenverfolgungen in der Grafschaft Hohenberg, der Reichstadt Reutlingen und der Fürstpropstei Ellwangen* (Stuttgart 1998), p. 406; Midelfort (1972) 180, assumes a lower proportion of women.
73. K. Wohlschlegel, 'Deutschordenskommende Mergentheim', in Lorenz and Schmidt (2004) 390.
74. M. Zeck, 'Reichsstadt Rottweil', in Lorenz and Schmidt (2004) 429. The territory of 'Rottweil' included the city of Rottweil and 27 villages.
75. Own calculation from data in M. Tschaikner, *'Der Teufel und die Hexen müssen aus dem Land...'. Frühneuzeitliche Hexenverfolgungen in Liechtenstein* (Liechtenstein 1998), pp. 100–11.
76. W. Behringer, *Mit dem Feuer vom Leben zum Tod. Hexengesetzgebung in Bayern* (München 1988).
77. Behringer (1997) 39, 68, 469.
78. Behringer (1997) 173.
79. Calculated from Behringer (1997) 58, 307, 318.
80. Calculated from G. Schwertl, 'Hexenprozesse im Pfleggericht Mitterfels', in *Verhandlungen des Historischen Vereins für Niederbayern* 116–17 (1990–1991), pp. 209–31. Freising: Behringer (1997) 354.
81. W. Behringer, 'Augsburg, Prince-bishopric of', in *EOW I* (2006) 67–68; Behringer (1994/1998); J. Durrant: 'Eichstätt, prince-bishopric of', in *EOW II* (2006) 307.
82. S. Kleinöder-Ströbel, *Die Verfolgung von Zauberei und Hexerei in den fränkischen Markgraftümern im 16.Jahrhundert* (Tübingen 2002), p. 21. The total number of accused of known gender was 102.
83. G. Mülleder, 'Salzburg, Arch-bishopric of', in *EOW IV* (2006), 1000. Schindler (1992), pp. 258–60.
84. Calculated from the data of U. Schönleitner, *Zauberei und Hexenprozesse in Österreich* (Wien 1986/87), p. 33. This high execution rate, however, is largely determined by the severe sentences in the Sorcerer-Jack trials.
85. E.M. Kern, 'Austria', in *EOW I* (2006) 72. On witch persecution in general see also H. Dienst, Hexenprozesse auf dem Gebiet der heutigen Bundesländer Vorarlberg, Tirol (with Südtirol), 'Salzburg, Nieder- und Oberösterreich sowie des Burgenlandes', in H. Valentinitsch (ed.), *Hexen und Zauberer. Die große Verfolgung – ein europäisches Phänomen in der Steiermark* (Graz/Wien 1987), pp. 265–90.
86. F. Byloff, *Hexenglaube und Hexenverfolgung in den österreichischen Alpenländern* (Leipzig 1934), p. 161.
87. This figure is the proportion in % without the cases of unknown gender.
88. D. Raser, 'Zauberei- und Hexenprozesse in Niederösterreich', in *Unsere Heimat* 60 (1989), 17–25. Schönleitner (1986/87) 41–2.
89. Calculated by the number of trials that are conserved in the central archives of Carinthia and other sources. The gender of 14 persons is unknown, see Chapter 8.

90. Schulte (2000) 246.
91. H. Rabanser: *Hexenwahn. Schicksale und Hintergrund. Die Tiroler Hexenprozesse* (Innsbruck 2006), pp. 99–100. H. Rabanser, Sagenhafte Hexer und ihre historische Fassbarkeit, in *Tiroler Heimat* 69 (2005), pp. 177–98.
92. M. Kosir, 'Slovenia', in *EOW IV* (2006) 1052.
93. Schönleitner (1986/87) 128.
94. M. Wilde, *Die Zauberei- und Hexenprozesse in Kursachsen* (Köln 2003), p. 308.
95. K. Lambrecht, *'Zur Ausrottung der Teufelssekte...', Frühneuzeitliche Hexenverfolgung in den schlesischen Territorien* (Stuttgart 1993), pp. 35–8.
96. K. Lambrecht, *Hexenverfolgung und Zaubereiprozesse in den schlesischen Territorien* (Köln 1995), p. 349.
97. See the names in W.G Soldan and H. Heppe, *Geschichte der Hexenverfolgung,* vol 2, (reprint Kettwig 1986), pp. 45–51.
98. H. Schwillus, *Kleriker im Hexenprozeß. Geistliche als Opfer der Hexenprozesse* (Würzburg 1992), pp. 10–86.
99. Calculated according to data in Appendix of B. Gehm, *Die Hexenverfolgung im Hochstift Bamberg und das Eingreifen des Reichshofsrat zur ihrer Beendigung* (Hildesheim 2000), pp. 292–363. The figures differ slightly from those given by: R.S. Walinski-Kiehl, *Prosecuting Witches in Early Modern Germany, with the special Reference to the Bishopric of Bamberg, 1595–1680*, unpublished PD thesis (Portsmouth 1981), p. 43, calculated from table 2/p. 101. R.S. Walinski-Kiehl, '"Godly States"', Confessional Conflict and Witch-Hunting in Early Modern Germany, in *Mentalities/Mentalités* (5.2.1988), p. 19.
100. W. *Nieß* (1982) 3, 44–5, 103- 106, 126–8, 142, 169–170, 177–8, 183–4, 233–4, 265, 271, 277, 301. The remaining 4% is accounted for by people of unknown gender.
101. S. Schleichert, 'Hexenprozesse in der Landgrafschaft Hessen-Kassel', in *Hessisches Jahrbuch für Landesgeschichte* 43 (1993), pp. 65–9.
102. T. Lange and J.R. Wolf, 'Hexenverfolgung zur Zeit Georg I.', in *Archiv für hessische Geschichte und Altertumskunde* 52 *(*1994), pp. 139–98.
103. I. Koppenhöfer, *Die mitleidslose Gesellschaft. Studien zu Verdachtsgenese, Ausgrenzungsverhalten und Prozeßproblematik im frühneuzeitlichen Hexenprozeß in der alten Grafschaft Nassau und...Nassau- Dillenburg (1559–1687),* (Frankfurt 1995), p. 90.
104. A. Vater, *Hexenverfolgung in den nassauischen Grafschaften im 16. und 17. Jahrhundert* (Marburg 1988), pp. 111–13.
105. R. Füssel, *Hexenverfolgungen in Thüringer Raum* (Hamburg 2003), pp. 200, 217.
106. G. Schormann, *Der Krieg gegen die Hexen* (Göttingen 1991), pp. 36–7, 62.
107. R. Decker, 'Die Hexenverfolgung im Herzogtum Westfalen', in *Westfälische Zeitschrift* 131–132/(1981–82), pp. 348–9, 386; R. Decker, 'Die Hexenverfolgung im Herzogtum Westfalen', in A. Bruns (ed.), *Hexen. Gerichtsbarkeit im kurkölnischen Sauerland* (Schmallenberg-Holthausen 1984), p. 218.
108. P.A. Heuser, 'Die kurkölnischen Hexenprozesse des 16.und 17.Jahrhunderts in geschlechtergeschichtlicher Perspektive', in Ahrendt-Schulte et al. (2002), pp. 137–8.
109. Heuser in Ahrendt-Schulte et al. (2002) 144–9.
110. R. Fuchs, *Hexenverfolgung an Ruhr und Lippe* (Münster 2002), p. 146.
111. R. Decker, 'Paderborn, Prince-Bishopric of', in *EOW III* (2006) 869.

112. C. Meier, 'Die Anfänge der Hexenprozesse in Lemgo', in Wilbertz et al. (1994) p. 88; R. Walz, *Hexenglaube und magischen Kommunikation im Dorf der frühen Neuzeit,* (Paderborn 1993), p. 70.
113. I. Kloppenburg, 'Die soziale Funktion städtischer Hexenprozesse. Die lippische Residenzstadt Detmold 1599–1669', in *Wilbertz et al.* (1994) 185.
114. I. Ahrendt-Schulte, 'Hexenprozesse als Spiegel von Alltagskonflikten', in Lorenz and Bauer (1995) 350; U. Bender-Wittmann, 'Hexenprozesse in Lemgo 1628–37', in P. Krutisch and I. Großmann (eds), *Der Weserraum zwischen 1500 und 1650* (Marburg 1993), p. 238.
115. G. Gersmann, 'Münster, Bishopric of', in *EOW III* (2006) 794.
116. Calculated from the data in G. Wilbertz, 'Hexenprozesse und Zaubereiglaube im Hochstift Osnabrück', in *Osnabrücker Mitteilungen* 84 (1978), p. 40.
117. H. Stebel, *Die Osnabrücker Hexenprozesse* (Osnabrück 1997), pp. 18, 151–4.
118. Calculated from G. Schormann, 'Hexenverfolgung in Schaumburg', in *Niedersächsisches Jahrbuch für Landesgeschichte* 45 (1973), p. 163.
119. J. Scheffler et al., 'Umrisse und Themen der Hexenforschung in der Region', in Wilbertz et al. (1994) 19.
120. G. Schormann, *Hexenprozesse in Nordwestdeutschland* (Hildesheim 1977), p. 87; G. Schwerhoff, 'Hexerei, Geschlecht und Regionalgeschichte', in Wilbertz et al. (1994) 325.
121. Schormann (1977) 57.
122. J. Wook, 'Hexenverfolgung im Bistum Verden', in *Praxis Geschichte* 4 (1991), pp. 38–43.
123. K. Möeller, *Dass Willkür über Recht ginge. Hexenprozesse in Mecklenburg im 16. und 17.Jahrhundert* (Bielefeld 2007), pp. 224–31.
124. C.O. Endler, 'Hexen und Hexenverbrennungen im Lande Ratzeburg', in *Mitteilungen des Heimatbundes für das Fürstentum Ratzeburg* 5 (1923), pp. 1–16.
125. Schulte (2001) 82, 97–104.
126. H. Schilling, *Die Stadt in der Frühen Neuzeit* (München 1993), pp. 4–14.
127. G. Schwerhoff, 'Vom Alltagsverdacht zur Massenverfolgung', in *Geschichte in Wissenschaft und Unterricht* 46 (1995), p. 364.
128. R. Rogge, 'Hexenverfolgung in Hamburg? Schadenszauber im Alltag und in der Justiz', in *Geschichte in Wissenschaft und Unterricht* 46 (1995), pp. 381–401.
129. For more precise figures on Lübeck see Chapter 7 of this study.
130. Calculated from the information in H. Schwarzwälder, 'Die Geschichte des Zauber- und Hexenglaubens in Bremen', in *Bremisches Jahrbuch 46* (1959), p. 225.
131. F. Irsigler, 'Zauberei- und Hexenprozesse in Köln, 15.-17. Jahrhundert', in Franz and Irsigler (1996), p. 171.
132. W. Behringer, '"Erhob sich das ganze Land zu ihrer Ausrottung", Hexenprozesse und Hexenverfolgung in Europa' in v. Dülmen (1987), p. 163.
133. Behringer (1997) 47–49.
134. Own evaluation from data in D. Vanysacker, *Hekserij in Brugge* (Brugge 1988), Bijlage, pp. 151–64.
135. J. Dillinger, 'Hexenverfolgung in Städten', in Franz and Irsigler (1998), p. 134.
136. G. Schormann, 'Städtische Gesellschaft und Hexenprozeß', in C. Meckseper (ed.), *Stadt im Wandel. Kunst und Kultur der Bürgertums in Norddeutschland 1150 bis 1650*, vol 4, (Stuttgart 1985) pp. 179–81.

137. R. Flagmeier, 'Hexenprozesse und sozialer Wandel in Korbach', in *Geschichtsblätter für Waldeck* 79(1991) 89.
138. Dupont-Bouchat (1978) 139.
139. G. Jerouschek, *Die Hexen und ihr Prozeß. Die Hexenverfolgung in der Reichsstadt Esslingen* (Esslingen 1991), p. 286.
140. A. Wittkampf, 'Das Hexenwesen in kleineren Reichsstädten', in R.A. Müller (ed.), *Reichsstädte in Franken,* vol. 2, (München 1987), pp. 100–7, Rowlands (2003) 160. Rothenburg had very few executions. Only three of 65 alleged persons went to the stake: Rowlands (2003) 7.
141. Midelfort (1972) 32.
142. Rita Voltmer's research results to Luxembourg are soon to be published.
143. These figures are provisional as there has not yet been any comprehensive research on East Friesia and Western Pomerania. Nevertheless, it is already evident that the male proportion was low. Möller (2002) 105; M. Skoruppa, 'Hexenverfolgung in Ostfriesland- eine Übersicht', in Ländliche Akademie Krummhörn (ed.), *Beiträge zur Hexenverfolgung in Ostfriesland* (Krummhörn 2002), pp. 30–50.
144. Morris (1991) 145–53.
145. M. Nenonen, *Noituus, taikuus ja noitavainot. Ala-Satakunnan, Pohjois-Pohjanmaan ja Viipurin Karjalan maaseudulla vuosina 1620–1700* (Helsinki 1992), pp. 444–50.
146. These data are from Nenonen (1992) 108.
147. P. Kamber, 'Croyances et peurs: La sorcellerie dans le Pays de Vaud (XVIe–XVIIe siècles)' in F. Flouck et al. (eds), *De l'Ours à la Cocarde : Régime bernois et révolution en pays de Vaud* (Lausanne 1998), pp. 247–56.
148. Total number of all known accused persons.
149. Distribution among accused of known gender.
150. For data on the Holy Roman Empire, see own calculations in this study.
151. The data on witch hunts in Europe are taken from the following works: O. Fiorvardardóttir, 'Iceland', in *EOW II* (2006), 533.; E. Naess, 'Norway', in Ankarloo and Henningsen (1990) 371–8; similar conclusions are reached by: R. Hagen, *Hekser* (Oslo 2003), pp. 272–3. P. Sörlin, *'Wicked arts'. Witchcraft and Magic Trials in Southern Sweden* 1635–1754 (Leiden 1999), p. 221; B. Ankarloo, 'Sweden: The Mass Burnings (1668–1676)', in Ankarloo (1990), 310; M. Madar, 'Estonia I: Werewolves and Poisoners, in Ankarloo and Henningsen (1990), 267; Heikkinnen and Kervinen', in Ankarloo and Henningsen (1990) 319–21; K.S. Jensen, *Troldom i Danemark 1500–1588* (København 1988), p. 94; J.C.V Johansen, *'Da Djaevelen var ude'... Troldom i det 17. århundredes Danmark,* (Odense 1991), p. 62; H. de Waardt, *Toverij en samenleving. Holland 1500–1800* (Rotterdam 1991), p. 139; Muchembled (1994) 115. M. Gijswijjt-Hofstra's figures for the province 'Zeeland' were not included as these comprised slander as well as witchcraft accusations, see M. Gijswijjt-Hofstra, *Witchcraft before Zeeland. Magistrates and Church Council* (Rotterdam 1991) 110–11; Sharpe (1996) 110, 114; C. Larner, *Enemies of God. The Witch Hunt in Scotland* (Baltimore/London 1981), p. 91; Goodare und Maxwell-Stuart criticize this high figure, saying it should be reduced by several hundred, see J. Goodare, 'Larner, Christina', in *EOW III* (2006) 627, P.G. Maxwell-Stuart, *'Scotland',* in *EOW IV* (2006) 1019; A. Soman, Le procès de la sorcellerie au parlement de Paris (1565–1640), *Annales ESC*

32 (1977), p. 798; Biesel (1997) 361; Monter (1997) 564. Monter (1976) 119 p.; M. Tschaikner, 'Graubünden (Grisons)', in *EOW II* (2006) 455–56. P. Kamber (1998), 249. S. Cirac Estopinán, *Los processos de hecheria en la Inquisición de Castilla la Nueva* (Madrid 1942), pp. 186–201; A. Gari Lacruz: *Brujeria e inquisitión en el Alto Aragón en la primera mitad del siglo XVII* (Zaragoza 1991), p. 218; Levack (1995) 134; E.W. Monter and J. Tedeschi, 'Towards a Statistical Profile of the Italian Inquisitions', in G. Henningsen and J. Tedeschi (eds), *The Inquisition in Early Modern Europe* (Dekalb 1989), p. 135, R. Martin, *Witchcraft and the Inquisition in Venice 1550–1650* (Oxford 1979) 226; G.M. Panizza, 'Piedmont', in *EOW III* (2006) 900–01, O. di Simplicio, 'Siena new state', in *EOW IV* (2006) 1036; I.Sz.Kristóf, 'Hungary', in *EOW II* (2006) 517–518. T. Vedris, 'Croatia, north-west', in *EOW I* (2006) 235. V. Kivelson, 'Through the Prism of Witchcraft: Gender and Social Change in Seventeenth-Century Muscovy', in B. Evanset et al. (eds), *Russia's Women, Accommodation, Resistance, Transformation,* (Berkeley 1991), p. 83. Lavrov cast doubts on Kivelson's data, as the rural archives have not been evaluated and the proportions of women may be higher: A. Lavrov. 'Russische Zauberer und ukrainische Zauberinnen', in *Jahrbücher für Geschichte Osteuropas* 53(2005), pp. 177–195.

4 Witch-hunts and the Male Witch: A Chronology

1. The figures are calculated from Decker (1984) 213–218; Gebhard (1989) 233–237; Schönleitner (1986) 210–22. Schulte (2000) 246; Dupont-Bouchat (1978) 127, whose figures are now considered too low, see R. Voltmer (2006) 677.
2. Calculated from the data in Nieß (1982) 44–5, 126–8, 142, 169–70, 177–8, 183, 233–4, 265, 271, 277, 301.
3. Schulte (2001) 69, 98.
4. Schwerhoff, (1995) 367.
5. Midelfort (1972) 179.
6. Midelfort (1972) 9, 72–4.
7. Midelfort (1972) 182–4.
8. Figures follow Midelfort (1972) 182.
9. Slightly altered for ease of understanding from Soldan/Heppe (1880/1986) 51.
10. Voltmer/Weisenstein (1996) 23, 301–8.
11. H. Vogel, *Der große Schongauer Hexenprozeß und seine Opfer, 1589–1592* (Schongau 1989), pp. 56–68.
12. Midelfort (1972) 179–80.
13. Figures calculated from Decker (1984) 213–18.
14. Heuser (2002) 139.
15. Calculated from Gehm (2000) 69–71, 110–11. Slightly different figures in Walinski-Kiehl (1981) 101.
16. Gebhard (1989) 233–38.
17. Calculated from the figures in Rochelandet (1992) Appendix.
18. Calculated from the figures in Schönleitner (1986) 223–247. The study reflects the level of research reached in 1987 and does not claim to be definitive. Although more recent research might reveal different figures, there is

no doubt as to the validity of classifying the region one of low intensity persecution.

19. Calculated from the information in Nieß (1982) 44–45, 126–8, 142, 169–70, 177–8, 183, 233–4, 265, 271, 277, 301. The remaining figures are accounted for by people of unknown sex.
20. Figures calculated from Schormann (1973) 144–159.
21. Figures calculated from Wilbertz (1978) 33–50.
22. Schulte (2001) 67.
23. Midelfort (1972) 121–63.
24. Exceptions are, for example, the small county of Namur in the Spanish Netherlands, Vorarlberg in the Alps and several territories in the southwest of the empire.

5 Men as Potential Witches in Demonological Treatises

1. J. Hansen, *Zauberwahn. Inquisition und Hexenprozeß im Mittelalter und die Entstehung der großen Hexenverfolgung* (München 1900/reprint Frankfurt 1998); N. Cohn, *Europe's Inner Demons, An Inquiry Inspired by the Great Witch Hunt* (London 1975); J.C. Schmitt, *Heidenspaß und Höllenangst: Aberglaube im Mittelalter* (Frankfurt 1993), pp. 98–157.
2. S. Clark, *Thinking with Demons. The Idea of Witchcraft in Early Modern Europe* (Oxford 1997), pp. 116, 130.
3. Numerous authors use Summers' translations. Yet Summers, a self-designated expert, was by no means always precise in his translations, particularly where gender was concerned. In his translation of Boguet's 'Discours Execrable des Sorciers', for example, there are numerous misunderstandings. It is regrettable that such a renowned historian as B.P. Levack still uses Summers' editions of Institor(is), Boguet and Guazzo see B. P. Levack (ed.), *The Witchcraft Sourcebook* (New York 2004) pp. 57, 77–81, 99–103. See also the discussion in Apps/Gow (2003) 114, n.19.
4. M.D. Bailey, *Battling Demons: Witchcraft, Heresy and Reform in the Late Middle Ages* (Pennsylvania 2003), p. 48; W. Tschacher, *Der Formicarius des Johannes Nider von 1437/38* (Aachen 2003), pp. 341–427; C. Chène in Osterero (1999) 222–65.
5. Jean Nider, *Formicarius*, V, 3, (1437) (in Latin) in M. Ostorero et al., *L'imaginaire du sabbat* (Lausanne 1999), traduction C. Chène, p. 146' '*Maleficus* dicitur quasi male faciens vel male fidem servans, et utrumque in maleficis, qui superstitionibus ex operibus proximum laedunt, satis reperitur,' (Italics by R.S.). Digitalised Latin version of 1480: http://inkunabeln.ub.uni-koeln.de
6. Nider, V, 3 (1437) 150 (Italics by R.S): '...domino Petro videlicet cive Bernensis in Lausanensi diocesi, qui multos *utriusque sexus* incineravit *maleficos* et alios fugavit e territorio dominii Bernensium.... Sunt igitur, vel noviter fuerunt... circa districtum Bernensis dominii quidam *malefici utriusque sexus...*'.
7. Nider, V/3 (1437) 151–7, V/4, 161–71, V/7 191–5.
8. Nider V/7 (1437) 194–6.V, 3, 152, V/4, 166–9.
9. Implied in M. Bailey, 'Nider, Johannes', in *EOW III* (2006) 827.
10. J. Nider, *Formicarius* (Köln 1480/Graz 1971), pp. 222–6.

11. See also Tschacher (2000) 436.
12. P. Mamoris, *Flagellum maleficorum*, (1462/Hansen 1901) 210.
13. N. Jacquier, *Flagellum haereticorum fascinariorum* (1458/Hansen 1901) 137, 'In hac autem fascinorum secta sive synagoga *conveniunt non solum mulieres, sed viri*, et quod deterius est, etiam ecclesiastici et religiosi ...'.
14. W. Rummel, Gutenberg, der Teufel und die Mutter Gottes von Eberhardsklausen, in Blauert (1990), pp. 101–108.
15. Kramer, literally translated, a small-scale merchant, Latinized his name, following the authors of Antiquity, using the Latin geneitive 'Institoris'. The literal translation in the nominative would be 'Institor'.
16. W. Behringer, *'Malleus Maleficarum'*, in *EOW III* (2006) 718; G. Jerouschek and W. Behringer, Das unheilsvollste Buch der Weltliteratur in Jerouschek and Behringer (eds), Heinrich Kramer (Institoris), *Der Hexenhammer. Malleus Maleficarum* (München 2000), pp. 22–26, 31–40.
17. H. Institoris, *Malleus maleficarum* (Speyer 1486) ed. and transl. by C. Mackay (Cambridge 2006) I/2, p. 71; emphasis added by R.S.
18. Institor(is) (1486/2006) 117, 119, 122.
19. Institor(is) (1486/2006), II/2/2, 374.
20. Institor(is) (1486/2006), II/1/13, 326.
21. Institor(is) (1486/2006), II/2/1, 367.
22. Institor(is) (1486), II/1/16, 339.
23. Institor(is) (1486), II/2/3, 380. Mackay translates the Latin adjective 'tempus muliebre' as 'womanly'.
24. Institor(is) (1486) II/1/9, 295: '... illa flagicia effeminatos viros ...'.
25. Nider (1437), V/3, 150; Institor(is) (1486) Latin version ed by C. Mackay I/11, 330; similar: II/1/2, 394.
26. Nider (1437) V/3 150, 154; Institor(is) (1486) 2/2, transl. Mackay 2/2, 234.
27. S. Anglo, 'Evident Authority and Authoritative evidence: the Malleus Maleficarum', in S. Anglo (ed.), *The damned Art* (London 1977), p. 6; Hansen (1900) 474.
28. Midelfort (1972) 22; Cohn (1975) 225.
29. Pohl (1988) 21, n. 124 and 215/n.70; Rochelandet (1992) 9. H. Valentinitsch, 'Hexenprozesse in und um Pettau (Ptuj) 1651/1652', in *Zeitschrift des Historischen Vereines für Steiermark* (1990), p. 77; M. Wutte, 'Hexenprozesse in Kärnten', in *Carinthia I*, 117 (1927), p. 37.
30. Behringer (2006) 722.
31. M. Luther, Dr, *Martin Luthers Werke, Kritische Gesamtausgabe* (Weimar 1883 pp.) (= WA) 10, 1,/591. The Weimar edition is used here. 'Item die Hexen, das sind die bösen Teufelshuren ...'.
32. J. Haustein, *Martin Luthers Stellung zum Zauber- und Hexenwesen* (Stuttgart 1990) pp. 44, 51–6, 62–3; 91–5. J. Haustein, 'Martin Luther als Gegner des Hexenwahns', in H. Lehmann and O. Ulbricht (eds), *Vom Unfug des Hexen-Processes. Gegner der Hexenverfolgung von Johann Weyer bis Friedrich Spee* (Wiesbaden 1992), p. 45.
33. Luther (1526) WA 16/551–2.
34. Haustein (1992) 35, 49–51.
35. Haustein (1990) 98–106.
36. Luther, WA 2/60–61. 'bei Zauberern und Zauberinnen', 'Das man gezaubert hat ... Das man sich mit dem Teufel verbunden hat'.

37. Luther, WA 16/551 p. 'Von der Zauberin...Es ist ein überaus gerechtes Gesetz, dass die Zauberinnen getötet werden, denn sie richten viel Schaden an, was bisweilen ignoriert wird...Dieses Gesetz von den Zauberinnen muss man dem zugefügten Schaden beistellen...Wo der Satan nicht hinkommt, kommt sein Weib hin, d.h. eine Zauberin. Zauberinnen sollen getötet werden, weil sie Diebe sind, Ehebrecher, Räuber, Mörder...'.
38. Luther, WA 29/487.
39. Haustein (1990) 33.
40. Luther, WA 24/84; WA 147/129, 'Auf erste greiffet er [der Teufel] den Menschen an, da er am schwechsten ist, nemlich die weibliche person, da ist Hevam und nicht Adam....Paulus ait: 'Adam non fuit seductus, sed Eva mulier' hoc est: mulier non erat tantae prudentiae ut Adam....Non animadvertit Sathanae insidias'.
41. Luther, WA 29/487.
42. Luther, WA 47/761.
43. M. Luther, *Martin Luthers Werke. Kritische Gesamtausgabe, Tischreden* (Weimar 1885 pp.), vol. 2, no. 2764 b, p. 643. For a balanced, unidealized and undistorted evaluation of Luther's image of women see: S. C. Karant-Nunn et al., *Luther on Women. A Sourcebook* (Cambridge 2003), pp. 10–13. In contrast Brauner (1995) 66–7. Here witches are portrayed as the female counterpart to the home-loving, virtuous Protestant housewife. Luther, however, does not express such a polarized view of women. On Luther and the acceptance of sexuality as a natural human trait, see J. Tonkin, Luther and women, in *Lutherjahrbuch* 57(1990), pp. 262–64. L. Roper, *Luther: Sex, Marriage and Motherhood,* http://www.warwick.ac.uk/fac/arts/History/teaching/protref/women/WR0911.htm (acc. June 2, 2007) A.P. Coudert also emphasizes the establishment of a new type of patriarchy through Protestantism in 'The Myth of the Improved Status of Protestant Women: The Case of the Witchcraze', in J. Brink et al. (eds), *The Politics of Gender in Early Modern Europe* (Kirksville 1989), pp. 61–89.
44. Luther, WA, Tischreden (1566), vol. 4/3979, 52. 'Anno 1538, den 25 August, ward viel geredet von Hexen und Zauberinnen...'.
45. General overview: P. Maxwell-Stuart, Daneau, Lambert in *EOW I* (2006) 246; O. Fatio, Lambert Daneau *1530–1595*, in J. Raitt (ed.), *Shapes of Religious Traditions in Germany, Switzerland and Poland 1560–1660* (New Haven 1981), pp. 105–119.
46. L. Daneau, *Dialogue très-utile-nécessaire pour ce temps. Auquel ce qui se dispute auiourd'hui des Sorciers et Eriges est traité bien amplement et resolu* (Paris 1573).
47. Daneau (1579) 58–70.
48. Daneau (1579) 24, 27–28, 45, 61, 77, 87, 100; pact with the devil : 37, 41, 57–58, 79.
49. Daneau (1579) 90: '...tout sorcier est digne de la haine publique de tout le monde et pourtant digne de mort'.
50. Daneau (1573) 82, 112, Daneau (1579) 67.
51. Daneau (1573) 76.
52. Daneau (1579) 67.
53. Daneau (1579) 103–10.
54. S. Meiger (1587) Q II, Y III, Z III.; B. Carpzov (1635) 324. H. Samson (1626) CIII c.
55. Schmidt (2004) 237–52.

56. H. Bullinger, *Wider die schwarzen kunst, abergleubigs sägnen, unwarhaffts warsagen und andere derglychen von gottverbottne künst*, Zentralbibliothek Zürich, Ms. F 63, 356r.-363v., hier zitiert nach http://www.unizh.ch/irg/schwarzkunst.html. (acc. July 7, 2007). Printed and disseminated in High German: H. Bullinger, 'Wider die schwartze Kunst...', in A. Sawr (ed.), *Theatrum de veneficis* (Frankfurt 1586), pp. 298–306.
57. Bruce Gordon, *'God killed Saul': Heinrich Bullinger and Jacob Ruef on the Power of the Devil in Edwards* (2002) 155–80.
58. Bullinger (1571) 362 r; (1586) 303. '...unter den weibern also sind, die nennet man Zauberinnen und Hexen...Die verläugnen auch Gottes und deß waren glaubens, verpfligten sich dem Teuffel...'.
59. Bullinger (1571) 362 r; (1586) 303. 'Zauberer sind, die man doch mit den Haupthandel den Hexen gleich, dann sie auch Hexenmeister genennet, und Bündnuß und verstendnuß mit dem Teufel machen, sich demselbigen verschreiben.'.
60. Bullinger (1571) 363v; (1586) 305.
61. J.C.V. Johannsen, 'Hemmingsen, Niels *(1513–1600)'*, in *EOW II* (2006) 481–482.
62. N. Hemmingsen, *Vermanunge von Den Schwartzkünstlerischen Aberglauben...* (Wittenberg 1586).
63. Hemmingsen (1586) E V v., H p., I f., K p. His work is not correctly paginated.
64. Hemmingsen (1586) C V v., LV v.
65. Hemmingsen (1586) D V b, O II; N. Hemmingsøn, *En Undervisning aff den hellige skrifft...* (København 1576), p. 10.
66. Hemmingsen (1586) K V c. 'Demnach muss auch gefragt, ob die *Zauberinnen* bei Nacht an einem gewissen Orte sich versammeln, wenn sie andere Gestalten angenommen haben und miteinander essen und trinken?', see also, J.C.V. Johansen, *'Denmark: The Sociology of Accusations'*, in Ankerloo and Henningsen (1990) 362.
67. Hemmingsen (1586) D V b.
68. Hemmingsen (1586) L V v.
69. Hemmingsøn (1576) 27.
70. Hemmingsen (1586) C V a.
71. Johansen (1991) 313.
72. U. Lange, *Untersuchungen zu Bodins Démonomanie* (Köln 1968), pp. 75, 155; J. L Pearl, *The Crime of Crimes. Demonology and Politics in France 1560–1620* (Waterloo 1999), p. 115.
73. S. Houdard, *Les sciences du diable. Quatre discours sur la sorcellerie* (Paris 1992), p. 103.
74. Clark (1997) 668–82.
75. The French edition of 1580 is used here: J. Bodin (Angevin), *De la Démonomanie Des Sorciers* (Paris 1580, reprint Hildesheim 1988), I/1, 1: '*Sorcier* est celuy qui par moyens Diaboliques sciemment s'efforce de parvenir à quelque chose'. R.A. Scott and J.L. Pearl (transl.a.ed) published an abridged translation in 1995, *On the Demon Mania of Witches* (Toronto 1995).
76. Bodin (1580) I/6, 47 p. (use of italics to show male and female demonstrative pronouns as referring to both sexes by R.S.): '... le mot de *Sorcier* n'est pas proprement dict de ceux qui gettent au sort pour sçavoir si bien ou mal leur adviendra, [combien que c'est une espece de Sorcelerie] ainsi principalement

pour *ceux et celles* qui gettent (d)es passages, ou enfouyent soubs l'essueil des estables certaines poudres maléfiques pour faire mourir ceux qui pas seront par dessus'.

77. Bodin (1580) III/1, 125: 'C'est pourquoy *les sorciers* qui sont contraints par Sathan de mal faire, tuer, empoisonner hommes et bestes'.
78. Bodin (1580) préface II/8 113, 114, 117, V/230, 236, 241.
79. Bodin (1580) V/238. 'A plus forte raison les contrats, conventions, sacrifices, adorations et détestables copulations *des Sorciers* avec les Démons non seulement sont volontaires, ainsi aussi d'une franche spontaneam volontatem'.
80. Bodin (1580) I/6 43, II/1 52, 59, II/7, 105, 107, V/227, 230.
81. In contrast to E.W. Monter, 'Inflation and witchcraft: The case of Jean Bodin', in T.K. Rabb and J.E. Siegel, *Action and Conviction in Early Modern Europe* (Princeton 1969), p. 385–86. It is correct that Bodin had not yet delivered a coherent and theoretical analysis of the witches' Sabbat, but this night gathering is derived from the statements of condemned witches and male witches and made a focus of his demonology.
82. Bodin (1580) II/4, 81 p. 'L'homme se voyant en la compagny de *grand nombre de sorciers et sorcières* incogneues,...' (italics by R.S.).
83. Bodin (1580) II/4, 82. 'elle eust fait la reverence au chef de l'assemblée qui estoit habillé en prince pompeusement et accompagné d'*une grande multitude d'hommes et de femmes* qui tous firent hommage au Maistre.' (italics by R.S.).
84. Bodin (1580) préface, II/4 80–92, IV/179, 185–186.
85. Bodin (1580) II/5, 82–83, III/5, 151, 133, IV/4, 193.
86. Bodin (1580) II/4, 79.
87. Bodin (1580) IV/4, 190.
88. In his standard work 'Six livres de la République' he assigned women a subordinate role in society, see C. Opitz-Belakhal, *Das Universum des Jean Bodin. Staatsbildung* (Frankfurt, 2004), esp. pp. 161–67.
89. Bodin (1580) V/224–26.
90. Bodin (1580) V/226.
91. Bodin (1580) V/225.
92. Houdard (1992) 96.
93. Southeast Germany: Behringer (1997) 226; Franche-Comté: Rochelandet (1992) 10; Holstein: A judge refers specifically to Bodin in a witch trial: Trial of Gretje Dwenger, StA Oldesloe, Act. VII C 46; Austria: H. Valentinitsch (1990) 77; Spanish Netherlands: Vanysacker (1988) 92.
94. Pearl (1999) 123.
95. J. Fischart, *De Magorum Daemonomania*...(Straßburg 1581). The 1591 edition was used for this study.
96. Fischart (1591) 103.
97. Fischart (1591) 101.
98. Fischart (1591) 266.
99. Fischart translates the Latin term 'lamia' by 'fiend' which, at the same time, is used to mean 'witch'. See: Fischart (1591) 270.
100. Fischart (1591) 1 (italics in the title by R.S.): 'Von eigentlicher Beschreibung oder Definition der Zauberer/Hexen und *Hexen und Hexenmeister'*. 'Fischart is not consistent in his terminology and sometimes uses, Zauberer' (sorcerer) for male witch; see explanation in Chapter 1, p. 00.

101. Fischart (1591) 112.
102. Fischart (1591) 129 confirmed in the subsequent remarks.
103. Fischart (1591) 135.
104. Fischart (1591) 157.
105. Fischart (1591) 162.
106. Fischart (1591) 171.
107. Fischart (1591) 200.
108. Fischart (1591) 217.
109. Fischart (1591) 225.
110. Fischart (1591) 234.
111. Fischart (1591) 130, *'unzählige Zauberer und Hexen in Deutschland...'*.
112. General overview: 'A. Rowlands, Goedelmann, Johann Georg (1559–1611)', in *EOW II* (2006) 448–9; J.G Godelmann, *Von Zäuberern, Hexen und Unholden* (Frankfurt 1592).
113. Godelmann (1592) 1/83–4, 2/240.
114. Godelmann (1592) 2/165 2/230.
115. Godelmann (1592) 2/203, 3/473.
116. Godelmann (1592) 3/345–99. S. Lorenz, 'Johann-Georg Godelmann – ein Gegner des Hexenwahns?', in R. Schmidt (ed.), *Beiträge zur Pommerschen und Mecklenburgischen Geschichte* (Marburg1981), pp. 61–105.
117. Godelmann (1592) 3/430–56; Clark (1997) 519.
118. Godelmann (1592) 1/82, 1/385.
119. Godelmann (1592) 1/83, 2/263, 3/434.
120. Godelmann (1592) 2/263.
121. Godelmann (1592) 3/451.
122. Clark (1997) 519; Lorenz (1981) 102–4.
123. A. Sawr, *Theatrum de veneficis* (Frankfurt 1586).
124. J. Vallick, *'Von Zauberern, Hexen und Unholden'*, in Sawr (1586) 54–69. W. Frijhoff, *'Jacob Vallick und Johann Weyer. Kampfgenossen, Konkurrenten oder Gegner?,'* in Lehmann and Ulbricht (1992) 67–74.
125. J. Ewich, *Von den Hexen* in Sawr (1586) 325–55; Schwarzwälder (1959) 171, 205.
126. *Allgemeine Deutsche Biographie*, vol. 30 (Leipzig 1890) 419.
127. Ewich (1586) 331, p. 334, 336; Sawr (1586) 207; Vallick (1586) 65.
128. Ewich (1586) 332, 336; Vallick (1586) 65 p.
129. Sawr (1586) 207.
130. Sawr (1586) 206 p.; Ewich (1586) 354 p.; Vallick (1586) 65–67.
131. Ewich (1586) 326.
132. Ewich (1586) 331.
133. Vallick (1586) 66.
134. Vallick (1586) 66.
135. Vallick refers to the frequently cited verse in the Book of Exodus in the Old Testament.
136. S. Meiger, *De Panurgia Lamiarum, Sagarum, Strigum ac Veneficarum, totiusque, cohortis Magicae Cacodaemonia libri tres* (Hamburg 1587), p. P IV, Q III, Kk III, Ss II.
137. D. Lohmeier, Die Hexenschrift des Samuel Meigerius, in Degn et al. (1983) 48.
138. Meiger (1587) N, D III.
139. Meiger (1587) V III v, X III v.
140. Meiger (1587) Aa. Cc II v, Mm v, V v.

141. Meiger (1587) X III vv.
142. Meiger (1587) A a.
143. Meiger (1587) Tt III, D II.
144. At least, not for Holstein: In book 3, Cc III, he speaks of 'Hexenmeistereye', but is referring here to the Catholic and southern German author, Molitor.
145. Meiger (1587) Bb II v.
146. Meiger (1587) E r, E.
147. Meiger (1587) E, E v. Meiger's list is incomplete as logically he should have named 10 commandments.
148. Meiger (1587) N: 'Gleichwohl der Zauberer und die Zauberin Menschen und Vieh töten und um die Gesundheit bringen, sind sie mit Recht als *Mörderinnen* am Leben zu strafen.' (Italics by R.S.).
149. J. Dillinger, 'Binsfeld, Peter (1546–1598)', in *EOW I* (2006) 122–4.
150. P. Binsfeld, *Tractat von Bekanntnuß der Zauberer und Hexen* (München 1592). The German editions of 1590 and 1592 and the Latin edition of 1589 were used for this study.
151. Binsfeld (1590) 52, 53, 57, 58. Binsfeld (1589) uses the term, 'malefici' throughout these chapters, see the Index.
152. Binsfeld (1592) 4, 29–31.
153. Binsfeld (1592) 26. Binsfeld (1589) 66: 'Malefici vel maleficae rem veneream habens cum Daemone'.
154. Binsfeld (1589) 77: '*Multi utriusque sexus* viri, mulieres, pueri et puellae confidentur id verum esse'.
155. Binsfeld (1592) 69, 68.
156. Binsfeld (1590) 38.
157. Binsfeld (1590), Titelblatt (italics by R.S.).
158. Binsfeld (1592) 18.
159. Binsfeld (1592) 55 v.
160. Binsfeld (1592) 19 v.
161. Binsfeld (1592) 21.
162. Dupont-Bouchat (1978) 80. E. Pauls, 'Zauberwesen und Hexenwahn am Niederrhein', in *Beiträge zur Geschichte des Niederrheins 13* (1898), p. 186.
163. W. Behringer, '*Meinungsbildende Befürworter und Gegner der Hexenverfolgung (15. bis 18. Jahrhundert)*', in Valentinitsch (1987) 223–5.
164. W. Monter and E. Peters, 'Rémy', Nicolas in *EOW IV* (2006) 955; Biesel (1997) 92–100. The German 1693 version and the Latin edition of 1597 were used for this study: N. Remigius, *Daemonolatriae libri tres* (Frankfurt 1597); *Daemonolatria oder Beschreibung von Zauberern und Zauberinnen,* 3 parts, (Hamburg 1693).
165. Rémy (1693) 1/25, 101; 1/27, 172–4; 1/29, 118; 1/32,140.
166. L. Dintzer, *Nicolas Rémy et son œuvre démonologique* (Lyon 1936), pp. 33–6.
167. Remy (1597) 2/9, 253: 'Quid causa sit, quod diabolus *Maleficorum* saepe assensum postulat, ubi quid alicui calamitatis molitur.'.
168. The German translation of 1693, from which this English version stems, is a very free rendering.
169. Rémy (1597) 1/6, 27.
170. Rémy (1597) 1/19; Rémy (1693) 1/19, 57, 88, 115.
171. Rémy (1693) 1/66, 71, 76, 78.

172. Rémy (1597) 1/19, 126; Rémy (1693) 1/88.
173. Rémy (1597) 1/15, 109: 'Certe multo plura in faeminas exempla edi memini, quam in viros. Nec adeo est sine ratione, quod haec hominum colluvies frequentius in genere effertur faeminino, sagae, veratrices, lamiae, striges...', Rémy (1693) 1/15, 75.
174. Rémy (1597) 1/15, 108; Rémy (1693) 1/15, 74.
175. Rémy (1597) 2/1, 188; Rémy (1693) 1/129–31.
176. Rémy (1597) 3/12, 407: 'Equidem non verebor...*maleficorum* examinadorum usu exercitus ac confirmatus...Vidilicet...igni interficere'.
177. Briggs (1996).
178. Biesel (1997) 96.
179. Pauls (1898) 187.
180. Grimmelshausen, *Abenteuerlicher Simplicissimus* (1669, reprint München 1961), p. 118.
181. The English translation was used for this study: M. Del Rio, *Investigations into Magic, ed. a. transl. by P.G. Maxwell-Stuart* (Manchester 2000). As certain text sections of this opulent work were summarized in Maxwell-Stuart's edition, the Latin edition was also used: M. Del Rio, *Disquisitionum magicarum libri sex* (Köln 1633 and Mainz 1603). Biography: E. Fischer, *Die 'Disquisitionum magicarum libri sex' von M. Del Rio als gegenreformatorische Exempel-Quelle* (Frankfurt 1975), pp. 5–13.
182. Del Rio (transl. Maxwell-Stuart) 5.1/189; Del Rio (1633) V. I/695.
183. Del Rio (transl. Maxwell-Stuart) 3.1 5./132.
184. Del Rio (transl. Maxwell-Stuart) 5.1./234; Del Rio (1633) 633, V/775.
185. Del Rio (transl. Maxwell-Stuart) 2.15./89; Del Rio (1633) II/159.
186. Del Rio (transl. Maxwell-Stuart) 129, 190, 213; Del Rio (1633) II/171.
187. Del Rio (1633)II/172 pp. Delrio (transl. Maxwell-Stuart) 2/93.
188. Del Rio (transl. Maxwell-Stuart) 2.16./91; Del Rio (1633), II/171, 176.
189. These statements are in the original Latin text of 1603: Del Rio (1603) IV/C I, QII, 137. Unfortunately, Maxwell-Stuart summarized these passages in the English edition.
190. Del Rio (1603) IV/C I, QII, 137 'Ideò mulieres citiùs imaginantur, sed viri minus pertinaciter imaginationes forent,cumque illae minus ratione polleant, minus etiam prudentiae habeant, proclivius est daemoni eas simiItudine falsa et apparente decipere.'
191. Clark (1997) 116.
192. Italics by R.S.
193. Levack (1995) 64; Fischer (1975) 142–3. For the wide-reaching reception in Austria, Luxembourg and Franche-Comté: Byloff (1934) 62, Dupont-Bouchat (1978) 82, Rochelandet (1992) 10. These are all regions in which higher proportions of men were prosecuted.
194. H. Boguet, *Discours Execrable Des Sorciers* (Rouen 1606); H. Boguet, *Discours des sorciers* (Lyon 1610). Both editions were used because Boguet's statements occasionally varied in the different works. The 1603 edition is available digitally:www.gallica.bnf.fr>Boguet. For the biography: F. Bavoux, *Boguet, Grand Juge de la Terre de St. Claude* (Besançon 1958), pp. 5–19.
195. Boguet (1606) 277 p.
196. Boguet (1606) 11–12, 54–7.

197. Boguet (1606) 117 pp.: 'Chapitre XXII: Si les *sorciers* font de la gresle', 'Chapitre XXIII: De la poudre des *sorciers*' (italics by R.S.).
198. Boguet (1606) 54: 'Chapitre XI. De l'accouplement du Demon avec *la Sorcière et le Sorcier'.*
199. Boguet (1606) 17–22.
200. Boguet (1606) 55: '... Et comme *le sorcier* n'est pas moins adonnné à ce plaisir que *la sorcière,* c'est pourquoy il se met aussi en femme pour luy complaire' (italics by R.S.).
201. Boguet (1606) 107 p.
202. Boguet (1606) 76–126.
203. Boguet (1606) 311.
204. Boguet (1610), no. 22, 48.
205. Rochelandet (1997) 19.
206. D. Meder, *Acht Hexenpredigten (Leipzig 1605); General Overview:* R. Schulte, 'Meder, David (1545–1616)', in *EOW III* (2006) 742.
207. Meder (1605) 15 a.
208. Meder (1605) 7 a.
209. Meder (1605) 45 a.
210. Meder (1605) 54 a, 112 a.
211. Meder (1605) 26 a.
212. Meder (1605) 27 a.
213. Meder (1605) 69 a.
214. Midelfort (1972) 48.
215. Meder (1605) 114 p.
216. Meder (1605) 39–40 a.
217. H. Samsonius, *Neun außerlesene und Wohlbegründete Hexen-Predigt* (Riga 1626), p. E II.
218. For a biography: 'Samson, H.', in *Allgemeine Deutsche Biographie,* Band 30 (Leipzig 1890), pp. 312–15.
219. Clark (1997) 438, compares the significance of Samson with William Perkins, the Puritan expert in the field of witchcraft.
220. Samson (1626) E III.
221. Samson (1626) K III c.
222. Samson (1626) C III.
223. Samson (1626) X II.
224. It is surprising that Clark (1997) 116 p., thinks that Samson neglected the question of gender specificity. In fact, Samson deals explicitly with this issue, in contrast to other authors.
225. Samson (1626) C II.
226. Samson (1626) C II.
227. Samson (1626) E.
228. Samson (1626) E II.
229. Samson (1626) E Iv, vv; E II v, vv; G II vv; G III vv; G IV v; N vv; J IV v, vv.
230. Samson (1626) C III vv., D III vv.
231. Samson (1626) E r.
232. Clark (1997) 209, comes to the same conclusion.
233. Samson (1626), K III vv.
234. Samson (1626) F III v, H III vvv, X III. 'Zaubergesindlein', 'Satans- und Drachengesindlein'.

235. H. von Schultheiß, *Eine Außführliche Instruction wie in Inquisition Sachen des grewlichen Lasters der Zauberey gegen Die Zauberer ... zu procedieren* (Köln 1634). A biography can be found in: R. Decker, 'Der Hexen-Richter Dr. Heinrich v. Schultheiß (1580–1646) aus Scharmede', in D. Grohmann (ed.), *750 Jahre Stadt Salzkotten* (Paderborn, 1996), pp. 1045–60.
236. Schultheiß (1634) title; Decker (1981–82) 339–86, Schormann (1991) 83.
237. Schultheiß (1634) 17–21.
238. Schultheiß (1634) 15 p.
239. Schultheiß (1634) 79, 99–101.
240. Schultheiß (1634) 177–236.
241. Schultheiß (1634) 230: 'An socium et socios habuerit?'.
242. Schultheiß (1634) 252.
243. Schultheiß (1634) 253.
244. Schultheiß (1634) 21, 27–31, 63, 86, 88, 91, 99, 111–13, 121, 138, 142, 152, 161, 236, 264, 298, 328, 344, 349–353, 357, 363, 365, 386, 388, 402, 406, 428, 466–68. Fewer women, however: 60, 84, 96, 104, 177, 329, 404, 446, 481 489.
245. Schultheiß (1634) 291.
246. Decker (1996) 6.
247. W. Schild, 'Carpzov, B.', in *Deutsche Biographische Enzyklopädie*, vol. 2 (Minden/London 1995), pp. 286–87. W. Trusen, 'Benedict Carpzov und die Hexenverfolgung in Recht und Kriminalität', in E. Schlüchter and K. Laubenthal (eds), *Festschrift für Friedrich Wilhelm Krause* (Köln 1990), pp. 19–35.
248. *Practicae Novae Imperialis Saxonicae Rerum Criminalium in partes III* (Wittenberg 1635). The Wittenberg edition of 1646 was used here.
249. Carpzov (1646) I/48/1.
250. S. Lorenz, 'Benedict Carpzov und die Hexenverfolgung', in G. Jerouschek et al. (ed.), *Benedict Carpzov. Neue Perspektiven zu einem umstrittenen sächsischen Juristen* (Tübingen 2000), p. 105; W. Sellert, Benedict Carpzov – Ein fanatischer Strafjurist und Hexenverfolger, in Lehmann/Ulbricht (1992) 325–30.
251. Carpzov (1636) I/48/34, 314: '... ante omnia docere ac demonstrare necesse habebit, venefic*os* venefic*as*que que varia morborum genera ... inferre posse'.
252. Carpzov (1646), Buch I/48/47, 315: 'Negari non potest, Magos et Sagas pactum habere cum Diabolo ...'.
253. Carpzov (1646) I/49/44, 324: 'Taliter ergò concumbentes Maleficos ac Sagas cum Daemone siquidem cum eo pactae fuerint'.
254. Carpzov (1646) I/49/29, 323.
255. Carpzov (1646) I/49/45, 324.
256. Carpzov (1646) I/48/58, 317: 'Quamvis non negem, Sagas ac Lamias saepe etiam praestigiis occupatas phantasia tantum conventibus Diabolicis, commessationibus et choreis interesse sibi videri ... Sagas utroque modo quandoque illusore dormientes, vana imagitione, et quandoque vere conventibus adesse Carpzov is very much in the defensive when he argues, for example: Ideoque nec absurde affirmatur Striges et Lamias corporaliter ad conventus diabolicos avolare'. See Carpzov (1646) I/317.

257. Carpzov (1646) I/49/53, 324: '...omnium Strigarum et Maleficorum cuiuscumque generis...'.
258. Carpzov (1646) I/49/30, 322.
259. Carpzov (1646) I/49/53, questio 15.
260. Schild (1995) 287.
261. T. Robisheaux, 'Zur Rezeption Benedict Carpzovs im 17.Jh', in Eiden and Voltmer (2002) 526, 534, p. 539.
262. J. Weyer, *Von Teufelsgespenst, Zauberern und Gifftbereytern. Schwartzkünstlern, Hexen und Unholden* (Frankfurt 1586). For this study I have used the German edition of 1586. Abridged English translation: B.J. Kohl/H.C.E.Midelfort (eds) *On witchcraft. An abridged Translation of Johann Weyer's, 'De praestigiis daemonum'* (Asheville 1998).
263. M. Valente, Weyer, 'Johann (1515–1588)', in *EOW IV* (2006) 1193–95.
264. Weyer (1586) III/166, 169, 199. see also S. Clark, 'Glaube und Skepsis in der deutschen Hexenliteratur von Johann Weyer bis Friedrich von Spee', in Lehmann/Ulbricht (1992) 23; S. Anglo, 'Melancholia and Witchcraft: The debate between Wier, Bodin and Scot', in P. Gerlo (ed.), *Folie et Déraison à la Renaissance* (Bruxelles 1976), pp. 209–25.
265. G.C. Davidson and J.M. Neale, *Klinische Psychologie* (München/Baltimore 1984), p. 15.
266. Weyer (1586) III/162.
267. Weyer (1586) II/80.
268. Weyer (1586) III/162, 157, IV/416.
269. Weyer (1586) Apologia, 519.
270. H. Lehmann/O. Ulbricht, *'Motive und Argumente von Gegnern der, Hexenverfolgung von Weyer bis Spee'*, in Lehmann and Ulbricht (1992) 12.
271. Weyer (1586) VI/400.
272. Weyer (1586) II/84.
273. Clark in Lehmann and Ulbricht (1992) 23.
274. H.C.E. Midelfort, *'Johann Weyer in medizinischer, theologischer und rechtsgeschichtlicher Hinsicht'*, in Lehmann and Ulbricht (1992) 63–4.
275. Godelmann (1584) 162–4, 212–14.
276. F. Spee, *Cautio criminalis, Seu de processibus contra sagas* (Rinteln 1631). The English translation was used here: *Friedrich Spee von Langenfeld, Cautio Criminalis, or a Book on Witch-Trial*s (transl. by M. Hellyer) (Charlotteville 2003). The German translation of 1631 was also used: *Cautio criminalis oder Rechtliches Bedenken wegen der Hexenprozesse* (1631/München 1982).
277. J.F. Ritter, *Friedrich von Spee 1591–1635* (Trier 1977). H.J. Zwetsloot, *Friedrich Spee und die Hexenprozesse* (Trier 1954); A. Arens (ed.), *Friedrich Spee im Licht der Wissenschaften* (Mainz 1984); T.G.M. Oorschot, (ed.): *Friedrich Spee (1591–1635* (Bielefeld 1993); D. Brockmann and P. Eicher (eds), *Die politische Theologie Friedrich von Spees* (München 1991).
278. J.M. Battafarano, 'Spees Cautio in Brockmann and Eicher (1991) 231; H.D. Kittsteiner, Spee – Thomasius – Becker: 'Cautio criminalis'und prinzipielles Argument', in Brockmann and Eicher (1991) 214.
279. Spee (transl. Hellyer) 200–20; Spee (1631/1982) 12, 31, 114, 154, 186, 233–5, 280–6.
280. Spee (transl. Hellyer) 24; Spee (1631/1982) 12.

281. Spee (transl. Hellyer) 15, 16, 18, 197, 198, 201; Spee (1631/1982) 1, 248, 256.
282. Spee (transl. Hellyer) 75; Spee (1631/1982) 82.
283. C. Opitz, 'Hexenverfolgung als Frauenverfolgung', in C. Opitz (ed.), *Der Hexenstreit* (Freiburg 1995),pp. 254–6.
284. Spee (transl. Hellyer) 125; Spee (1631/1982) 153.
285. Spee (transl. Hellyer) 148; Spee (1631/1982) 186.
286. Spee (1631/1982) 248.
287. H. Wunder, 'Friedrich Spee und die verfolgten Frauen', in Brockmann and Eicher (1991) 117–31.
288. Behringer (2004) 180 p.; S. Lorenz, Die Rezeption der cautio criminalis in der Rechtswissenschaft zur Zeit der Hexenverfolgung, in Oorschot (1993) 130–153.
289. Burgundy: Rochelandet (1992) 70; Austria: Dienst in Zöllner (1986) 71; Paderborn: R. Decker, *Die Hexen und ihre Henker. Ein Fallbericht* (Freiburg 1994), p. 259.
290. Clark (1997) 116, 130. The arguments put forward now by Apps and Gow (2003) 37 pp. supported and augmented those I presented in 'Hexenmeister' (2000).
291. Apps and Gow (2003) 104. In their chapter on contemporary demonology, the authors refer, with one exception, to Catholic authors and, unfortunately, do not include Protestant or, specifically, Lutheran writers.
292. A glance at the following chapter illustrates this clearly (1486/Latin version 2006): I/5, 261, 268, 272, 277. He repeatedly alternates between the two genders in a description of the same matter. Institor(is) (1486/Latin version 2006): I/5, 261, 268, 272, 277.
293. Apps and Gow (2003) also highlighted this issue.
294. See also Clark (1997) 139, 142, 529.
295. The interrogation catalogue for Saxony-Coburg included, for example, questions relating to attendance at the witches' Sabbat; this triggered off a heated discussion among Protestant jurists and theologians betwen the proponents of persecution and moderate persecution sceptics, see: Behringer (1995) 354–6.
296. Although Stephen's main argument is controversial and disputable, he does discuss the idea of intercourse with the Devil on a dual-gender level, i.e. he includes cases of alleged male witches in his analysis, W. Stephens, *Demon Lovers: Witchcraft, Sex, and the Crisis of belief* (Chicago, 2002), pp. 5, 8,16, 20, 23, 54, 114, 133, 191, 281, 353.
297. R. van Dülmen, 'Imaginationen des Teuflischen. Nächtliche Zusammenkünfte, Hexentänze, Teufelssabbate', in v. Dülmen (1987) 94–130. N. Jacques-Chaquin and M. Préaud (eds), *Le sabbat des sorciers en Europe (XVe–XVIIIe siècles)* (Paris 1992); A. Soman, *Le sabbat des sorciers: preuve juridique*, pp. 85–99; R. Briggs, *Le Sabbat des sorciers en Lorraine*, pp. 155–81; E. Biesel, *Les descriptions du sabbat dans les confessions des inculpés lorrains et trévirois*, pp. 183–97; R. Walinski-Kiehl, *La chasse aux sorcières et le sabbat des sorcières dans les évêches de Bamberg et Würzburg* (vers 1590-vers 1630), pp. 213–25.
298. Binsfeld (1589), Title page.
299. Binsfeld (1589), Title page.
300. Institoris (1486) 2.2.8. See the Latin version ed. by Mackay (2003) 555.

301. Del Rio (1599/1600) V/775, 781; Schultheiß (1634) 22.
302. Boguet (1606) 214 : 'Tu ne permettras point que les sorciers vivent'.
303. Daneau (1573) 38: 'Moyse, qui les [this personal pronoun refers to the previous noun, "les sorciers"] a condamnez par les condammements de Dieu en Exod, chap. 22'.
304. Bullinger (1586) 305.
305. Samson (1626) C II; Ewich (1586) 347; Sawr (1586) 204; Meiger (1587) C I, D II v, F IV; Godelmann (1584) III/434; Hemmingsen (1586) O II; Carpzov (1635) 314, No. 40.
306. W. Wyporska, 'Exodus 22.18 (22:17)', in *EOW I* (2006) 337 p. confirmed and further substantiated the points I made in 'Hexenmeister' (2000).
307. 'Die Zeuberinnen soltu nicht leben lassen', in M. Luther, *Die gantze Heilige Schrifft Deudsch* (Wittenberg 1545), p. 163. This edition of 1545 is the last Bible translation to appear in Luther's lifetime.
308. This information was provided by Dr A. Hess, lecturer in the Hebrew language at the Institute of Theology, University of Kiel. Both the Catholic and the Protestant church have agreed on this version in the uniform translation of the Bible, see Bischöfe Deutschlands u.a. and Rat der evangelischen Kirche (eds), *'Die Bibel. Altes und Neues Testament* (Stuttgart 1980). Exodus 22, 18, p. 74 is translated there as: 'You shall not permit a witch to live'.
309. Weyer (1586) II/79–84.
310. 'Maleficos non patieris vivere', see P. Gasquet and H. Quentin (eds), *Biblia sacra iuxta Latinam vulgatam versionem* (reprinted Rom 1929), p. 193.
311. W. Sauer-Geppert, 'Bibelübersetzungen: Übersetzungen ins Deutsche', in *Theologische Realenzyklopädie,* (Berlin/New York 1980) VI, 242.
312. J. Schmidt, 'Bibelübersetzungen', in J. Höfer and K. Rahner (eds), *Lexikon für Theologie und Kirche,* vol. 2 (Freiburg 1958), pp 375–402.
313. B. Hall, 'Bibelübersetzungen: Übersetzungen ins Französische', in *Theologische Realenzyklopädie* (1980) VI, 254–6.
314. J. Bugenhagen, *De Biblia...yn dyth dudesche ulittich uthgesettet.* (Lübeck 1533), p. 56.
315. B. Stolt, 'Bibelübersetzungen: Übersetzungen ins Dänische', in *Theologische Realenzyklopädie* (1980) VI, 246.
316. J. Piscator, Biblia. *Das ist: Alle Bücher der H. Schrift des alten und neuren Testaments* (Herborn 1604), p. 238.
317. See the article on Piscator in *Allgemeine Deutsche Biographie,* vol. 26, (Berlin 1970), pp. 180–1.
318. E. Peters, *The Magician, the Witch and the Law* (Philadelphia 1978), pp. 16–18, 67–9.
319. Clark (1997) 536; Blauert (1989) 24–36.
320. Institor(is) (1486/2003, transl. by C. Mackay) I/71. In order to avoid misunderstandings, Mackay's term 'sorcerer' has been replaced by the term agreed upon for the purposes of this book 'witch'.
321. Binsfeld (1590) 76.
322. Del Rio (transl. Maxwell-Stuart) 5.5./210.
323. Hansen (1900) 271–3.
324. R. Schulte, 'Jean Gerson (1363–1429)', in *EOW II* (2006) 437–8.; Peters (1978) 17, 143–5.
325. H. Fründ in M. Ostorero (1999) 30.

326. The correspondence is given in Hansen's (1901) collection of sources p. 30–31. 'Ubi facultas locusque tutus dabitur per legitimas inquisitones et processus ... contra ... receptatores et fautores *haereticorum maleficorum* ... procedatis'. The words in question are in the Latin genitive (Italics by R.S.).
327. Hansen (1900) 275–7, 411.
328. H. Fründ (1430/1999) 30, 32, 40.
329. Innozenz VIII. (1484) in Behringer (1995) 88 (Italics by R.S.).
330. J. Tinctor(is) and J. Taincture, 'Contra sectam Vaudensium, Paris um 1450', reproduced in J.P. Davidson, *Hexen in der nordeuropäischen Kunst 1470–1750* (Düsseldorf 1988) figure 2. Tinctor(is) was Professor of Theology und Rector of the University of Cologne. As a canon in Tournai he experienced one of the first mass trials in Arras and by publishing this picture in his manuscript wanted to give a graphic portrayal of the heresy of the vaudois.
331. Boguet (1606) 374–7.
332. Bernard Gui, *Das Buch der Inquisition* (ed. and transl. by M. Pawlik) (Augsburg 1999), pp. 124, 136.; A. Patschovsky, *Der Passauer Anonymus* (Stuttgart 1968), p. 87; P. Biller, *The Waldenses 1170–1530* (Aldershot 2001) pp. 132, 274, 280.
333. C. Auffarth; *Die Ketzer* (München 2005) p. 118; Biller (2001) 125–158; Utz-Tremp (1999) unpaginated introduction; Patschovsky (1968) 70–73.
334. To this extent, it is possible to confirm Monter's hypothesis on the connection between the persecution of heretics and that of witches in the theological context.
335. Ginzburg, Hexensabbat (1980) 78–80, neglects this palpable root of the witches' Sabbat and in this case cannot avoid the criticism of one-dimensionality.

6 Magic and Gender in Popular Culture

1. H.P. Broedel has shown how elements of popular belief found their way into one of the most widespread works of learned culture, see *The Malleus Maleficarum and the Construction of Witchcraft: Theology and Popular Belief* (Manchester 2003); G. Schwerhoff, Die Erdichtung der weisen Männer. Gegen falsche Übersetzungen von Hexenglauben und Hexenverfolgung in Lorenz and Bauer (1995) 413–415.; P. Burke, *Helden, Schurken und Narren. Europäische Volkskultur in der frühen Neuzeit* (Stuttgart 1981- German transl. of P. Burke, *Popular culture in Early Modern Europe*, New York 1978), p. 41. M. Mauss' analysis of the connection between magic and religion is still considered excellent: M. Mauss: *Esquisse d'une théorie générale de la magie* (Paris 1903). The conflicts described in Ginzburg's discussion of Muchembled are now outdated, see H. Eiden, Die Unterwerfung der Volkskultur? Muchembled und die Hexenverfolgungen, in Voltmer (2005) 23–40; C. Ginzburg: 'Deciphering the Sabbath' versus R. Muchembled, 'Satanic Myths and Cultural Reality', in Ankarloo and Henningsen (1990) 121–160.
2. D. Harmening, *Superstitio. Überlieferungs- und theoriegeschichtliche Untersuchungen zur kirchlich-theologischen Aberglaubensliteratur des Mittelalters* (Berlin 1979), pp. 43–75.

3. A. Gurjewitch, *Das Weltbild des mittelalterlichen Menschen* (München 1980), pp. 352–99; Schmitt (1993) 45–50, 136; R. Künzel, 'Paganisme, syncrétisme et culture religieuse populaire au Haut Moyen Age. Reflexions de méthode, in *Annales ESC 4–5* (1992), pp. 1055–69. Kieckhefer (1976) 47–92.
4. Labouvie (1991) 57–67.
5. H. Dienst, 'Zur Rolle von Frauen in magischen Vorstellungen und Praktiken', in W. Affeldt (ed.), *Frauen in Spätantike und Frühmittelalter* (Sigmaringen 1990), p. 193.
6. M. Blöcker, *Frauenzauber – Zauberfrauen in Opitz* (1995) 99–127; H. Mordek and M. Glatthaar, 'Von Wahrsagerinnen und Zauberern. Ein Beitrag zur Religionspolitik Karls des Großen', in *Archiv für Kulturgeschichte 75* (1993), pp. 33–64.
7. Behringer (2004) 31.
8. The Latin version of the 'corrector' is cited here as in Schmitz (1898) pp. 424–43, Nos 64 and 154: 'Fecisti quod quaedam mulieres facere solent...'
9. 'Consuluisti magos, et in domum tuam induxisti exquirendi aliquid arte malefica, aut expiandi causa, vel paganorum consuetudinem sequens, divinos, qui tibi divinarent, ut futura ab eis requireres quasi a propheta, et illos qui sortes exercent, vel qui per sortes sperant se futura praescire, vel illos qui vel augurriis vel incantationibus inserviunt, ad te invitasti?...' No. 60, Schmitz (1898) 422.
10. 'Fecisti ligaturas et incantationes, et illas varias fascinationes quas nefarii homines, subulci vel bubulci, et interdum venatores faciunt dum dicunt diabolica carmina super panem aut super herbas', Schmitz (1898) 423.
11. For example: LAS AR Eiderstedt (1614); AR Steinburg (1625); AR Reinbek (1639–40); AR Segeberg (1651); AR Ahrenbök (1674–75).
12. Report written by the pastor of Siek, see LAS AR 111 (1639–40).
13. Walz (1993) 257–68.
14. *Schleswig* was a Danish fiefdom; *Holstein* belonged to the Holy Roman Empire. These two territories were bound by a common contract. Schleswig is nevertheless included in this investigation in order to increase the amount of data and size of the sample, thus improving the statistical significance of the conclusions.
15. LAS 104 (1674–75).
16. LAS 390/520 (1668–71).
17. Walz (1993) 306–14, 335–40.
18. The sources are to be found almost exclusively in the Landesarchiv (State Archives) of Schleswig-Holstein and the historical records index of the Seminar of European Ethnology at the University of Kiel. They are listed in the Appendix.
19. K. Kramer, *Volksleben in Holstein (1550–1800)* (Kiel 1987), p. 283.
20. LAS AR 102 (1592).
21. LAS AR 102 (1592); AR 103 (1615); AR 104 (1623 und 1625); Reichsarchiv Kopenhagen: Film 43161, Amt Apenrade 1648; Gerichtsprotokoll Eutin, 275/459 (1673); AR 107 (1681); AR 107 (1681/82); AR 112 (1689/90); AR 108 (1704/05); KA Ratzeburg, AP Ratzeburg (1726–30).
22. Sander (1991) 69–73.
23. LAS AR 112 (1650–51).

24. LAS AR 104 (1632) 275/456; AP Eutin (1624–64) 168 (1670); 275/457, AP Eutin (1657); AP Kaltenhof 276/1231.
25. LAS 163 (1624).
26. LAS 163 (1624).
27. M. Mitterauer, 'Geschlechtsspezifische Arbeitsteilung und Geschlechterrollen in ländlichen Gegenden Mitteleuropas', in I. Martin and R. Zoepffel (eds), *Historische Anthropologie,* vol. 2 (Freiburg 1989), pp. 819–909.
28. O. Højrup, 'Die Arbeitsteilung zwischen Männern und Frauen in der bäuerlichen Kultur Dänemarks', in *Ethnologia Skandinavica* (1975), p. 24; S. Wiegelmann, 'Bäuerliche Arbeitsteilung in Mittel- und Nordeuropa. Konstanz oder Wandel', in *Ethnologia Skandinavica* (1975), pp. 7–9.
29. The German historian Heide Wunder has pointed out a number of times the causality between female-specific magic offences and women's role in traditional female domains, Wunder (1992) 192–203.
30. The sources give the names and abodes of over 50 cunning folk, a quarter to a third of them male.
31. Thus, for this northern German region it is not possible to support Labouvie's thesis that there was a tendency to ascribe 'black magic' to women and 'white magic' to men.

7 The Persecution of Male Witches in Holstein

1. H. Laffert, *Peinliche Fälle, deren Verlauff, Erörterung und Abhelffung in kurtz-verfassten Berichten* (Lüneburg 1702), p. 165. The author cites original documents.
2. Laffert (1702) 166.
3. Laffert (1702) 166.
4. Laffert (1702) 167.
5. Pinneberg belonged to the County of Schauenburg upon Weser from 1390 to 1640, when it fell again to Holstein. The small county of Rantzau which came into being in 1650 returned to Holstein in 1726.
6. U. Lange, *Geschichte Schleswig-Holsteins* (Neumünster 1996), pp. 153–91; Schilling (1993) 11; K. Wegemann, 'Die Volkszahl Schleswig-Holsteins seit dem Mittelalter', in *Zeitschrift der Gesellschaft für Schleswig-Holsteinische Geschichte* 47 (1917), p. 66.
7. See for more details: Schulte (2001) 35–40; Further: D. Unverhau, 'Akkusationsprozeß-Inquisitionsprozeß. Indikatoren für die Intensität der Hexenverfolgung in Schleswig-Holstein?', in Degn et al. (1983), pp. 59–142; B. Hoffmann, 'Die Hexenverfolgung in Schleswig-Holstein zwischen Reformation und Aufklärung', in *Schriften des Vereins für schleswig-holsteinische Kirchengeschichte* II, 34–5 (1978), p. 132; R. Heberling, 'Zauberei- und Hexenprozesse in Schleswig-Holstein-Lauenburg', in *Zeitschrift der Gesellschaft für Schleswig-Holsteinische Geschichte* 45 (1915), pp. 116–248.
8. Schulte (2001) 41–3.
9. ER provided by the University of Rostock, 12.1.1620, in S. Lorenz, *Aktenversendung und Hexenprozeß. Dargestellt am Beispiel der Juristenfakultät Rostock und Greifswald (1570/82–1630)* vol. 2 (Frankfurt 1982) pp. 589–90.
10. Lorenz (1982–83) vol. 2/1 and 2/2.

11. Kieler Varbuch 1465–1565 in H. Luppe (ed.), *Mitteilungen des Vereins für Kieler Stadtgeschichte* 17 (1899), pp. 82–84.
12. Trial of an unknown soldier, in 'Chronik eines Rendsburger Bürgers', in *Magazin für die neuere Historie und Geographie, von A.F. Büsching* (Halle 1783), p. 329. This execution did not, however, mark the end of all the trials. In 1735 a local court indicted two women, one of whom was expelled from the country; LAS 119/No. 80.
13. The number of the persons in verifiable trials has now (2007) risen to 453. The difference between this and the data presented in 2000 is, however, so small that the proportions have either remained the same or changed only slightly.
14. W. Brehmer, 'Lübeckische Hexenprocesse im 17. Jahrhundert', in *Mittheilungen des Vereins für Lübeckische Geschichte und Alterthumskunde* 6 (1893) 38–40; 6 (1893) 33–40; 4 (1889–90) 80. J.R. Becker, *Umständliche Geschichte der kaiserlichen und Heiligen Römischen Reiches freyen Stadt* (Lübeck 1805), p. 108–10. Becker was obviously able to work with the original material, only some of which is still available today.
15. Schulte (2001) 43–5, 96; Sources: *Mauritius* (1669), pp. 71–80; LAS 65.1/112 a, LAS 11/164, LAS 7/6195, 6353 (1689–90, 1686–91); KA Warder (1666–1698) XI, 2.
16. Even one of the largest trials, held in 1686, was initiated by the villagers of East Holstein; see the trials in Schmoel and Övelgönne: LAS 65–1/112a und LAS 11/164.
17. Details: Schulte (2001) 84–88.
18. Based on 316 records; 59% mentions.
19. Trial of Gesche Böttchers (1682), LAS 7/1758.
20. Confession of Rips Aleke (1619), LAS 102.1/163, fol. 82–86; Lorenz (1982–83) 2/1, pp. 584–5.
21. Confession of Grete Carstens (1620), LAS 102.1/163, fol. 97–8.
22. Trial of Anna Pape 1611, LAS 3/381.
23. Trial of four persons in Trenthorst, AHL Altes Senatsarchiv, Interna Landgüter IX, Trenthorst, fasc. 5, 1613.
24. Trial of Trineke Ewers 1676, StA Wilster, Acta II K 592 fol 698 pp. and 593 (Kriminalsachen).
25. LAS 7/1770.
26. Court records for the district of Eutin, LAS 275/458, 1660–67.
27. Trials of 1612 in Bergedorf, HSA 415–1, Bergedorf I, Lübecker Senatsakten betreffend, vol. 130, Fasc.a.
28. Lorenz (1982–83) 1, 368–70, 396–98.
29. Trial of Elsche Volbiers 1652, LAS 119/80.
30. Eichstätt (two connected trials): Behringer (1987) 239; Baden-Baden: Midelfort (1972) 133; Bamberg: Walinski-Kiehl (1993) 219; Trier: Voltmer/Weisenstein (1996) 240–242.
31. Dülmen (1987) 127.
32. Based on data relating to 172 women and 36 men. This total of 208 persons makes it possible to qualify types of maleficium; double entries were possible.
33. H. Institoris, *Malleus maleficarum* (Speyer 1486, Latin text, ed. by C. Mackay, Cambridge 2006) 425.

34. Based on 316 trials, 279 of women and 37 of men.
35. Confession of Anneke Rehben (1577), LAS 400.5/789, No. 25. 82.
36. StA Rendsburg A X 6, 236 a.
37. LAS 3/381.
38. LAS 102.1/163, fol. 64 p.
39. ER provided by the University of Rostock, 21.2.1619, in Lorenz (1982–83) 2/1, 577 p.
40. ER provided by the University of Rostock, 26.3.1622/11.1.1623, in Lorenz (1982–83) 2/1, 616/628.
41. LAS 119/80 (1643).
42. LAS 119/80 (1652).
43. J. Kinder, *Urkundenbuch zur Chronik der Stadt Plön* (Plön 1890), pp. 162–3.
44. LAS 7/1758 (1667).
45. LAS 7/1758; 'Grave, Über einen Hexenprocess im Jahre 1667', in *Schleswig-Holstein-Lauenburgische Provinzialberichte* 7 (1817), pp. 174–88.
46. Edict, 29.8.1689, see T. Götze, 'Aus alten Akten und Urkunden', in *Lauenburgische Heimat* 1 (1925), pp. 26–7.
47. LAS 3/381; ER provided by the University of Rostock, 16.8./17.10.1603, in Lorenz (1982–83) 2/1, 271, 277.
48. LAS 3/381.
49. Meiger (1587) O q. III v (italics by R.S.).
50. AHL Urfehdensammlung, Nr. 443 a. 446 (1544).
51. LAS 400.5/107, 197 a., Nr. 789, 24.
52. AHL Urfehdensammlung, vol. I, 552 und 553 (8.6.1588).
53. See the court records for 1588, printed in A. Michelsen (ed.), *Urkundensammlung der Schleswig-Holstein-Lauenburgischen Gesellschaft für vaterländische Geschichte*, vol. I (Kiel 1839), p. 411.
54. Michelsen (1839) 412; Lorenz (1982–83) 2/1, 169.
55. Trial of Catharina Gnaustes and Gorries Egge, StA Mölln, Nr. 818 (Kriminalgerichtsprotokolle 1572–1663); AHL Altes Senatsarchiv, Externa, Deutsche Territorien, Nr. 2778; Unverhau (1983) pp. 103, 138.
56. AHL Urfehdensammlung, vol. 2, No. 1278 (19.6.1645).
57. AHL Dom-Trauregister, 1576 bis 1615, 54 (1.5.1604).
58. H. Gerholz, *Berufsbezeichnungen* (Lübeck 1972), p. 45.
59. J. H. Zedler, *Großes vollständiges Universallexikon,* Band 43 (1743), p. 1007; R. v. Dülmen, Kulturelles Handeln und sozialer Prozeß (Köln 1993), pp. 257–8.
60. AHL Altes Senatsarchiv, Interna, Landgüter XI Trenthorst, Fasc. 5.
61. AHL Altes Senatsarchiv, Interna, Landgüter XI Trenthorst, Fasc. 5, p. 4.
62. Confession of Nuppenow, AHL Altes Senatsarchiv, Interna, Landgüter XI, Trenthorst, Fasc. 5, p. 5.
63. AHL Altes Senatsarchiv, Interna, Landgüter XI, Trenthorst, Fasc. 5, p. 4 v-3 v, p. 16v-21r.
64. LAS AR Rendsburg 104, 1615; O. Mensing (ed.) *Die Bauernchronik des Hartich Sierck aus Wrohm (1615–1664)* (Flensburg 1925), pp. 59–60.
65. ER provided by the University of Rostock, 12.1.1620, in Lorenz (1983) 2/1, 588–99.
66. ER provided by the University of Rostock, 11.7.1603, in Lorenz (1983) 2/1, 268.
67. Testimony of Anna Bauernvogts and Krileke Smitkers in Kinder (1892) 47.

68. Testimony of Lewin Fillmann, in Kinder (1892) 245.
69. Testimonies of Aßmus Stender and Margreta Valentinß, in Kinder (1892) 245.
70. Confession of Jochim Emecke, 9.6.1635, in Kinder (1892) 247.
71. Communication written by the magistrate of Tremsbüttel, 7.9.1652, LAS 7/1758.
72. Magistrate's communication of 26.8.1652, LAS 7/1758.
73. Magistrate's communication of 9.11.1652, LAS 7/1758.
74. Confession of Marcus Schneekloth, 11.10.1654, LAS 119/80.
75. See Baptism and Death Register of the district of Stakendorf in *Die Heimat 39* (1929) 117; D. Unverhau, 'Wahr, daß sie eine Hexe sey Zauberfälle zwischen Hexerei und Aberglauben aus dem Gebiet des Klosters Preetz (1643–1735)', in *Schleswig-Holstein* 3 (1981), pp. 8–12.
76. Confession of Marcus Schneekloth vom 11.10.1654, LAS 119/80.
77. O. Mensing, *Schleswig- Holsteinisches Wörterbuch* (Neumünster 1931) vol. 2, p. 22; vol. 4, p. 1.
78. LAS 119/80.
79. Mauritius (1669), consilium XXVI, 349.
80. Testimony of the daughter of the neighbour, in Mauritius (1669) 349.
81. Confession of Grundt, in Mauritius (1669) 350.
82. On the dishonourable nature of shoemakers, see Dülmen (1992) 270.
83. J.Z. Hartmann, *Protocollum Inquisitionis in Sachen des inquirierenden Gerichts des Klosters Preetz wider Andreas Brehmer Inquisition in puncto ligaturae magicae* (Hamburg/Kiel 1729), pp. 126, 147.
84. Hartmann (1729) 154.
85. Hartmann (1729) 171.
86. Hartmann (1729) 175.
87. Schulte (2001) 86.
88. Confession of Krohn in H. Harten, Hexenprozesse im Lauenburgischen (1681) in *Lauenburgische Heimat* 9 (1955), p. 40.
89. Harten (1955) 36–40.
90. See the description of this trial at the beginning of this chapter.
91. A pastor's report in *Schleswig-Holstein-Lauenburgische Landesberichte* 2 (1847), pp. 218–19.
92. *Schleswig-Holsteinisch-Lauenburgische Landesberichte* (1847) p. 220.
93. Büsching (1783) 329.
94. A good deal of what Owen Davies has to say about the English cunning-folk also applies to Holstein in the 16th and 17th centuries, although here they did not practise these arts as their main occupation, see O. Davies: *Witchcraft, Magic and Culture 1736–1951* (Manchester 1999), pp. 214–29.
95. W. Jacobeit, *Schäfer in Zentraleuropa* (Berlin 1987), p. 26.
96. K.S. Kramer, Ehrliche/Unehrliche Gewerbe, in A. Erler and E. Kaufmann (eds), *Handwörterbuch zur deutschen Rechtsgeschichte*, vol. 1 (Berlin 1971), pp. 855–858; Dülmen (1992) 194–214; B. Roeck, *Außenseiter, Randgruppen, Minderheiten. Fremde in Deutschland in der Frühen Neuzeit* (Göttingen 1993), pp. 106–14.
97. *Zedlers Universallexikon*, vol. 13 (1735), p. 3259.
98. Lorey (1998) 194–98.
99. See for France: R. Mandrou, La France au 17e et 18e siècles (Paris 1970), p. 315; C. Garrett, 'Witches and Cunning Folk in the Old Régime', in

J. Beauroy et al. (eds), *The Wolf and the Lamb. Popular Culture in France from the Old Regime to the 20*th *century* (Stanford 1976), p. 60. For parts of the Empire: Raith (2004) 227; Briggs (1996) 99–133; E. Labouvie, *Verbotene Künste. Volksmagie und ländlicher Aberglaube in Dorfgemeinden des Saarraums (16.-19. Jahrhundert)* (St. Ingbert 1992), p. 181.

100. In this point I concur with Monter (2006) 713–715. In the mid-18th century herdsmen in the Brunswick region represented only 7% of all households; calculated from R.V. Dülmen, Kultur und Alltag in der Frühen Neuzeit, vol. 2 (München 1995), p. 18. In Holstein they represented with 16 % of the persecuted clearly more than their proportion in the population. The demographic data for the early modern period needed for more precise regional comparisons are not available.
101. Van Dülmen, vol.2 (1993) 39.
102. Court accounts of Ahrensbök and Trittau, LAS 108/1229 a. LAS 111/1618–19; Kreisarchiv Ratzeburg, AP Brüchebuch Ratzeburg (1753).
103. Communication of the town of Lübeck, 15.7.1603, AHL Altes Senatsarchiv, Interna, Lübisches Recht 94/11.
104. Letter from the relatives, 5.8.1603, AHL Altes Senatsarchiv, Interna, Lübisches Recht 94/11.
105. Verdict of the Imperial Chamber Court, 12.1.1604, AHL Altes Senatsarchiv, Interna, Lübisches Recht 94/11.
106. All records in: HSA 415–1, Lübecker (Senats-)Akten betreffend Bergedorf I, vol. 130. fasc. A; further: D. Unverhau, 'Aufruhr und Rebellion im Amt Bergedorf wegen eines Zauberers und dreier Zauberinnen im Jahre 1612', in *Zeitschrift für Hamburgische Stadtgeschichte* 68 (1982), pp. 1–22.
107. LAS 15/2656.
108. ER provided by the University of Rostock, 12.6.1627, in Lorenz (1982–83) 2/1, 657.
109. ER provided by the University of Rostock, 30.6. a.1.7.1625, in Lorenz (1982–83) 2/1, 641, 650.
110. LAS 260/579.
111. Confession of Hans Struck, 20.6.1646, in LAS 260/579.
112. E. Waschinski, *Währung, Preisentwicklung und Kaufkraft des Geldes in Schleswig-Holstein von 1226–1864* vol. 2 (Neumünster 1952), Tabelle 12 a.
113. LAS, 275/456, 14.7.1646.
114. LAS 275/456, 21.7.1646.
115. W. Dittmer, *Das Sassen-und Holstenrecht in practischer Anwendung auf einige im 16ten Jahrhundert vorgekommene Civil- u. Criminalfälle* (Lübeck 1843), p. 149.
116. ER provided by the University of Rostock, 10.1.1600 in Lorenz (1982–83) 2/1, 234.
117. ER provided by the University of Rostock, 23.12.1574, in Lorenz (1982–83) 2/1, 112.
118. Quoted as in P. Aye, *Aus Eutins vergangenen Tagen. Vorträge gehalten im hiesigen Bürgerverein* (Eutin 1891–1892), p. 144.
119. Aye (1891–1892) 143–6.
120. StA Kiel: Protocollum civitatys Chiloniensis de Anno 1674–78 (Obergerichtsprotokoll Nr. 7).

121. Confession of Busch, in Chronik des Asmus Bremer, Urteil des Kieler Obergerichts, 30.6.1676, p. 689.
122. Chronicle of Asmus Bremer, p. 690; Further: D. Unverhau: *Kieler Hexenfälle des 16. und 17. Jahrhunderts*, (Kiel 1980), p. 27.
123. Tax register of 1673 for the town of Kiel, see J. Grönhoff, Kieler Bürgerbuch (Kiel 1958), p. 96.
124. KA Preetz, Register of Deaths, Bornhöved, 3.12.1678.
125. KA Preetz, Register of Deaths, Bornhöved, 21.8.1687; F.M. Meier, 'Hexenprozesse in Holstein im 17. Jahrhundert', in *Schleswig-Holsteinische Blätter für Polizei und Kultur* 1 (1799), pp. 79–85.
126. S. Göttsch, 'Schadenszauber – zur Disziplinierung leibeigener Untertanen', in *Kieler Blätter zur Volkskunde* 23 (1991), p. 60, 64.
127. S. Göttsch, *'Alle für einen Mann ...', Leibeigene und Widerständigkeit in Schleswig-Holstein im 18. Jahrhundert* (Neumünster 1981), pp. 108–10, 117–19.
128. Mauritius (1669) 74–5, 79.
129. Written request by the inhabitants of a village, printed in: R. Schmidt, 'Über die klösterlich-Preetzische Probstei in *Neue Schleswig-holsteinische Provinzialberichte* (1812), p. 71.
130. Mauritius (1669) 71.
131. Letter from the Faculty to the monastery, in Meier (1799) 76.
132. Mauritius (1669) 78–9; Further: Unverhau (1981) 10.
133. KA Warder XI/2; Bericht des Pastors Wilhelmi 1674, printed in *Wagrisch-Fehmarner Blätter*, 16.4.1864.
134. LAS 268/675.
135. Request of Clauß Kohler, in LAS 268/675.
136. LAS 268/675. ER provided by the University of Greifswald of 28.5. 30.5., 13.8, 11.9.1669.
137. LAS 11/164, 7/3530 a. 3529, 65–1/112.
138. LAS 11/164, fasc. 43.
139. Testimony of the pastor on the estate, 4.5.1686 in: LAS 11/164, fasc. 43.
140. Confession of Hinrich Markmann, 10.6.1686, in LAS 65–1/112 a.
141. Testimony of Christoph von Rantzau, LAS 11/164, fasc. 3.
142. Jacobsen (1996) 134–136.
143. W. Prange, *Christoph Rantzau auf Schmoel und die Schmoeler Leibeigenschaftsprozesse* (Neumünster 1965), pp. 15–32.

8 Carinthia. Wanted: Beggar, Male

1. KLA GV-SA 35 Lg. Paternion (1658); see also A. v. Jaksch, 'Ein Hexenprocess in Paternion im Jahre 1662', in *Carinthia I*, 83 (1893), pp. 17–18. Von Jaksch was wrong, however, about the date of the trial.
2. S. Gosler, *Hexenwahn und Hexenprozesse in Kärnten* (Graz 1955), pp. 94–6; Wutte (1927) 49–50; Byloff (1934) 95.
3. E. Bruckmüller, *Sozialgeschichte Österreichs* (Wien 1985), pp. 217–19.
4. C. Fraess-Ehrfeld, *Geschichte Kärntens. Die ständische Epoche*, vol. 2 (Klagenfurt 1994), pp. 674–6.
5. T. Winkelbauer, 'Ständefreiheit und Fürstenmacht', vol. 2 in *Österreichische Geschichte 1522–1699* (Wien 2003), p. 271.

6. Wutte (1927) 30.
7. M. Wutte, 'Das kärntische Bannrichteramt', in *Carinthia I,* 102 (1912), pp. 115–36.
8. M. Wutte, 'Gerichtsbräuche im Lg. Paternion', in *Carinthia* I, 98 (1908), pp. 41–2.
9. Gosler (1955) 182.
10. KLA GV-SA 35 Herrschaft Grünberg (1492); see also Gosler (1955) 46–9.
11. Own calculations complementary to the data of Schönleitner (1986–7) 248–78, plus the figures for 1715/23: see Sarman (1995) 47–56.
12. Schönleitner (1986–87) 248–78; Wutte (1927), 66; Byloff (1934) 131; Gosler (1955) 140; G. Sarman, Der Bettler und Zauberer Christian Wucher und das letzte Todesurteil in einem Kärntner Hexenprozeß (1723) in *Carinthia* 187 (1997), pp. 480–82.
13. KLA GV-SA Fasz. 35 Lg. St. Leonhard (1725/26).
14. Own calculations complementary to the data from Schönleitner (1986–87) 248–78 and Sarman (1995) 47–50.
15. Schönleitner (1986–87) 266.
16. KLA GV-SA Fasz. 35 (f.e. 1602, 1650, 1651, 1669–70); Byloff (1934) 63, 90, 103; Wutte (1927) 43, 57, 65; K. Baron v. Hauser, Aus dem Archive, in Carinthia I 71(1881), pp. 153–5.
17. Exceptions: Georg Eder was accused of arson in 1667 and Sebastian Rumbl of harm to livestock, KLA HA Paternion Fasz. 14 and KLA AHS B 1322, fol. 97.
18. KLA GV-SA Fasz. KLA GV-SA Fasz. 35 Lg. St. Leonhard (1725/26) 35 Lg. Spittal (1666); Literature: Wutte (1927) 54.
19. KLA HA Lodron C 117/Ld XXIII/44 (1653).
20. Byloff (1934) 131.
21. Gosler (1955) 106.
22. M. Freiherr v. Aichelburg, 'Der Proceßs des Peter Enzi', in *Carinthia I,* 81 (1891), p. 78.
23. Gosler (1955) 75.
24. KLA GV-SA Fasz. 35 Lg. Spittal (1653) and Lg. Althofen (1664).
25. Trial of 'Stehe-Peter', who was named as a werewolf: KLA GV-SA Fasz. 35 Lg Spittal (1666); KLA HA Porcia Fasz. XXIII a, Nr. 98 (1669).
26. KLA GV-SA Fasz. 35 Stadtgericht Wolfsberg (1705–06), in detail: M. Swatek, 'Die Wolfbanner. Der Wolfberger Hexenprozeß von 1705/06', in *Carinthia I* 193 (2003), pp. 315- 43, esp. 323.
27. F. Byloff, 'Wolfsbannerei', in *Oberdeutsche Zeitschrift für Volkskunde* 2 (1927), p. 133. It should be noted that the trial took place in Obdach, in neighbouring Styria.
28. Trials of Gertrud und Christine (1673), Eva N (1660); Maidl Merthl (1705), see Swatek (2003) 327; Wutte (1927) 42, 59.
29. KLA GV-SA Fasz. 35 Lg. Keutschach (1605 a. 1658); Literature: Jaksch (1884) 14; Wutte (1927) 58.
30. Aichelburg (1891) 78.
31. KLA HA Porcia Fasz. CVIII, Nr. 213/13 U (1676); Literature: Wutte (1927) 55.
32. KLA GV-SA Fasz. 35 Lg. Weissenegg (1685).
33. KLA GV-SA Fasz. 35 Lg. Weissenegg (1666).
34. KLA HA Paternion Fasz. 14 (1667); Literature: Gosler (1955) 112.

35. Gosler (1955) 106.
36. The complete question catalogue is given in Gosler (1955) 201–2.
37. KLA GV-SA Fasz. 35 Sg. Wolfsberg (1674).
38. KLA GV-SA Fasz. 35 Lg. Spittal (1653) and Lg. Keutschach (1720). Confessions of Blasius Kofler, 1653, and Bartlmä Droscheter, 1720, given in Gosler (1955) 85–6, 145.
39. See: Sarman (1997) 481 p.
40. KLA GV-SA Fasz. 35 Lg. Paternion (1658); Copy of the question catalogue: Jaksch (1893), 17–18.
41. Wutte (1927) 4–5.
42. KLA GV-SA Fasz. 35 Lg. Althofen (1721); Hauser (1881) 188.
43. Jaksch (1893) 14.
44. KLA GV-SA Fasz. 35 Lg. Straßburg (1658); Literature: Wutte (1927) 49, 53, 67.
45. See Hauser (1881) 121; Wutte (1927) 41, 49–53, 58 p.; Gosler 64, 72, 75 f., 85 p., 92–94, 145 on the many descriptions of the witches' Sabbat.
46. KLA GV-SA Fasz. 35 Lg. Althofen (1719–21); Court record, 12.9.1721, in Hauser (1881) 187–8.
47. KLA GV-SA Fasz. 35 Lg. Spittal (1653); Literature: Wutte (1927) 53–4.
48. Schönleitner (1986–87) 63 arrives at different figures; however, the personal histories and, in particular, the nicknames clearly indicate the vagrant lives these people led.
49. Gosler (1955) 141–2.
50. KLA HA Porcia Fasz. CVII No 213/13U (1686); further cases: Gosler (1955) 132–3.
51. Jaksch (1894) 13–14.
52. C. Fraess-Ehrfeld (1994) 485; Gosler (1955) 54, 59.
53. KLA GV-SA Fasz. 35 Lg. Paternion (1662); Literature: Jaksch (1893) 9–14.
54. KLA GV-SA Fasz. 35 Lg. Weissenegg/Sg. Straßburg (1705); Literature: Swatek (2003) 328.
55. See, for example, the case of a beggar in Styria described in H. Valentinitsch, 'Bettlerverfolgung und Zaubereiprozesse in der Steiermark', in *Mitteilungen des Steiermarkischen Landesarchivs* 35–36 (1986), p. 115.
56. Jaksch (1894) 12–14.
57. KLA GV-SA Fasz. 35 Lg. Straßburg (1666); Literature: Wutte (1927) 58–9.
58. Wutte (1927) 56.
59. Jaksch (1894) 43–4.
60. KLA GV-SA Fasz. 35 Lg. Althofen (1653) (1664).
61. KLA GV-SA Fasz. 35 Lg. Althofen (1631) (1676); Literature: Hauser (1881) 121.
62. KLA HA Porcia Fasz. CVIII Nr. 213/13U (1676); Literature: Byloff (1934) 120.
63. KLA GV-SA Fasz. 35 (1653, 1666)); Literature : Byloff (1934) 102; Wutte (1927) 51.
64. Hauser (1881) 122.
65. KLA HA Porcia Fasz. XXII No. 97 (1646); Literature: Wutte (1927) 41.
66. KLA GV-SA Fasz. 35 Sg. Straßburg (1688); KLA AHS B 1322, fol. 97; Literature: Hauser (1881) 125.
67. KLA GV-SA Fasz. 35 Lg. Spittal and Sg. Wolfsberg (1646); for further cases, see Wutte (1927) 37 p. Similar observations have been made for trials in other Austrian territories, see Schindler (1992) 299, Valentinitsch (1986) 109.

68. KLA GV-SA Fasz. 35 (1719–21), Court record of the trial on 12.9.1712 from Hauser (1881) 186. I have altered the order of the statements for the sake of clarity.
69. Wutte (1927) 32, 50–55 gives a very good overview.
70. Sarman (1997) 461–4; Dienst (1987) 271–6; Valentinitsch (1987) 312–14.; Dienst (1986) 85–6.; Byloff (1934) 47, 88, 101, 116, 145.
71. Valentinitsch (1987) 312–13.; Byloff (1934) 88.
72. Schindler (1992) 262, 268.
73. E. Bruckmüller, *Sozialgeschichte Österreichs* (Wien 1985), pp. 215–64; R. Sandgruber, *Ökonomie und Politik. Österreichische Wirtschaftsgeschichte vom Mittelalter bis zur Gegenwart* (Wien 1995), pp. 103–34.
74. Sandgruber (1995) 115. This comparatively slight recession might explain why persecution levels in Carinthia were lower than in Styria.
75. Fraess-Ehrfeld (1994) 674.
76. H. Lehmann, Das Zeitalter des Absolutismus (Stuttgart1980), p. 144.
77. R. Jütte, *Poverty and Deviance in Early Modern Europe* (Cambridge 1994), pp. 146–50. Dülmen (1992) vol.2, pp. 202, 218, 225, 238–40, 280–2.; E. Schubert, 'Mobilität ohne Chance: Die Ausgrenzung des fahrendes Volk', in W. Schulze(ed.), *Ständische Gesellschaft und soziale Mobilität*, (München 1988), pp. 113–64; C. Sachße and F. Tennstedt, *Geschichte der Armenfürsorge in Deutschland* (Stuttgart 1980), pp. 28–38, 101–14, 122, 131.
78. Jütte (1994) 146.
79. T. Winkelbauer (2003) 245–66.
80. H. Stekl, Gesellschaftliche Außenseiter im barocken Österreich, in K. Gutkas, *Prinz Eugen und das barocke Österreich* (Wien 1985), p. 226.
81. Sandgruber (1995) 134–5.
82. Jaksch (1894) 12.
83. Jaksch (1894) 13.
84. KLA HA Porcia Fasz. XXII Nr. 97(1630).
85. KLA GV-SA Fasz. 35 Lg. Spittal (1666); Literature: Wutte (1927) 54 p.
86. KLA GV-SA Fasz. 35 Lg. Spittal (1653); Literature : Wutte (1927) 51.
87. KLA GV-SA Fasz. 35 Lg. Paternion (1658); Literature: Wutte (1927) 50.
88. KLA GV-SA Fasz. 35 Lg. Straßburg (1653) Lg. Spittal (1676); Literature: Wutte (1927) 55–6.
89. KLA GV-SA Fasz. 35 Lg. Althofen (1691); Court records, 10.7.1691, in Hauser (1881) 185.
90. *Ludwig Moratori's Gedanken über die Abschaffung des Bettelns und Verpflegung der Armen*. Translated and duplicated by Peter Obladen (Wien 1780), p. 30.
91. U. Danker, *Räuberbanden im Alten Reich um 1700* (Frankfurt 1988), p. 379.
92. Sachße/Tennstedt (1980) 109.
93. P. Chaunu, *Europäische Kultur im Zeitalter des Barock* (Zürich 1968), p. 131.
94. Byloff (1934) 43–4.
95. Quoted from Byloff (1934) 48; also Valentinitsch (1986) 299.
96. H. Bräuer, *'und hat seithero gebetlet'. Bettler und Bettlerwesen in Wien und Niederösterreich zur Zeit Kaiser Leopold* I. (Wien1996) 228; Schindler (1992) 295–7; Valentinitsch (1986) 106.
97. Quoted from Wutte (1927) 47.
98. Valentinitsch (1986) 108.

99. An example of the exact court costs, which had to be borne by the lord of the manor, is given in: Trial of Thomas Hauser: KLA HA Mittertrixen LV/ Nr. 242 Sch 59 (1685).
100. Report of a Prince's official, cited in: Hauser (1881) 183.
101. Jütte (1994) 41, 149 p., Tabelle 2. This does not exclude the possibility that women were also mobile; for a vivid study of a female vagrant, see H. Valentinitsch, Frauen unterwegs. Eine Fallstudie zur Mobilität von Frauen in der Steiermark um 1700, in Wunder/Vanja (1996), pp. 223–36.
102. Wutte (1927) 47.
103. KLA GV-SA Fasz. 35 Lg. Althofen (1674); Wutte (1927) 42.
104. Wutte (1927) 41.
105. KLA GV-SA Fasz. 35 Lg. Spittal (1666); Literature: Gosler (1955) 110.
106. Jaksch (1894) 43.
107. KLA HA Porcia Fasz. CVIII Nr. 213/13U (1676); Wutte (1927) 55.
108. KLA GV-SA Fasz. 35 Lg. St. Leonhard (1725/26); Swatek (2003) 339–340.
109. G.E. Schäfer, *Spiel, Spielraum und Verständigung. Untersuchung zur Entwicklung von Spiel und Phantasie im Kindes- und Jugendalter* (Weinheim 1986), pp. 251–89.
110. P. Segl, *Ketzer in Österreich* (Paderborn 1984), p. 349.
111. W. Maleczek, Die Ketzerverfolgungen im österreichischen Hoch- und Spätmittelalter, in E. Zöllner (ed.), *Wellen der Verfolgung in der österreichischen Geschichte* (Wien 1986), pp. 28–9.
112. Byloff (1934) 13.

9 Male Witches, Feminized Men or Shamans?

1. Walinski-Kiehl (1981), pp. 102–111; Gehm (2000), pp. 188–200, 270; Voltmer (2008).
2. Schulte in Rowlands/Grundy (2008) forthcoming; Walinski-Kiehl (1981) 106–8.
3. Johannes Bergmann, *Disputatio philosophica de mulieribus* (Wittenberg 1629) cited from: R. Bake and B. Kiupel, 'Städtische Frauen- und Männerbeziehung im 18. Jahrhundert', in *Praxis Geschichte* 1 (1995), p. 28.
4. W. Schmale, *'Geschlecht und Kultur'* (Wien 2000), pp. 30–5; M. Dinges, *Hausväter, Priester und Kastraten. Zur Konstruktion von Männlichkeit im Spätmittelalter und FrüherNeuzeit* (Göttingen 1998), pp. 13–19. Clark (1997) 31–42 overestimates this dual classification of the gender characteristics for the early modern period.
5. Walinski-Kiehl (2004) 254–71.
6. See also Apps/Gow (2003) 136.
7. Fischart (1591) 103. The term, 'Hexin' occurs frequently in Fischart, e.g. 108, 110, 111, 114, 191 (italics by R.S.).
8. Cited from Keller (1989) 91.
9. G. E. V. Rüling, *Auszüge einiger merkwürdiger Hexen-Prozesse aus dem 17.Jahrundert im Fürstenthum Calenberg* (Göttingen 1786), p. 34 for the Hanover region; *Elsässische Monatschrift für Geschichte und Volkskunde* 3 (1912), p. 452 for Alsace in present-day France; Labouvie (1991) 78 for

the Saar region; C. Waas, 'Ein Hexenprozeß aus "der guten alten Zeit"', in Preußische Jahrbücher 132 (1908) p. 43 and 56 G.K. Horst, *Zauberbibliothek*, vol. 1 (Mainz 1821), p. 199 for Hesse; A. Bach, *Hexenprozesse in der Vogtei Ems* (Wiesbaden 1923), p. 35 for the Nassau region; trial of 'the Meyersche', in LAS AR Ahrensbök 108/1199 (1638–39) for Holstein; J. Lilienthal, *Die Hexenprozesse in Braunsberg nach den Criminalacten des Braunsberger Archivs* (Königsberg 1861), p. 134 for Prussia. The translators of Rémy also frequently used the term 'Hexin', see Rémy (1697) 66, 157, 217, 226, 238.

10. Cited from Soldan/Heppe (1880/1986) 45.
11. Trial of men and women in Lintheim and Hesse, copied by Horst (1821) 203. Further: M. Raab, 'Der große Hexenprozeß von Geisling von 1689–1691', in *Verhandlungen des Vereins für Oberpfalz und Regensburg* 65 (1915), p. 93. The term 'Hexenpersonen' (witch people) was widespread; for some examples, see F. Leitschuh, *Beiträge zur Geschichte des Hexenwesens in Franken* (Bamberg 1883), p. 40, K. Kélé, *Hexenwahn und Hexenprozesse in der ehemaligen Reichstadt und Landvogtei Hagenau* (Hagenau 1893), p. 155.
12. Statement made by the accused Hans Leber of Dieburg (1627), cited from Gebhardt (1989) 178.
13. Question catalogue of 1612, see Pohl (1988) 305.
14. Cited from Gebhardt (1989) 159.
15. Confession of Michael Haisch (1663), cited from H. Pöschko, Der Prozeß des Michael Haisch, in *Praxis Geschichte* 4 (1991), p. 26.
16. General study: E. Pócs, *Between the Living and the Dead: A Perspective on Witches an Seers in the Early Modern Age* (Budapest 1999); see also: C. Ginzburg (1990), esp. pp. 153–5; G. Klaniczay, *Heilige, Hexen, Vampire* (Berlin 1990), pp. 29–50.
17. R. Hutton, *Shamans. Siberian Spirituality and the Western Inspiration* (London 2001/2007), pp. VII-VIII, 43–110.
18. States of trance and ecstasy are not necessarily elements of a shaman's work, see Hutton (2001/2007) esp. 110; R.N. Hamayon, 'Are, Trance, Ecstasy' and Similar Concepts Appropriate in the Study of Shamanism, *Shaman: An International Journal for Shamanistic Research* 2 (1993), esp. p. 7; K.E. Müller, *Schamanismus. Heiler, Geister, Rituale* (München 1997), pp. 19–21, 40–5, 80–2, 88–91; Further: J. Halifax, *Shamanistic voices* (New York 1979), pp. 22–24; M. Eliade, *Schamanismus und archaische Ekstasetechnik* (Zürich 1956), esp. pp. 180–208.
19. Müller (1997) 31–33.
20. W. Behringer is of the opinion that shamanism was practised by preachers of the Waldenses and attempts to account for the persecution of men in the Alps by this tradition. However, this explanation does not go very far towards explaining the phenomenon, since even the author himself concedes that there cannot have been more than a few shamans in the region, see Behringer (2005) 180.
21. Behringer (1994).
22. H. Ammann, 'Die Hexenprozesse im Fürstenthum Brixen', in *Forschungen zur Geschichte Tirols und Vorarlbergs* 34 (1890) 145–66. I. Zingerle, *Barbara Pachlerin, die Sarnthaler Hexe und Mathias Perger, der Lauterfresser* (Innsbruck 1858), pp. 23–54.
23. H.d. Waardt, 'Cunning-folk' in *EOW I* (2006) 237–9.

24. See also the critical comments by G. Henningsen, 'The white sabbat and Other Archaic Patterns of Witchcraft', in *Acta Ethnographica Hungarica* 37 (1991–92), p. 302.
25. R. Hagen, 'shamanism' in *EOW IV* (2006), p. 1031, Hutton (2001/2007) 147–9.
26. R. Hagen, 'Traces of Shamanism in the Witch Trials of Norway', in H.d. Waardt, et al. (ed.), *Dämonische Besessenheit: Zur Interpretation eines kulturhistorischen Phänomens* (Bielefeld 2005), pp. 307–25; K. Tegler, Till Blåkulla med kropp och själ. Schamanistika föreställningar i svenska trolldomsprocesser, in L. Oja (ed.) *Vägen til Blåkulla* (Uppsala 1997), esp. pp. 48–58; E. Pócs, 'Possession phenomena, possession-systems: some east-central European examples', in E. Pócs/G. Klaniczay (eds), *Communicating with the Spirits* (Budapest 2005), pp. 84–154.

10 The Power of the 'Witch Folk' and the Rulers

1. S. Clark, 'Inversion, Misrule and the Meaning of Witchcraft', in *Past and Present* 97 (1980), pp. 98–127.
2. Binsfeld (1592) 37: 'Die Zauberer machen Verbindung mit dem Teufeln zu Schaden der Menschen und Verderbung aller Dinge... Die Zauberer verbinden sich mit dem Teufel zum Verderben des menschlichen Geschlechts'.
3. Boguet (1606) Préface, unpaginated: '... un nombre infini ... que l'on voit surcroitre tous les jours'.
4. Boguet (1606) Préface.
5. Boguet (1602) in the translation by M. Summers (1929) 32. It is by no means certain that these were actually Boguet's words, as this statement does not appear in the 1606 and 1610 editions. It is extremely difficult, even in France, to access the 1602 edition.
6. Schultheiß (1634) 8.
7. Bodin (1580) 219. 'J'ai dict... que le Sathan a des Sorciers de toutes qualités....'.
8. Bodin (1580) 212.
9. Bodin (1580) Préface a. p. 212 v. Bodin cites this last figure as information given by the male witch, Trois Eschelles' who he describes many times in his work.
10. N. Jacques-Chaquin, 'Demoniac Conspiracy', in Graumann and Moscovici (1987), p. 83.
11. H. Haag, 'Der Teufel im Judentum und Christentum', in *Saeculum* 34 (1983), pp. 248–58.
12. D. Groh, 'The Temptation of Conspiracy', in Graumann and Moscovici (1987) 1–38.
13. Groh (1987) 4.
14. H. Zukier, '*The Conspiratorial Imperative*', in Graumann and Moscovici (1987) 93–9.
15. S. Moscovici, 'The Conspiracy Mentality', in Graumann and Moscovici (1987) 154.
16. D.G. Pruitt, 'Conspiracy Theory in Conflict Escalation', in Graumann and Moscovici (1987) 199–201.

17. C.F. Graumann, 'History and Social Psychology – A synopsis', in Graumann and Moscovici (1987) 245–51.
18. Cited from the ecclesiastical councillors according to Dillinger (1999) 145, 447; R. Voltmer, Jagd auf 'böse Leute'. Hexenverfolgungen in der Region um den Laacher See, in http://www.historicum.net (acc. October 25, 2007).
19. B. Roeck, *Gegenreformation und Dreißigjähriger Krieg 1555–1648* (Stuttgart 1996), pp. 8–10; B. Roeck, Christlicher Idealstaat und Hexenwahn, in *Historisches Jahrbuch* 108/(1988), pp. 379–405.
20. The connection between deviant behaviour and witch persecutions has been questioned, see Walz (1993). One must, however, also ask whether behaviour which was perceived as deviant is always ascertainable from legal sources, since such perceptions were not necessarily expressed in court cases.
21. Roeck (1988) 398; N. Elias, Über den Prozeß der Zivilisation, vol. 2: (Frankfurt 1978), pp. 312–434; G. Oestreich, Geist und Gestalt des frühmodernen Staates (Berlin 1969), pp. 188–90. I adhere to the idea of 'social disciplining' here, since the essential elements of this thesis have not been shaken by recent criticism in research literature: R. Voltmer, Gegen die Unzucht. Nachtridentinische Sittenreform, Kriminalisierung und Verfolgung devianter Sexualität im Erzbistum Trier, in H.G. Borck et al. (eds), Unrecht und Recht. Kriminalität und Gesellschaft im Wandel, 1500–2000 (Koblenz 2002), pp. 481–511; H. Schnabel-Schüle, Überwachen und Strafen im Territorialstaat (Köln 1997) p. 165–168; H. Schilling, 'Kirchenzucht und Sozialdisziplinierung im frühneuzeitlichen Europa'. Beiheft der Zeitschrift für historische Forschung 16 (1994), pp. 11–40; G. Lottes, 'Disziplin und Emanzipation. Das Sozialdisziplinierungskonzept und die Interpretation der frühneuzeitlichen Geschichte', Westfälische Forschungen 42 (1992), pp. 63–74; M. Prinz, 'Herrschaft, Religion und Volk', in Westfälische Forschungen 42 (1992), pp. 1–25.

Selected Bibliography

This bibliography is confined to books and articles that have been cited more than once in the Notes

Archives/sources

France

Archives Départementales du Doubs à Besançon

Série 2 B (Parlement de Dôle) numéros: 1285, 2271, 2437/55, 2465/77, 2470, 2515, 2516/222–223, 2519/103–119, 2473/94, 2547, 2493.

Série B 15940 (Baillage de Quingey et Pontarlier).

Série 10 F (Fonds Bavoux) numéros: 4, 5, 7, 10, 11, 13, 17, 18, 21, 37, 42, 54, 69, 76, 84.

Archives Départementales de Haute Saône à Vesoul

Série (Régistres d'arrêts) B 5040/131, 5048/43, 5048/232, 5049, 5050, 5051, 5057, 5119, 9677.

Germany

Landesarchiv Schleswig-Holstein

Abt./no.: 3/381; 7/575, 592, 784, 1558, 1572, 1756, 1758, 1770, 1771, 2645, 2647, 3024, 3392, 3396, 3404, 3529, 3530, 5467, 5471, 6144, 6157, 6195, 6353; 11/164; 15/784, 1752, 1753, 1758, 1887, 2089, 2645, 2647, 2649, 2656; 65–1/112 a; 111/248; 119/80; 133/166; 173/151, 152, 153, 155; 210/1552; 217/87, 89; 260/579; 268/673, 675, 887; 275/456, 457, 579; 390/264, 271.

Historical records index of the Seminar of European Ethnology at the University of Kiel (Administrative accounts and penal records)

LAS Abt./no.: B VI 1 (1686–93); 275/456–60 (1624–1712); 108 (1638–1753); AR 106 (1616–63); AR 107 (1646–82); 163 (1591–1696); 275 Nr. 584–627 (1663–1711); 180 AR 87 (1581); 167 (1692–96); 168 (1597–1788); AR 105 (1712 - 21); AR 101 (1560); AR 112 (1641–1701); AR 113 (1651–56); AR 111 (1593–1703); AR 109 (1640–1728); AR 104 (1585–1671); 162 (1580–1681); AR 110 (1560–1663); AR 103 (1606–48); AR 102 (1585–1616); 161 (1643/44); AR 111 (1608–1705); 142/1-12 (1729–87), 30–32 (1650–92); 125.20/8 (1644). Other archives: KrA Ratzeburg, AP (1723–56), GP Niendorf (1723–31); RA Kopenhagen, Film 43156, 43161 (1616–50); StA Wilster, Man. 11 b/273, Man. III b/396 ; StA Kiel, XXII/l, Gerichtsbuch 1611; StA Oldenburg A 1 12/4; StA Plön, Altarchiv, Nr. 189 (1674); KA Meldorf, Acta IV/99 a.

Town/city, church and private archives: Archiv der Hansestadt Lübeck

Dom-Trauregister, 1576–1615; Altes Senatsarchiv, Interna, Landgüter, Lübisches Recht 94/11, Kämmerei, Ritzerauer Landgerichtsprotokolle 1561–1698; St. Johannis Jungfrauenkloster/Nr. 275, 662, 1003, 1033; Urfehdensammlungen 1–1305 (1301–1663). *KA Warder*: XI, Nr. 2; *KA Lübeck*: H. Jimmerthal, Geschichte der St. Marienkirche zu Lübeck (1857); *KA Preetz*: Kirchenbuch Bornhöved (1678–1687); *Privatarchiv Drews Fehmarn*: Landgerichtsprotokollbuch Fehmarn 1626; *StA Kiel*: Protocollum civitatys Chiloniensis de anno 1666–73; *StA Mölln*: Nr. 818 (1572–1663); *StA Rendsburg*: A X 6/221, 222, 236 a; X 7/237, 239, 240–263a, 246–279, 270; *StA Bad Oldesloe*: Ac VII C 46–49; *StA Wilster*: Acta II K 591, 592, 593, 619; *Staatsarchiv Hamburg*: 415–1: Bergedorf I, Lübecker Senatsakten betreffend, vol. 130, Amt Bergedorf II/Nr. 4688 (1675–78).

Austria

Kärntner Landesarchiv (Archives for Carinthia)

GV-SA Faszikel 35 (Geschichtsverein Kärnten Sammelarchiv);
AHS (Allgemeine Handschriftenreihe) 467, B 1322;
HA (Herrschaftsarchive): Lodron C117, Porcia Faszikel XXII, XXIII, CVIII, Mittertrixen Faszikel LV, B166, Paternion Faszikel 14–30, 89–92.

Primary printed sources

Binsfeld, Petrus, *Tractatus de confessionibus Maleficorum et Sagarum* (Trier 1589); *Tractat von Bekanntnuß der Zauberer und Hexen*, München 1592.

Bodin, Jean (Angevin), *De la Démonomanie Des Sorciers*, Paris 1580.

Boguet, Henry, *Discours Execrable Des Sorciers*. Ensemble leur Proces, faits depuis 2 ans en ça, en divers endroicts de France, Rouen 1606/Lyon 1610.

Bullinger, Heinrich, Wider die schwartze Kunst, Abergläubigs segnen, unwahrhafftigs warsagen, und andere dergleichen von Gott verbottene Kunst in Sawr (1586), pp. 298–306; Wider die schwarzen kunst, H[einrych] B[ullinger].*Actorum XIX*. Zentralbibliothek Zürich, Ms. F 63, 356r–363v., see http://www.unizh.ch/irg/schwarzkunst.html (acc. 3 March 2007).

Carolina Die peinliche Gerichtsordnung Kaiser Karls V. und des Heiligen Römischen Reichs von 1532, ed. by C. Schroeder, Stuttgart 2000.

Carpzov, Benedict, *Practica Nova Imperialis Saxonicae Rerum Criminalium in partes III*, Wittenberg 1635/1647.

Daneau, Lambert, *Dialogue tres-utile-necessaire pour ce temps. Auquel ce qui se dispute auiourd'hui des Sorciers et Eriges est traité bien amplement et resolu*, Paris 1573.

—— *Deux traictez nouveaux fort utiles pour ce temps, le premier touchant les sorciers*, Genève 1579.

—— *Ein Gespräch von Zauberern, welche man lateinisch sortilegos oder sortiarias nennet*, in Sawr (1586).

Del Rio, Martín, *Disquisitionum magicarum libri sex quibus continentur accurata curiosarum artium, et vanarum superstitionum confutatio*, Köln 1633/Mainz 1603.

—— *Investigations into Magic*, ed, a. transl. by P.G. Maxwell-Stuart, Manchester 2000.

Ewich, Johann, Von der Hexen. Die man gemeiniglich Zauberin nennet, oder auff niedersächsisch Toverschen, in: Sawr (1586), pp. 325–355.

Fischart, Johann, *Daemonomania. Vom außgelasenen Wütigen Teuffelsheer, Allerhand Zauberern, Hexen und Hexenmeistern, Unholden, Teuffelsbeschwörern, Warsagern, Schwartzkünstlern, Vergifftern, Augenverblendern*, Straßburg 1581.

Fründ, Hans, Die Chronik des Hans Fründ in Ostorero, Martine/Paravicini Bagliani, Agostino/Utz-Tremp, Kathrin (eds), *L'imaginaire du sabbat. Edition critique des textes les plus anciens* (1430 c.–1440 c.), Lausanne 1999, pp. 29–45.

Gervasius von Tilbury, *Otia Imperialia*, ed. by F. Liebknecht, Hannover 1856.

Godelmann, Johann Georg, *Von Zäuberern, Hexen und Unholden*. (Frankfurt 1592).

Hansen, Joseph (ed.), *Quellen zur Untersuchung des Hexenwahns und der Hexenverfolgung im Mittelalter*, Bonn 1901.

Hartmann, Joann Zacharias, *Protocollum Inquisitionis in Sachen des inquirierenden Gerichts des Klosters Preetz wider Andreas Brehmer* (Hamburg/Kiel 1729).

Hemmingsøn, Niels (= Hemmingsen, N.): *En Undervisning aff den hellige skrifft huad man døme skal om den store og gruelige Guds bespottelse, som skeer met trolddom, signelse, manelse oc anden saadon Guds hellige Naffns ov ords vanbrug*, København (Kopenhagen) 1576.

—— *Vermanunge von Den Schwartzkünstlerischen Aberglauben*, Wittenberg 1586.

Institoris (Kramer), Heinrich, *Malleus maleficarum* (Speyer 1486) vol.1: latin, vol.2: trans. by C. Mackay, Cambridge 2006.

Kinder, Johannes (ed.), *Urkundenbuch zur Chronik der Stadt Plön*. Urkunden und Akten, Plön 1890.

Laffert, H., *Peinliche Fälle*, Lüneburg 1702.

Luther, Martin, *Die gantze Heilige Schrifft Deudsch*, Wittenberg 1545.

—— Dr Martin Luthers Werke, *Kritische Gesamtausgabe*, Weimar 1883 f., several vols.

—— Dr Martin Luthers Werke. *Kritische Gesamtausgabe*, Tischreden, Weimar 1885.

Martène, Edmund and Durand, Ursuni (eds), *'Bonifatius, sermo XV. De abrenunciatione in baptismate', in Veterum Scriptorum et monumenterium Historicorum*, Tomus IX, Paris 1733.

Mauritius, Ericus, *Consiliorum Chiloniensium Specimen sive Responsa de Jure*, Chiloni 1669.

Meder, David, *Acht Hexenpredigten*, Leipzig 1605.

Meiger, Samuel, *De Panurgia Lamiarum, Sagarum, Strigum ac Veneficarum*, Hamburg 1587.

Nider, Johannes, *Formicarius*, Köln 1480, Graz 1971.

(French translation in, Ostorero, Martine, Paravicini Bagliani, Agostino and Utz-Tremp, Kathrin (eds), *L'imaginaire du sabbat. Edition critique des textes les plus anciens (1430 c.–1440 c.)* Lausanne 1999, pp. 122–99.

Rémy, Nicolas, *Daemonolatriae libri tres Nicolai Remigii serenissimi ducis Lotharingi consiliis interioribus et in eius ditione Lotharingia cognitoris publici*, Frankfurt a.M. 1597.

—— *Daemonolatria oder Beschreibung von Zauberern und Zauberinnen*, Hamburg 1693.

Samson, Herrmann, *Neun außerlesenen und Wohlbegründete Hexen-Predigt.*, Riga 1626.

Sawr, Abraham (ed.), *Theatrum de veneficis*, Frankfurt 1586.

Schmitz, Hermann J. (ed., *Die Bußbücher und das kanonische Bußverfahren nach handschaftlichen Quellen dargestellt,* Düsseldorf 1898.

Schultheiß, Heinrich von, *Eine Außführliche Instruction wie in Inqusition Sachen des grewlichen Lasters der Zauberey gegen Die Zauberer der göttlichen Majestät und der Christenheit Feinde ... zu procedieren,* Köln 1634.

Spee, Friedrich von, *Cautio criminalis oder rechtliches Bedenken wegen der Hexenprozesse,* (latin: 'Cautio criminalis, seu de processibus contra sagas' Rinteln 1631), transl. by J. F. Ritter von, München 1982.

Tholoson, Claude, 'Ut magorum et maleficiorum errores', in Ostorero et al. (1999), pp. 362–416.

Vallick, Jacob, 'Von Zauberern, Hexen und Unholden', in: Sawr (1586), pp. 54–69.

Voltmer, Rita and Weisenstein, Karl (eds), *'Das Hexenregister des Claudius Musiel. Ein Verzeichnis von hingerichteten und besagten Personen aus dem Trierer Land (1586–1594),* Trier 1996.

Weyer, Johann, *Von Teufelsgespenst, Zauberern und Gifftbereytern. Schwartzkünstlern, Hexen und Unholden,* Frankfurt 1586.

Zedler, Johann Heinrich (ed.), *Großes vollständiges Universallexikon aller Wissenschaften und Künste,* Halle/Leipzig 1732–54, several vols.

Secondary literature

Ahrendt-Schulte, Ingrid, (with Bauer, D.R, Lorenz, S., Schmidt, J.M) (eds), *Geschlecht, Magie und Hexenverfolgung,* Bielefeld 2002.

Aichelburg, Max Freiherr von, 'Der Proceßs des Peter Enzi', in: *Carinthia I,* 81/1891, pp. 76–80.

Amundsen, Karin, 'The Duke's Devil and Doctor Lambe's darling: A Case Study of the Male Witch in Early Modern England', *PSI-SIGMA Historical Journal 2* (2004) (http://www.unlv.edu/student_orgs/psisigma/PAT% 20Articles/Amundsen.pdf);

Anglo, Sydney, 'Evident Authority and Authoritative Evidence: The Malleus Maleficarum', in: Anglo, S. (ed.), *The Damned Art. Essays in the Literature of Witchcraft,* London 1977, pp. 1–31.

Ankarloo, Bengt and Henningsen, Gustav (eds), *Early Modern Witchcraft. Centres and Peripheries,* Oxford 1990.

Apps, Lara and Gow Andrew, *Male Witches in Early Modern Europe,* Manchester 2003.

Bailey, Michael, 'Nider, Johannes', in *EOW III* (2006) 826–8.

——*Battling demons, Witchcraft, Heresy and Reform in the Late Middle Ages,* Pennsylvania 2003.

Baroja, Julio Carlo, 'Witchcraft and Catholic Theology', in: Ankarloo and Henningsen (1990), pp. 19–43.

Barry, Jonathan, Hester, Marianne and Roberts, Gareth (eds): *Witchcraft in Early Modern Europe,* Cambrige 1996.

Bavoux, Francis, *La sorcellerie à Quingey,* Monaco 1947.

——'Les Loups-Garous en Franche-Comté', in *Heures Comtoises* 4/1952, pp. 3–8.

——Boguet, *Grand Juge de la Terre de St. Claude,* Besançon 1958.

——*Les procès inédits de Boguet en matière de sorcellerie dans la grande judicature de Saint-Claude, XVIe–XVIIe,* Dijon 1958.

Becker, Johann R., *Umständliche Geschichte des kaiserlichen und Heiligen Römischen Reiches freyen Stadt Lübeck*, Band 3, Lübeck 1805.

Behringer, Wolfgang, *Hexenverfolgung in Bayern. Volksmagie, Glaubenseifer und Staatsraison in der Frühen Neuzeit, München* 1997, 3rd edn., (English translation of the former edition: *Witchcraft Persecutions in Bavaria: Religious Zealotry and Reason of State in Early Modern Europe*, Cambridge 1997).

—— *Chonrad Stoeckhlin und die Nachtschar. Eine Geschichte aus der frühen Neuzeit, München/Zürich 1994* (engl. translation: The Shaman of Oberstdorf. Chonrad Stoeckhlin and the Phantoms of the Night Charlotteville 1998).

—— *Hexen- und Hexenprozesse*, München 1995, (3rd edn).

—— *Das unheilvollste Buch der Weltliteratur. Zur Enstehungsgeschichte des Malleus Maleficarum und zu den Anfängen der Hexenverfolgung in Heinrich Kramer (Institoris): Der Hexenhammer. Malleus Maleficarum*, transl from latin by Wolfgang Behringer, Günter Jerouschek, Werner Tschacher, München 2000.

—— *Witches and Witch-hunts. A Global History*, Cambridge 2004.

—— 'How Waldensians Became Witches, Heretics and Their Journey to the other World', in Klaniczay and Pócs (2005), pp. 155–92.

Bethencourt, Francisco, 'Portugal: A Scrupulous Inquisition', in Ankarloo and Henningsen (1990), pp. 403–22.

—— 'Un univers saturé de magie, L'Europe méridionale', in Muchembled (1994), pp. 159–94.

Bever, Edward, 'Old Age and Witchcraft in Early Modern Europe', in Stearns, Peter N. (Ed.), *Old Age in Preindustrial Society*, New York 1982, pp. 150–90.

Biller, Peter, *The Waldenses 1170–1530: Between a Religious Order and a Church*, Aldershot 2001.

Biesel, Elisabeth, *Hexenjustiz, Volksmagie und soziale Konflikte im lothringischen Raum*, Trier 1997.

Blauert, Andreas, *Frühe Hexenverfolgungen. Ketzer-, Zauberei und Hexenprozesse des 15. Jahrhunderts*, Hamburg 1989.

—— (ed.), *Ketzer, Zauberer, Hexen. Die Anfänge der europäischen Hexenverfolgung*, Frankfurt 1990.

Blécourt, Willem de, 'The Making of the Female Witch. Reflections on Witchcraft and Gender in the Early Modern Period', *Gender and History* 12/2000, pp. 287–309;

—— 'Four centuries of Frisian Witch-doctors', in Gijswijt-Hofstra and Friijhoff (1991), pp. 157–66.

—— 'Spuren einer Volkskultur oder Dämonisierung? Kritische Anmerkungen zu Ginzburgs "Die Benandanti"', in Kea, *Zeitschrift für Kulturwissenschaften* 5/1993, pp. 17–29.

—— 'Mangels Beweisen. Über das Ende der Verfolgung in Niederländisch und Spanisch-Geldern 1590–1640', in Lorenz and Bauer (1995), pp. 77–95.

Blécourt, W. de and Waardt, Hans de: Das Vordringen der Zaubereiverfolgungen in den Niederlanden, Rhein, Maas und Schelde entlang, in: Blauert (1990), pp. 182–216.

Brauner, Sigrid, *Fearless Wives and Frightened Shrews. The Construction of the Witch in Early Modern Germany*, Massachusetts 1995.

Brehmer, W., 'Lübeckische Hexenprocesse im 17. Jahrhundert', in: *Mittheilungen des Vereins für Lübeckische Geschichte und Alterthumskunde 6/1893*, no. 3, pp. 38–40; 6/1893, no. 3, pp. 33–40; 4/1889–90, p. 80.

Briggs, Robin, 'Women as victims? Witches, Judges and Community', in: *French History* 5/1991, pp. 438–50.

——*Communities of Belief, Oxford* 1989.

——*Witches and Neighbours. The Social and Cultural Context of European Witchcraft*, London 1996.

——*The Witches of Lorraine*, Oxford 2008.

Brockmann, Doris and Eicher, Peter (eds), *Die politische Theologie Friedrich von Spees*, München 1991.

Brouette, Emile, 'La sorcellerie dans le comté de Namur au début de l'époque moderne (1509–1546)', in *Annales de la société archéologique de Namur* 42/1953–54, pp. 359–420.

Bruckmüller, Ernst, *Sozialgeschichte Österreichs*, Wien 1985.

Bruns, Alfred (ed.), *Hexen. Gerichtsbarkeit im kurkölnischen Sauerland, Schmallenberg-Holthausen* 1984.

Burghartz, Susanne, 'Hexenverfolgung als Männerverfolgung? Zur Gleichsetzung von Hexen als Frauen am Beispiel der Luzerner und Lausanner Hexenprozesse des 15. und 16. Jahrhunderts', in: Opitz (1995), pp. 147–738; (English transl.: The equation of women with witches: A case study of witchcraft trials in Lucerne and Lausanne in the fifteenth and sixteenth centuries, in Evans, Richard J.: *The German Underworld: Deviants and Outcasts in German History.* London 1988, pp. 57–74).

Burke, Peter, 'The Comparative Approach to European Witchcraft', in Ankarloo and Henningsen (1990), pp. 435–41.

——Helden, *Schurken und Narren. Europäische Volkskultur in der frühen Neuzeit*, Stuttgart 1981/(German transl. of P. Burke, *Popular Culture in Early Modern Europe*, New York 1978).

Byloff, Fritz, *Hexenglaube und Hexenverfolgung in den österreichischen Alpenländern*, Leipzig 1934.

——*Wolfsbannerei in Oberdeutsche Zeitschrift für Volkskunde 2* (1927), pp. 130–138.

Clark, Stuart, 'Inversion, Misrule and Meaning of Witchcraft', in: *Past and Present* 97/1980, pp. 98–127.

——Protestant Demonology, 'Sin, Superstition and Society (1520–1630)', in Ankarloo and Henningsen (1990), pp. 45–81.

—— 'Glaube und Skepsis in der deutschen Hexenliteratur von Johann Weyer bis Friedrich von Spee', in Lehmann and Ulbricht (1992), pp. 15–33.

—— *Thinking with Demons. The Idea of Witchcraft in Early Modern Europe*, Oxford 1997.

Coudert, Allison P., *'Female Witches'*, in *EOW II* (2006), pp. 367–83.

—— 'The Myth of the Improved Status of Protestant Women: The Case of the Witchcraze', in Brink, J. and et al., (eds), *The Politics of Gender in Early Modern Europe*, Kirksville 1989, pp. 61–89.

Davidson, Jane, *Hexen in der nordeuropäischen Kunst 1470–1750*, Düsseldorf 1988.

Davies, Owen, *Witchcraft, magic and Culture 1736–1951*, Manchester 1999

Decker, Rainer, 'Die Hexenverfolgung im Hochstift Paderborn', in: *Westfälische Zeitschrift* 128/1978, pp. 314–56.

——'Die Hexenverfolgung im Herzogtum Westfalen', in *Westfälische Zeitschrift* 131–2/1981–82, pp. 339–86.

—— 'Die Hexenverfolgung im Herzogtum Westfalen', in Bruns, A. (ed.) (1984), pp. 91–118.

—— 'Der Hexen-Richter Dr. Heinrich v. Schultheiß (ca. 1580–1646) aus Scharmede', in: Grohmann, D.(ed.), *750 Jahre Stadt Salzkotten*, Paderborn 1996.

Degn, Christian and Lehmann, Hartmut and Unverhau, Dagmar (eds): *Hexenprozesse. Deutsche und skandinavische Beiträge*, Neumünster 1983.

Delsalle, Paul, *La Franche-Comté au temps des Archeducs Albert et Isabelle 1598–1633*, Bescancon 2002.

Dienst, Heide, Magische Vorstellungen und Hexenverfolgungen in den österreichischen Ländern (15.und 18. Jahrhundert), in Zöllner (1986), pp. 70–94.

—— 'Hexenprozesse auf dem Gebiet der heutigen Bundesländer Vorarlberg, Tirol (mit Südtirol), Salzburg, Nieder- und Oberösterreich sowie des Burgenlandes', in: Valentinitsch (1987), pp. 254–85.

Dillinger, Johannes, Binsfeld, Peter (1546–1598) in *EOW I* (2006) 122–24.

—— 'Schwäbisch-Österreich', in Lorenz and Schmidt (2004), pp. 283–94.

—— 'Böse Leute', *Hexenverfolgungen in Schwäbisch-Österreich und Kurtrier im Vergleich*, Trier 1999.

—— Hexenverfolgung in Städten, in Franz and Irsigler (1998), pp. 129–65.

Dintzer, Lucien, *Nicolas Rémy et son œuvre démonologique*, Lyon 1936.

Dittmer, G.W., *Das Sassen- und Holsten-Recht, in practischer Anwendung auf einige im 16ten Jahrhundert vorgekommene Civil- und Criminalfälle nach den im Archive des St. Johannis-Klosters zu Lübeck aufbewahrten Protokolle*... Lübeck 1843.

Dülmen, Richard van (ed.), *Hexenwelten. Magie und Imagination*, Frankfurt 1987.

—— *Gesellschaft der Frühen Neuzeit: Kulturelles Handeln und sozialer Prozeß. Beiträge zur historischen Kulturforschung, Wien* 1993.

—— *Kultur und Alltag in der Frühen Neuzeit, drei Bände*, München 1990–94.

Dupont-Bouchat, Marie-Sylvie, *'La répression de la sorcellerie dans le Duché du Luxembourg aux XVIe et XVIIe siècles'*, in Dupont-Bouchat et al. (1978), pp. 40–184.

Dupont-Bouchat, Marie-Sylvie, Frijoff, Willem and Muchembled, Robert (eds): *Prophètes et sorciers dans les Pays-Bas, XVIe–XVIIe siècles*, Paris 1978.

Durrant, Jonathan, Eichstätt, prince-bishopric of, in *EOW II* (2006), pp. 307–08.

Edwards, Kathryn A. (ed.), *Werewolves, Witches and Wanderings Saints. Traditional Belief and Folklore in Early Modern Europe*, Kirksville 2002.

Eiden, Herbert/Voltmer, Rita (eds), *Hexenprozesse und Gerichtspraxis*, Trier 2002.

Eiden, H., 'Die Unterwerfung der Volkskultur? Muchembled und die Hexenverfolgungen', in Voltmer (2005) 23–40.

Eliade, Mircea, *Schamanismus und archaische Ekstasetechnik*, Zürich 1956.

—— Occultism, *Witchcraft and Cultural fashions. Essays in Comparative Religions*, Chicago 1976.

Encyclopedia of Witchcraft. *The Western Tradition*, ed. by Richard M. Golden, 4 vols, Santa Barbara 2006 (=EOW).

Febvre, Lucien, *Histoire de Franche-Comté*, Paris 1922.

Fraess-Ehrfeld, *Claudia: Geschichte Kärntens*, 2 vols., Klagenfurt 1994.

Franz, Gunther and Irsigler, Franz (eds), *Hexenglaube und Hexenprozesse im Raum Rhein-Mosel-Saar*, Trier 1996.

—— *Methoden und Konzepte der historischen Hexenverfolgung*, Trier 1998.

Frijhoff, Willem, 'Prophétie et société dans les Provinces-Unies aux XVIIe–XVIIe siècles', in Dupont-Bouchat et al. (1978), pp. 265–362.

—— 'Jacob Vallick und Johann Weyer. Kampfgenossen, Konkurrenten oder Gegner?', in Lehmann and Ulbricht (1992), pp. 65–88.

Füssel, Ronald, *Hexenverfolgungen in Thüringer Raum*, Hamburg 2003.

Garrett, Clark, 'Women and Witches: Pattern of Analysis', in: *Signs 3*, 1977, pp. 461–470.

Gaskill, Malcolm, 'The Devil in the Shape of a Man: Witchcraft, Conflict and Belief in Jacobean England', *Historical Research*, 71 (1998) pp. 142–71.

Gebhard, Horst, *Hexenprozesse im Kurfürstentum Mainz des 17. Jahrhunderts*, Mainz 1989.

Gehm, Britta, *Die Hexenverfolgung im Hochstift Bamberg und das Eingreifen des Reichshofsrat zu ihrer Beendigung*, Hildesheim 2000.

Gersmann, Gudrun, 'Münster, bishopric of', in *EOW III* (2006) pp. 794–5

Gijswijt-Hofstra, Mariijke and Friijhoff, Willem (eds), *Witchcraft in the Netherlands from the Fourteenth to the Twentieth Century*, Rotterdam 1991.

Ginzburg, Carlo, *Die Benandanti. Feldkulte und Hexenwesen im 16. und 17. Jahrhundert*, Frankfurt 1980.

—— Hexensabbat. Entzifferung einer nächtlichen Geschichte, Berlin 1990.

Golden, Richard M. (ed.), *Encyclopedia of Witchcraft. The Western Tradition*, 4 vols, Santa Barbara 2006 (=EOW).

Goodare, Julian, 'Larner, Christina', in *EOW III* 2006, pp. 627–8.

—— 'Women and the Witch-Hunt in Scotland', *Social History*, 23, 1998, pp. 288–308.

Gosler, Sieglinde, *Hexenwahn und Hexenprozesse in Kärnten. Von dem Ende des 15. Jahrhunderts bis zum ersten Drittel des 18. Jahrhunderts*, Graz 1955.

Graumann, Carl Friedrich and Moscovici, Serge (eds), *Changing Concepts of Conspiracy*, New York 1987.

Gutkas, Karl (ed.), *Prinz Eugen und das barocke Österreich*, Wien 1985.

Gijswijjt-Hofstra, Marijke and Frijhoff, Willem (eds): *Witchcraft in the Netherlands from the 14th to the 20th*, Rotterdam 1991.

Hagen, R., 'Shamanism' in *EOW IV* (2006) 1029–31.

—— 'Traces of Shamanism in the Witch Trials of Norway, in H. d. Waardt, et al. (eds), *Dämonische Besessenheit: Zur Interpretation eines kulturhistorischen Phänomens* (Bielefeld 2005), pp. 307–25.

Halifax, Joan, *Shamanistic Voices*, New York 1979.

Hansen, Joseph, *Zauberwahn. Inquisition und Hexenprozeß im Mittelalter und die Entstehung der großen Hexenverfolgung*, München/Leipzig 1900.

Harf-Lancner, Laurence, 'La métamorphose illusoire: Des théories chrétiennes de la métamorphose aux images médivales du loup-garou, in: *Annales ESC 40*', 1985, pp. 208–26.

Harmening, Dieter, *Superstitio. Überlieferungs- und theoriegeschichtliche Untersuchungen zur kirchlich-theologischen Aberglaubensliteratur des Mittelalters*, Berlin 1979.

—— *Zauberei im Abendland. Vom Anteil der Gelehrten am Wahn der Leute*, Würzburg 1991.

Hauser, Karl Baron von, 'Aus dem Archive', in *Carinthia I*, 71/1881, pp. 118–26, 152–6, 181–90.

Haustein, Jörg, *Martin Luthers Stellung zum Zauber- und Hexenwesen*, Stuttgart 1990.

——*'Martin Luther als Gegner des Hexenwahns'*, in: Lehmann and Ulbricht (1992), pp. 35–53.

Heberling, Richard, Zauberei- und Hexenprozesse in Schleswig-Holstein-Lauenburg, in: *Zeitschrift der Gesellschaft für Schleswig-Holsteinische Geschichte* 45/1915, pp. 116–248.

Heikkinnen, Antero and Kervinen, Timo: Finland: The Male Domination, in: Ankarloo and Henningsen (1990), pp. 319–38.

Henningsen, Gustav (with Ankarloo, Bengt) (eds), *Early Modern Witchcraft. Centres and Peripheries*, Oxford 1990.

——'The White Sabbat and Other Archaic Patterns of Witchcraft', in *Acta Ethnographica Hungarica* 37 (1991–92), pp. 293–304.

Hester, Marianne, 'Patriarchal reconstruction and witch-hunting', in: Barry et al. (1996), pp. 288–306.

Heuser, Peter A, 'Die kurkölnischen Hexenprozesse des 16.und 17.Jahrhunderts in geschlechtergeschichtlicher Perspektive',in Ahrendt and Schulte (2002), pp. 137–38.

Hoffmann, Birgit, 'Hexenverfolgung in Schleswig-Holstein zwischen Reformation und Aufklärung', in *Schriften des Vereins für Schleswig-Holsteinische Kirchengeschichte* II, 34–35/1978, pp. 110–72.

Holmes, Clive, 'Women: Witnesses and Witches', in *Past and Present* 140/1993, pp. 45–78.

Horst, Georg Konrad, *Zauberbibliothek oder von Zauberei, Hexen und Hexenprocessen, Dämonen, und Gespenstern*, vol.1, Mainz 1821.

Houdard, Sophie, *Les sciences du diable. Quatre discours sur la sorcellerie*, Paris 1992.

Irsigler, Franz, 'Zauberei- und Hexenprozesse in Köln, 15.-17. Jahrhundert, in: Franz and Irsigler (1996), pp. 169–79.

——'Hexenverfolgungen vom 15. bis 17. Jahrhundert', in: Franz/Irsigler (1998), pp. 3–20.

Jacques-Chaquin, Nicole and Préaud, Maxime (ed.), *Le sabbat des sorciers en Europe (XVe–XVIIIe siècles)*, Paris 1993.

Jaksch, August von, 'Ein Hexenprocess in Paternion im Jahre 1662', in *Carinthia I*, 83/1893, pp. 9–18.

——'Hexen und Zauberer', in: *Carinthia I*, 84/1894, pp. 7–15, pp. 43–53.

Jensen, Karsten Sejr, *Troldom i Danemark 1500–1588*, København 1988.

Jerouschek, Günter (with Schild, Wolfgang and Gropp, Walter (eds), *Benedict Carpzov. Neue Perspektiven zu einem umstrittenen sächsischen Juristen*, Tübingen 2000.

Johansen, Jens C.V., Denmark: 'The Sociology of Accusations', in: Ankarloo and Henningsen (1990), pp. 339–65.

——'Da Djaevelen var ude...', *Troldom i det 17. århundredes Danmark*, Odense 1991.

Jütte, Robert, *Poverty and Deviance in Early Modern Europe*, Cambridge 1994.

Karant-Nunn S.C. and M. E. Wiesner-Hanks (eds), *Luther on Women. A Sourcebook*, Cambridge 2003.

Kamber, Peter, 'Croyances et peurs: La sorcellerie dans le Pays de Vaud (XVIe–XVIIe siècles)', in F.Flouck et al. (eds), *De l'Ours à la Cocarde: Régime bernois et révolution en pays de Vaud*, Lausanne 1998, pp. 247–56.

——La chasse aux sorciers aux sorcières au XVIe siècle dans le pays de Vaud, Aspects quantitatifs (1581–1620), *Revue historique vaudoise* 90/1982, pp. 21–33.

Keller, Wilhelm Otto (ed.), *Hexer und Hexen in Miltenberg und der Cent Bürgstadt – Beiträge zur Geschichte der Hexenprozesse am südlichen Untermain*, Miltenberg 1989.

Kent, Elisabeth, 'Masculinity and Male Witches in Old and New England, 1593–1680', *History Workshop Journal*, 60 (2005), pp. 69–92.

Kern, Edmund M., 'Austria', in *EOW* (2006) 70–5.

Kieckhefer, Richard, *European Witch Trials. Their Foundations in Popular and Learned Culture*, 1300–1500, London 1976.

—— *Repression of Heresy in Medieval Germany*, Pennsylvania University Press 1979.

—— *Magie im Mittelalter*, München 1992.

—— 'Magie et sorcellerie en Europe au Moyen Age', in Muchembled (1994), pp. 17–44.

Kivelson, Valerie, 'Male Witches and gendered Categories in Seventeenth-century Russia', *Comparative Studies in Society and History* 45 (2003), pp. 606–31.

—— 'Through the Prism of Witchcraft: Gender and Social Change in Seventeenth – Century Muscovy', in: Evanset et al. (eds): *Russia's Women, Accomodation, Resistance, Transformation*, Berkeley 1991, pp. 74–94.

Klaniczay, Gábor (with Pócs, Eva), *Communicating with the Spirits* (Budapest 2005).

—— 'Hungary, The Accusations and the Universe of Popular Magic', in Ankarloo and Henningsen (1990), pp. 219–55.

—— Heilige, Hexen, *Vampire. Vom Nutzen des Übernatürlichen*, Berlin 1990.

Kleinöder-Ströbel, Susanna, *Die Verfolgung von Zauberei und Hexerei in den fränkischen Markgraftümern im 16. Jahrhundert*, Tübingen 2002.

Kramer, Karl Sigismund, *Volksleben in Holstein (1550–1800)*, Kiel 1987.

Labouvie, 'Eva: Männer im Hexenprozeß. Zur Sozialanthropologie eines "männlichen" Verständnisses von Magie und Hexerei', in: *Geschichte und Gesellschaft* 16/1990, pp. 56–78. (english transl.: Men in Witchcraft Trials: Towards a Social Anthropology of, "Male" Understandings of Magic and Witchcraft', in U. Rublack (ed.), *Gender in Early Modern History*, Cambridge 2002, pp. 49–68.

—— Zauberei und Hexenwerk. *Ländlicher Hexenglaube in der frühen Neuzeit*, Frankfurt 1991.

Lambrecht, Karen, 'Tabu und Tod. Männer als Opfer frühneuzeitlicher Verfolgungswellen, in Ahrendt and Schulte (2002), pp. 193–208.

—— *Hexenverfolgung und Zaubereiprozesse in den schlesischen Territorien*, Köln 1995.

Lange, Ursula, *Untersuchungen zu Bodins Démonomanie*, Köln 1968.

Larner, Christina, *Enemies of God. The Witch Hunt in Scotland*, Baltimore 1981.

—— *Witchcraft and Religion: The Politics of Popular Belief*, Oxford 1984.

Lavrov, Alexander, 'Russische Zauberer und ukrainische Zauberinnen. Zaubereiprozesse von 1700 bis 1740 als historische Quelle', in *Jahrbücher für Geschichte Osteuropas* 53/2005, pp. 177–19.

Lees, Clare, A. (ed.), *Medieval masculinities. Regarding Men in the Middle Ages*, Minneapolis 1994.

Lehmann, Hartmut, *Das Zeitalter des Absolutismus. Gottesgnadentum und Kriegsnot*, Stuttgart 1980.

—— 'Hexenprozesse in Norddeutschland und in Skandinavien im 16., 17. und 18. Jahrhundert. Bemerkungen zum Forschungsstand', in Degn et al. (1983), pp. 9–13.

——(with Ulbricht, Otto) (eds), 'Vom Unfug des Hexen-Processes'. *In Gegner der Hexenverfolgungen von Johann Weyer bis Friedrich Spee*, Wiesbaden 1992.

Lehmann, H. and Ulbricht, O., 'Motive und Argumente von Gegnern der Hexenverfolgung von Weyer bis Spee', in: Lehmann/Ulbricht (1992), pp. 1–14.

Levack, Brian P., *The Witch-Hunt in Early Modern Europe*, 3rd edn, London 2006.

Lorenz, Sönke, 'Johann-Georg Godelmann – ein Gegner des Hexenwahns?', in: Schmidt, R. (ed.): *Beiträge zur Pommerschen und Mecklenburgischen Geschichte*, Marburg 1981, pp. 61–105.

——*Aktenversendung und Hexenprozeß. Dargestellt am Beispiel der Juristenfakultät Rostock und Greifswald (1570/82–1630)*, 3 Bände, Frankfurt 1982.

——'Die Rezeption der cautio criminalis in der Rechtswissenschaft zur Zeit der Hexenverfolgung', in Oorschot (1993), pp. 130–53.

——(with Schmidt, J.M.)(eds), *Wider alle Hexerei und Teufelswerk. Die europäische Hexenverfolgung und ihre Auswirkung auf Südwestdeutschland*, Ostfildern 2004.

——*Hexen und Hexenverfolgung im deutschen Südwesten*, Ostfildern 1994.

Lorenz, S. and Bauer, D.R. (eds), *Das Ende der Hexenverfolgung*, Stuttgart 1995.

——Hexenverfolgung. *Beiträge zur Forschung unter besonderer Berücksichtigung des südwestdeutschen Raumes*, Würzburg 1995.(= 1995 a)

Lorey, Elmar, *Henrich der Werwolf. Eine Geschichte aus der Zeit der Hexenprozesse mit Dokumenten und Analysen*, Frankfurt 1998.

Madar, Maia, 'Estonia I: Werewolves and Poisoners', in: Ankarloo and Henningsen (1990), pp. 257–72.

Mährle, Wolfgang, 'Fürstprobstei Ellwangen', in J. Dillinger et al. *Zum Feuer verdammt. Die Hexenverfolgungen in der Grafschaft Hohenberg, der Reichstadt Reutlingen und der Fürstpropstei Ellwangen*, Stuttgart 1998.

Martin, Ruth, *Witchcraft and the Inquisition in Venice 1550–50*, Oxford 1979.

Mauss, Marcel, *Esquisse d'une théorie générale de la magie*, Paris 1903.

Maxwell-Stuart, Peter, 'Scotland', in *EOW IV* (2006), pp. 1018–20; 'Daneau', in *EOW I* (2006), pp. 246.

——Wizards. *A History*, Brimscombe 2004.

Midelfort, H.C. Eric, *Witch hunting in Southwestern Germany 1562–1684: The Social and Intellectual Foundations*, Stanford 1972.

——'Johann Weyer in medizinischer, theologischer und rechtsgeschichtlicher Hinsicht', in Lehmann and Ulbricht (1992), pp. 53–64.

—— 'Alte Fragen und neue Methoden in der Geschichte des Hexenwahns', in Lorenz and Bauer (1995a), pp. 13–30.

'Modestin, Georg/Tremp, Kathrin Utz: Zur spätmittelalterlichen Hexenverfolgung in der heutigen Westschweiz in Zeitenblicke 1/2002', see http://www.zeitenblicke.historicum. net/2002/01/Modestin/modestin.html

'Montballyu, Jos (R.Opsommer), Flandern-Hexenverfolgung' (acc. 15 March, 2007), in G. Gersmann et al.(eds), *Lexikon der Geschichte der Hexenverfolgung*, see: http://www.historicum.net/themen/hexenverfolgung/lexikon.

——Die Hexenprozesse in der Grafschaft Flandern (1495–1692), in Eiden and Voltmer (2002), pp. 287–96.

Monter, William, 'Male Witches' in *EOW III* (2006) pp. 711–713; (with E.Peters): 'Rémy, Nicolas', in *EOW IV* (2006) 955–6.

——'Toads and eucharists: the male witches of Normandy, 1564–1660', *French Historical Studies* 20 (1997), p. 563–95.

Monter, William, *Witchcraft in France and Switzerland. The Borderlands During the Reformation*, Ithaca/London 1976.

—— (with J. Tedeschi) 'Towards a statistical profile of the Italian inquisitions, sixteenth to eighteenth century', in G.Henningsen and J. Tedeschi (eds), *The Inquisition in Early Modern Europe*, Dekalb 1989.

Moeller, Katrin, *Dass Willkür über Recht ginge. Hexenprozesse in Mecklenburg im 16. und 17.* Jahrhundert, Bielefeld 2007.

Muchembled, Robert:

—— *Sorcières, justice et société aux 16e et 17e siècles*, Paris 1987.

—— 'Satanic Myths and Cultural Reality', in Ankarloo and Henningsen (1990), pp. 121–60.

—— *Le roi et la sorcière. L'Europe des bûchers (XVe aux XXIIIe siècles)*, Paris 1993.

—— (ed.), *Magie et sorcellerie en Europe du Moyen Age à nos jours*, Paris 1994.

—— 'Terres de contrastes: France, Pays-Bas, Provinces-Unies', in Muchembled (1994), pp. 99–132.

Nenonen, Marko, 'Envious are all the people, witches watch at every gate. Finnish witches and witch trials in the 17th century', in *Scandinavian Journal of History* 18/1993, pp. 77–91.

—— *Noituus, taikuus ja noitavainot, Ala-Satakunnan, Pohjois-Pohjanmaan ja Viipurin Karjalan maaseudulla vuosina 1620–1700*, Helsinki 1992 (with English summary).

Nieß, Walter, *Hexenprozesse in der Grafschaft Büdingen*, Büdingen 1982.

Oates, Caroline, 'Metamorphosis and Lycanthropy in Franche-Comté, 1521–1643', in Feher, M. (ed.), *Fragments for a History of the Human Body, Part One*, New York 1989, pp. 305–63.

Oorschot, Theo G.M (ed.), *Friedrich Spee (1591–1635)* Bielefeld 1993.

Opitz, Claudia (ed.), *Der Hexenstreit. Frauen in der frühneuzeitlichen Hexenverfolgung*, Freiburg 1995.

Ostorero, M., 'Fôlatrer avec les démons', *Sabbat et chasse aux sorciers à Vevey* (1448), Lausanne 1995.

Paravy, Pierrete, *De la Chrétienté romaine à la Réforme en Dauphiné*, 2 vols, Rome 1993.

Pearl, Jonathan L., *The Crime of Crimes. Demonology and Politics in France 1560–1620*, Waterloo 1999.

Peters, Edward, *The Magician, the Witch and the Law*, Philadelphia 1978.

Pócs, Éva (with.G. Klaniscay), *Communicating with the Spirits* (Budapest 2005).

—— 'Why witches are women', in *Acta Ethnographica Hungarica* 48/2003, pp. 367–83.

—— *Between the Living and the Dead. A Perspective on Witches and Seers in Early Modern Age*, Budapest 1999.

Pohl, Herbert, *Hexenglaube und Hexenverfolgung im Kurfürstentum Mainz*, Stuttgart 1988.

Rabanser, Hansjörg, *Hexenwahn. Schicksale und Hintergrund. Die Tiroler Hexenprozesse*, Innsbruck 2006.

Raser, Dorothea, *Zauberei- und Hexenprozesse in Niederösterreich, in: Unsere Heimat* 60 (1989), pp. 14–41.

Rochelandet, Brigitte, *Destins des femmes en Franche-Comté*, Bescançon 2005.

—— La Répression de la sorcellerie aux XVIe et XVIIe siècles, thèse de doctorat, 2 vols, Besançon 1992.

—— *Sorcières, Diables et Bûchers en Franche-Comté*, Besançon 1997.

Roeck, Bernd, *'Christlicher Idealstaat und Hexenwahn. Zum Ende der europäischen Hexenverfolgungen'*, in: *Historisches Jahrbuch* 108/1988, pp. 379–405.

Roper, Lyndal, *Witch Craze. Terror and Fantasy in Baroque Germany*, New Haven 2004.

Rowlands, Alison, (with J. Grundy) (eds), *Witchcraft and Masculinities*, Basingstoke 2008.

—— *Witchcraft Narratives in Germany: Rothenburg, 1561–1652*, Manchester 2003.

Rummel, Walter, Gutenberg, der Teufel und die Mutter Gottes von Eberhardsklausen. Erste Hexenverfolgung im Trierer Land, in: Blauert (1990), pp. 91–117.

—— Bauern, Herren und Hexen. *Studien zur Sozialgeschichte sponheimischer und kurtrierischer Hexenprozesse* (1574–1664), Göttingen 1991.

Sachße, Christoph and Tennstedt, Florian: *Geschichte der Armenfürsorge in Deutschland. Vom Spätmittelalter bis zum Ersten Weltkrieg*, Stuttgart 1980.

Sandgruber, Roman, *'Luxusindustrie und Massenarmut. Merkantilistische Wirtschaftspolitik und Güterproduktion in Österreich'*, in Gutkas (1985), pp. 203–11.

—— *Ökonomie und Politik. Österreichische Wirtschaftsgeschichte vom Mittelalter bis zur Gegenwart*, Wien 1995.

Sarman, Gerhard, 'Der Bettler und Zauberer Christian Wucher und das letzte Todesurteil in einem Kärntner Hexenprozeß (1723)', in *Carinthia*, 187/1997, pp. 461–94.

—— 'Ihme zur Straff und andern zum abscheuhen und exempl', in 'Der Maria Saaler Hexenprozeß gegen den Bettler Christian Wucher 1720–23', Wien 1995.

Schild, Wolfgang, *Die Geschichte der Gerichtsbarkeit*, Hamburg 1997.

Schindler, Norbert, *Widerspenstige Leute. Studien zur Volkskultur in der Frühen Neuzeit*, Frankfurt 1992, pp. 258–314, (English translation: *Rebellion, Community and Custom in Early Modern Germany*, Cambridge 2002.

—— 'Die Ramigsteiner Bettlerhochzeit 1688/89. Armut, Sexualität und Hexenpolitik in einem Salzburger Bergwerksort des 17. Jahrhunderts', in *Historische Anthropologie* 2/1994, pp. 165–92.

Schmidt, J.M., *Die Kurpfalz*, in Lorenz and Schmidt (2004), pp. 237–52.

Schmitt, Jean-Claude, *Heidenspaß und Höllenangst: Aberglaube im Mittelalter*, Frankfurt 1993.

Schönleitner, Ulrike, *Zauberei- und Hexenprozesse in Österreich. Geisteswissenschaftliche Diplomarbeit*, Wien 1986/87.

Schormann, Gerhard, Hexenverfolgung in Schaumburg, *Niedersächsisches Jahrbuch für Landesgeschichte*, 45/1973 pp. 145–63.

—— *Hexenprozesse in Nordwestdeutschland*, Hildesheim 1977.

—— 'Städtische Gesellschaft und Hexenprozeß', in: Meckseper, C. (ed.), *Stadt im Wandel. Kunst und Kultur der Bürgertums in Norddeutschland 1150 bis 1650*, Band 4, Stuttgart 1985, pp. 175–87.

—— *Der Krieg gegen die Hexen. Das Ausrottungsprogramm des Kurfürsten von Köln*, Göttingen 1991.

Schulte, Rolf, *Hexenmeister. Die Verfolgung von Männern im Rahmen der Hexenverfolgung im Alten Reich, 1530–1730*, Frankfurt 2000.

Schulte, Rolf, *Hexenverfolgung in Schleswig-Holstein*, vom 16. bis 18. Jahrhundert, Heide 2001.

—— 'Okkulte Mächte, Hexenverfolgung und Geschlecht in Afrika', in Schmidt, Burghard and Schulte, Rolf (eds), *Witchcraft in subsaharian Africa/Hexenverfolgung und magische Vorstellungswelten im modernen Afrika*, Hamburg 2008.

Schwerhoff, Gerd, 'Hexerei, Geschlecht und Regionalgeschichte', in: Wilbertz et al. (1994), pp. 325–53.

Schwillus, Harald, *Kleriker im Hexenprozeß. Geistliche als Opfer der Hexenprozesse des 16. und 17.* Jahrhunders in Deutschland, Würzburg 1992.

Sharpe, Jim, *'Les Iles Britanniques: une vue d'ensemble'*, in Muchembled (1994), pp. 133–58.

—— *Instruments of Darkness. Witchcraft in England 1550–1750*, London 1997.

Simplicio, Oscar do, *Siena New State in EOW IV* (2006) 1034–36.

Sörlin, Per, *'Wicked arts', Witchcraft and Magic Trials in Southern Sweden 1635–1754*, Leiden 1999.

Soldan, Wilhelm Georg and Heppe, Heinrich: *Geschichte der Hexenverfolgung*, 1880, reprint Kettwig 1986.

Soman, Alfred, 'Le procès de la sorcellerie au Parlement de Paris (1565–1640)', in *Annales ESC* 32/1977, pp. 790–815.

—— 'Le sabbat des sorciers: Preuve Juridique', in Jacques-Chaquin and Préaud (1992), pp. 85–99.

—— *Sorcellerie et Justice Criminelle. Le Parlement de Paris (16e-18e siècles)*, Hampshire 1992.

Stephens, Walter, *Demon Lovers: Witchcraft, Sex, and the Crisis of belief*, Chicago 2002.

Swatek, M., 'Die Wolfbanner. Der Wolfberger Hexenprozeß von 1705/06', in *Carinthia* I 193 (2003), pp. 315–43.

Tovio, Raisa M., 'Women at Stake. Interpretations of Women's Role in Witchcraft and Witch Hunts from the early 20th Century to the present', in ARV. *Nordic Yearbook of Folklore* 62 (2006), pp. 187–205.

Tschacher, Werner, *Der Formicarius von Johannes Nider von 1437/38. Studien zu den Anfängen der europäischen Hexenverfolgungen im Spätmittelalter*, Aachen 2000.

Tschaikner, Manfred, *'Der Teufel und die Hexen müssen aus dem Land...' Frühneuzeitliche Hexenverfolgungen in Liechtenstein*, Liechtenstein 1998.

—— 'Vorarlberg', in Lorenz (1994), pp. 231–43.

Unverhau, 'Dagmar: Kieler Hexen und Zauberer zur Zeit der großen Verfolgung (1530–1676)', in *Mitteilungen der Gesellschaft für Kieler Stadtgeschichte* 68/1981, pp. 41–96.

—— '"Wahr, daß sie eine Hexe sey". Zauberfälle zwischen Hexerei und Aberglauben aus dem Gebiet des Klosters Preetz (1643–1735)', in Schleswig-Holstein 3 (1981), pp. 8–12.

—— 'Aufruhr und Rebellion im Amt Bergedorf wegen eines Zauberers und dreier Zauberinnen im Jahre 1612', in *Zeitschrift für Hamburgische Stadtgeschichte* 68/1982, pp. 1–22.

—— 'Akkusationsprozeß, Inquisitionsprozeß, Indikatoren für die Intensität der Hexenverfolgung in Schleswig-Holstein', in Degn et al.(1983), pp. 59–142.

Utz-Tremp, Kathrin, *Waldenser, Wiedergänger, Hexen und Rebellen. Biographien zu den Waldenserprozessen von Freiburg im Üchtland* (1399 und 1430), Freiburg/Schweiz 1999.

Valentinitsch, Helfried (ed.), *Hexen und Zauberer. Die große Verfolgung – ein europäisches Phänomen in der Steiermark*, Graz 1987.

—— 'Die Verfolgung von Hexen und Zauberern im Herzogtum Steiermark – eine Zwischenbilanz', in Valentinitsch (1987), pp. 297–316.

—— 'Hexenprozesse in und um Pettau (Ptuj) 1651/1652', in *Zeitschrift des Historischen Vereines für Steiermark* 1990, pp. 61–79.

Vanysacker, Dries, 'Netherlands, southern', in *EOW III* 2006, pp. 813–18.

—— Hekserij in Brugge. *De magische leefwereld van een stadsbevolkering, 16de–17de eeuw*, Brugge 1988.

Voltmer, Rita, 'Witch-hunters, Witch-finders and Kings of the Sabbat: The Prominent Role of Men in the Mass persecutions of Trier, St. Maximin, Luxembourg and the Eifel-territories, in Rowlands and Grundy (2008).

—— 'Luxembourg, duchy of, in *EOW III* (2006) 677–680; St.Maximin, Prince Abbey of', in *EOW IV* (2006), pp. 1082–83.

—— *Hexenverfolgung und Herrschaftspraxis*, Trier 2005.

—— Jagd auf böse Leute. 'Hexenverfolgungen in der Region um den Laacher', see, in http://www.historicum.net

—— (with Eiden, H.) (eds), *Hexenprozesse und Gerichtspraxis*. Trier 2002.

—— Gegen die Unzucht, 'Nachtridentinische Sittenreform, Kriminalisierung und Verfolgung devianter Sexualität im Erzbistum Trier, in H.G. Borck et al. (ed.), *Unrecht und Recht. Kriminalität und Gesellschaft im Wandel, 1500–2000* (Koblenz 2002), pp. 481–511.

——(with Weisenstein, Karl), *Das Hexenregister des Claudius Musiel. Ein Verzeichnis von hingerichteten und besagten Personen aus dem Trierer Land* (1586–1594), Trier 1996.

Waardt, Hans.de, *Toverij en samenleving. Holland 1500–1800*, Rotterdam 1991.

Waite, Gary K., *Magic and Witchcraft in Early Modern Europe*, Basingstoke 2003.

Walinski-Kiehl, Robert, 'Males, "masculine honour", and Witch hunting in Seventeenth-century Germany', in *Men and Masculinities* 6(2004), pp. 254–271.

—— 'Prosecuting witches in early modern Germany, with the special reference to the Bishopric of Bamberg, 1595–1680', unpublished Ph D thesis, Portsmouth 1981.

—— '"Godly States" Confessional Conflict and Witch-Hunting in Early Modern Germany', in: *Mentalities/Mentalités*, 5.2 (1988), pp. 13–24.

——'La chasse aux sorcières et la sabbat des sorcières dans les évêches de Bamberg et Würzburg (vers 1590–vers 1630)', in Jacques-Chaquin and Préaud (1993), pp. 213–225.

Walz, Rainer, *Hexenglaube und magische Kommunikation im Dorf der frühen Neuzeit. Die Verfolgungen in der Grafschaft Lippe*, Paderborn 1993.

Wiesner-Hanks, Merry, '*Gender*', in *EOW II* (2006), pp. 407–11.

Wilbertz, Gisela, 'Hexenprozesse und Zauberglaube im Hochstift Osnabrück', in *Osnabrücker Mitteilungen, Mitteilungen des Vereins für Geschichte und Landeskunde von Osnabrück* 84 (1978), pp. 33–49.

Wilbertz, Gisela and Schwerhoff, Gerd/Scheffler, Jürgen. (eds), *Hexenverfolgung und Regionalgeschichte. Die Grafschaft Lippe im Vergleich*, Bielefeld 1994.

Winkelbauer, *Thomas, Österreichische Geschichte 1522–1699*, 2 vols, Wien 2003.

Wyporska, Wanda, 'Exodus 22.18 (22:17)', in *EOW II* (2006) pp. 337–8.

Wunder, Heide, 'Friedrich Spee und die verfolgten Frauen', in Brockmann and Eicher (1991), pp. 117–31.

Wunder, Heide, *'"Er ist Sonn", "sie ist Mond", Frauen in der Frühen Neuzeit'*, München 1992.

—— (with Vanja, Christina), *Wandel der Geschlechtsbeziehungen zu Beginn der Neuzeit*, Frankfurt 1991.

—— Weiber, Menscher, *Frauenzimmer. Frauen in der ländlichen Gesellschaft 1500–1800*, Göttingen 1996.

Wutte, Martin, 'Gerichtsbräuche im Landgericht Paternion', in: *Carinthia I*, 98/1908, pp. 41–7.

—— 'Das kärntische Bannrichteramt', in *Carinthia I*, 102/1912, pp. 115–36.

—— 'Hexenprozesse in Kärnten', in *Carinthia I*, 117/1927, pp. 27–67.

Index